BRIGGS LAND ™

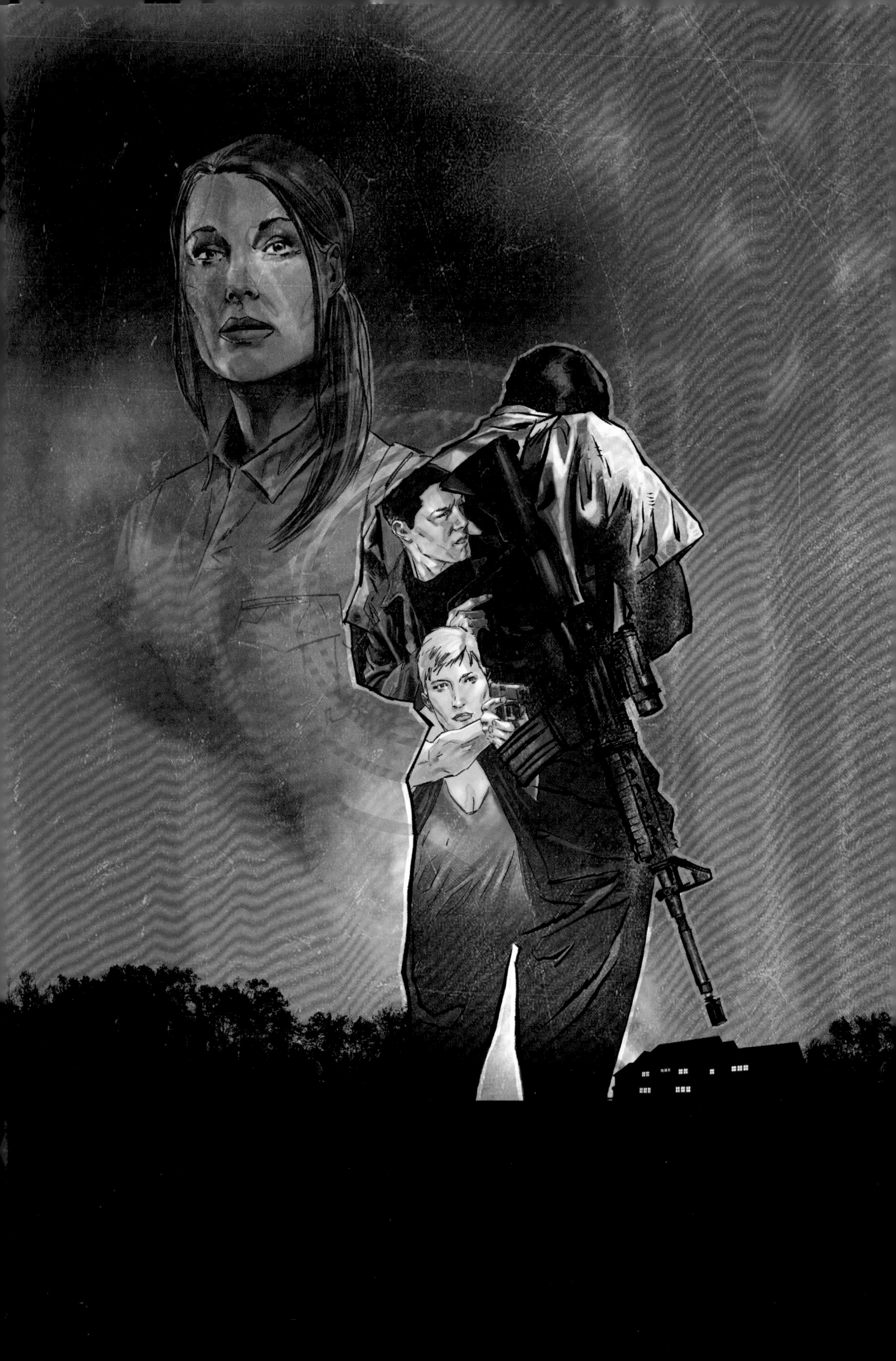

MACK CHATER

VOLUME 2
LONE WOLVES

SCRIPT / BRIAN WOOD

ART / MACK CHATER
VANESA R. DEL REY
WERTHER DELL'EDERA

COLORS / LEE LOUGHRIDGE

LETTERS / NATE PIEKOS OF BLAMBOT®

COVER / MACK CHATER AND BRIAN WOOD

CHAPTER BREAK ART / MATTHEW WOODSON
KIM JUNG GI
FIONA STAPLES
JG JONES
ROBERT SAMMELIN
BEN OLIVER
TRISTAN JONES

BRIGGS LAND CREATED BY BRIAN WOOD

BRIGGS▦LAND™

DARK HORSE BOOKS

PRESIDENT AND PUBLISHER / MIKE RICHARDSON
EDITOR / SPENCER CUSHING
ASSISTANT EDITOR / KEVIN BURKHALTER
COLLECTION DESIGNER / JUSTIN COUCH
DIGITAL ART TECHNICIAN / ALLYSON HALLER

SPECIAL THANKS TO BRIAN BOCKRATH AND BEN DAVIS OF AMC, JOHN HODGES AND RAVI NANDAN OF A24, ANGELA CHENG CAPLAN, HARRIS M. MILLER II, AND MEREDITH, AUDREY, AND IAN.

NEIL HANKERSON Executive Vice President / TOM WEDDLE Chief Financial Officer / RANDY STRADLEY Vice President of Publishing / NICK McWHORTER Chief Business Development Officer / MATT PARKINSON Vice President of Marketing / DAVID SCROGGY Vice President of Product Development / DALE LaFOUNTAIN Vice President of Information Technology / CARA NIECE Vice President of Production and Scheduling / MARK BERNARDI Vice President of Book Trade and Digital Sales / KEN LIZZI General Counsel / DAVE MARSHALL Editor in Chief / DAVEY ESTRADA Editorial Director / SCOTT ALLIE Executive Senior Editor / CHRIS WARNER Senior Books Editor / CARY GRAZZINI Director of Specialty Projects / LIA RIBACCHI Art Director / VANESSA TODD Director of Print Purchasing / MATT DRYER Director of Digital Art and Prepress / MICHAEL GOMBOS Director of International Publishing and Licensing

Briggs Land Volume 2: Lone Wolves

This volume collects the Dark Horse comic book series *Briggs Land: Lone Wolves* #1–#6, originally published June 2017–November 2017.

Published by Dark Horse Books
A division of Dark Horse Comics, Inc.
10956 SE Main Street
Milwaukie, OR 97222

DarkHorse.com

International Licensing: 503-905-2377
To find a comics shop in your area, visit the Comic Shop Locator Service at www.comicshoplocator.com

Library of Congress Cataloging-in-Publication Data

Names: Wood, Brian, 1972- author. | Chater, Mack, artist. | Del Rey, Vanesa
   R., artist. | Dell'Edera, Werther, artist. | Loughridge, Lee, colourist. |
   Piekos, Nate, letterer. | Woodson, Matthew, artist.
Title: Lone wolves / script, Brian Wood ; art, Mack Chater, Vanesa R. Del
   Rey, Werther Dell'Edera ; colors, Lee Loughridge ; lettering, Nate Piekos
   of Blambot ; cover and chapter break art, Matthew Woodson.
Description: First edition. | Milwaukie, OR : Dark Horse Books, 2018. |
   Series: Briggs Land ; Volume 2 | "This volume collects the Dark Horse
   comic book series Briggs Land: Lone Wolves #1-#6, originally published
   June 2017-November 2017"
Identifiers: LCCN 2017044017 | ISBN 9781506702100 (paperback)
Subjects: LCSH: Comic books, strips, etc. | BISAC: COMICS & GRAPHIC NOVELS /
   Crime & Mystery. | COMICS & GRAPHIC NOVELS / Literary. | COMICS & GRAPHIC
   NOVELS / General.
Classification: LCC PN6728.B69 W63 2018 | DDC 741.5/973--dc23
LC record available at https://lccn.loc.gov/2017044017

First edition: January 2018
ISBN 978-1-50670-210-0

10 9 8 7 6 5 4 3 2 1

Printed in China

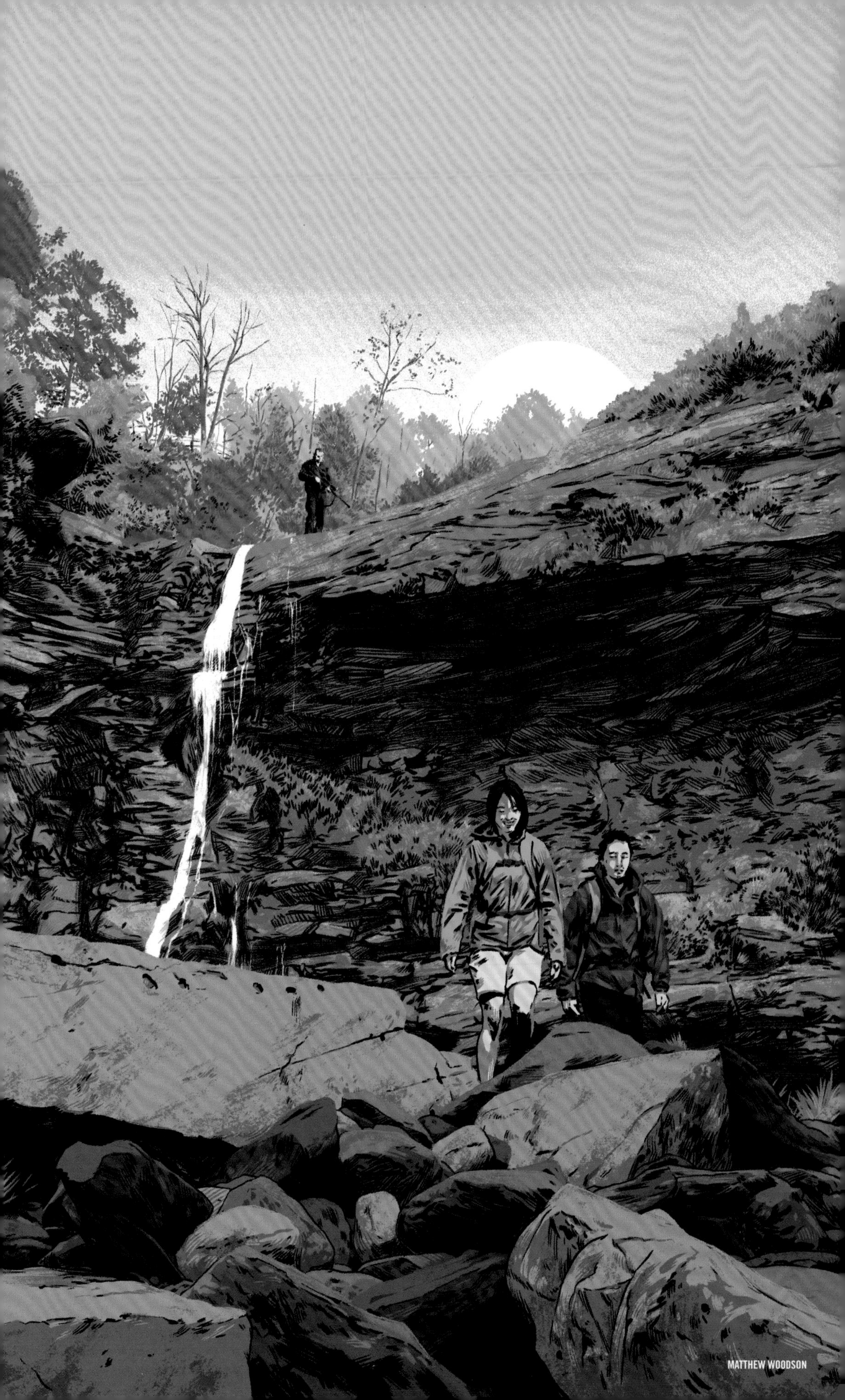
MATTHEW WOODSON

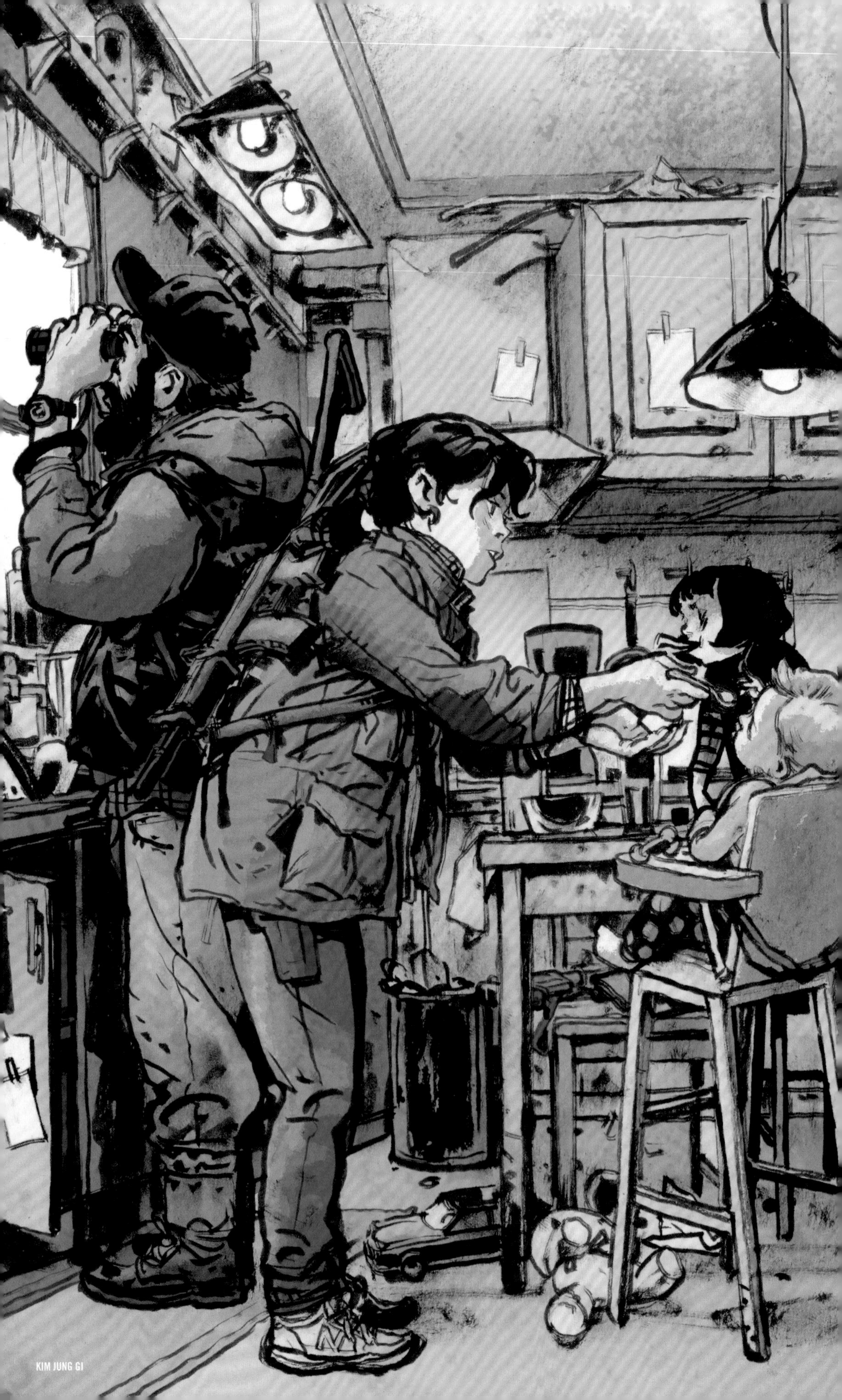

KIM JUNG GI

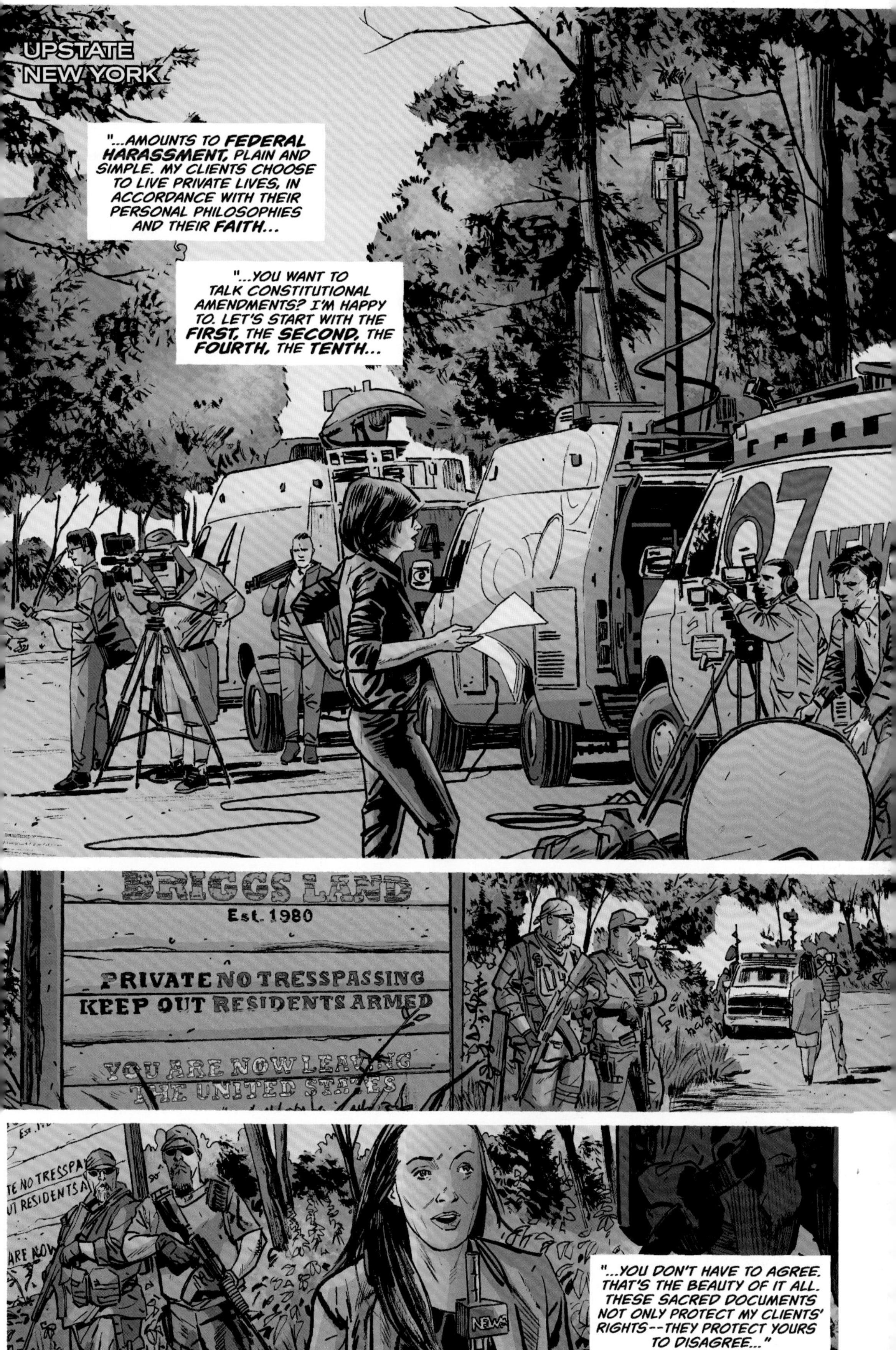
UPSTATE NEW YORK
"...AMOUNTS TO FEDERAL HARASSMENT, PLAIN AND SIMPLE. MY CLIENTS CHOOSE TO LIVE PRIVATE LIVES, IN ACCORDANCE WITH THEIR PERSONAL PHILOSOPHIES AND THEIR FAITH...
"...YOU WANT TO TALK CONSTITUTIONAL AMENDMENTS? I'M HAPPY TO. LET'S START WITH THE FIRST, THE SECOND, THE FOURTH, THE TENTH...
BRIGGS LAND
Est. 1980
PRIVATE NO TRESSPASSING
KEEP OUT RESIDENTS ARMED
YOU ARE NOW LEAVING THE UNITED STATES
"...YOU DON'T HAVE TO AGREE. THAT'S THE BEAUTY OF IT ALL. THESE SACRED DOCUMENTS NOT ONLY PROTECT MY CLIENTS' RIGHTS--THEY PROTECT YOURS TO DISAGREE..."

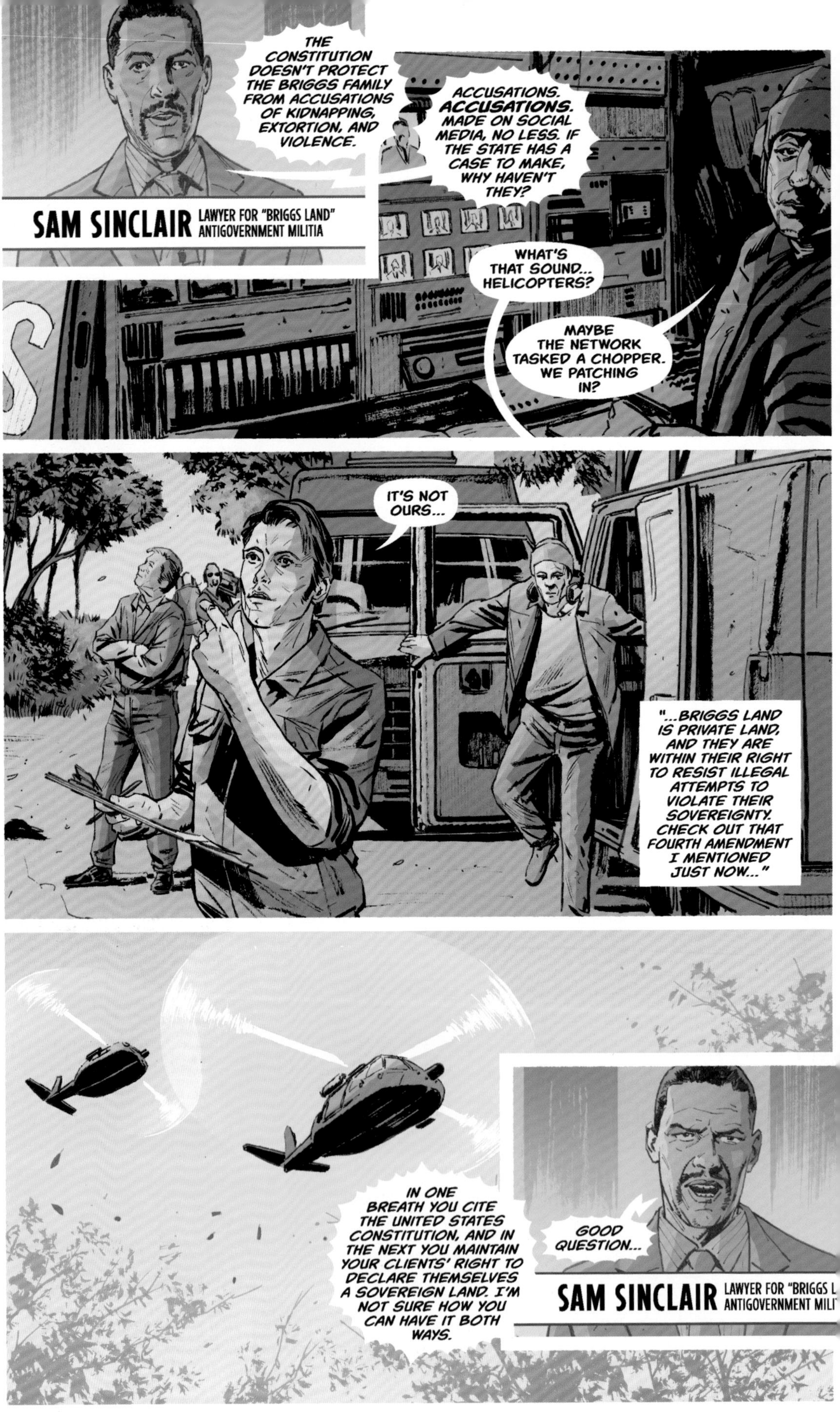
THE CONSTITUTION DOESN'T PROTECT THE BRIGGS FAMILY FROM ACCUSATIONS OF KIDNAPPING, EXTORTION, AND VIOLENCE.
SAM SINCLAIR LAWYER FOR "BRIGGS LAND" ANTIGOVERNMENT MILITIA
ACCUSATIONS. ACCUSATIONS. MADE ON SOCIAL MEDIA, NO LESS. IF THE STATE HAS A CASE TO MAKE, WHY HAVEN'T THEY?
WHAT'S THAT SOUND... HELICOPTERS?
MAYBE THE NETWORK TASKED A CHOPPER. WE PATCHING IN?
IT'S NOT OURS...
"...BRIGGS LAND IS PRIVATE LAND, AND THEY ARE WITHIN THEIR RIGHT TO RESIST ILLEGAL ATTEMPTS TO VIOLATE THEIR SOVEREIGNTY. CHECK OUT THAT FOURTH AMENDMENT I MENTIONED JUST NOW..."
IN ONE BREATH YOU CITE THE UNITED STATES CONSTITUTION, AND IN THE NEXT YOU MAINTAIN YOUR CLIENTS' RIGHT TO DECLARE THEMSELVES A SOVEREIGN LAND. I'M NOT SURE HOW YOU CAN HAVE IT BOTH WAYS.
GOOD QUESTION...
SAM SINCLAIR LAWYER FOR "BRIGGS L ANTIGOVERNMENT MILI

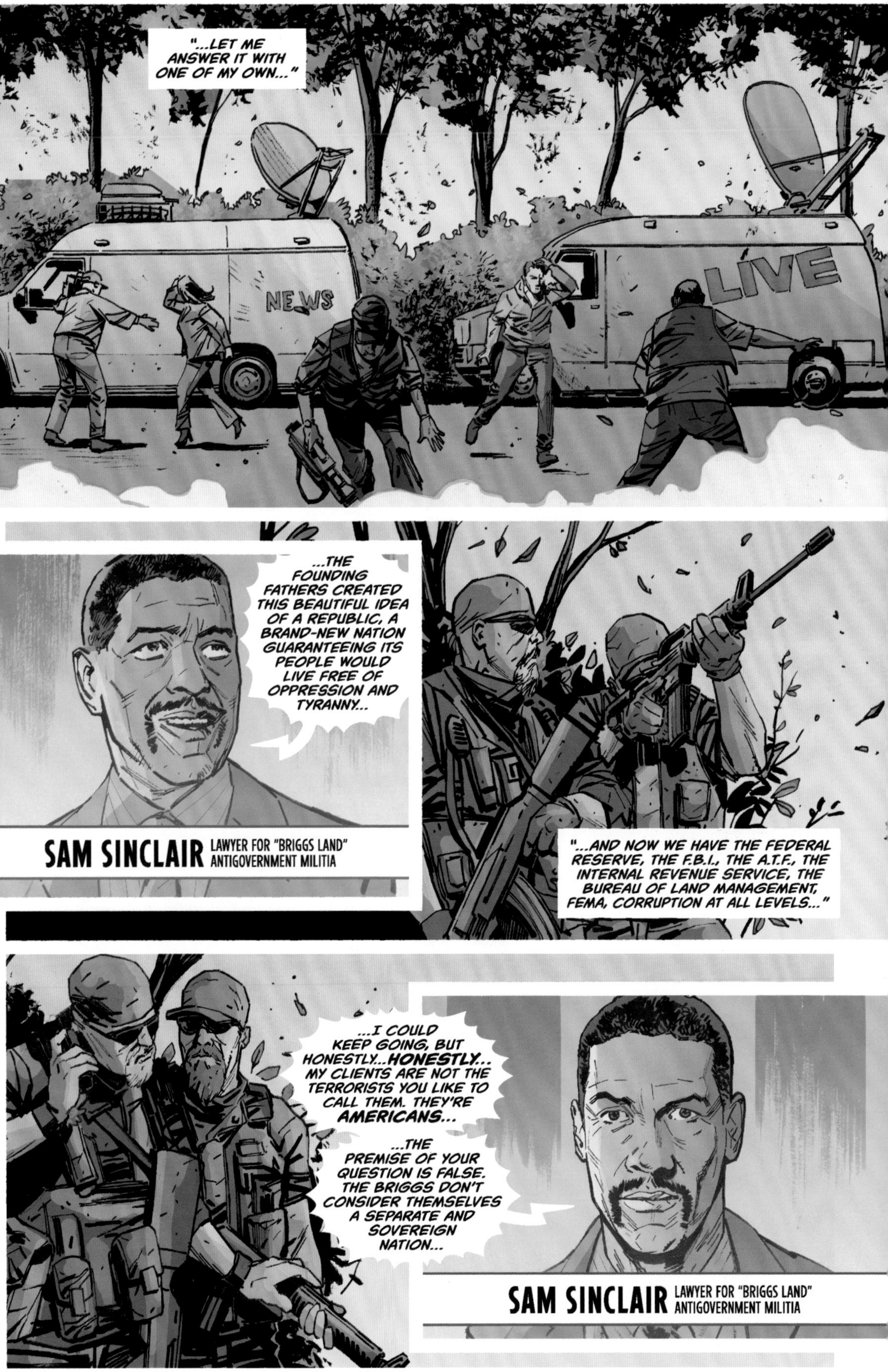
"...LET ME ANSWER IT WITH ONE OF MY OWN..."
NEWS
LIVE
...THE FOUNDING FATHERS CREATED THIS BEAUTIFUL IDEA OF A REPUBLIC, A BRAND-NEW NATION GUARANTEEING ITS PEOPLE WOULD LIVE FREE OF OPPRESSION AND TYRANNY...
SAM SINCLAIR LAWYER FOR "BRIGGS LAND" ANTIGOVERNMENT MILITIA
"...AND NOW WE HAVE THE FEDERAL RESERVE, THE F.B.I., THE A.T.F., THE INTERNAL REVENUE SERVICE, THE BUREAU OF LAND MANAGEMENT, FEMA, CORRUPTION AT ALL LEVELS..."
...I COULD KEEP GOING, BUT HONESTLY...HONESTLY... MY CLIENTS ARE NOT THE TERRORISTS YOU LIKE TO CALL THEM. THEY'RE AMERICANS...
...THE PREMISE OF YOUR QUESTION IS FALSE. THE BRIGGS DON'T CONSIDER THEMSELVES A SEPARATE AND SOVEREIGN NATION...
SAM SINCLAIR LAWYER FOR "BRIGGS LAND" ANTIGOVERNMENT MILITIA

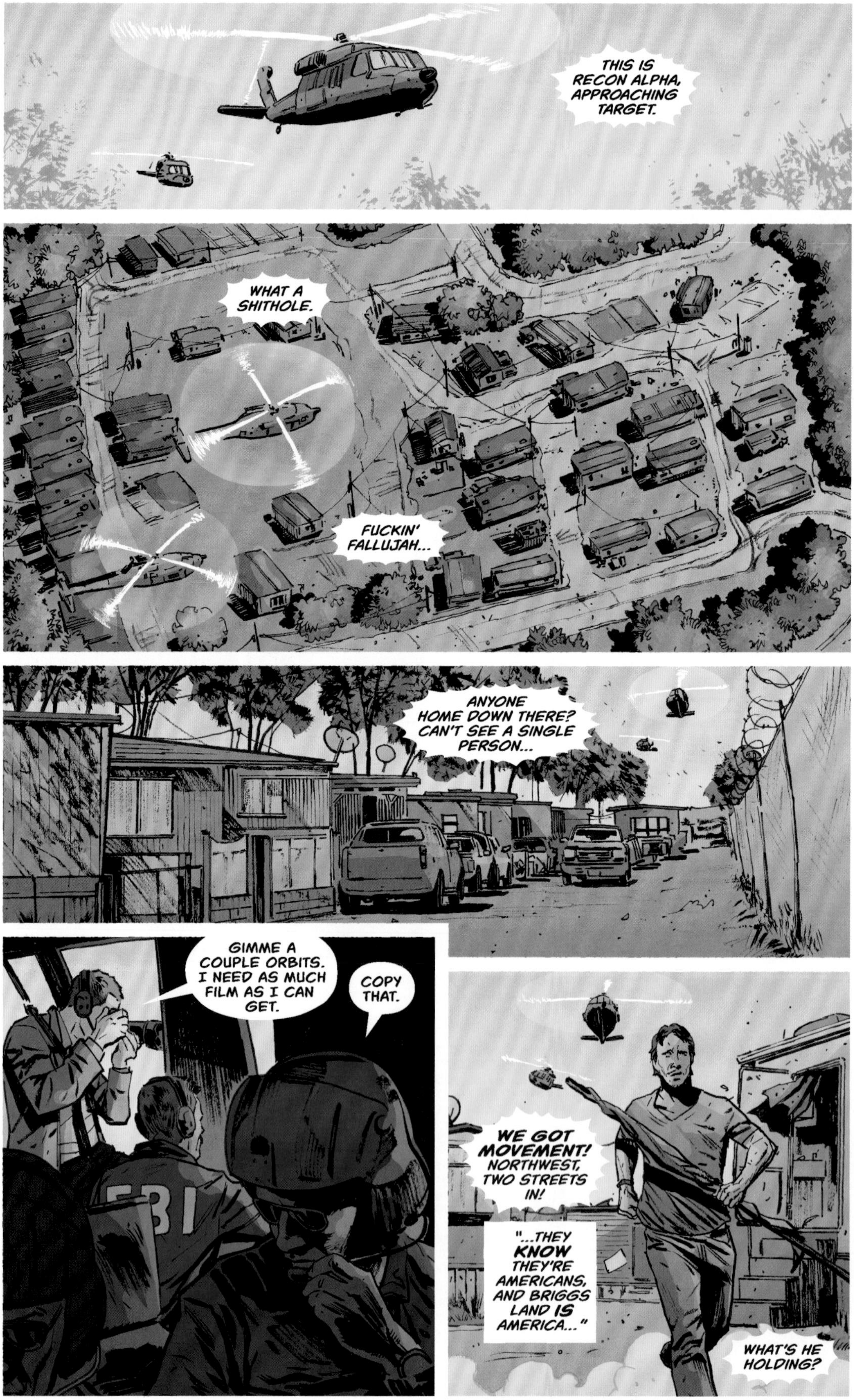

THIS IS RECON ALPHA, APPROACHING TARGET.
WHAT A SHITHOLE.
FUCKIN' FALLUJAH...
ANYONE HOME DOWN THERE? CAN'T SEE A SINGLE PERSON...
GIMME A COUPLE ORBITS. I NEED AS MUCH FILM AS I CAN GET.
COPY THAT.
FBI
WE GOT MOVEMENT! NORTHWEST, TWO STREETS IN!
"...THEY KNOW THEY'RE AMERICANS, AND BRIGGS LAND IS AMERICA..."
WHAT'S HE HOLDING?

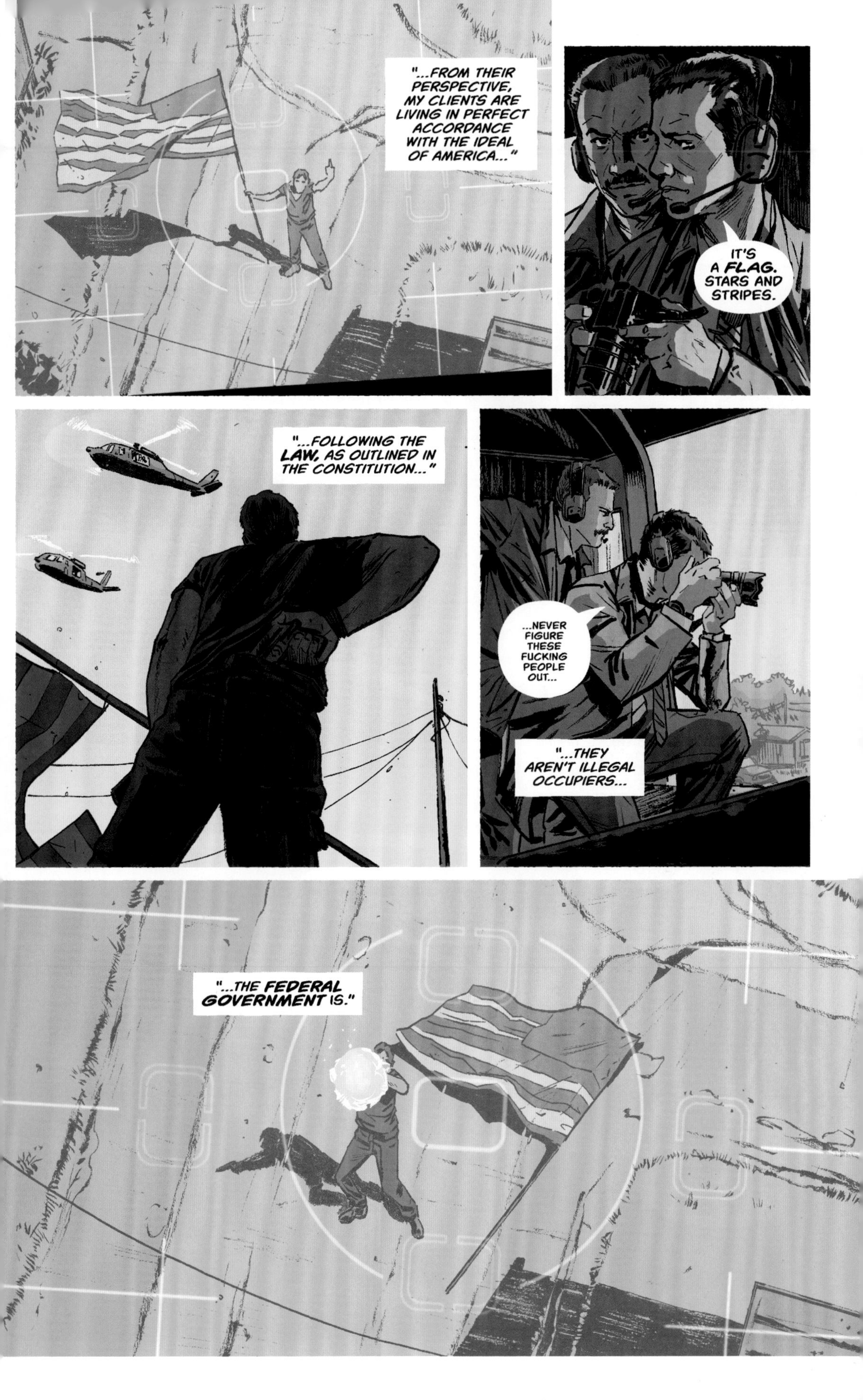
"...FROM THEIR PERSPECTIVE, MY CLIENTS ARE LIVING IN PERFECT ACCORDANCE WITH THE IDEAL OF AMERICA..."
IT'S A FLAG. STARS AND STRIPES.
"...FOLLOWING THE LAW, AS OUTLINED IN THE CONSTITUTION..."
...NEVER FIGURE THESE FUCKING PEOPLE OUT...
"...THEY AREN'T ILLEGAL OCCUPIERS...
"...THE FEDERAL GOVERNMENT IS."

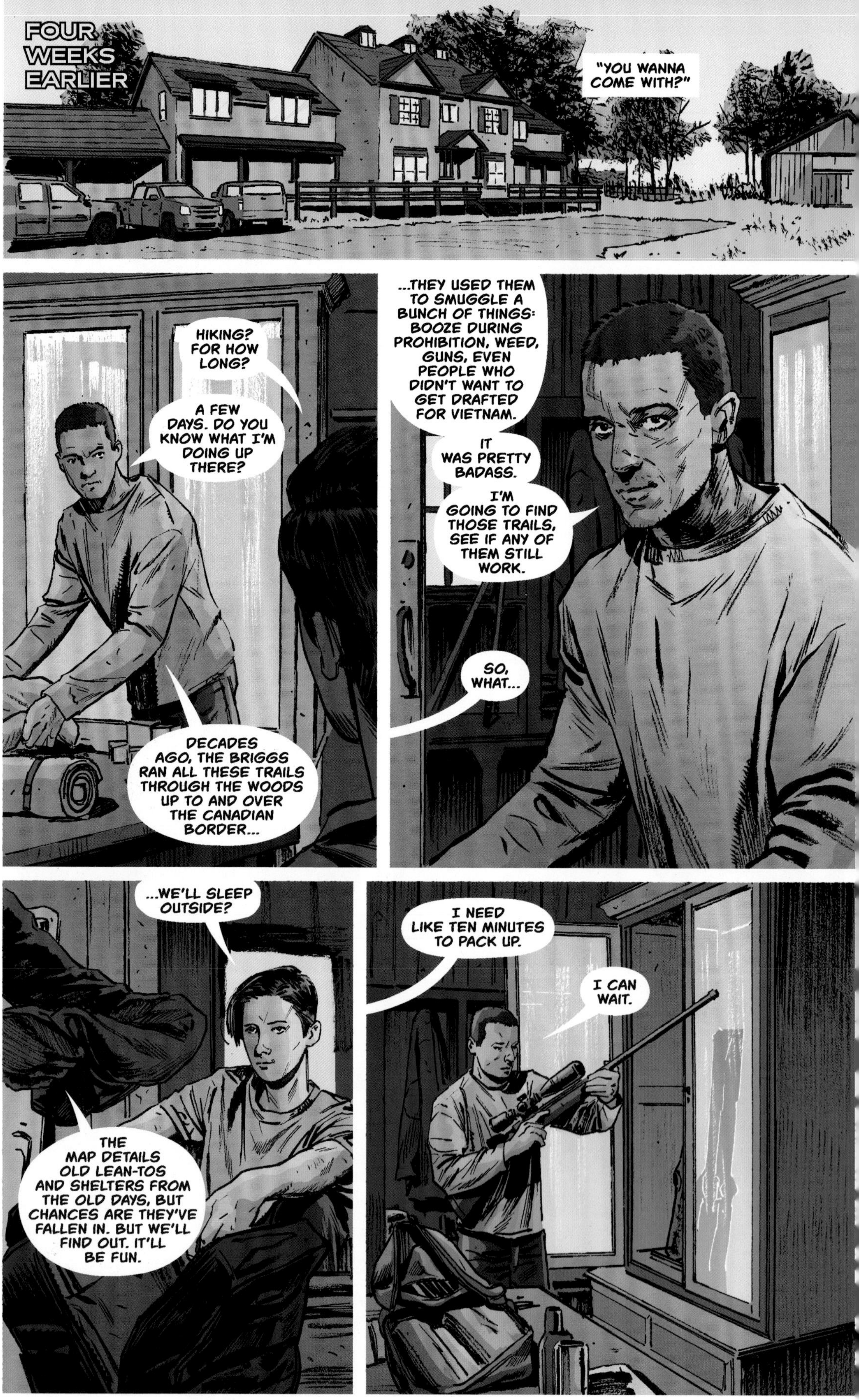
FOUR WEEKS EARLIER
"YOU WANNA COME WITH?"
HIKING? FOR HOW LONG?
A FEW DAYS. DO YOU KNOW WHAT I'M DOING UP THERE?
DECADES AGO, THE BRIGGS RAN ALL THESE TRAILS THROUGH THE WOODS UP TO AND OVER THE CANADIAN BORDER...
...THEY USED THEM TO SMUGGLE A BUNCH OF THINGS: BOOZE DURING PROHIBITION, WEED, GUNS, EVEN PEOPLE WHO DIDN'T WANT TO GET DRAFTED FOR VIETNAM.
IT WAS PRETTY BADASS.
I'M GOING TO FIND THOSE TRAILS, SEE IF ANY OF THEM STILL WORK.
SO, WHAT...
...WE'LL SLEEP OUTSIDE?
THE MAP DETAILS OLD LEAN-TOS AND SHELTERS FROM THE OLD DAYS, BUT CHANCES ARE THEY'VE FALLEN IN. BUT WE'LL FIND OUT. IT'LL BE FUN.
I NEED LIKE TEN MINUTES TO PACK UP.
I CAN WAIT.

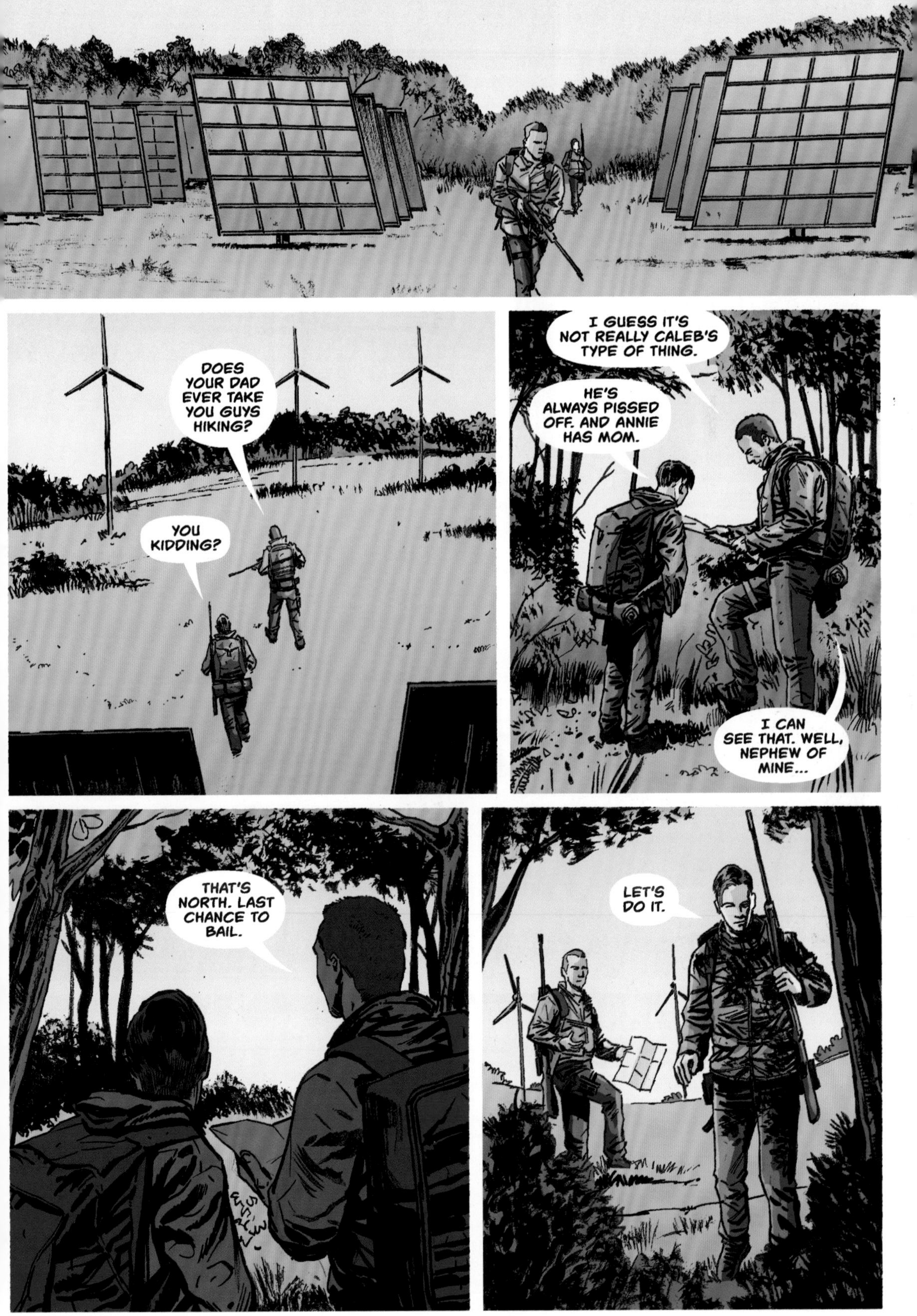
DOES YOUR DAD EVER TAKE YOU GUYS HIKING?
YOU KIDDING?
I GUESS IT'S NOT REALLY CALEB'S TYPE OF THING.
HE'S ALWAYS PISSED OFF. AND ANNIE HAS MOM.
I CAN SEE THAT. WELL, NEPHEW OF MINE...
THAT'S NORTH. LAST CHANCE TO BAIL.
LET'S DO IT.

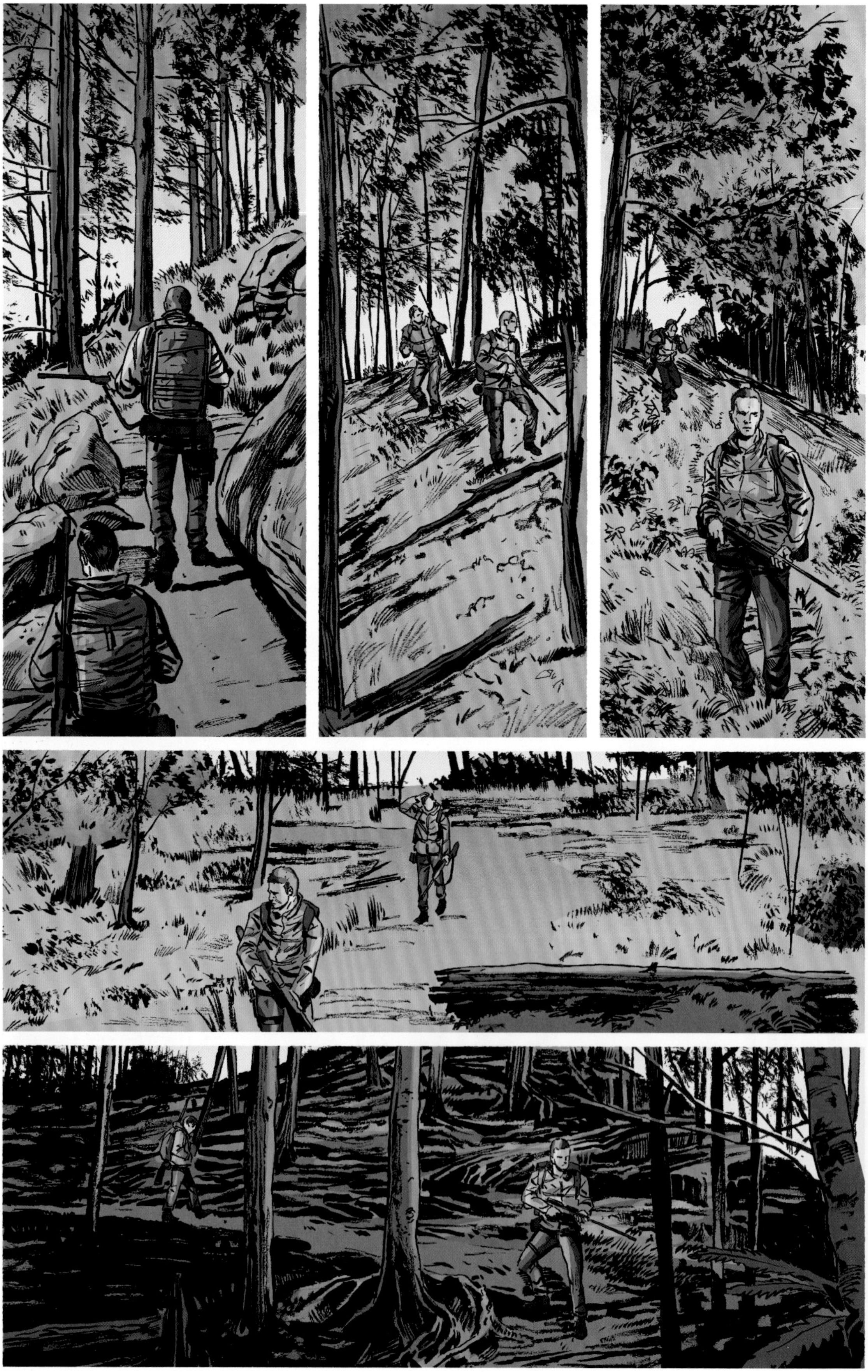

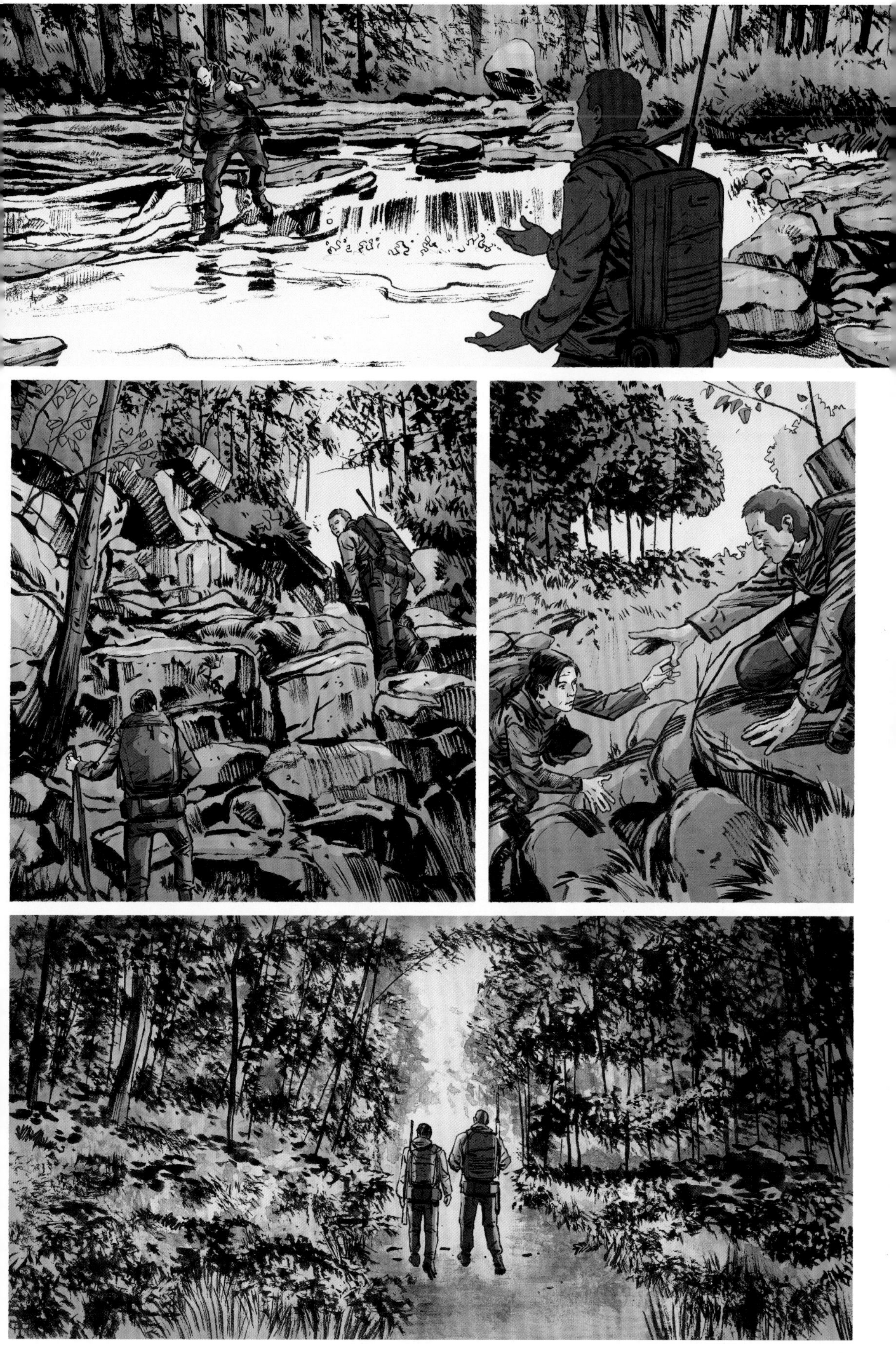

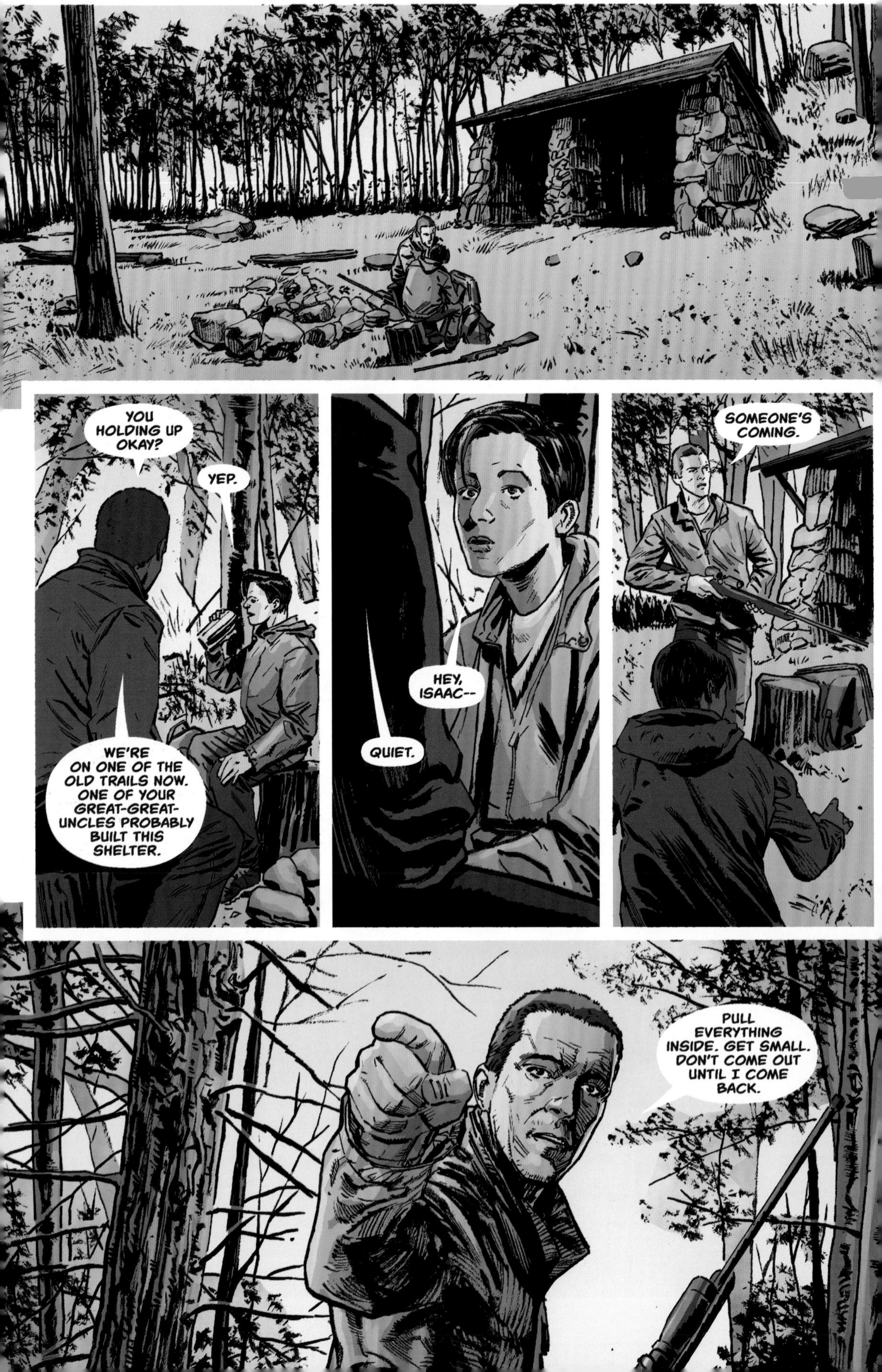
YOU HOLDING UP OKAY?
YEP.
WE'RE ON ONE OF THE OLD TRAILS NOW. ONE OF YOUR GREAT-GREAT-UNCLES PROBABLY BUILT THIS SHELTER.
HEY, ISAAC--
QUIET.
SOMEONE'S COMING.
PULL EVERYTHING INSIDE. GET SMALL. DON'T COME OUT UNTIL I COME BACK.

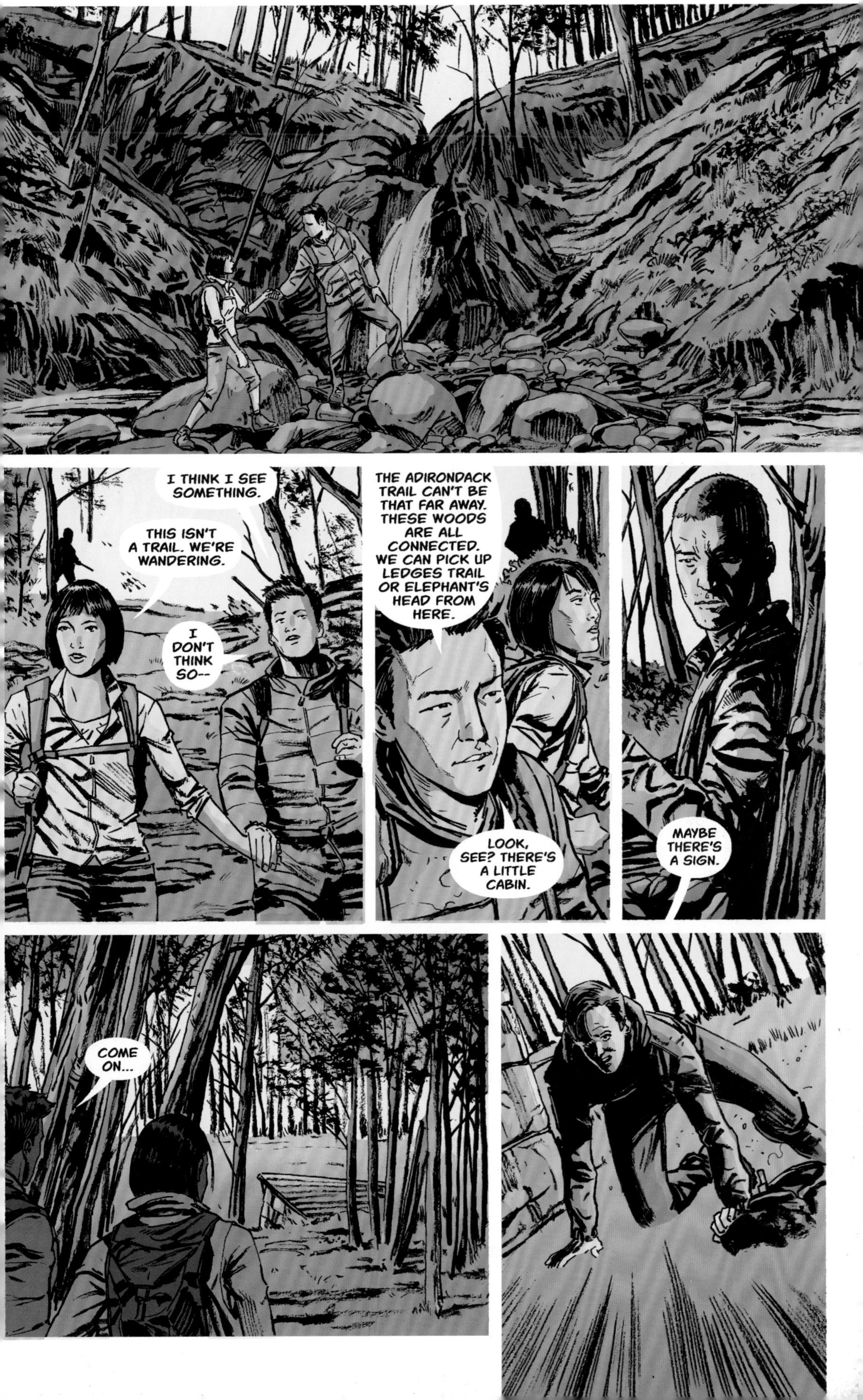
I THINK I SEE SOMETHING.
THIS ISN'T A TRAIL. WE'RE WANDERING.
I DON'T THINK SO--
THE ADIRONDACK TRAIL CAN'T BE THAT FAR AWAY. THESE WOODS ARE ALL CONNECTED. WE CAN PICK UP LEDGES TRAIL OR ELEPHANT'S HEAD FROM HERE.
LOOK, SEE? THERE'S A LITTLE CABIN.
MAYBE THERE'S A SIGN.
COME ON...

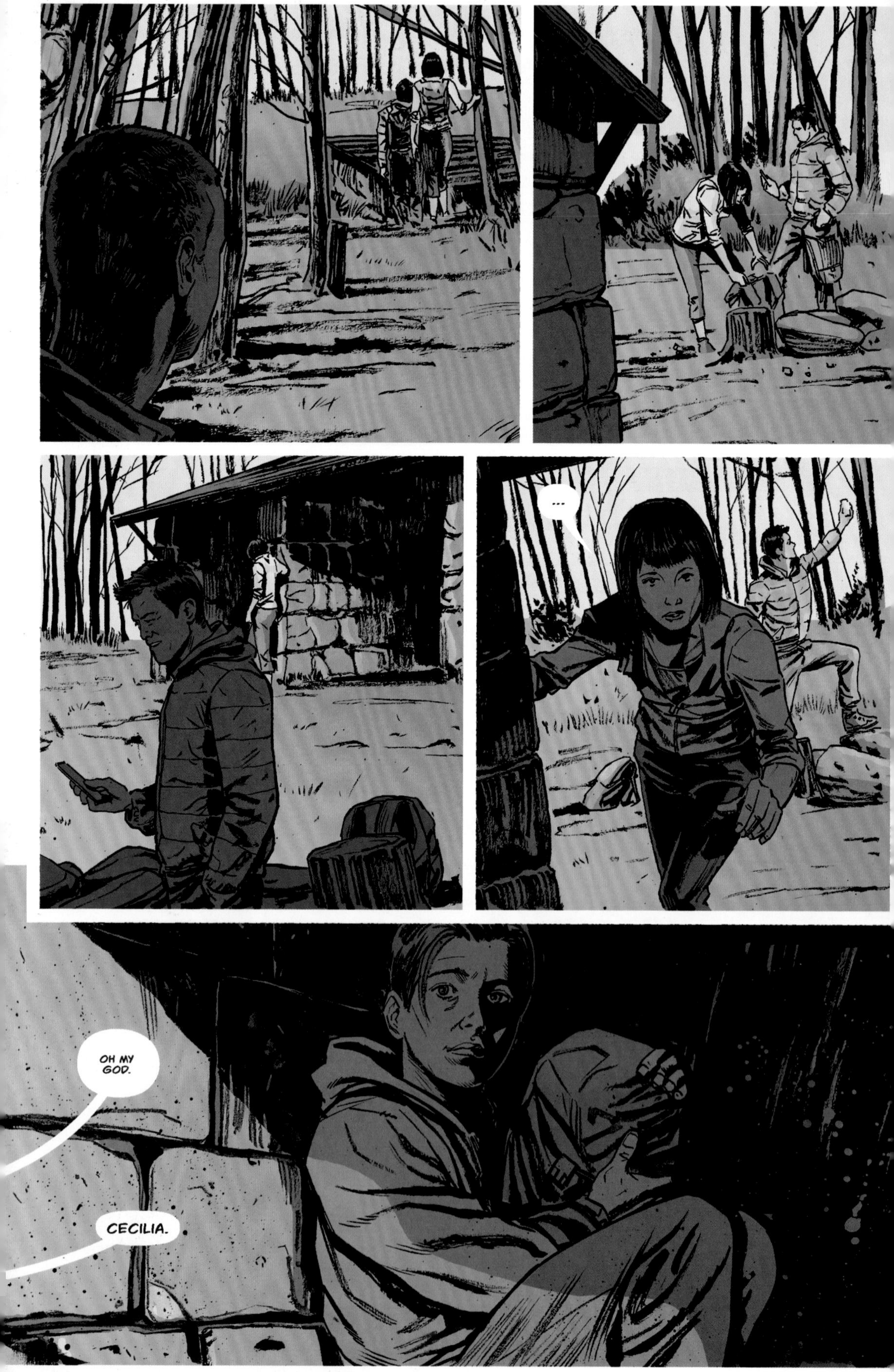
...
OH MY GOD.
CECILIA.

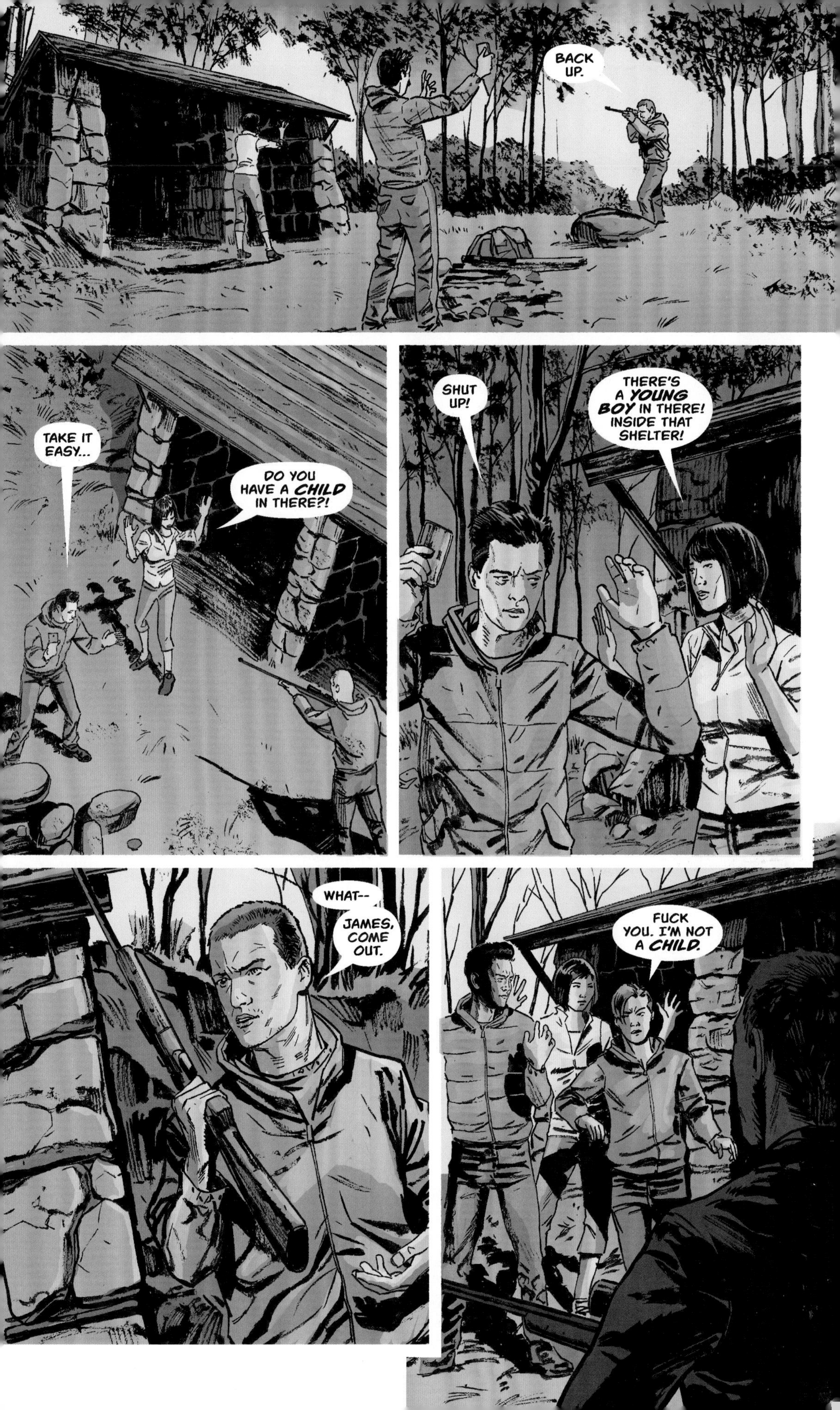
BACK UP.
TAKE IT EASY...
DO YOU HAVE A CHILD IN THERE?!
SHUT UP!
THERE'S A YOUNG BOY IN THERE! INSIDE THAT SHELTER!
WHAT--
JAMES, COME OUT.
FUCK YOU. I'M NOT A CHILD.

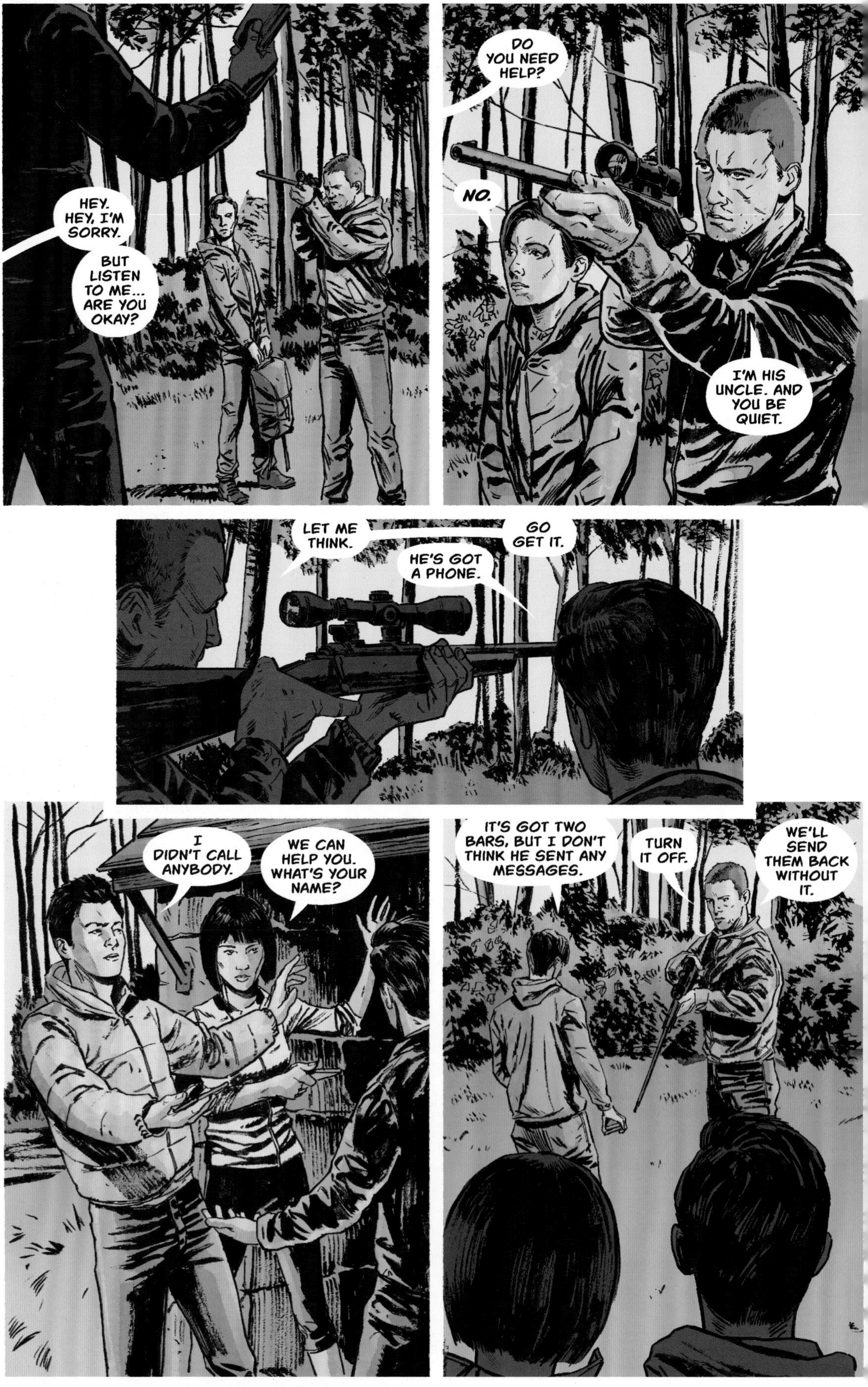
HEY. HEY, I'M SORRY.
BUT LISTEN TO ME... ARE YOU OKAY?
DO YOU NEED HELP?
NO.
I'M HIS UNCLE. AND YOU BE QUIET.
LET ME THINK.
HE'S GOT A PHONE.
GO GET IT.
I DIDN'T CALL ANYBODY.
WE CAN HELP YOU. WHAT'S YOUR NAME?
IT'S GOT TWO BARS, BUT I DON'T THINK HE SENT ANY MESSAGES.
TURN IT OFF.
WE'LL SEND THEM BACK WITHOUT IT.

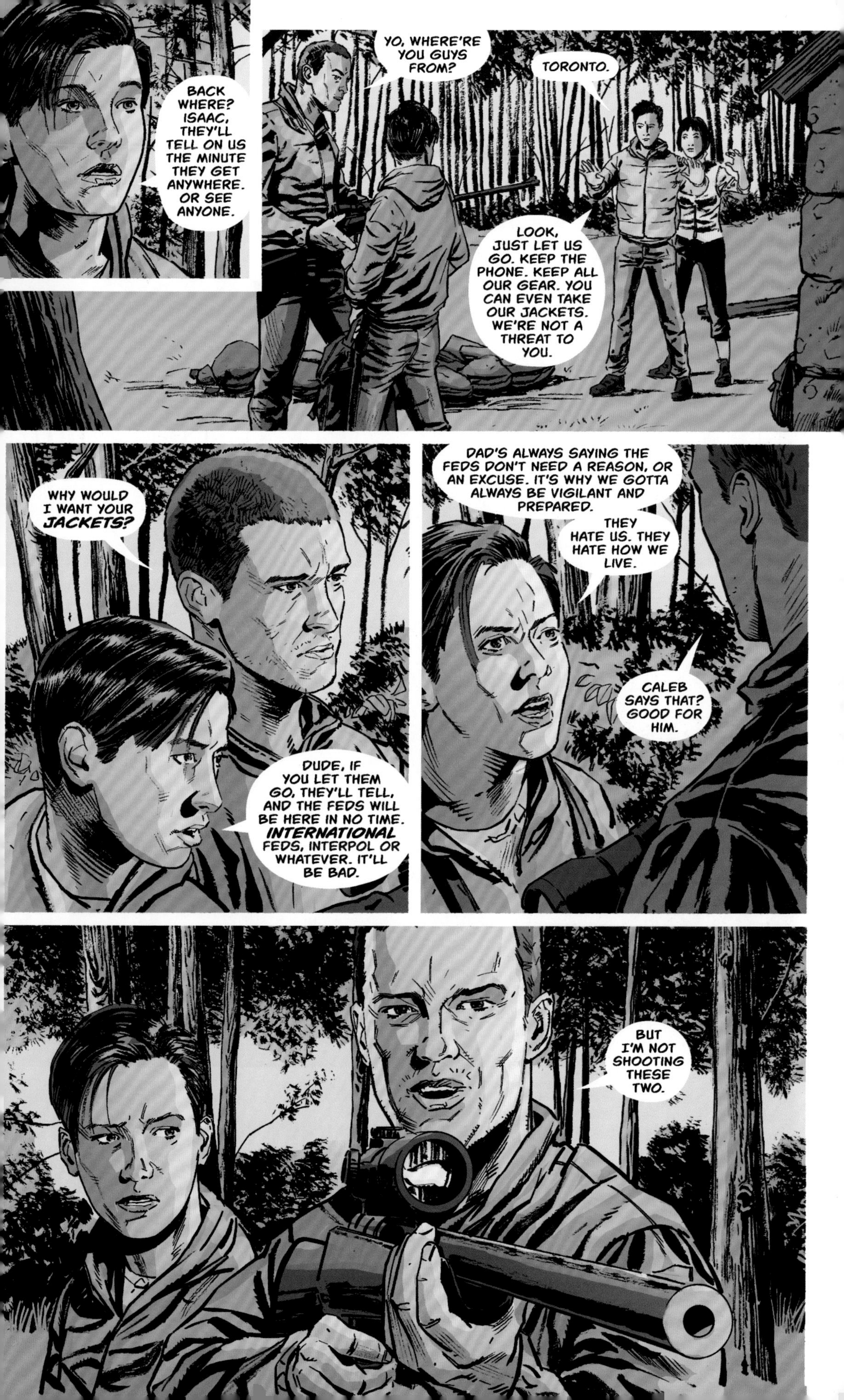
BACK WHERE? ISAAC, THEY'LL TELL ON US THE MINUTE THEY GET ANYWHERE. OR SEE ANYONE.
YO, WHERE'RE YOU GUYS FROM?
TORONTO.
LOOK, JUST LET US GO. KEEP THE PHONE. KEEP ALL OUR GEAR. YOU CAN EVEN TAKE OUR JACKETS. WE'RE NOT A THREAT TO YOU.
WHY WOULD I WANT YOUR JACKETS?
DUDE, IF YOU LET THEM GO, THEY'LL TELL, AND THE FEDS WILL BE HERE IN NO TIME. INTERNATIONAL FEDS, INTERPOL OR WHATEVER. IT'LL BE BAD.
DAD'S ALWAYS SAYING THE FEDS DON'T NEED A REASON, OR AN EXCUSE. IT'S WHY WE GOTTA ALWAYS BE VIGILANT AND PREPARED.
THEY HATE US. THEY HATE HOW WE LIVE.
CALEB SAYS THAT? GOOD FOR HIM.
BUT I'M NOT SHOOTING THESE TWO.

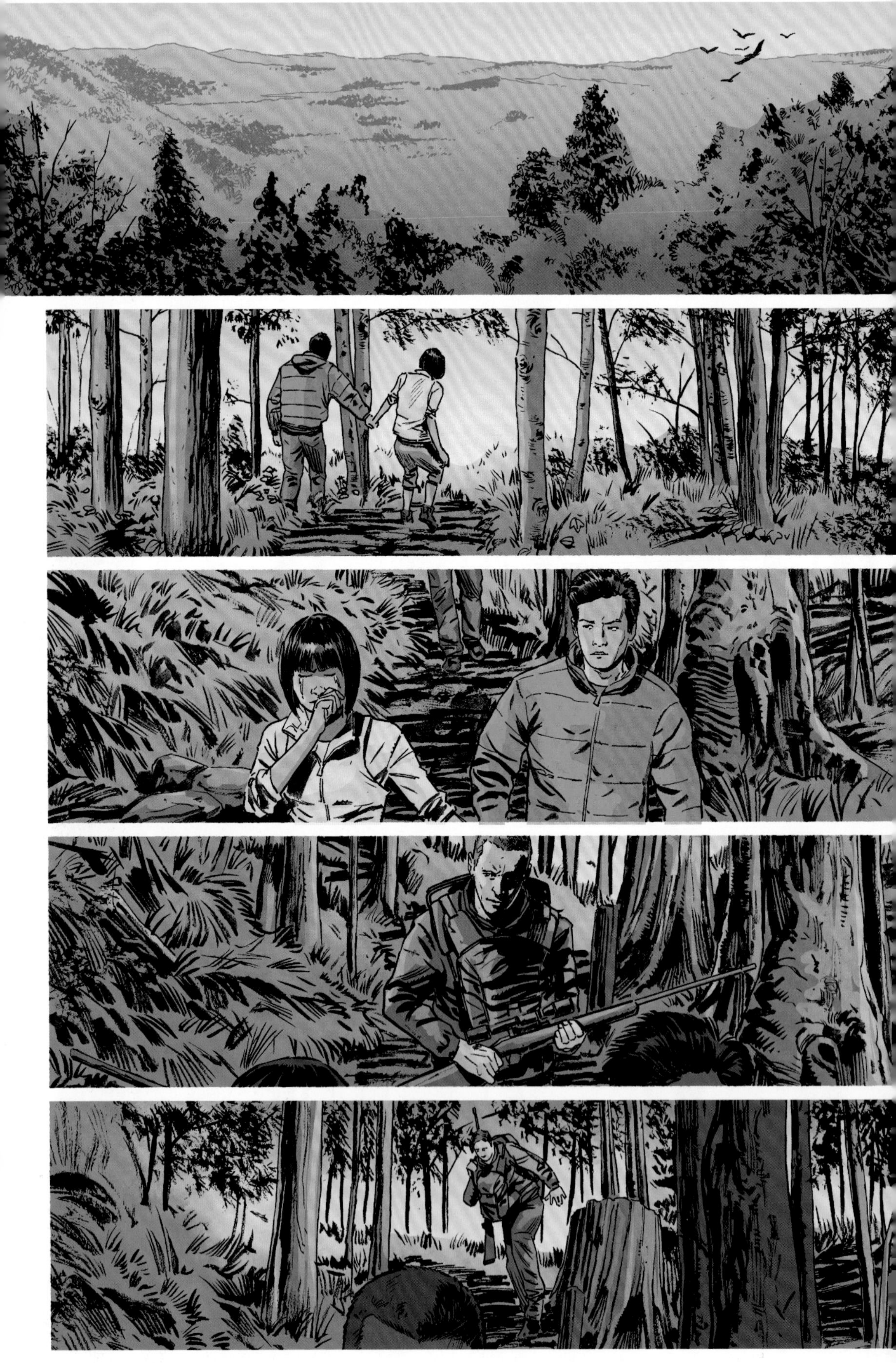

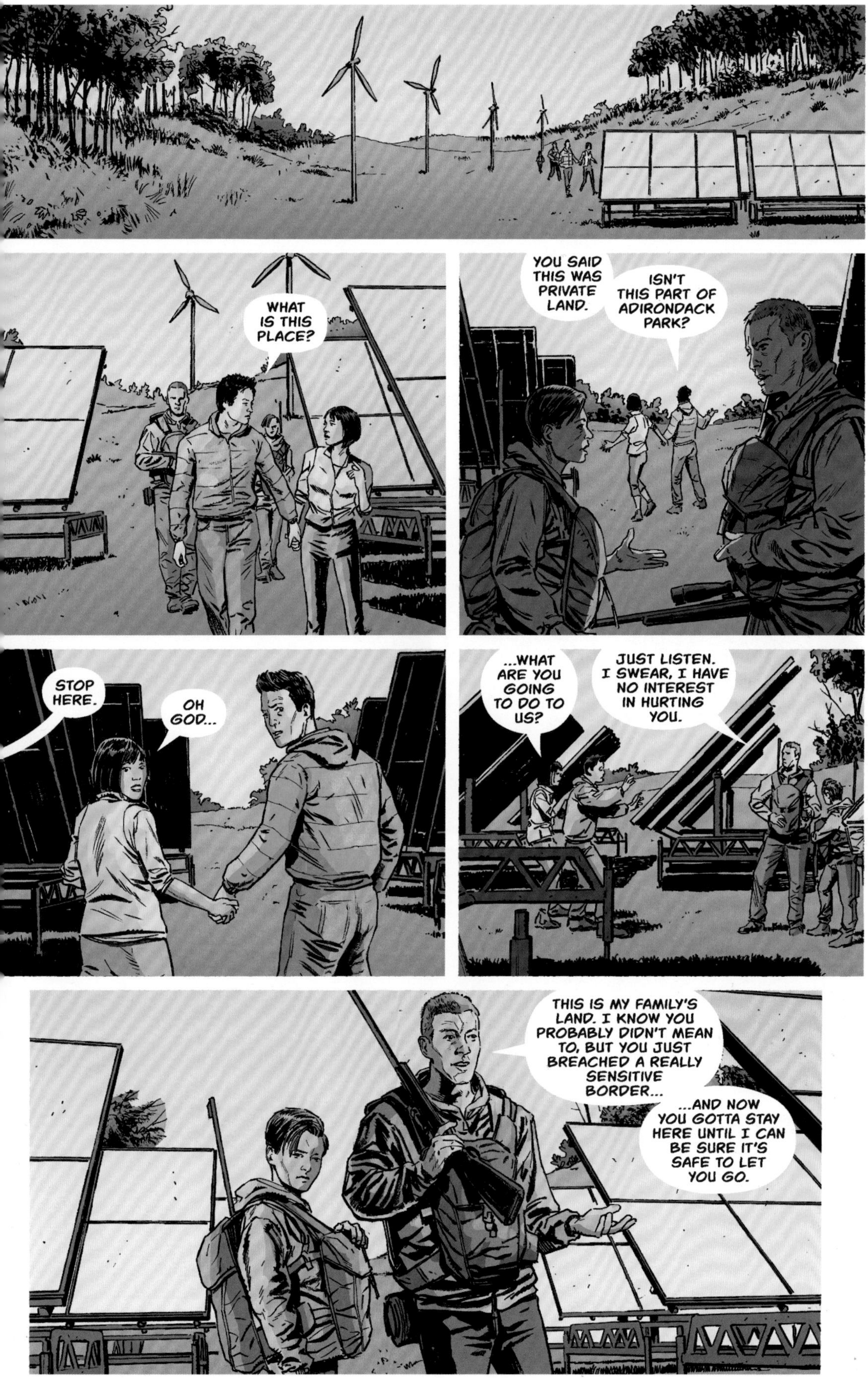
WHAT IS THIS PLACE?
YOU SAID THIS WAS PRIVATE LAND.
ISN'T THIS PART OF ADIRONDACK PARK?
STOP HERE.
OH GOD...
...WHAT ARE YOU GOING TO DO TO US?
JUST LISTEN. I SWEAR, I HAVE NO INTEREST IN HURTING YOU.
THIS IS MY FAMILY'S LAND. I KNOW YOU PROBABLY DIDN'T MEAN TO, BUT YOU JUST BREACHED A REALLY SENSITIVE BORDER...
...AND NOW YOU GOTTA STAY HERE UNTIL I CAN BE SURE IT'S SAFE TO LET YOU GO.

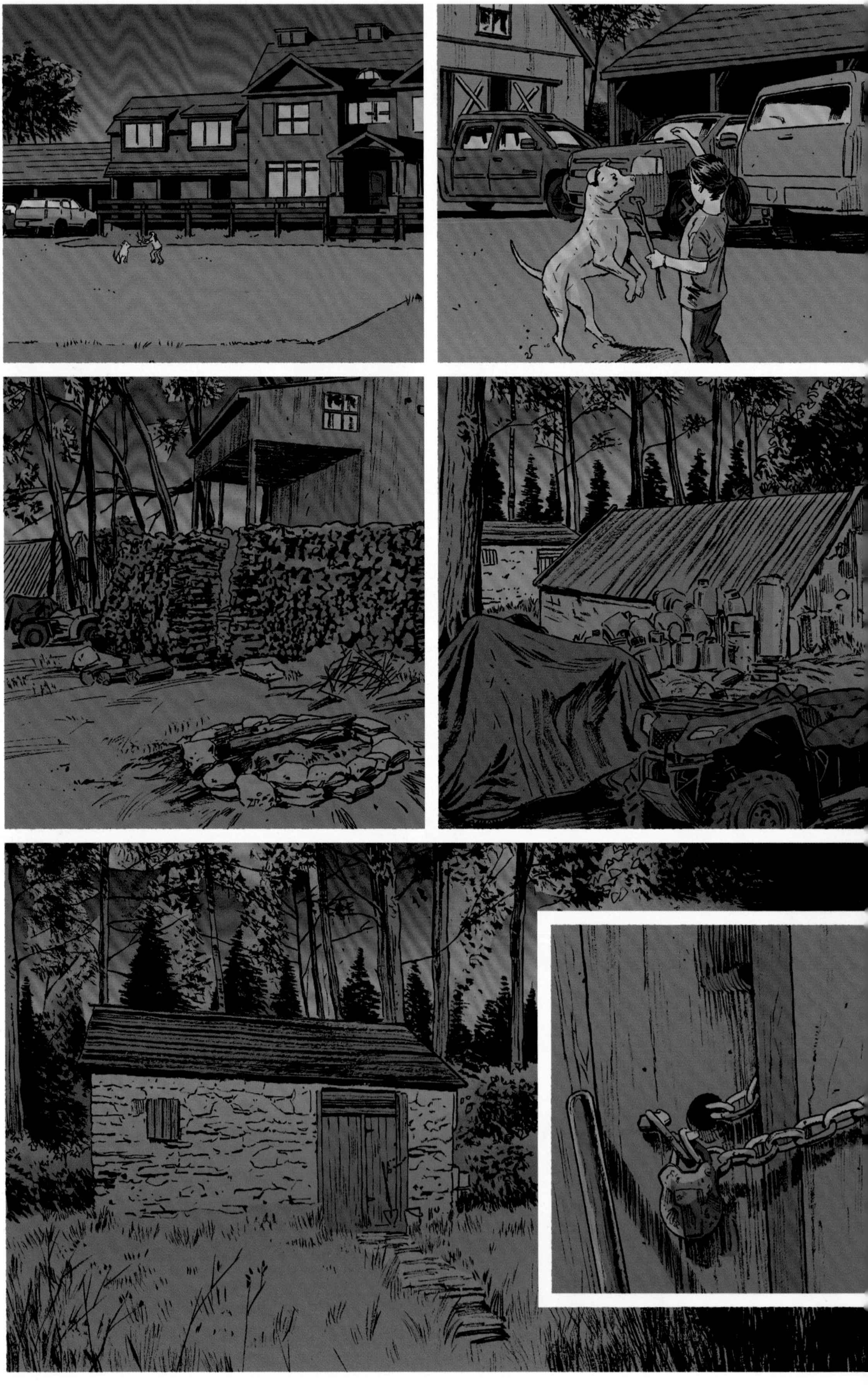

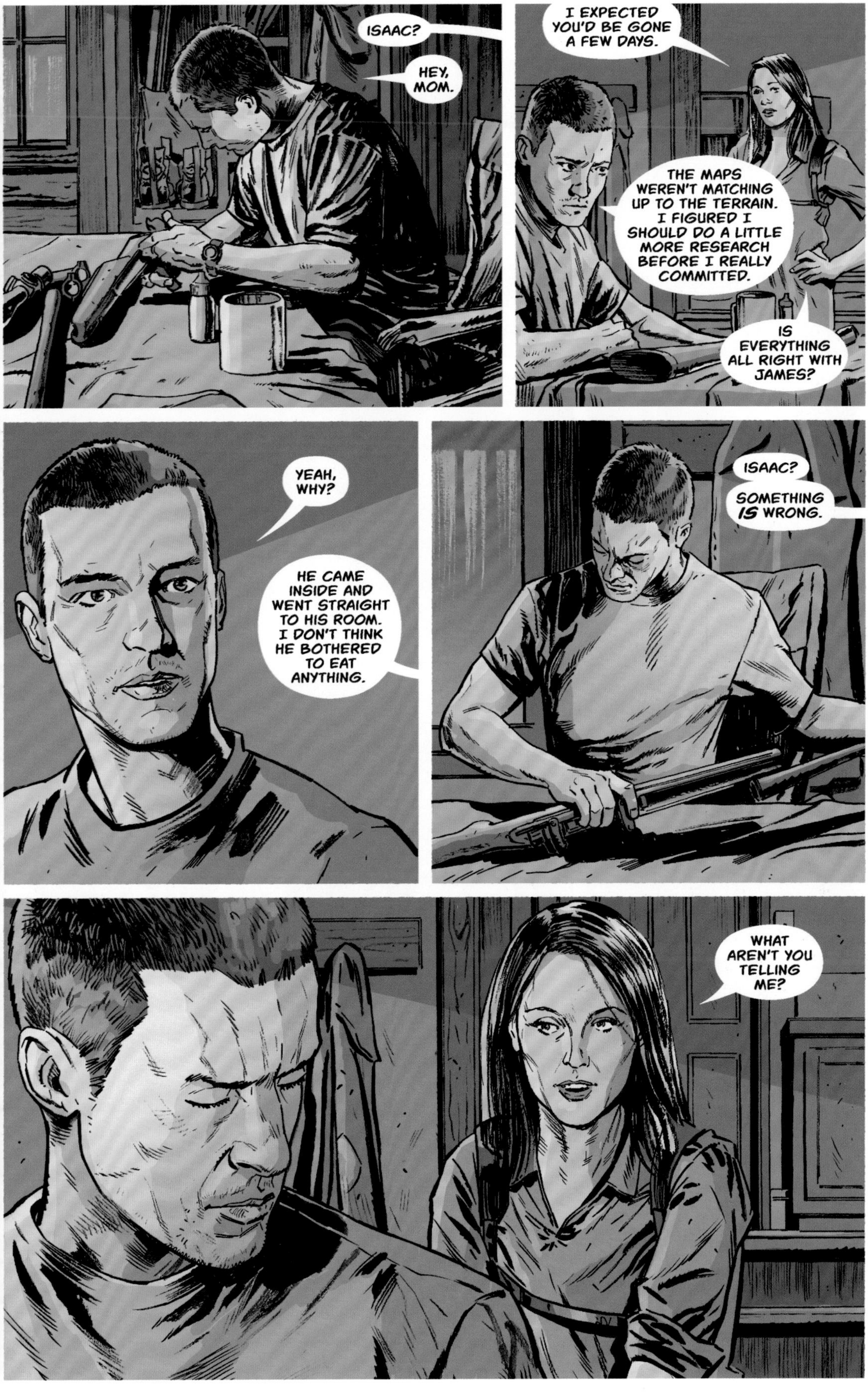
ISAAC?
HEY, MOM.
I EXPECTED YOU'D BE GONE A FEW DAYS.
THE MAPS WEREN'T MATCHING UP TO THE TERRAIN. I FIGURED I SHOULD DO A LITTLE MORE RESEARCH BEFORE I REALLY COMMITTED.
IS EVERYTHING ALL RIGHT WITH JAMES?
YEAH, WHY?
HE CAME INSIDE AND WENT STRAIGHT TO HIS ROOM. I DON'T THINK HE BOTHERED TO EAT ANYTHING.
ISAAC?
SOMETHING *IS* WRONG.
WHAT AREN'T YOU TELLING ME?

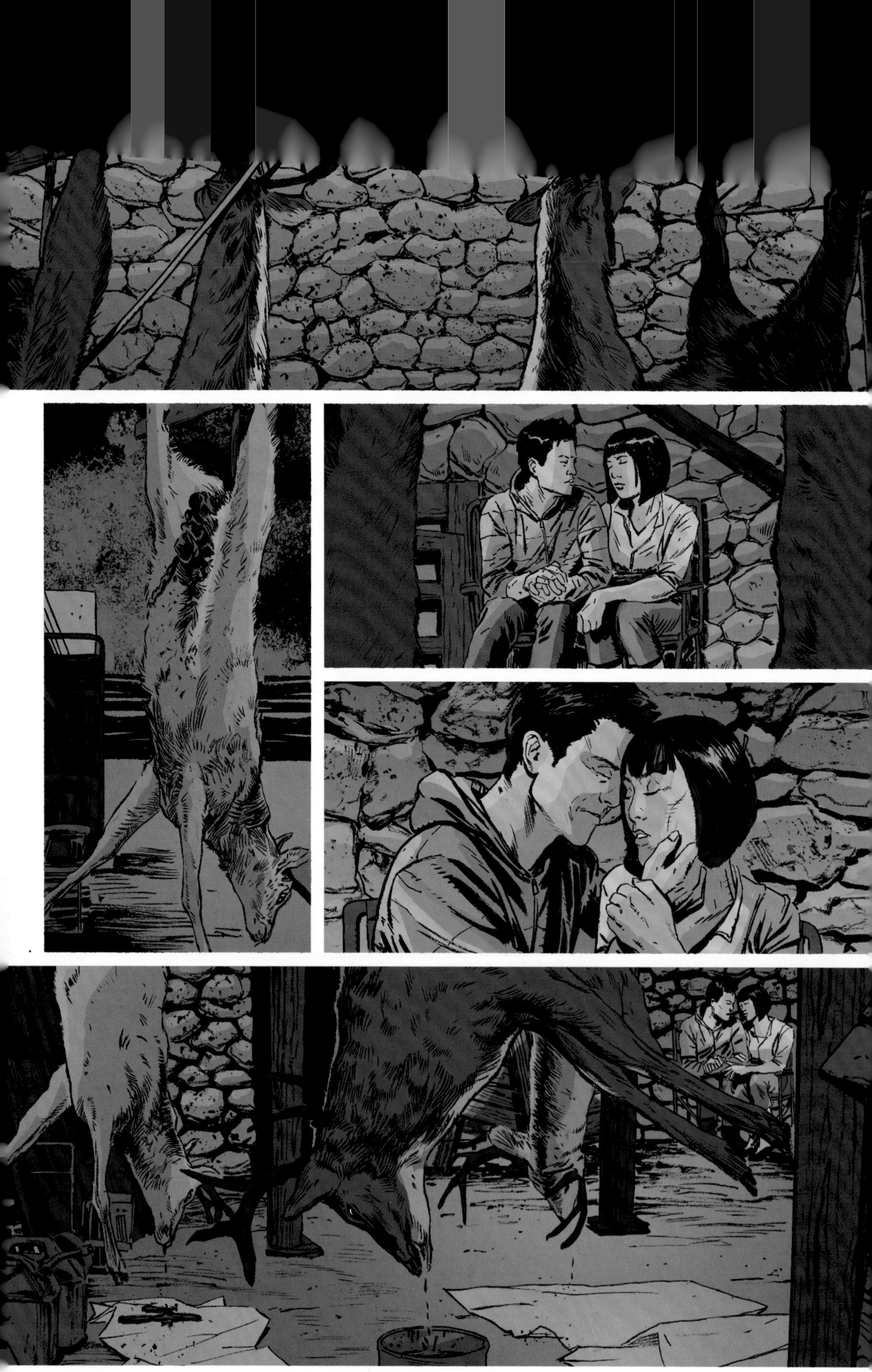

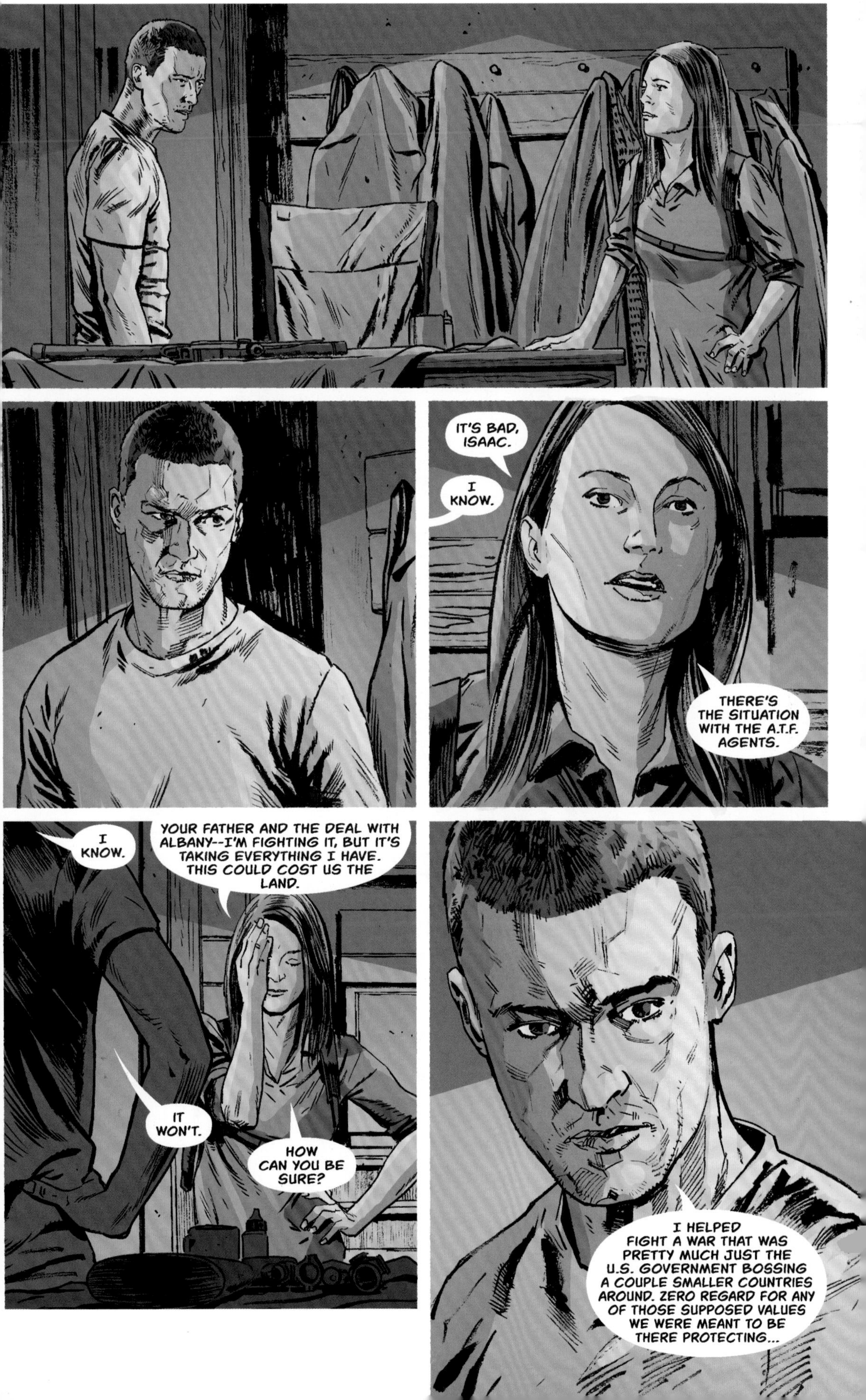
IT'S BAD, ISAAC.
I KNOW.
THERE'S THE SITUATION WITH THE A.T.F. AGENTS.
I KNOW.
YOUR FATHER AND THE DEAL WITH ALBANY--I'M FIGHTING IT, BUT IT'S TAKING EVERYTHING I HAVE. THIS COULD COST US THE LAND.
IT WON'T.
HOW CAN YOU BE SURE?
I HELPED FIGHT A WAR THAT WAS PRETTY MUCH JUST THE U.S. GOVERNMENT BOSSING A COUPLE SMALLER COUNTRIES AROUND. ZERO REGARD FOR ANY OF THOSE SUPPOSED VALUES WE WERE MEANT TO BE THERE PROTECTING...

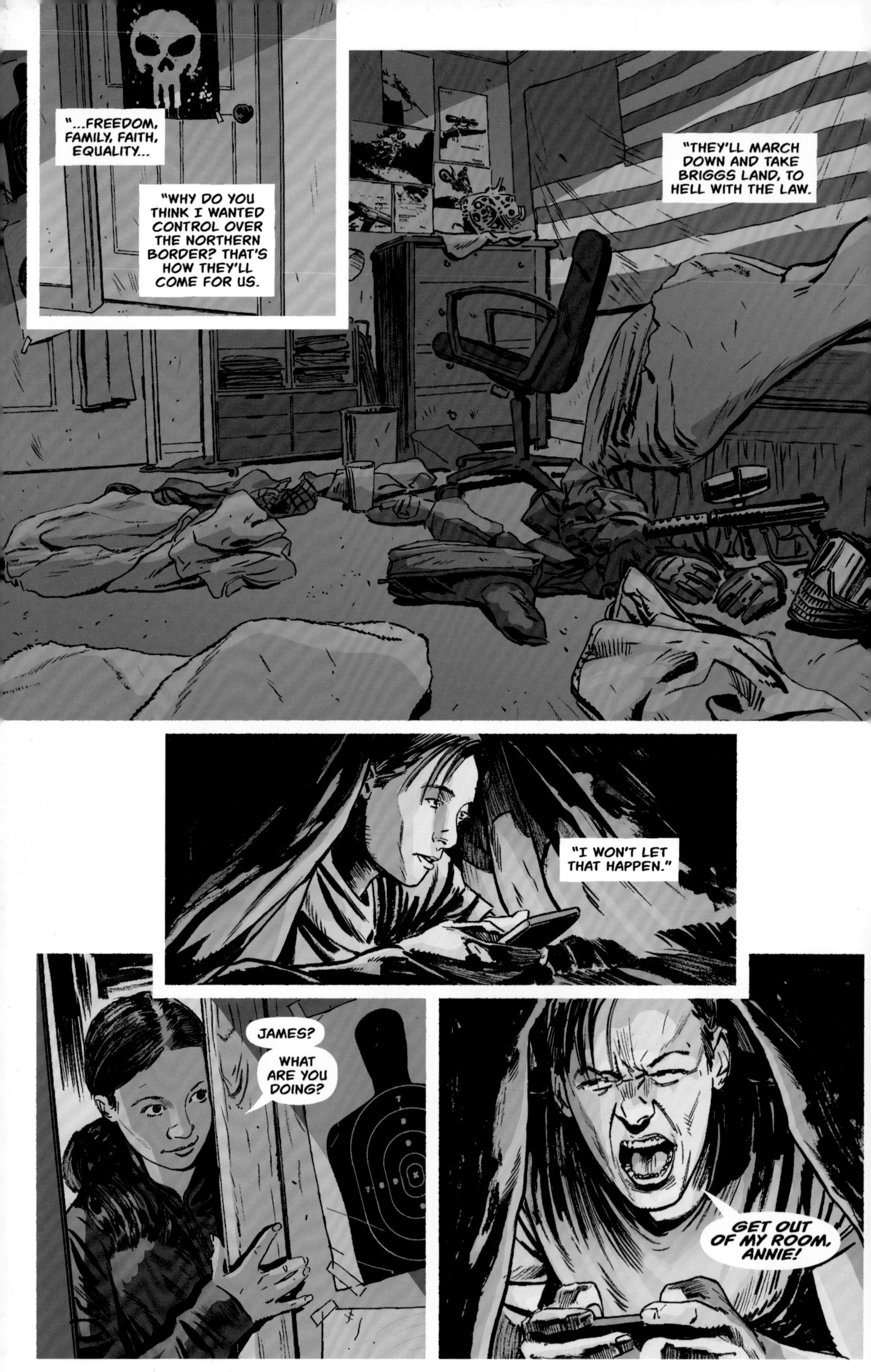
"...FREEDOM, FAMILY, FAITH, EQUALITY...
"WHY DO YOU THINK I WANTED CONTROL OVER THE NORTHERN BORDER? THAT'S HOW THEY'LL COME FOR US.
"THEY'LL MARCH DOWN AND TAKE BRIGGS LAND, TO HELL WITH THE LAW.
"I WON'T LET THAT HAPPEN."
JAMES?
WHAT ARE YOU DOING?
GET OUT OF MY ROOM, ANNIE!

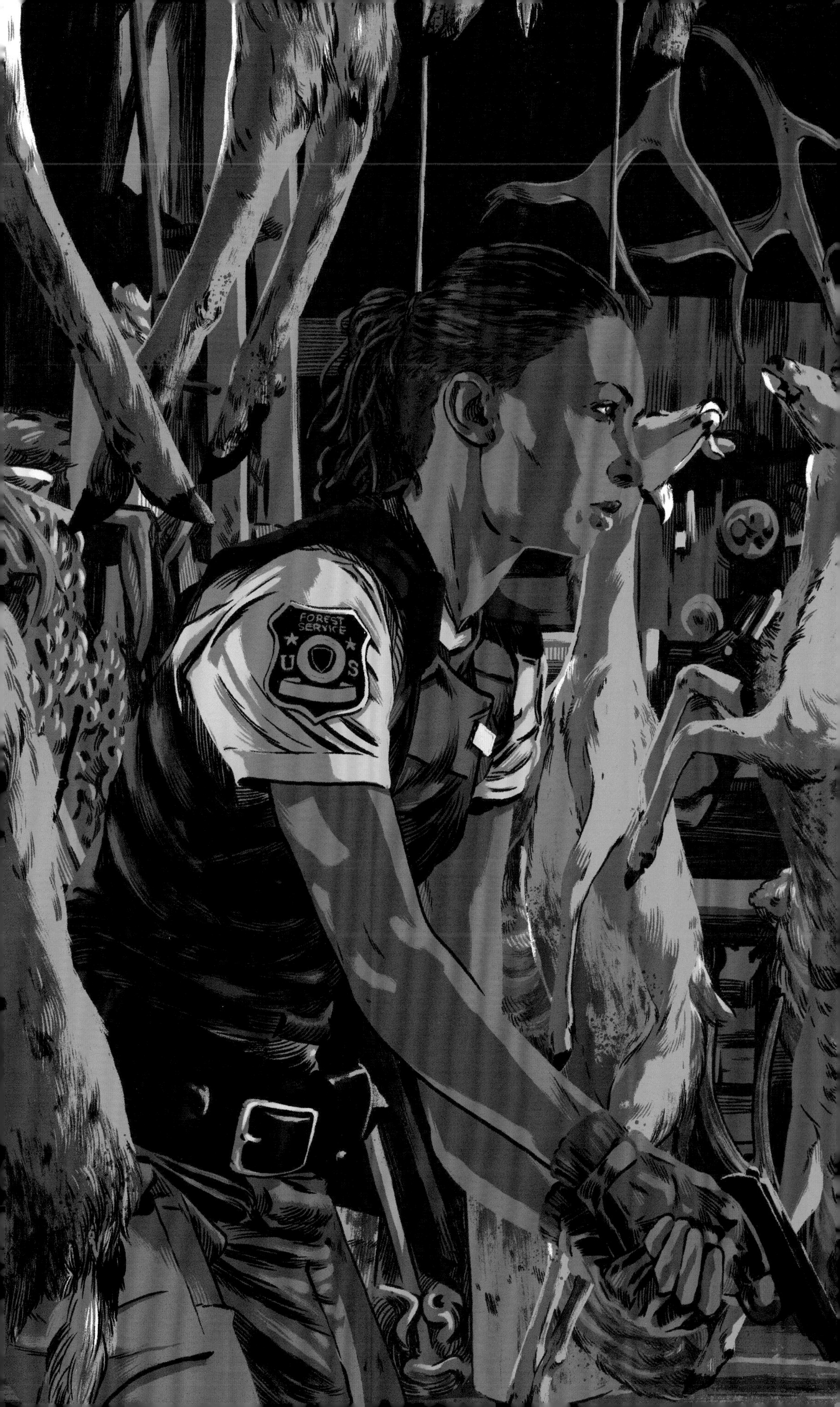
FOREST SERVICE
U S

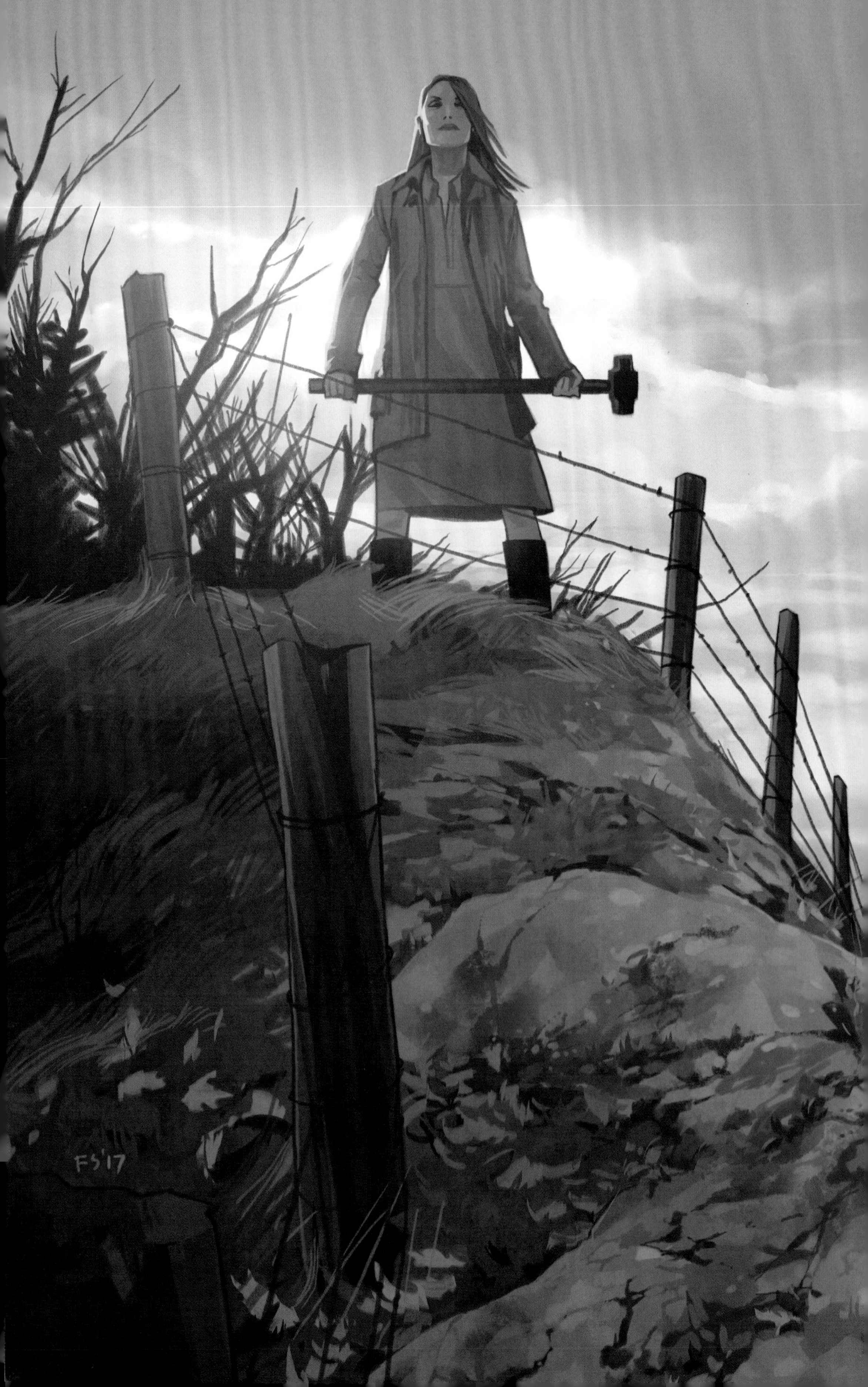
FS'17

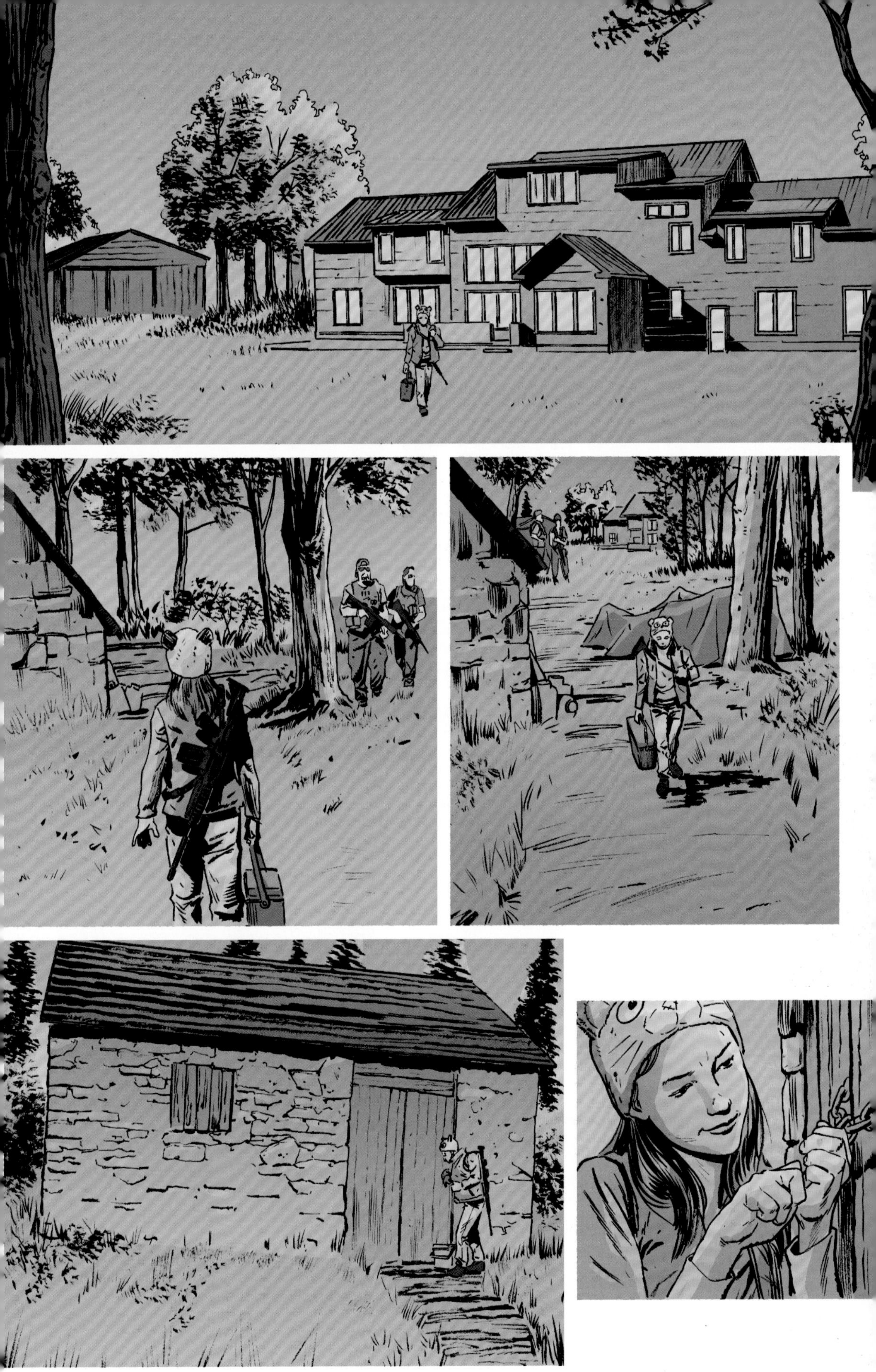

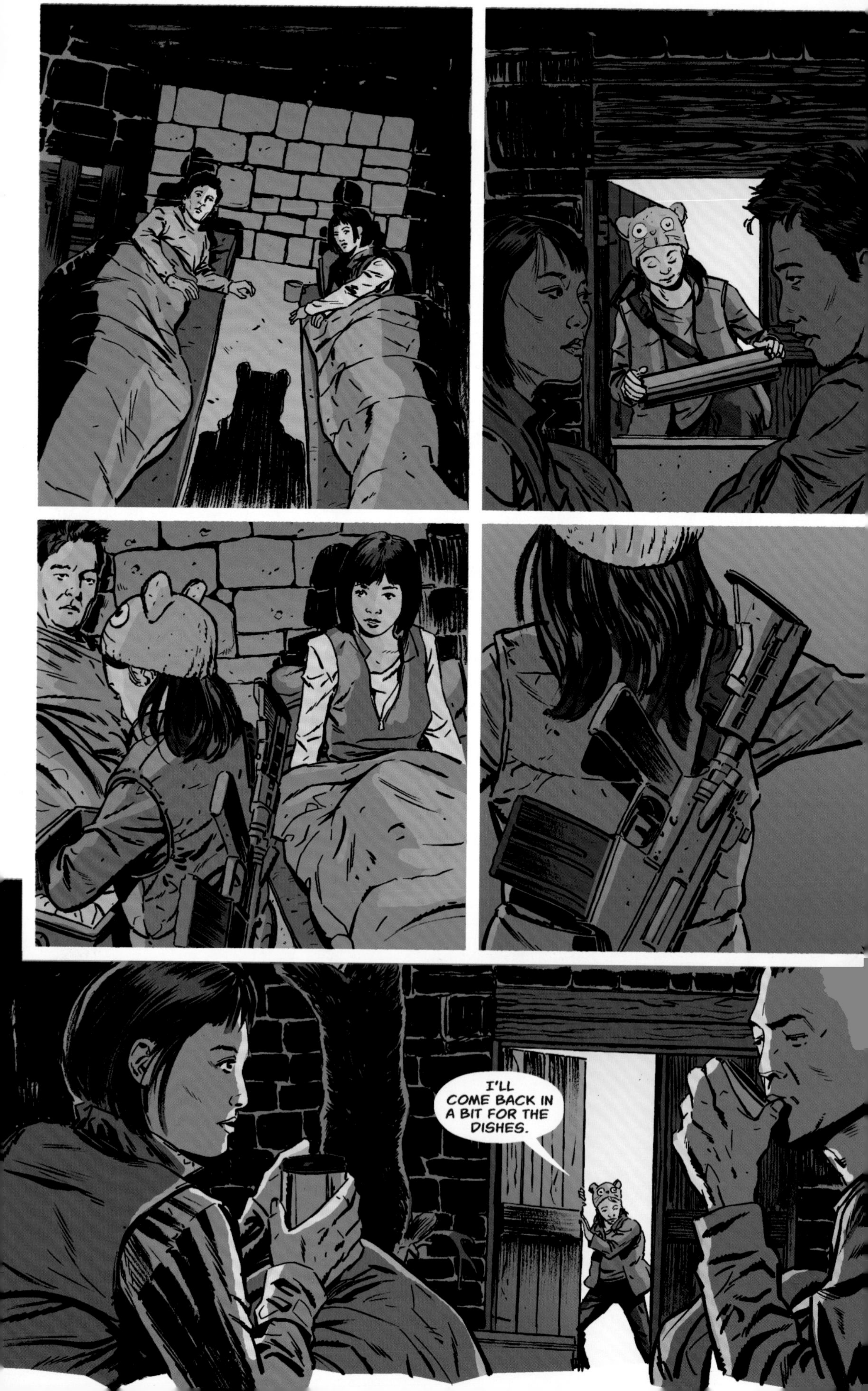
I'LL
COME BACK IN
A BIT FOR THE
DISHES.

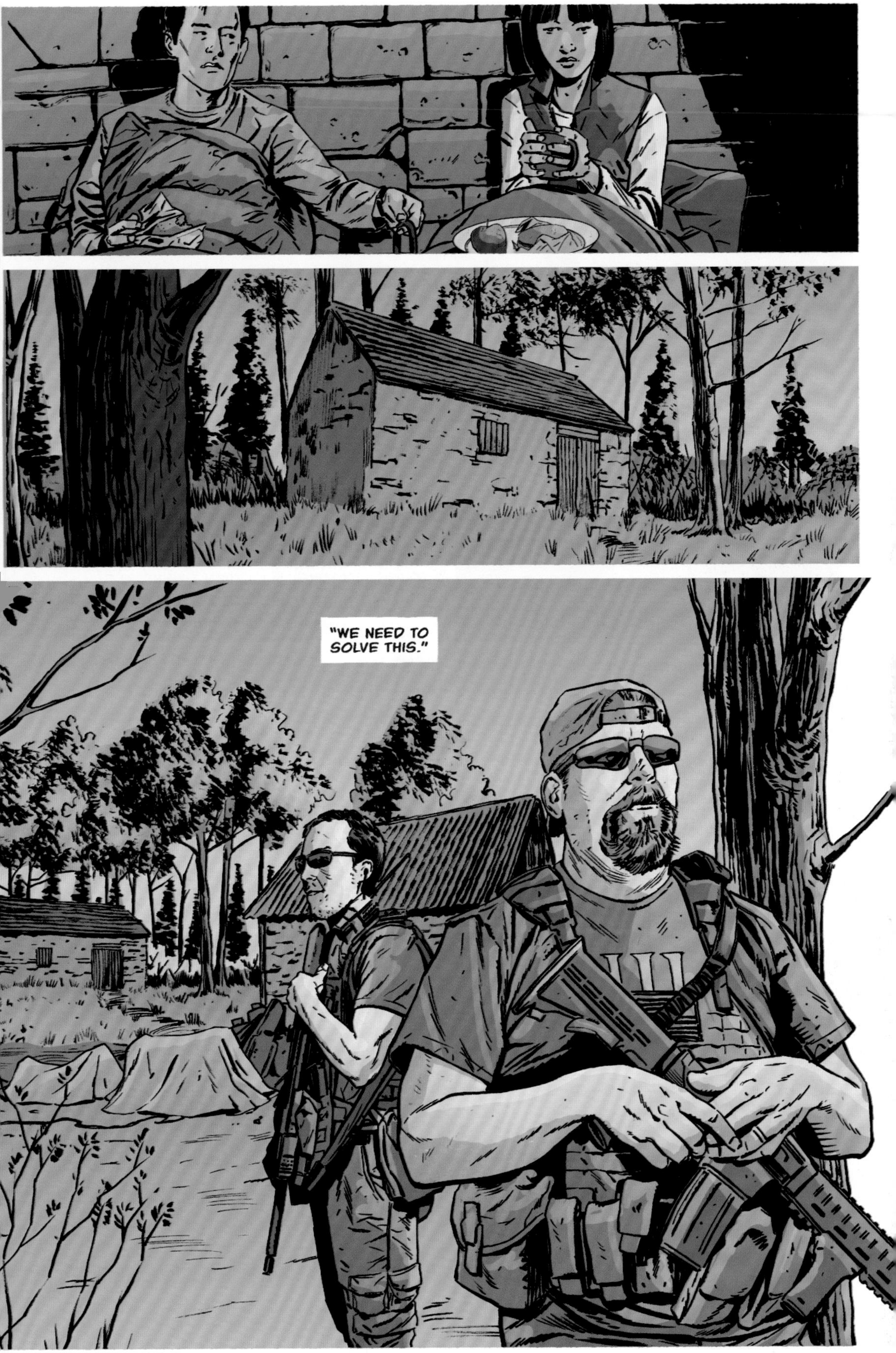
"WE NEED TO SOLVE THIS."

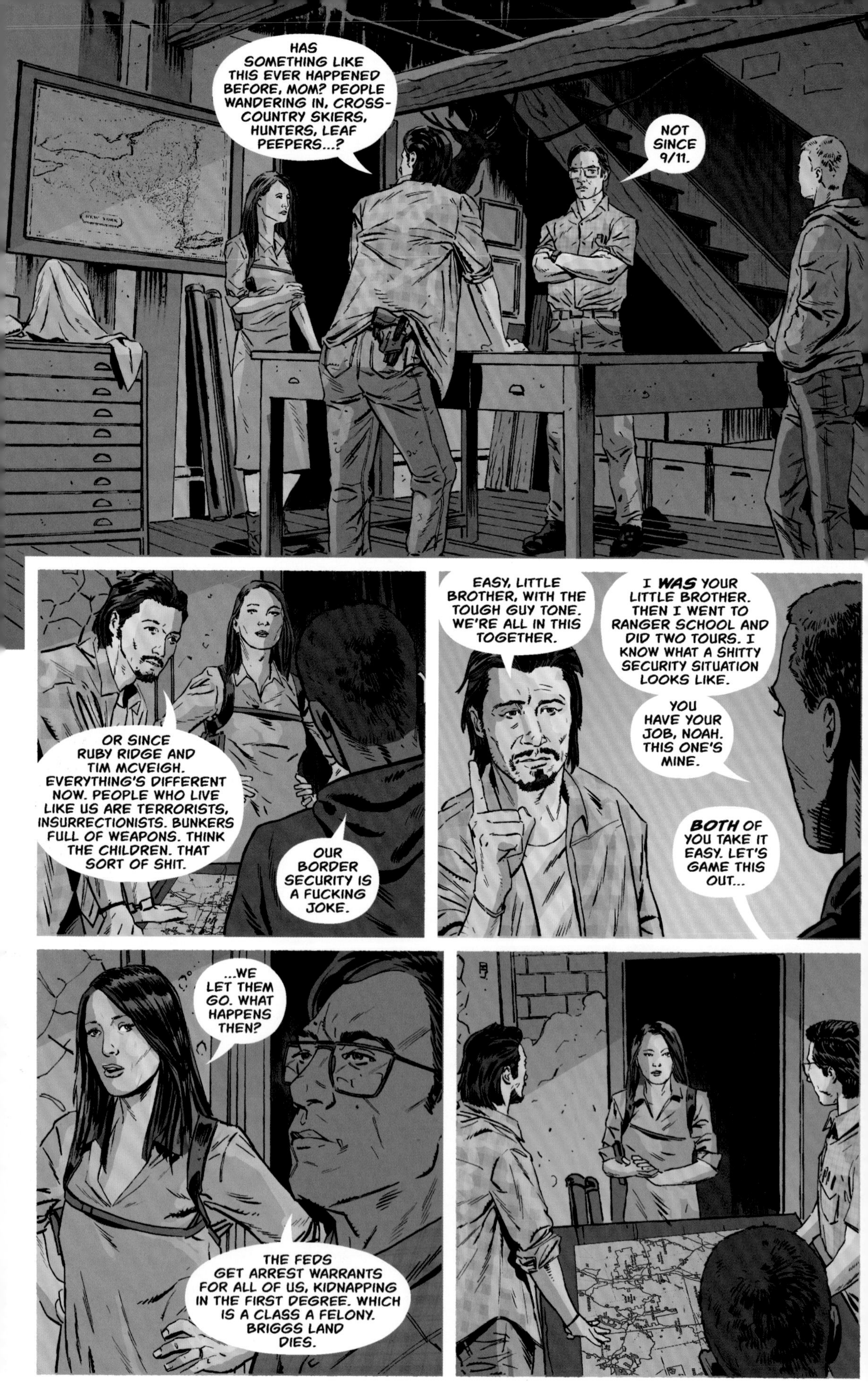
HAS SOMETHING LIKE THIS EVER HAPPENED BEFORE, MOM? PEOPLE WANDERING IN, CROSS-COUNTRY SKIERS, HUNTERS, LEAF PEEPERS...?
NOT SINCE 9/11.
NEW YORK
OR SINCE RUBY RIDGE AND TIM MCVEIGH. EVERYTHING'S DIFFERENT NOW. PEOPLE WHO LIVE LIKE US ARE TERRORISTS, INSURRECTIONISTS. BUNKERS FULL OF WEAPONS. THINK THE CHILDREN. THAT SORT OF SHIT.
OUR BORDER SECURITY IS A FUCKING JOKE.
EASY, LITTLE BROTHER, WITH THE TOUGH GUY TONE. WE'RE ALL IN THIS TOGETHER.
I *WAS* YOUR LITTLE BROTHER. THEN I WENT TO RANGER SCHOOL AND DID TWO TOURS. I KNOW WHAT A SHITTY SECURITY SITUATION LOOKS LIKE.
YOU HAVE YOUR JOB, NOAH. THIS ONE'S MINE.
BOTH OF YOU TAKE IT EASY. LET'S GAME THIS OUT...
...WE LET THEM GO. WHAT HAPPENS THEN?
THE FEDS GET ARREST WARRANTS FOR ALL OF US, KIDNAPPING IN THE FIRST DEGREE. WHICH IS A CLASS A FELONY. BRIGGS LAND DIES.

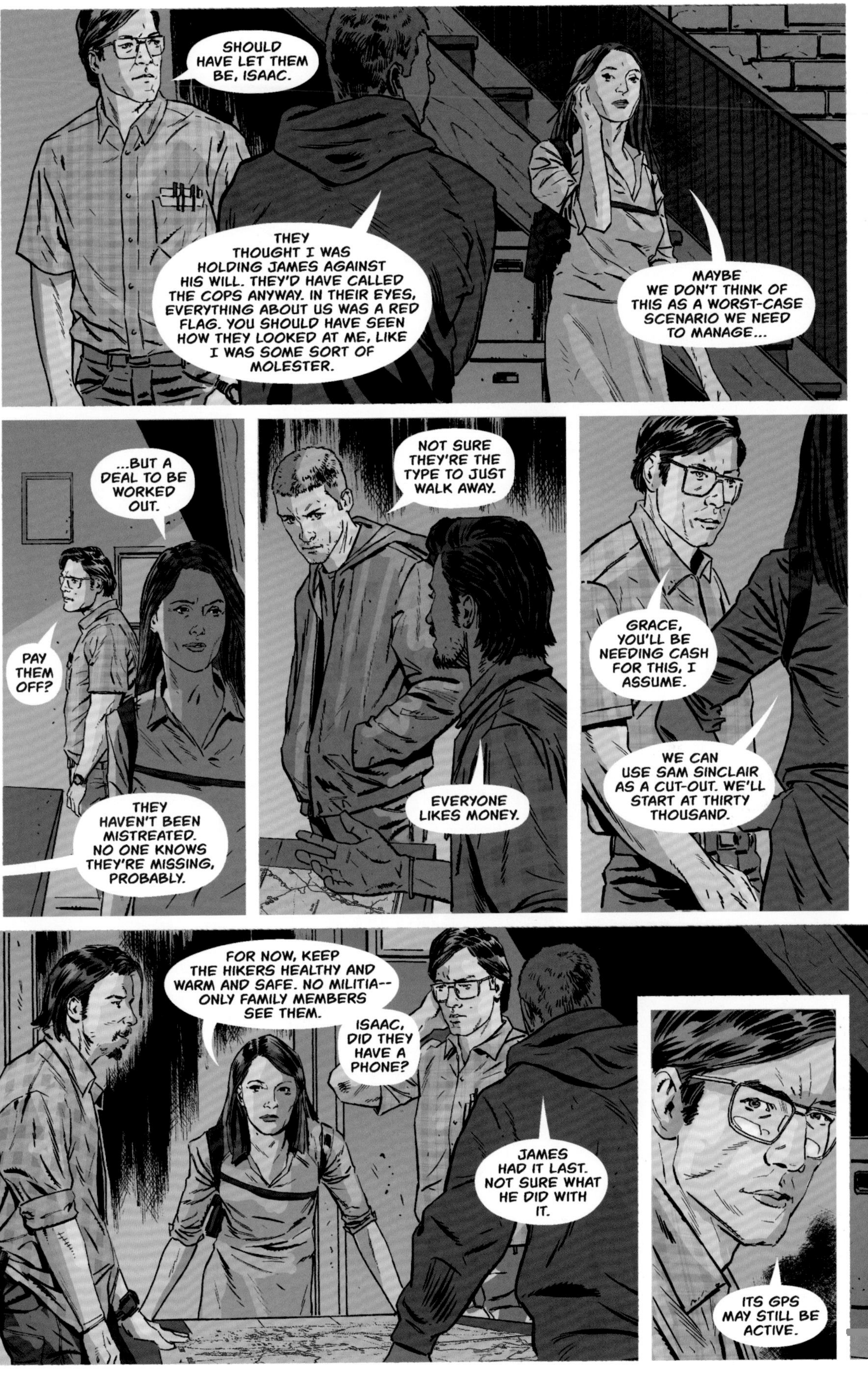
SHOULD HAVE LET THEM BE, ISAAC.
THEY THOUGHT I WAS HOLDING JAMES AGAINST HIS WILL. THEY'D HAVE CALLED THE COPS ANYWAY. IN THEIR EYES, EVERYTHING ABOUT US WAS A RED FLAG. YOU SHOULD HAVE SEEN HOW THEY LOOKED AT ME, LIKE I WAS SOME SORT OF MOLESTER.
MAYBE WE DON'T THINK OF THIS AS A WORST-CASE SCENARIO WE NEED TO MANAGE...
...BUT A DEAL TO BE WORKED OUT.
PAY THEM OFF?
THEY HAVEN'T BEEN MISTREATED. NO ONE KNOWS THEY'RE MISSING, PROBABLY.
NOT SURE THEY'RE THE TYPE TO JUST WALK AWAY.
EVERYONE LIKES MONEY.
GRACE, YOU'LL BE NEEDING CASH FOR THIS, I ASSUME.
WE CAN USE SAM SINCLAIR AS A CUT-OUT. WE'LL START AT THIRTY THOUSAND.
FOR NOW, KEEP THE HIKERS HEALTHY AND WARM AND SAFE. NO MILITIA-- ONLY FAMILY MEMBERS SEE THEM.
ISAAC, DID THEY HAVE A PHONE?
JAMES HAD IT LAST. NOT SURE WHAT HE DID WITH IT.
ITS GPS MAY STILL BE ACTIVE.

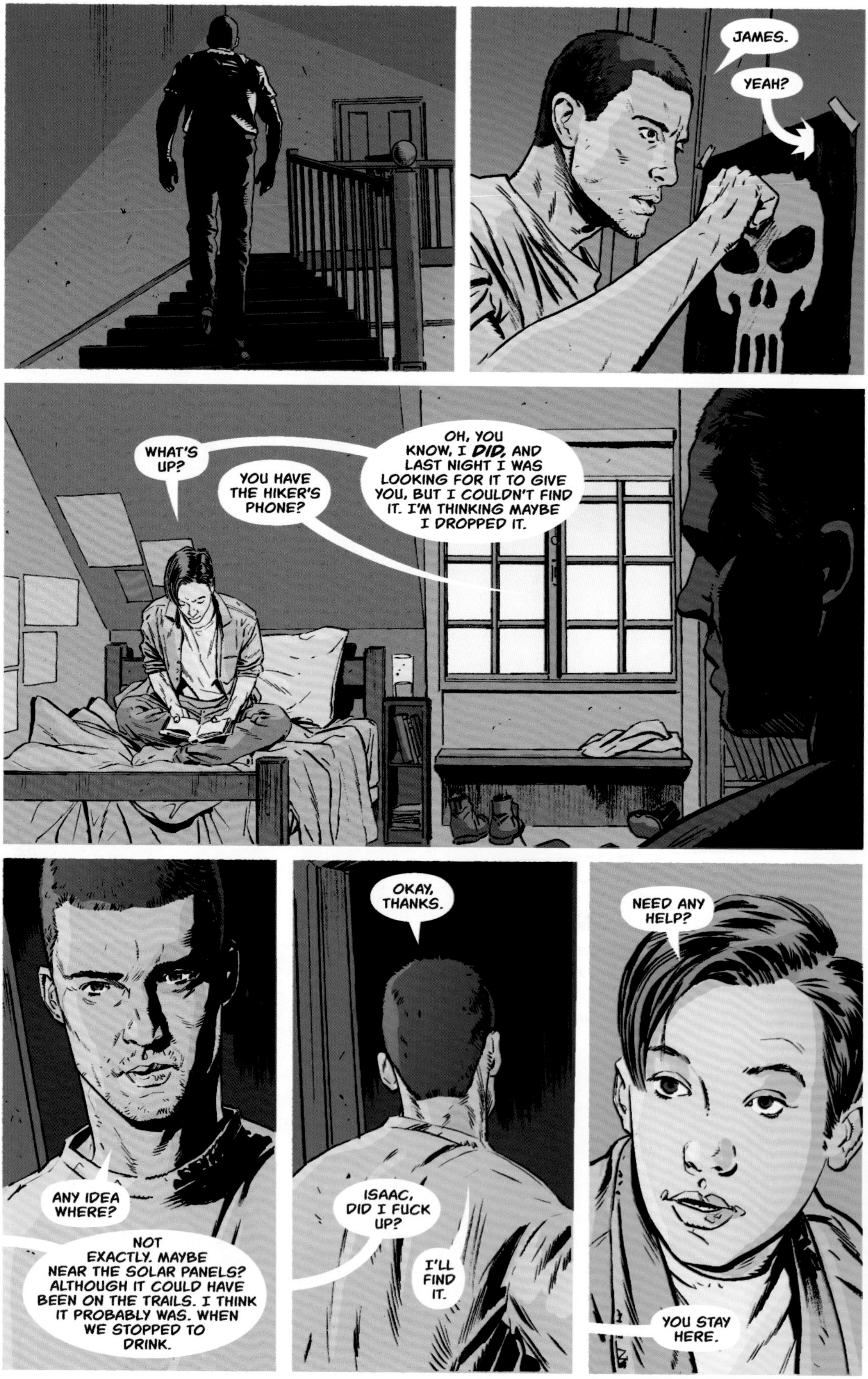
JAMES.
YEAH?
WHAT'S UP?
OH, YOU KNOW, I *DID,* AND LAST NIGHT I WAS LOOKING FOR IT TO GIVE YOU, BUT I COULDN'T FIND IT. I'M THINKING MAYBE I DROPPED IT.
YOU HAVE THE HIKER'S PHONE?
ANY IDEA WHERE?
NOT EXACTLY. MAYBE NEAR THE SOLAR PANELS? ALTHOUGH IT COULD HAVE BEEN ON THE TRAILS. I THINK IT PROBABLY WAS. WHEN WE STOPPED TO DRINK.
OKAY, THANKS.
ISAAC, DID I FUCK UP?
I'LL FIND IT.
NEED ANY HELP?
YOU STAY HERE.

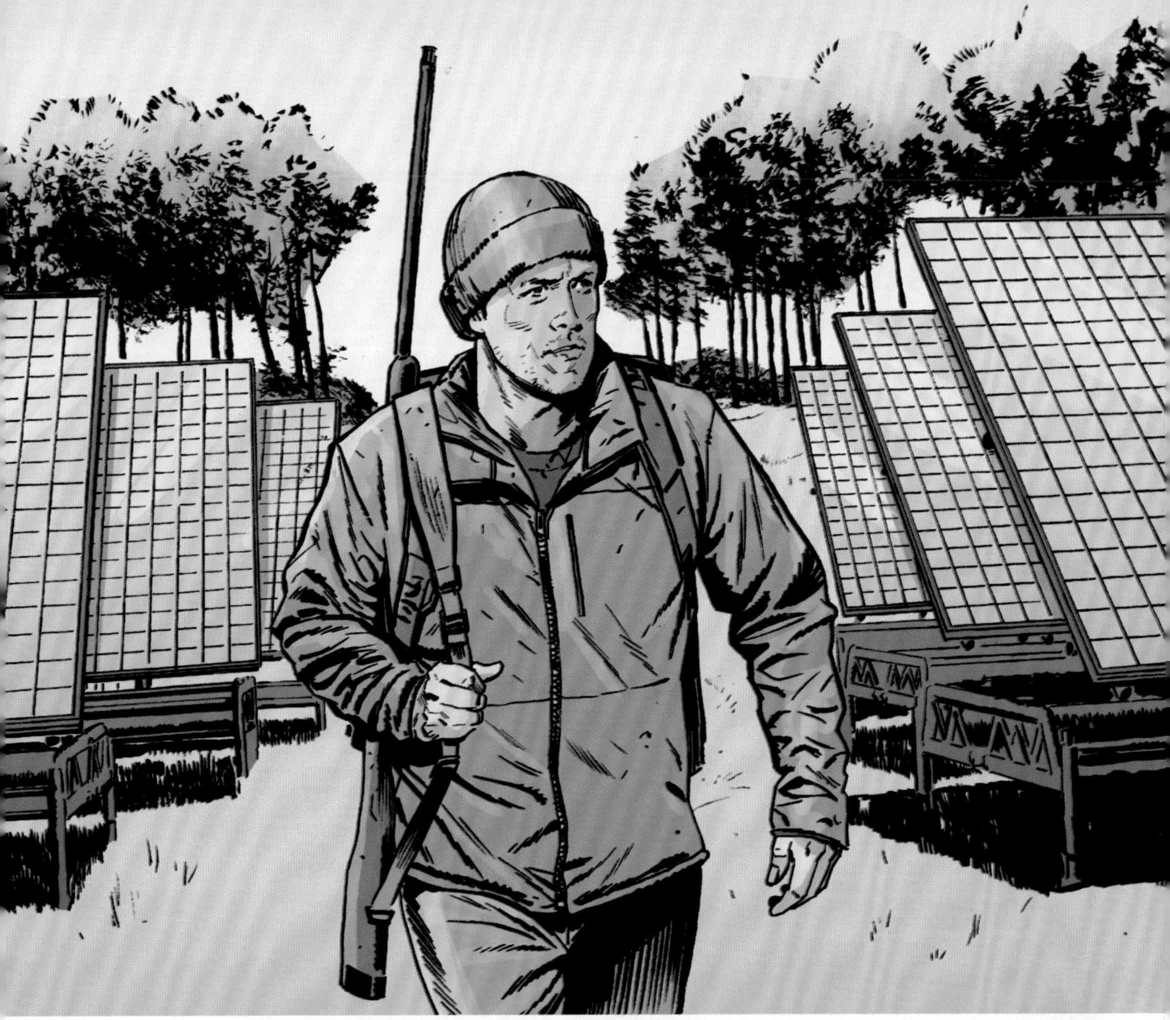
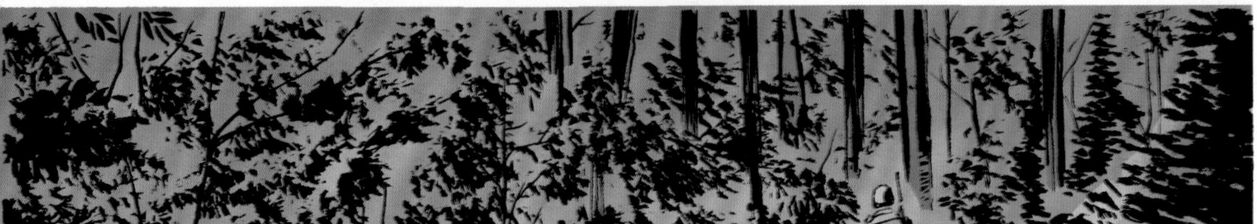
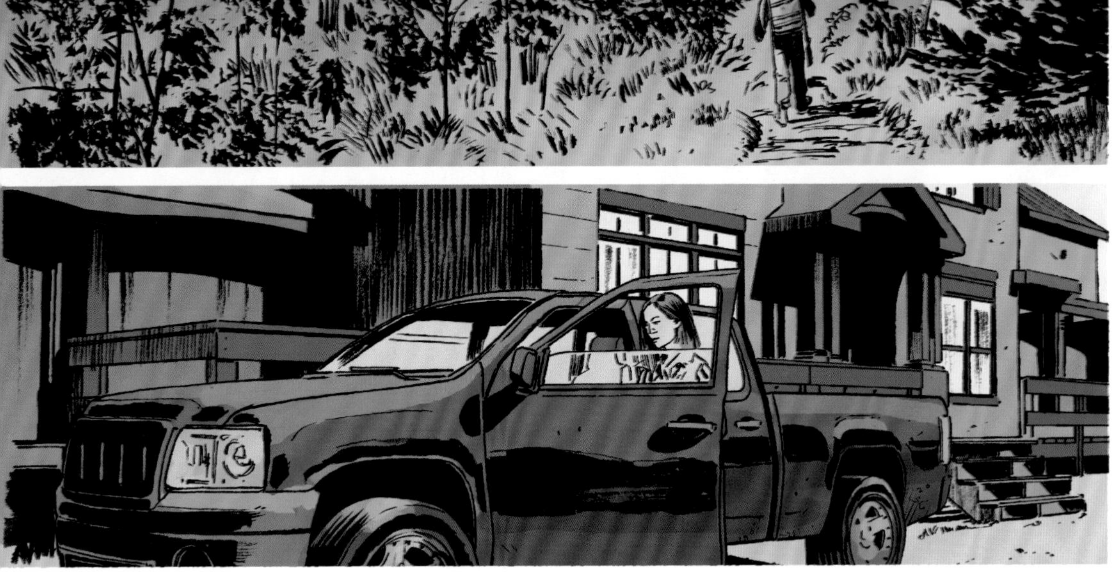

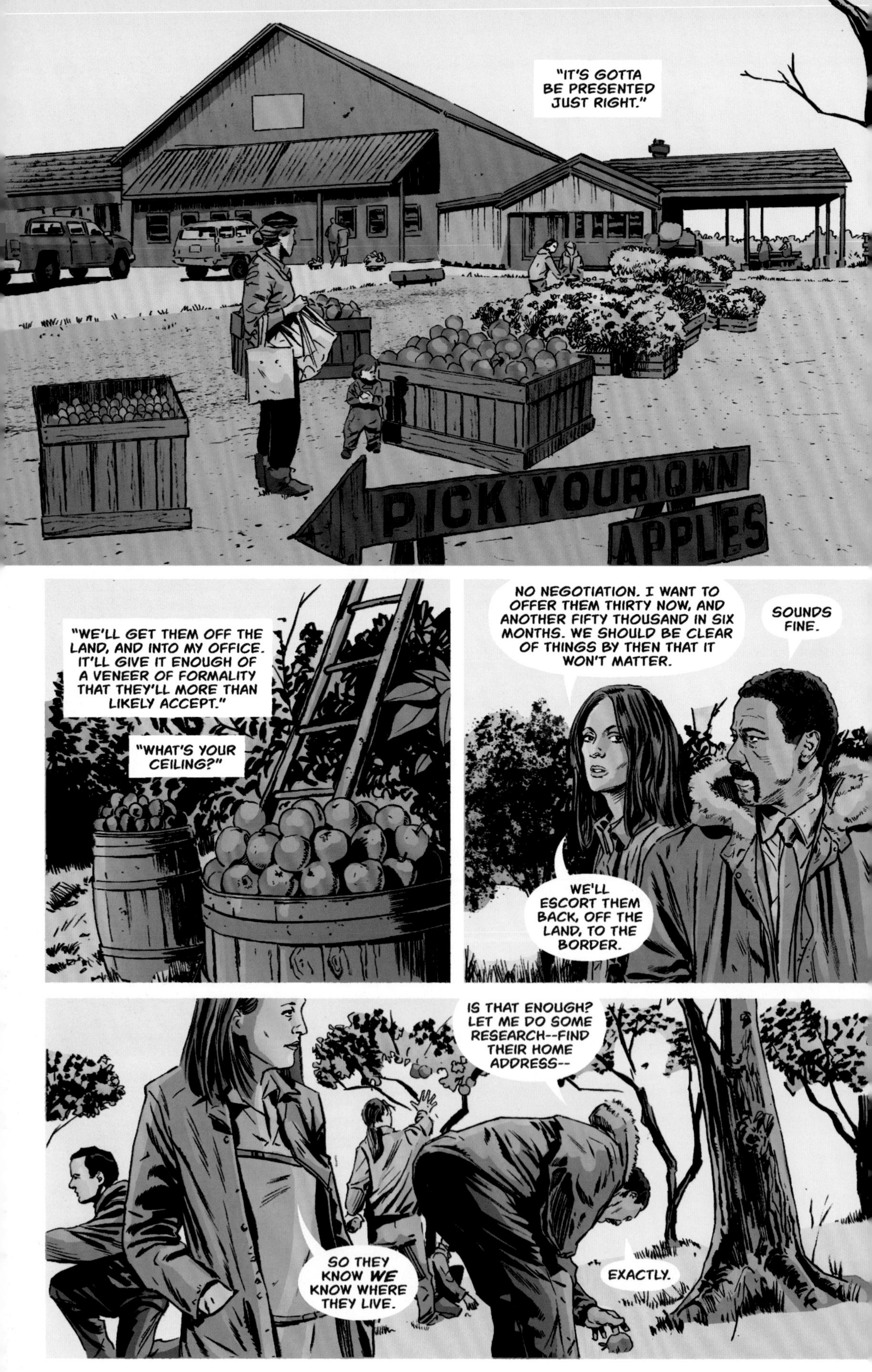

"IT'S GOTTA BE PRESENTED JUST RIGHT."
PICK YOUR OWN
APPLES
"WE'LL GET THEM OFF THE LAND, AND INTO MY OFFICE. IT'LL GIVE IT ENOUGH OF A VENEER OF FORMALITY THAT THEY'LL MORE THAN LIKELY ACCEPT."
"WHAT'S YOUR CEILING?"
NO NEGOTIATION. I WANT TO OFFER THEM THIRTY NOW, AND ANOTHER FIFTY THOUSAND IN SIX MONTHS. WE SHOULD BE CLEAR OF THINGS BY THEN THAT IT WON'T MATTER.
SOUNDS FINE.
WE'LL ESCORT THEM BACK, OFF THE LAND, TO THE BORDER.
IS THAT ENOUGH? LET ME DO SOME RESEARCH--FIND THEIR HOME ADDRESS--
SO THEY KNOW *WE* KNOW WHERE THEY LIVE.
EXACTLY.

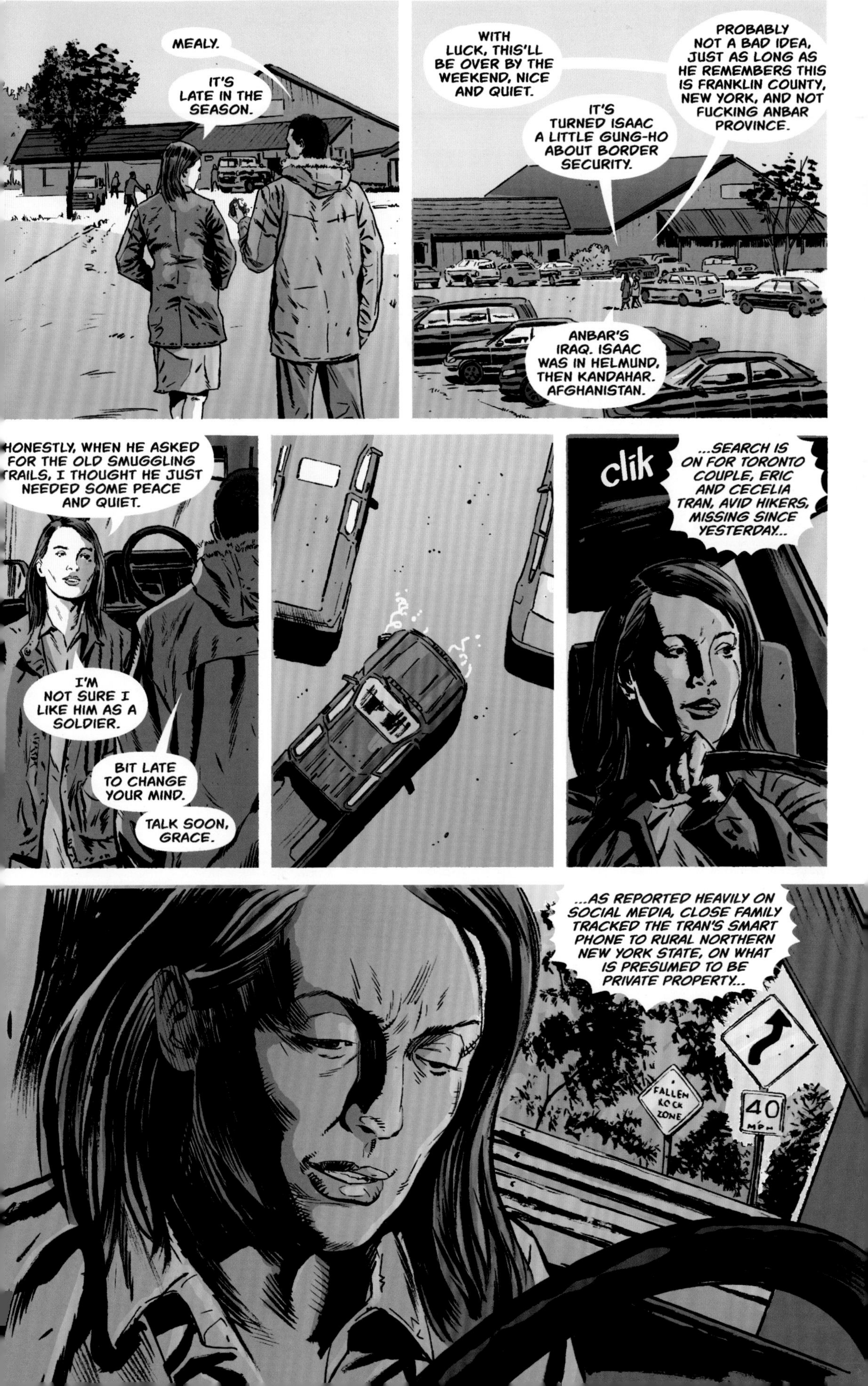
MEALY.
IT'S LATE IN THE SEASON.
WITH LUCK, THIS'LL BE OVER BY THE WEEKEND, NICE AND QUIET.
PROBABLY NOT A BAD IDEA, JUST AS LONG AS HE REMEMBERS THIS IS FRANKLIN COUNTY, NEW YORK, AND NOT FUCKING ANBAR PROVINCE.
IT'S TURNED ISAAC A LITTLE GUNG-HO ABOUT BORDER SECURITY.
ANBAR'S IRAQ. ISAAC WAS IN HELMUND, THEN KANDAHAR. AFGHANISTAN.
HONESTLY, WHEN HE ASKED FOR THE OLD SMUGGLING TRAILS, I THOUGHT HE JUST NEEDED SOME PEACE AND QUIET.
I'M NOT SURE I LIKE HIM AS A SOLDIER.
BIT LATE TO CHANGE YOUR MIND.
TALK SOON, GRACE.
clik
...SEARCH IS ON FOR TORONTO COUPLE, ERIC AND CECELIA TRAN, AVID HIKERS, MISSING SINCE YESTERDAY...
...AS REPORTED HEAVILY ON SOCIAL MEDIA, CLOSE FAMILY TRACKED THE TRAN'S SMART PHONE TO RURAL NORTHERN NEW YORK STATE, ON WHAT IS PRESUMED TO BE PRIVATE PROPERTY...
FALLEN ROCK ZONE
40 MPH

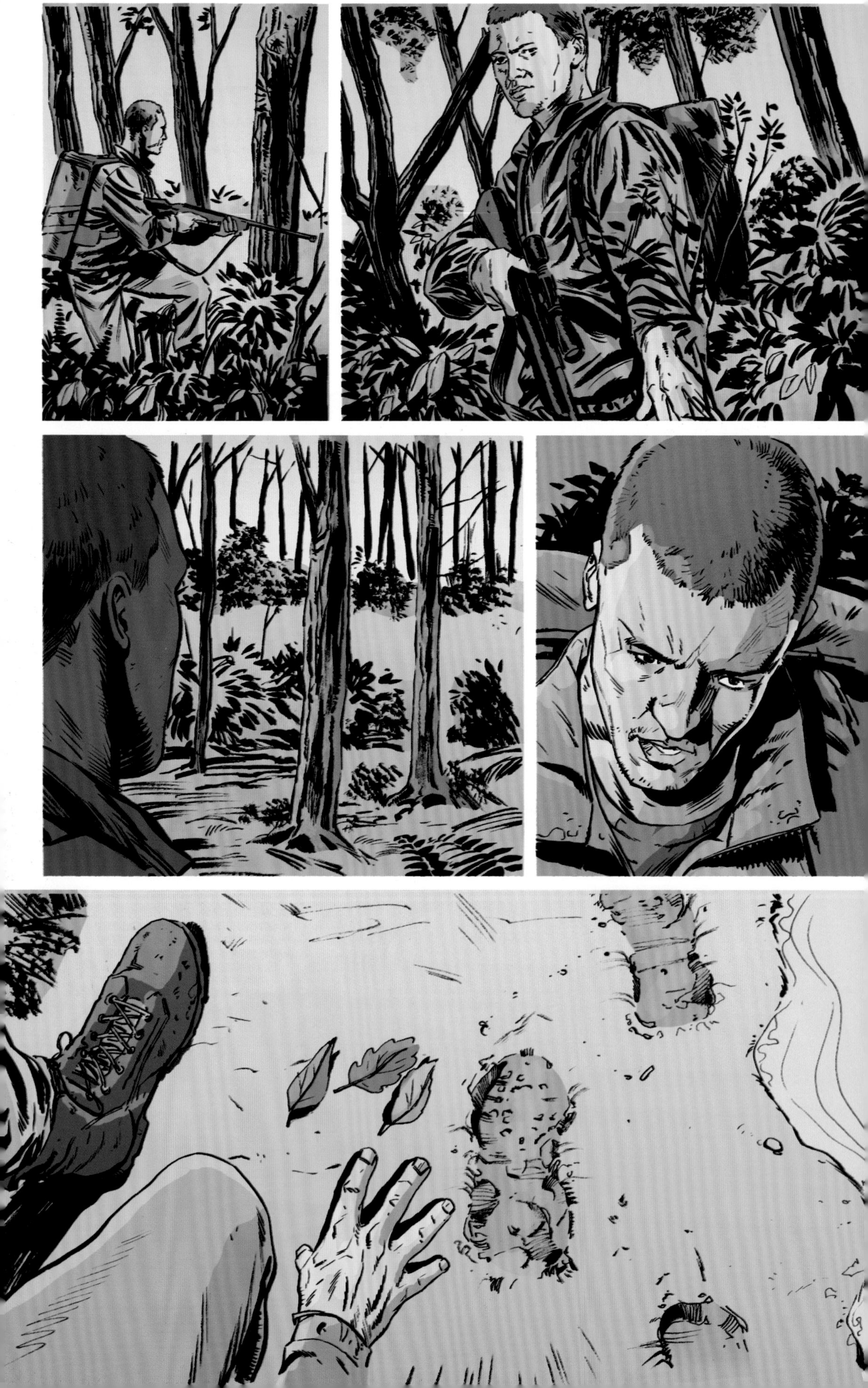

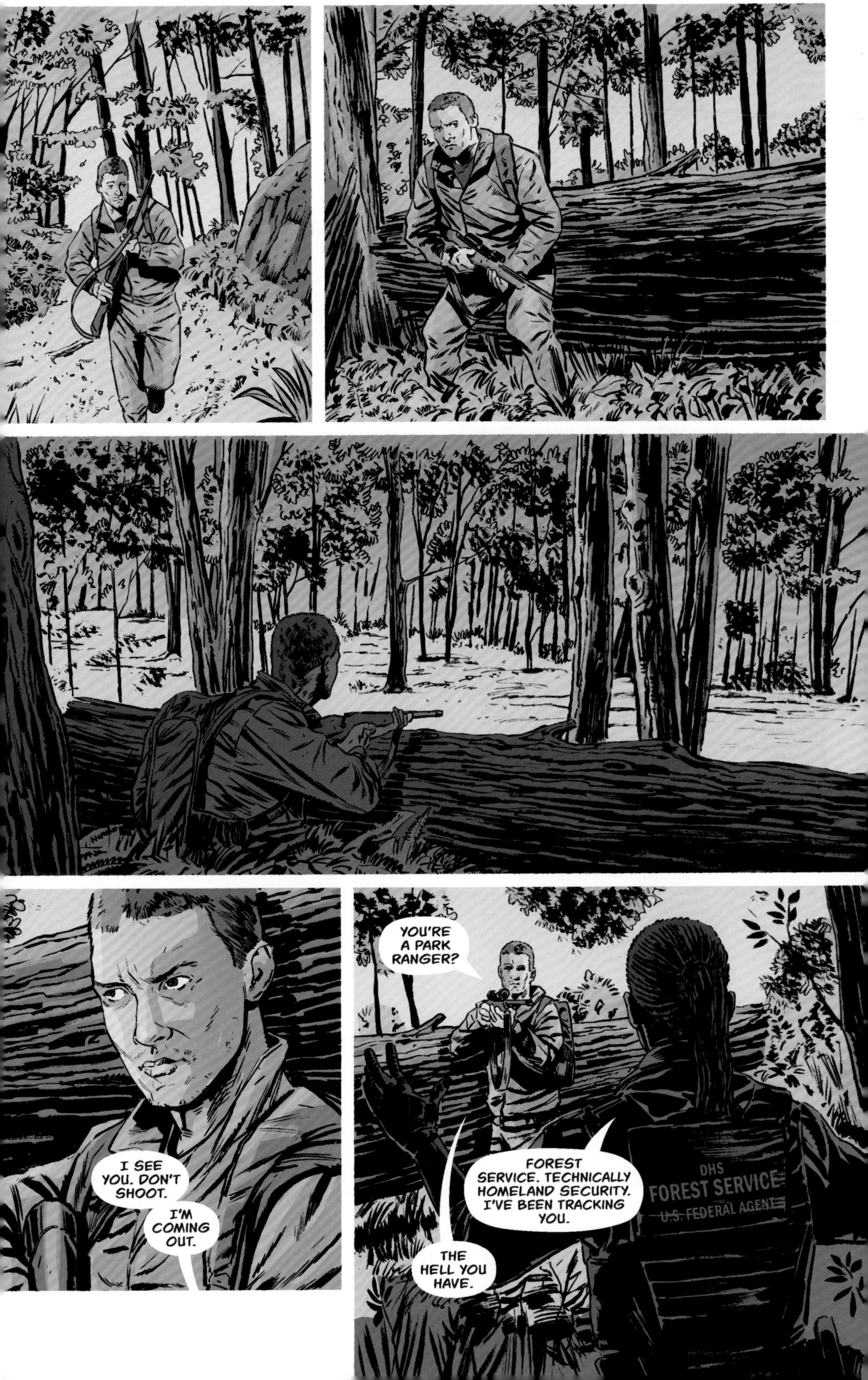
I SEE YOU. DON'T SHOOT.
I'M COMING OUT.
YOU'RE A PARK RANGER?
FOREST SERVICE. TECHNICALLY HOMELAND SECURITY. I'VE BEEN TRACKING YOU.
DHS
FOREST SERVICE
U.S. FEDERAL AGENT
THE HELL YOU HAVE.

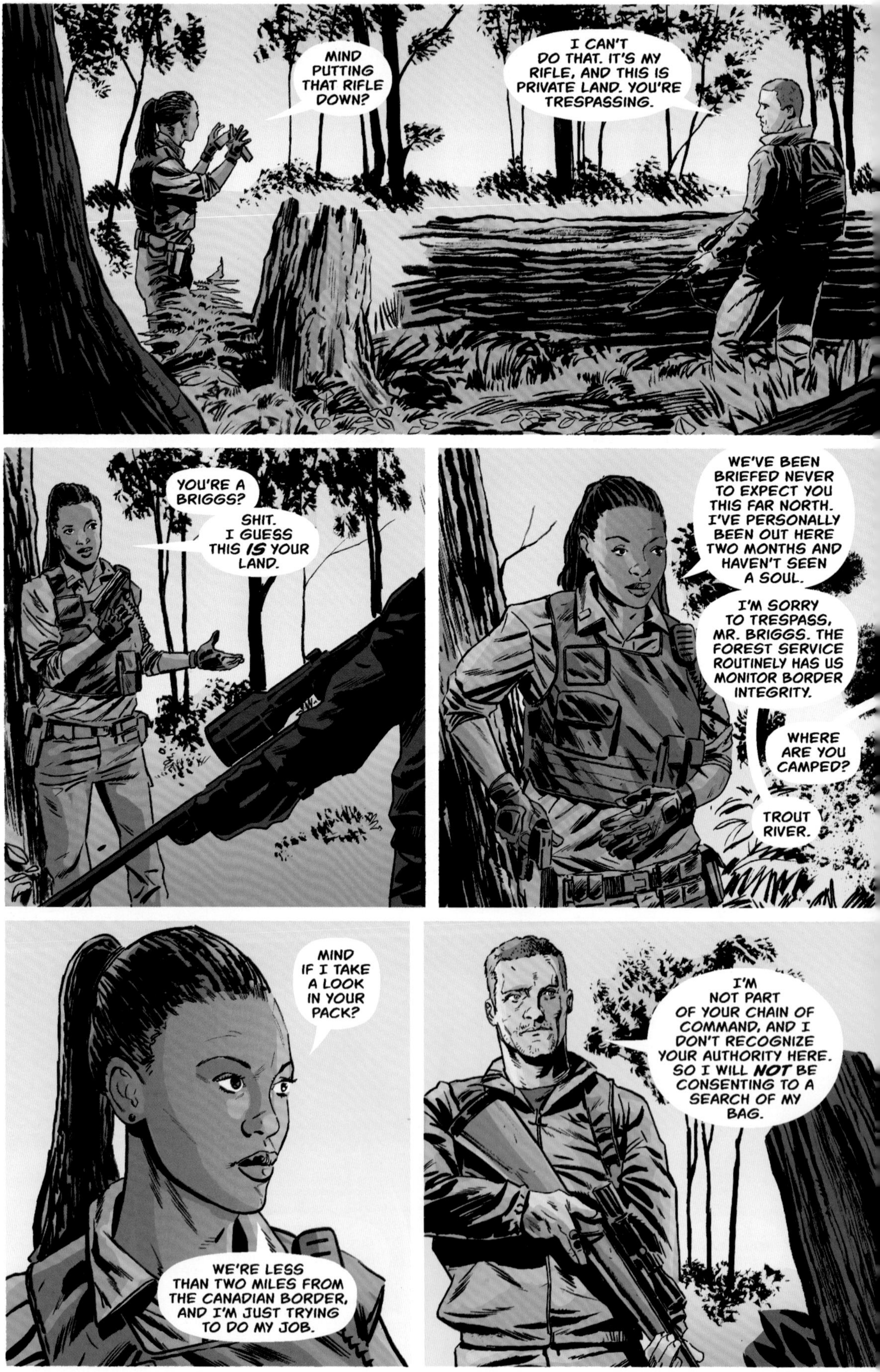
MIND PUTTING THAT RIFLE DOWN?
I CAN'T DO THAT. IT'S MY RIFLE, AND THIS IS PRIVATE LAND. YOU'RE TRESPASSING.
YOU'RE A BRIGGS?
SHIT. I GUESS THIS *IS* YOUR LAND.
WE'VE BEEN BRIEFED NEVER TO EXPECT YOU THIS FAR NORTH. I'VE PERSONALLY BEEN OUT HERE TWO MONTHS AND HAVEN'T SEEN A SOUL.
I'M SORRY TO TRESPASS, MR. BRIGGS. THE FOREST SERVICE ROUTINELY HAS US MONITOR BORDER INTEGRITY.
WHERE ARE YOU CAMPED?
TROUT RIVER.
MIND IF I TAKE A LOOK IN YOUR PACK?
WE'RE LESS THAN TWO MILES FROM THE CANADIAN BORDER, AND I'M JUST TRYING TO DO MY JOB.
I'M NOT PART OF YOUR CHAIN OF COMMAND, AND I DON'T RECOGNIZE YOUR AUTHORITY HERE. SO I WILL *NOT* BE CONSENTING TO A SEARCH OF MY BAG.

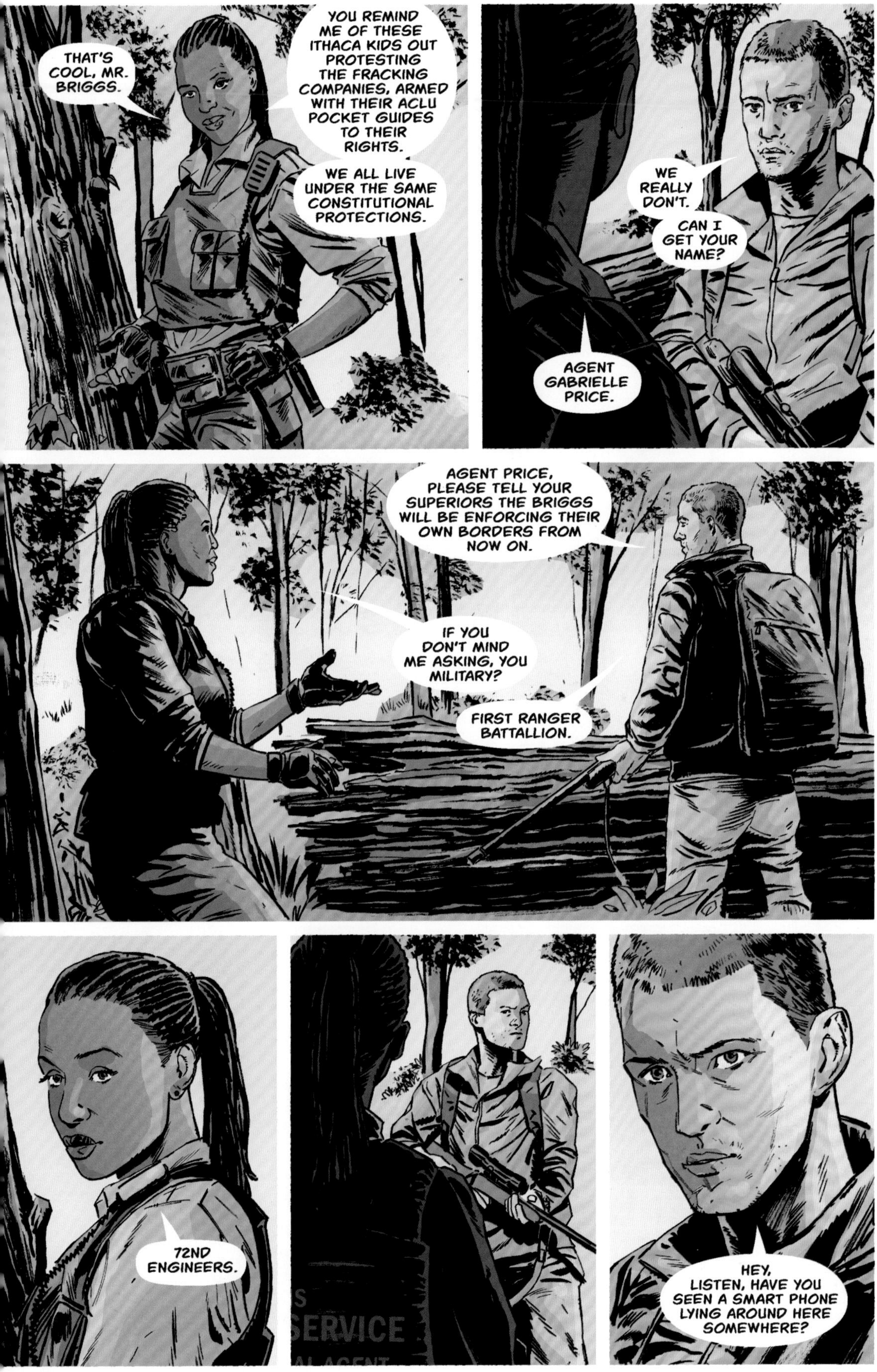
THAT'S COOL, MR. BRIGGS.
YOU REMIND ME OF THESE ITHACA KIDS OUT PROTESTING THE FRACKING COMPANIES, ARMED WITH THEIR ACLU POCKET GUIDES TO THEIR RIGHTS.
WE ALL LIVE UNDER THE SAME CONSTITUTIONAL PROTECTIONS.
WE REALLY DON'T.
CAN I GET YOUR NAME?
AGENT GABRIELLE PRICE.
AGENT PRICE, PLEASE TELL YOUR SUPERIORS THE BRIGGS WILL BE ENFORCING THEIR OWN BORDERS FROM NOW ON.
IF YOU DON'T MIND ME ASKING, YOU MILITARY?
FIRST RANGER BATTALION.
72ND ENGINEERS.
HEY, LISTEN, HAVE YOU SEEN A SMART PHONE LYING AROUND HERE SOMEWHERE?

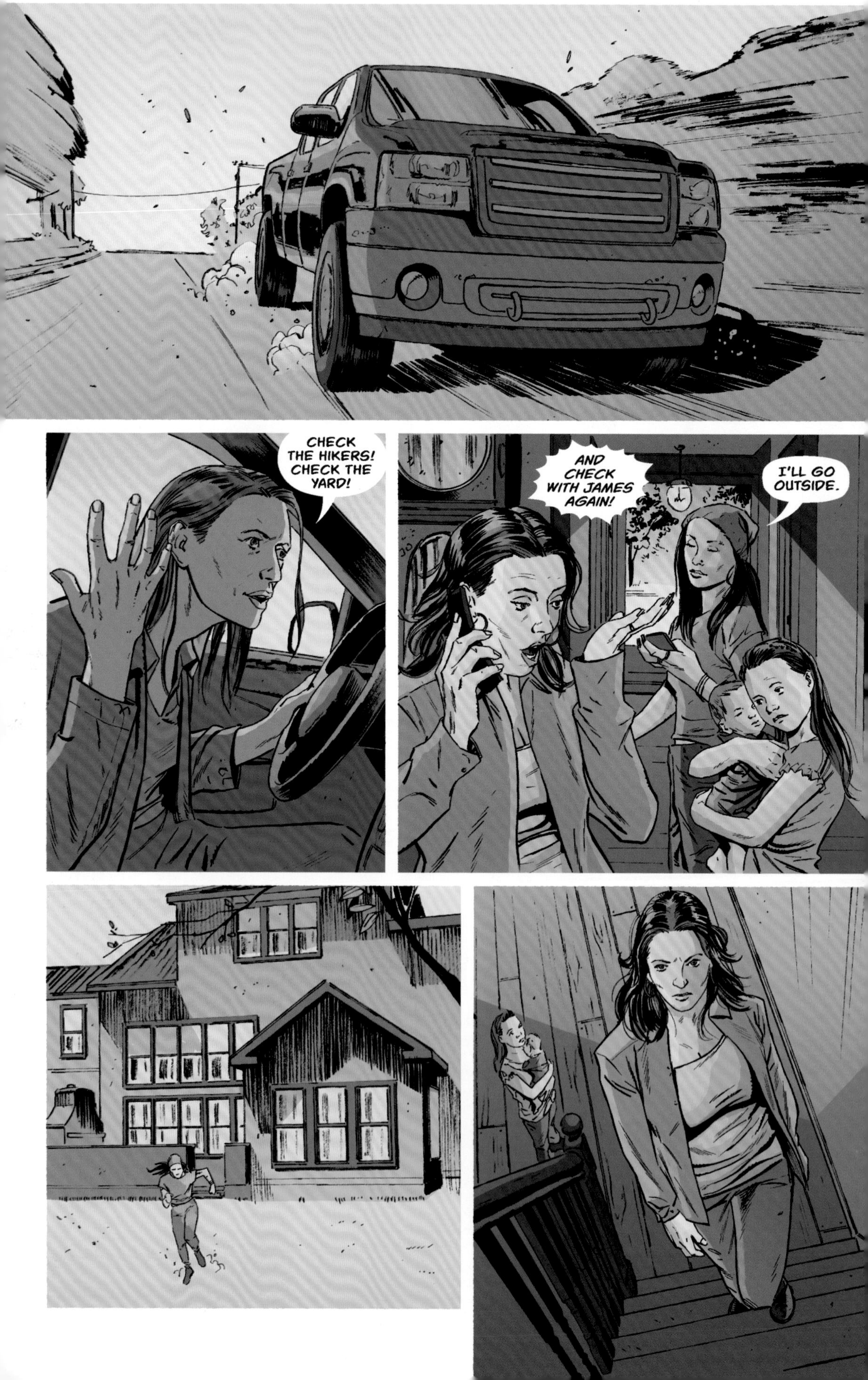
CHECK THE HIKERS! CHECK THE YARD!
AND CHECK WITH JAMES AGAIN!
I'LL GO OUTSIDE.

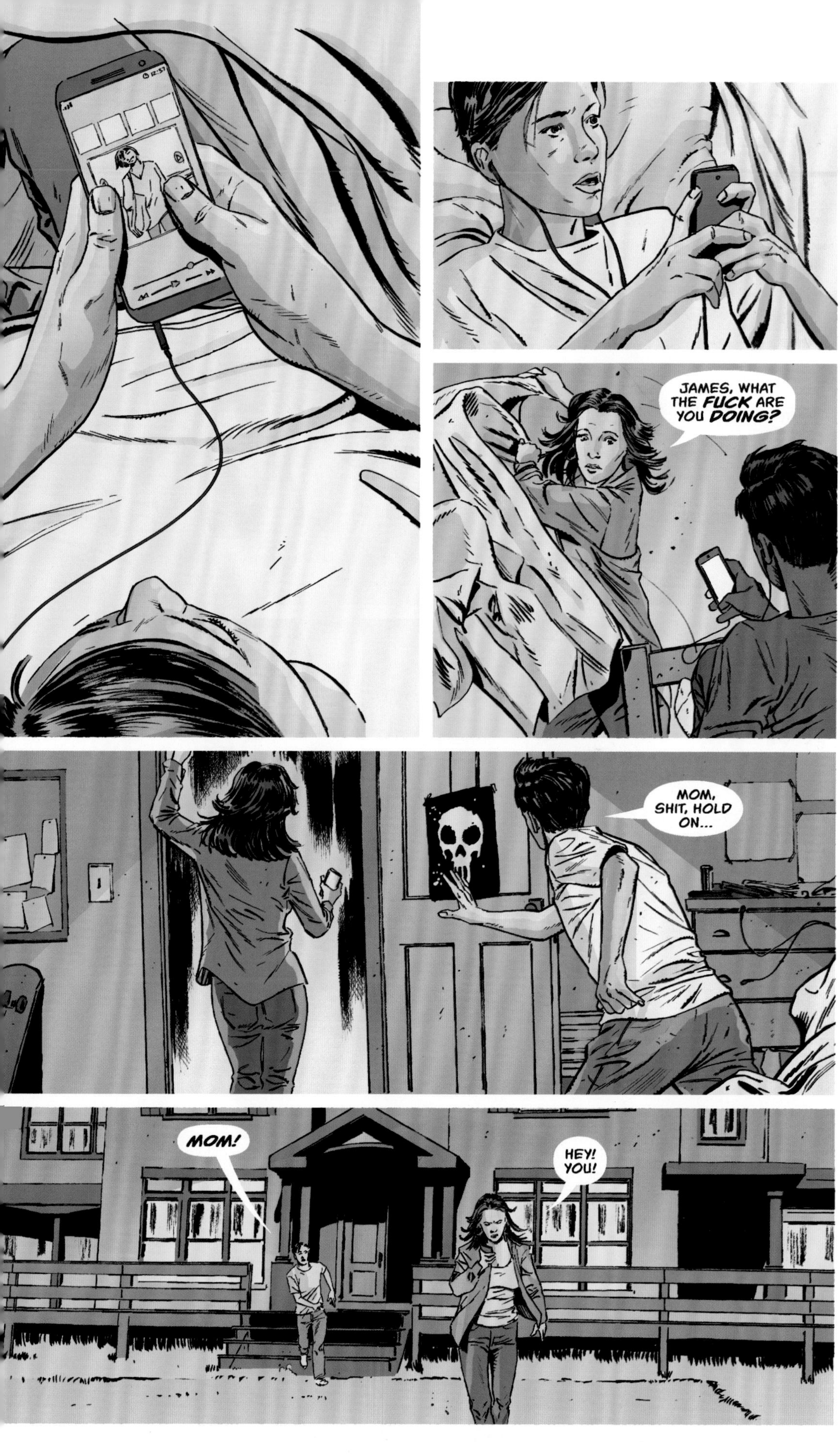
JAMES, WHAT THE FUCK ARE YOU DOING?
MOM, SHIT, HOLD ON...
MOM!
HEY! YOU!

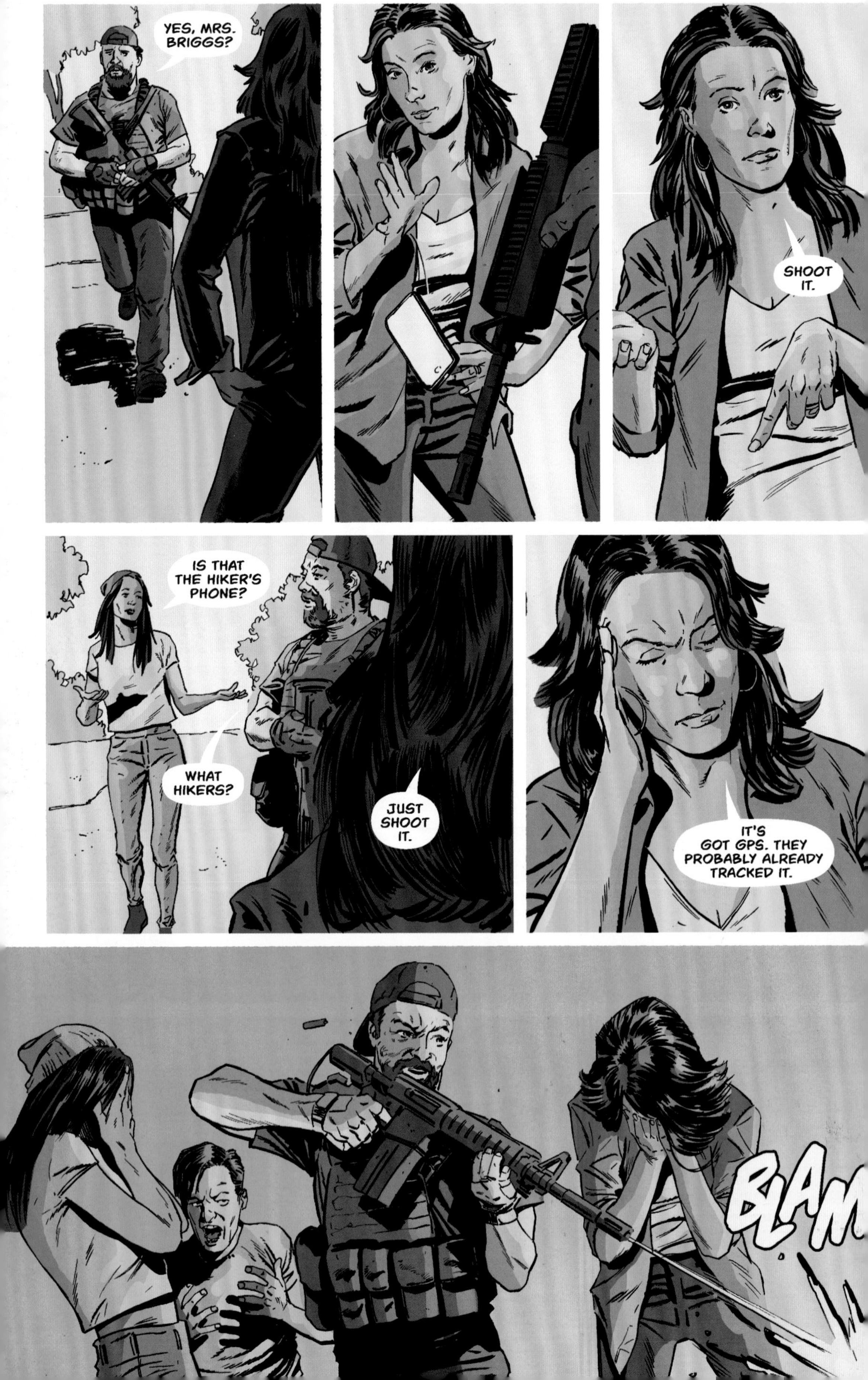
YES, MRS. BRIGGS?
SHOOT IT.
IS THAT THE HIKER'S PHONE?
WHAT HIKERS?
JUST SHOOT IT.
IT'S GOT GPS. THEY PROBABLY ALREADY TRACKED IT.
BLAM

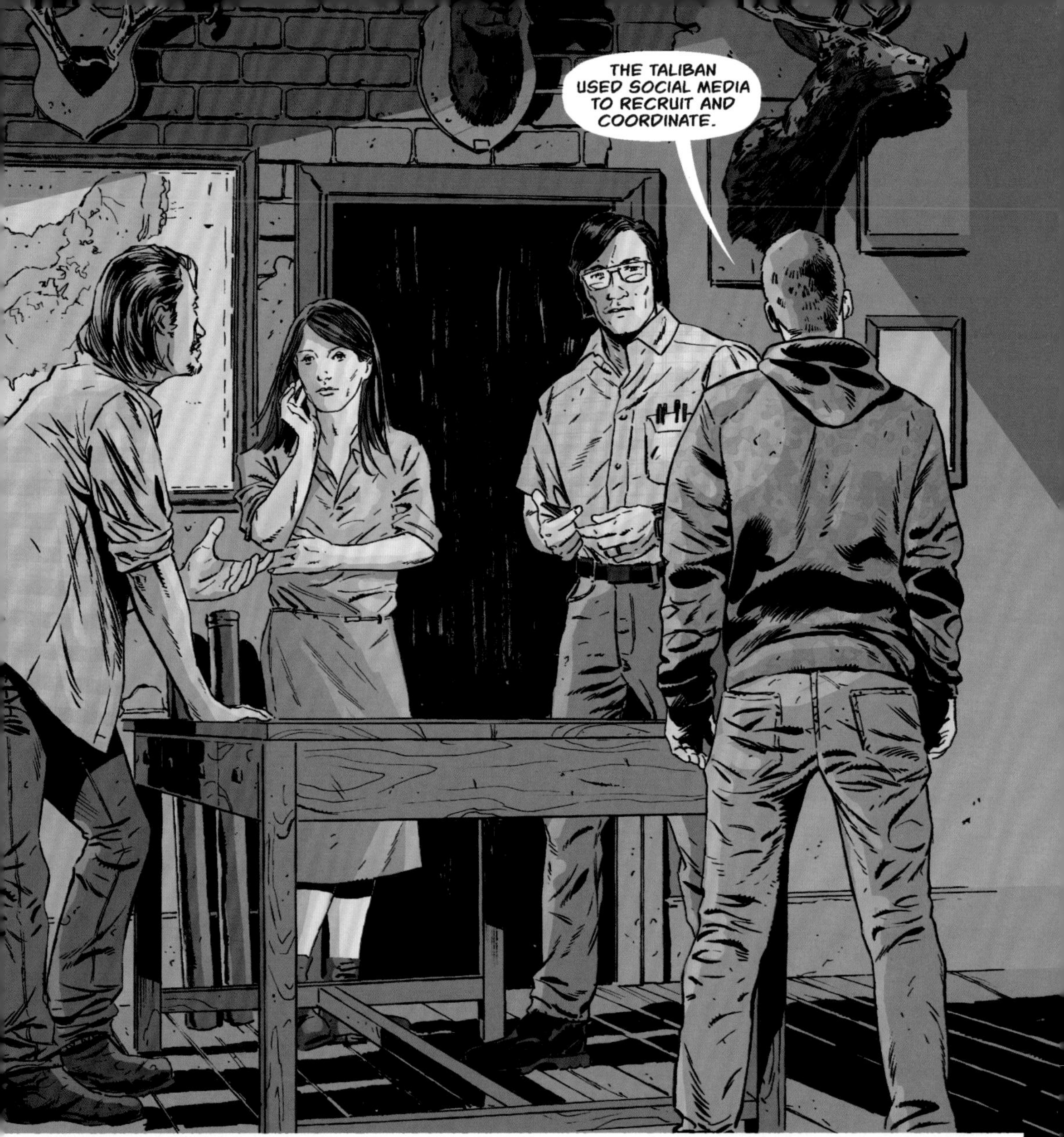
THE TALIBAN USED SOCIAL MEDIA TO RECRUIT AND COORDINATE.

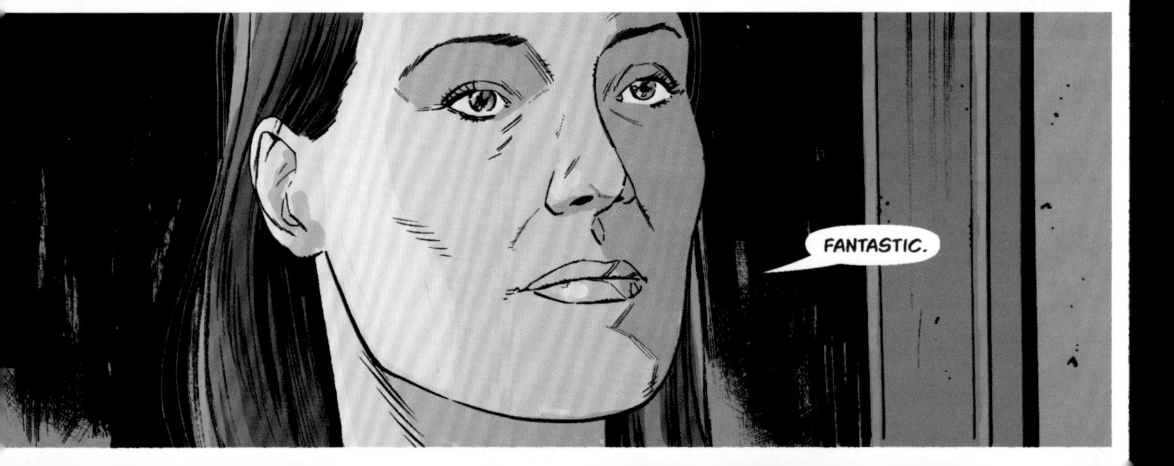
FANTASTIC.

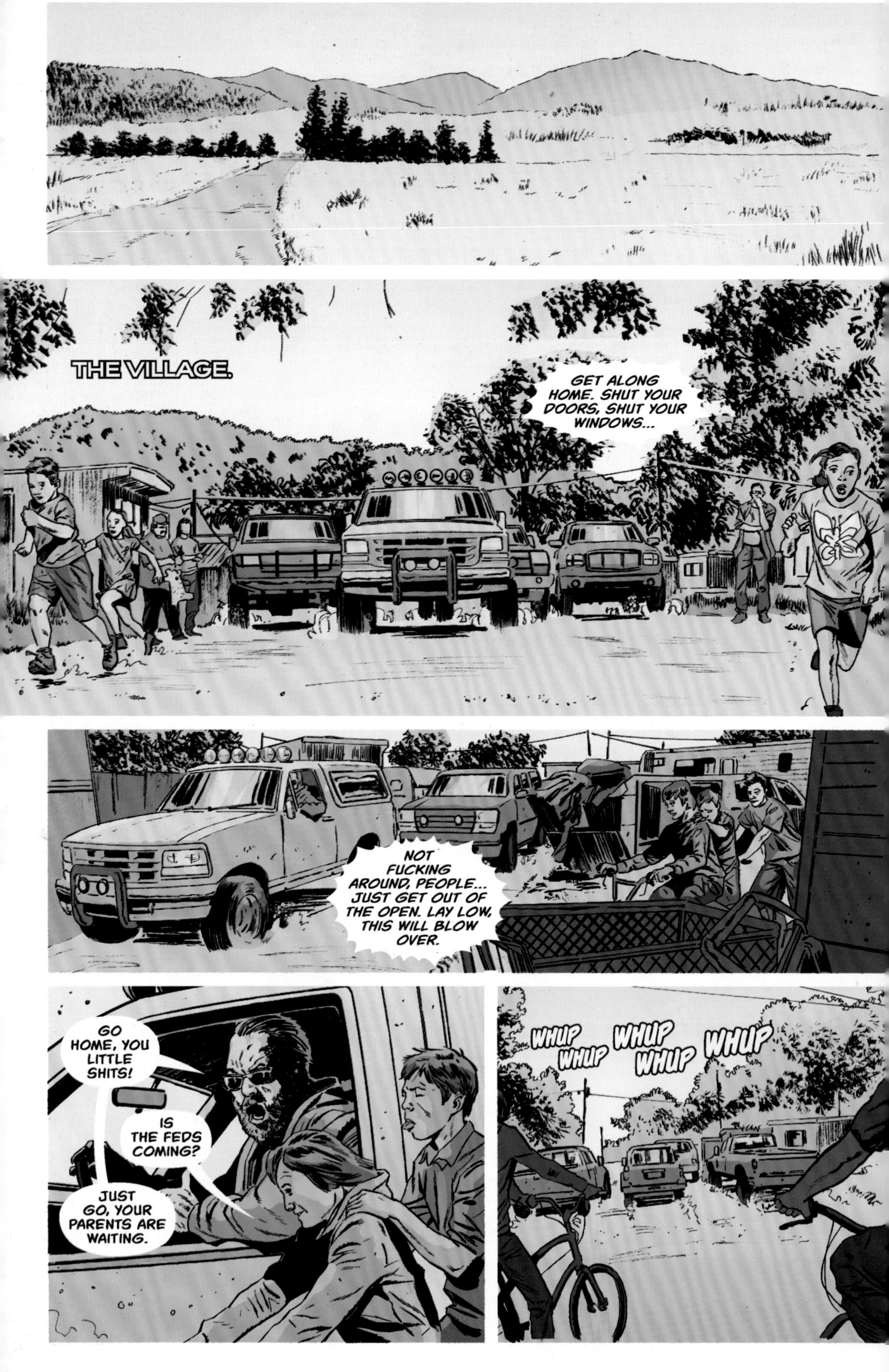
THE VILLAGE.
GET ALONG HOME. SHUT YOUR DOORS, SHUT YOUR WINDOWS...
NOT FUCKING AROUND, PEOPLE... JUST GET OUT OF THE OPEN. LAY LOW, THIS WILL BLOW OVER.
GO HOME, YOU LITTLE SHITS!
IS THE FEDS COMING?
JUST GO, YOUR PARENTS ARE WAITING.
WHUP WHUP WHUP WHUP WHUP

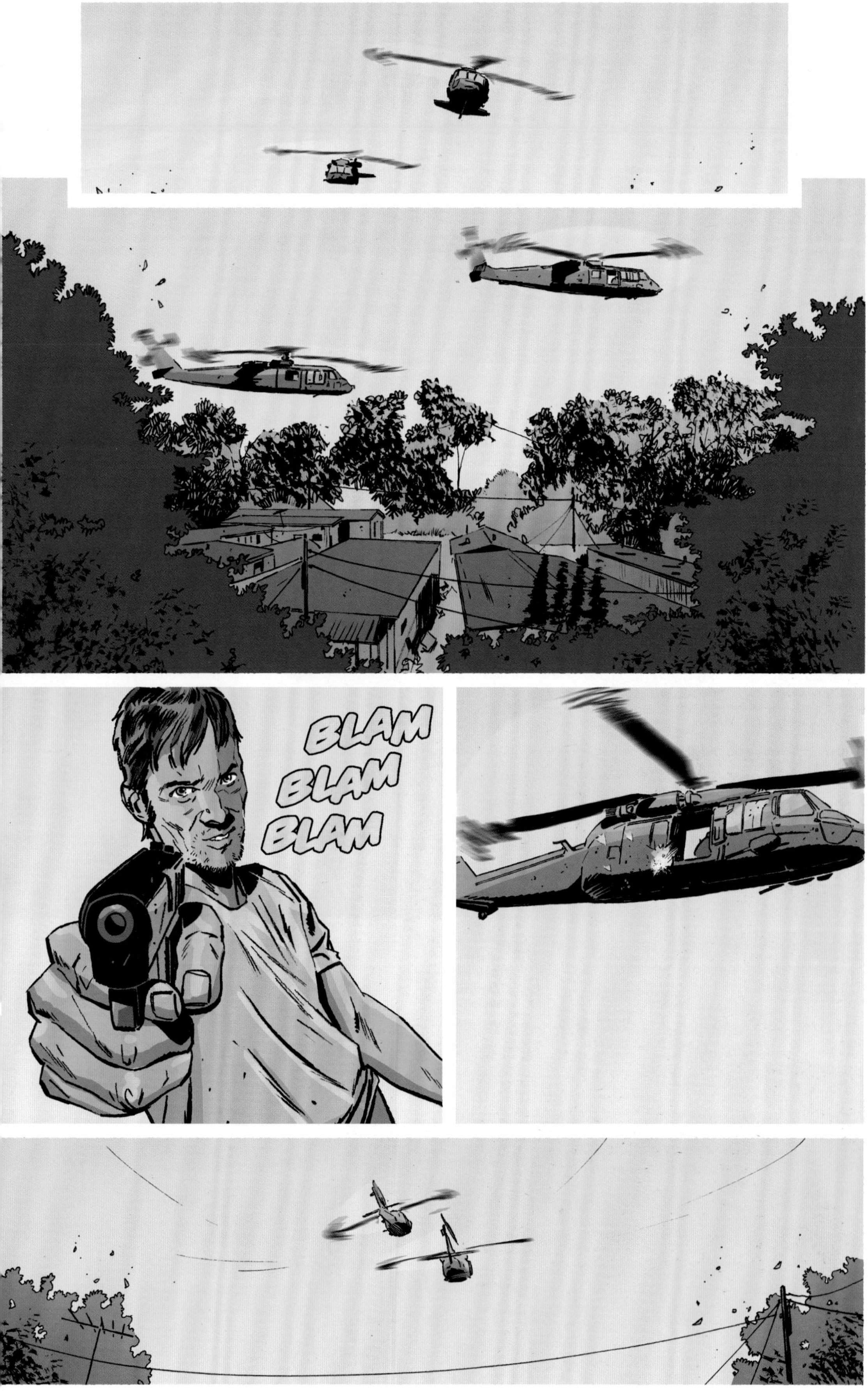
BLAM
BLAM
BLAM

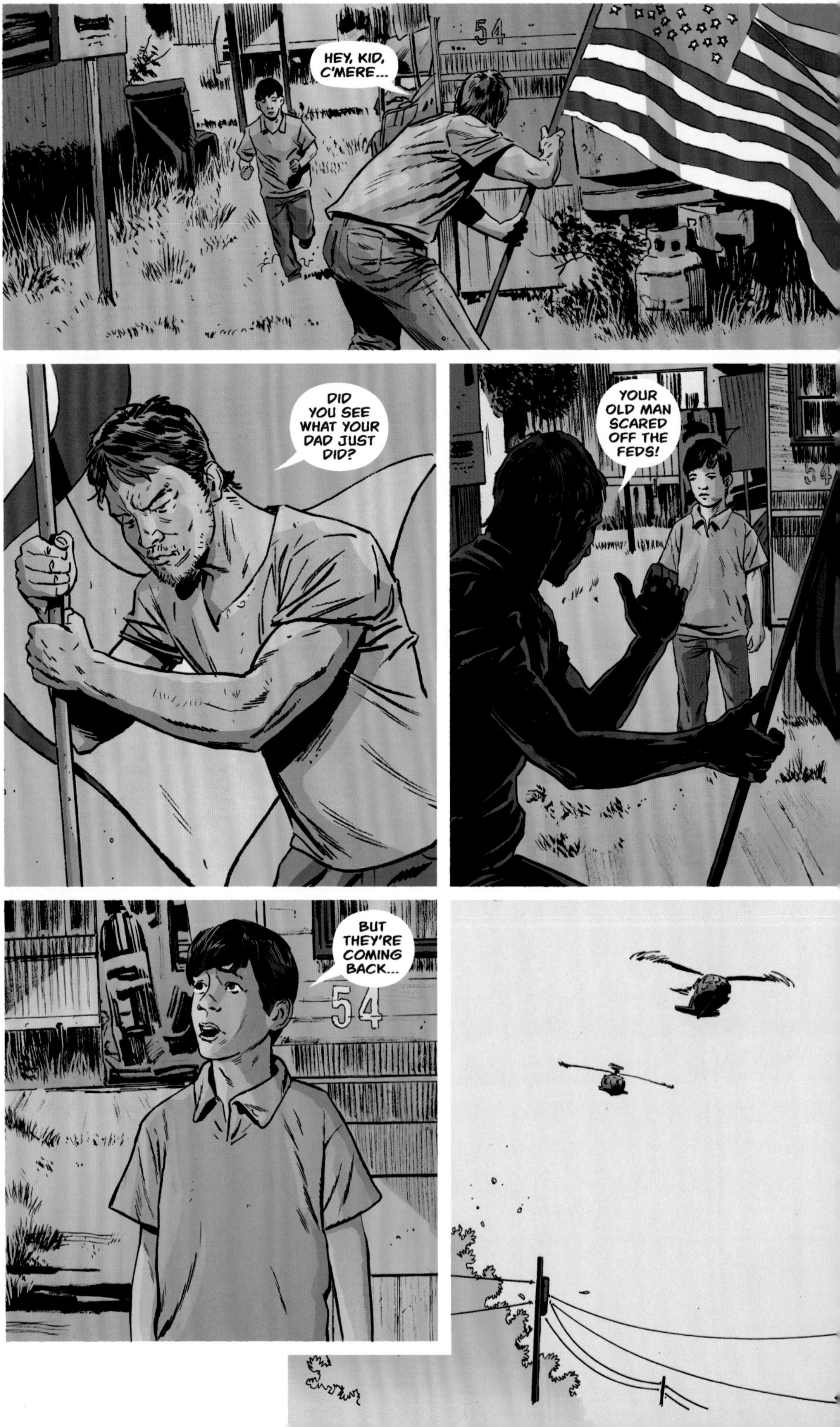
HEY, KID, C'MERE...
DID YOU SEE WHAT YOUR DAD JUST DID?
YOUR OLD MAN SCARED OFF THE FEDS!
BUT THEY'RE COMING BACK...

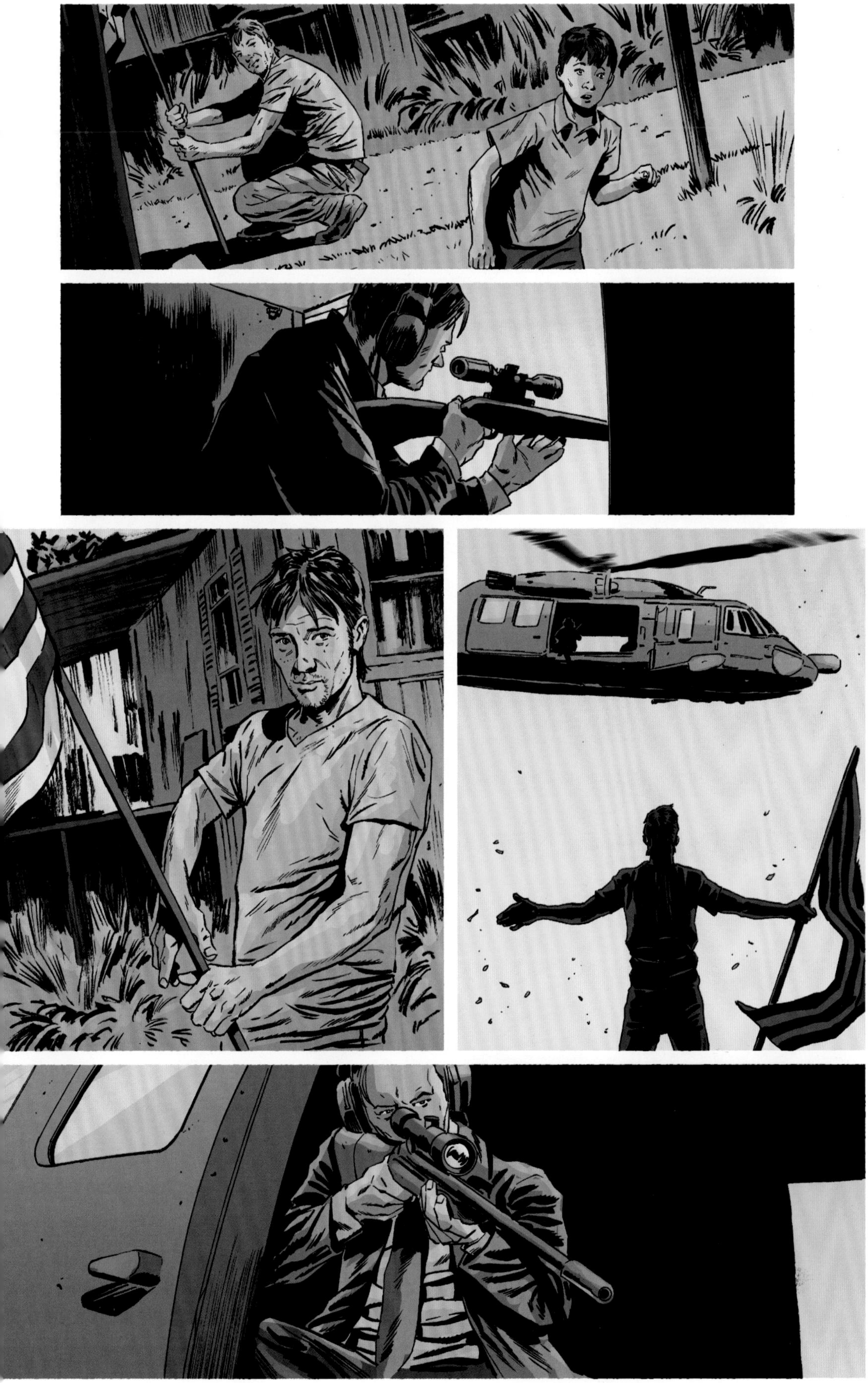

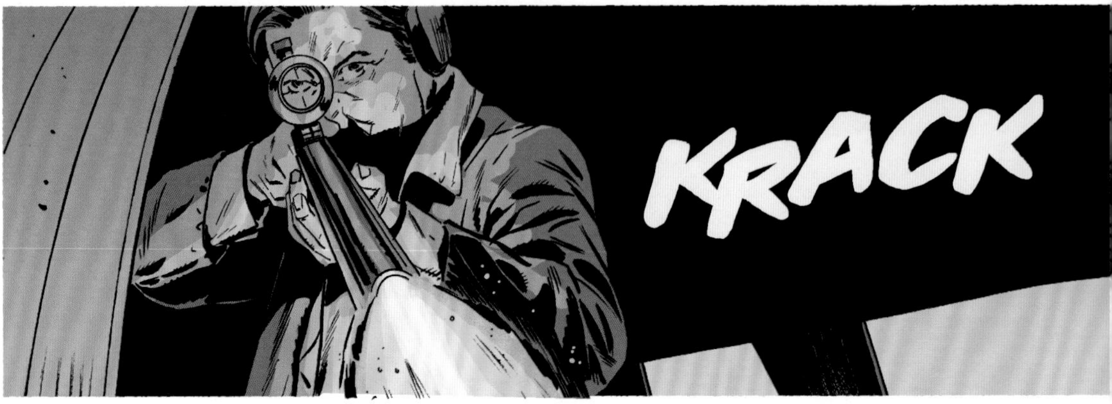
KRACK

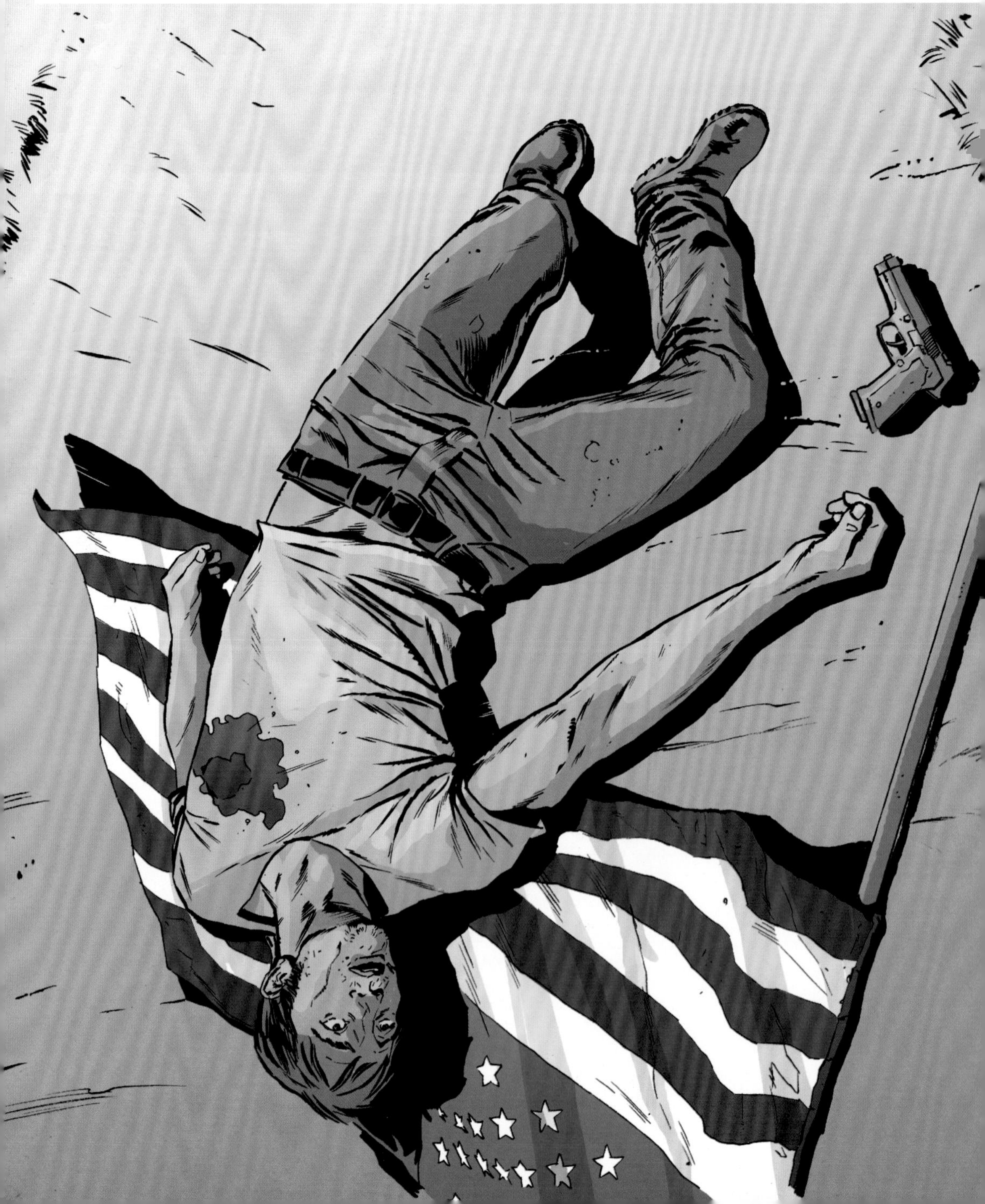

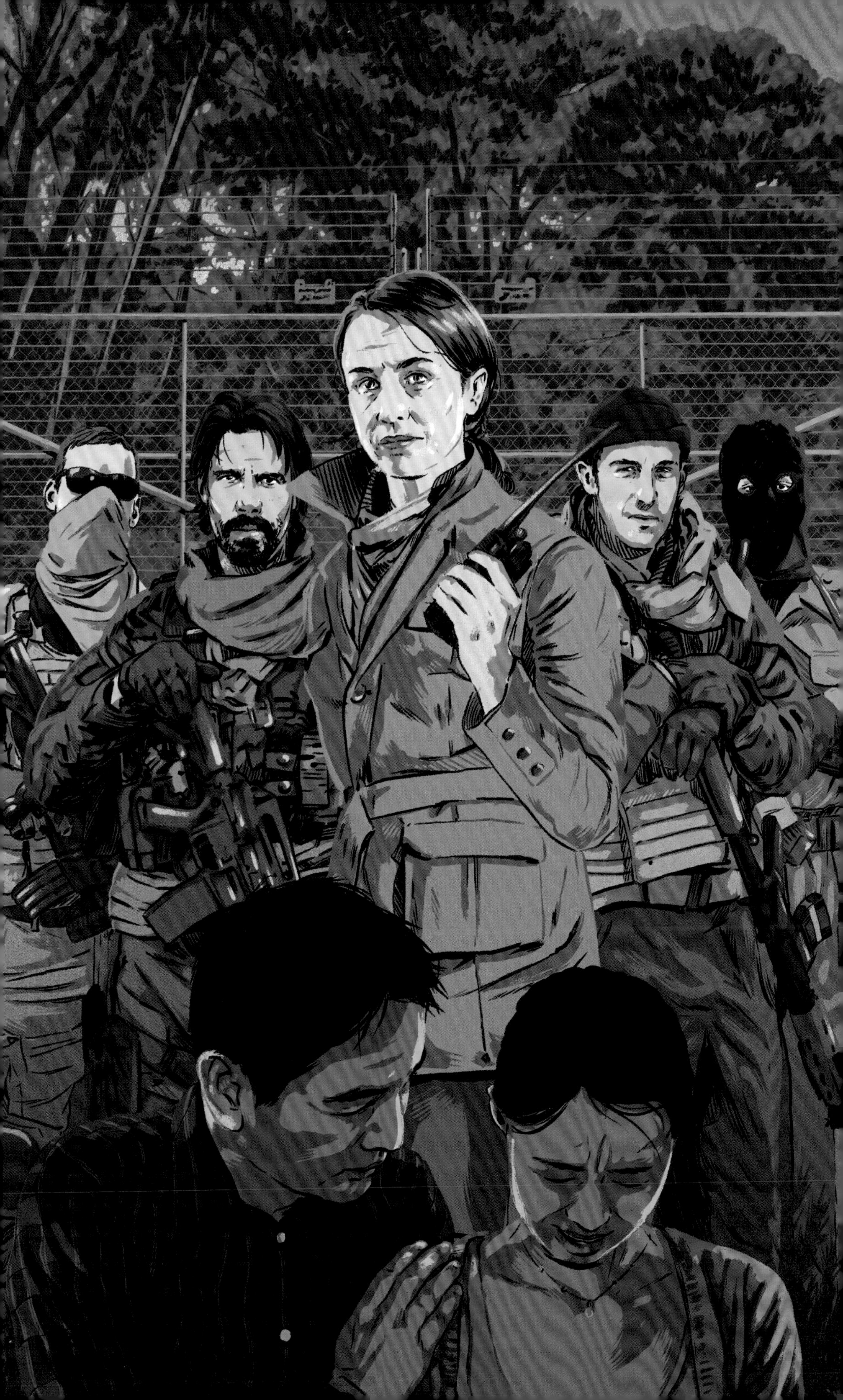

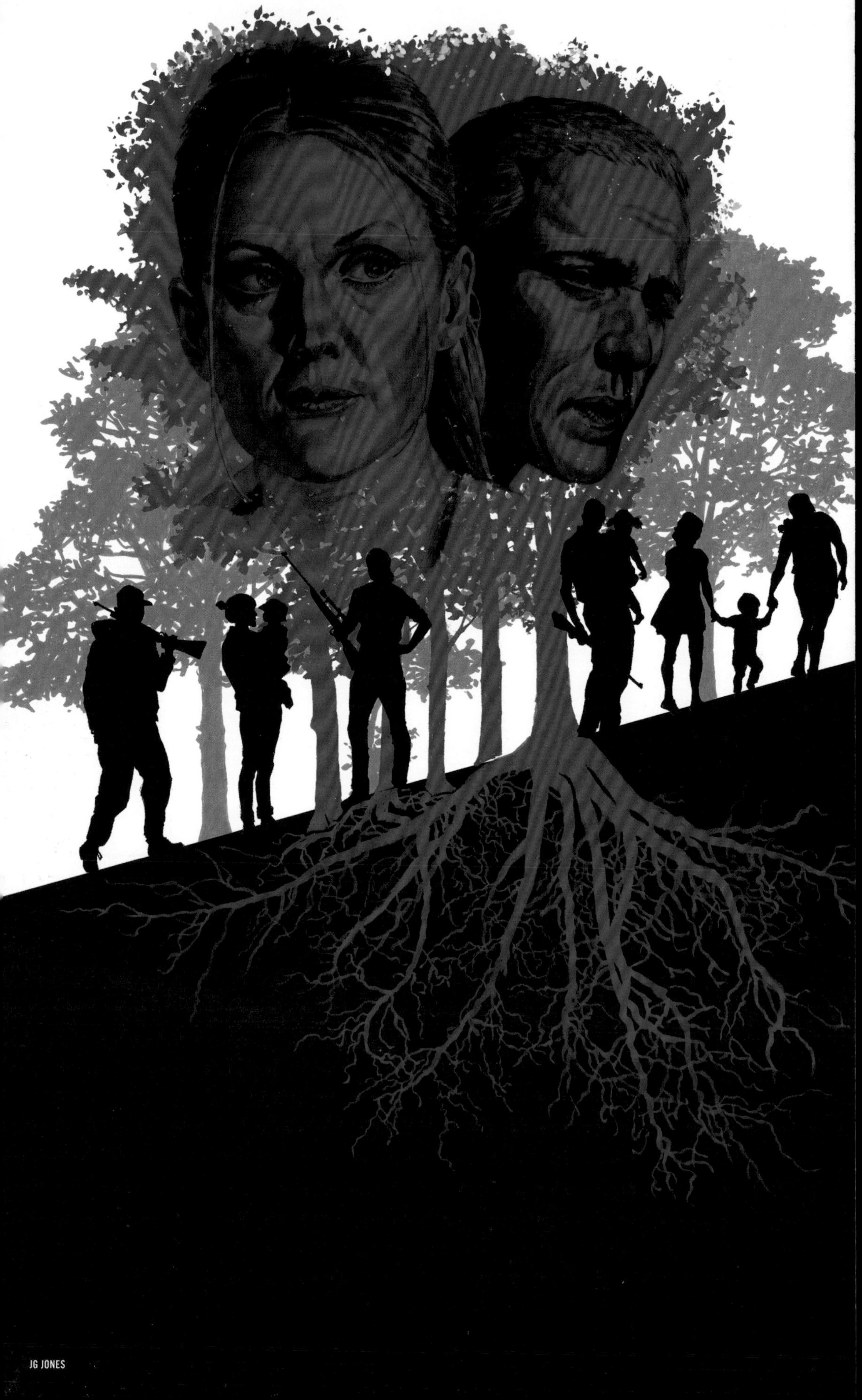
JG JONES

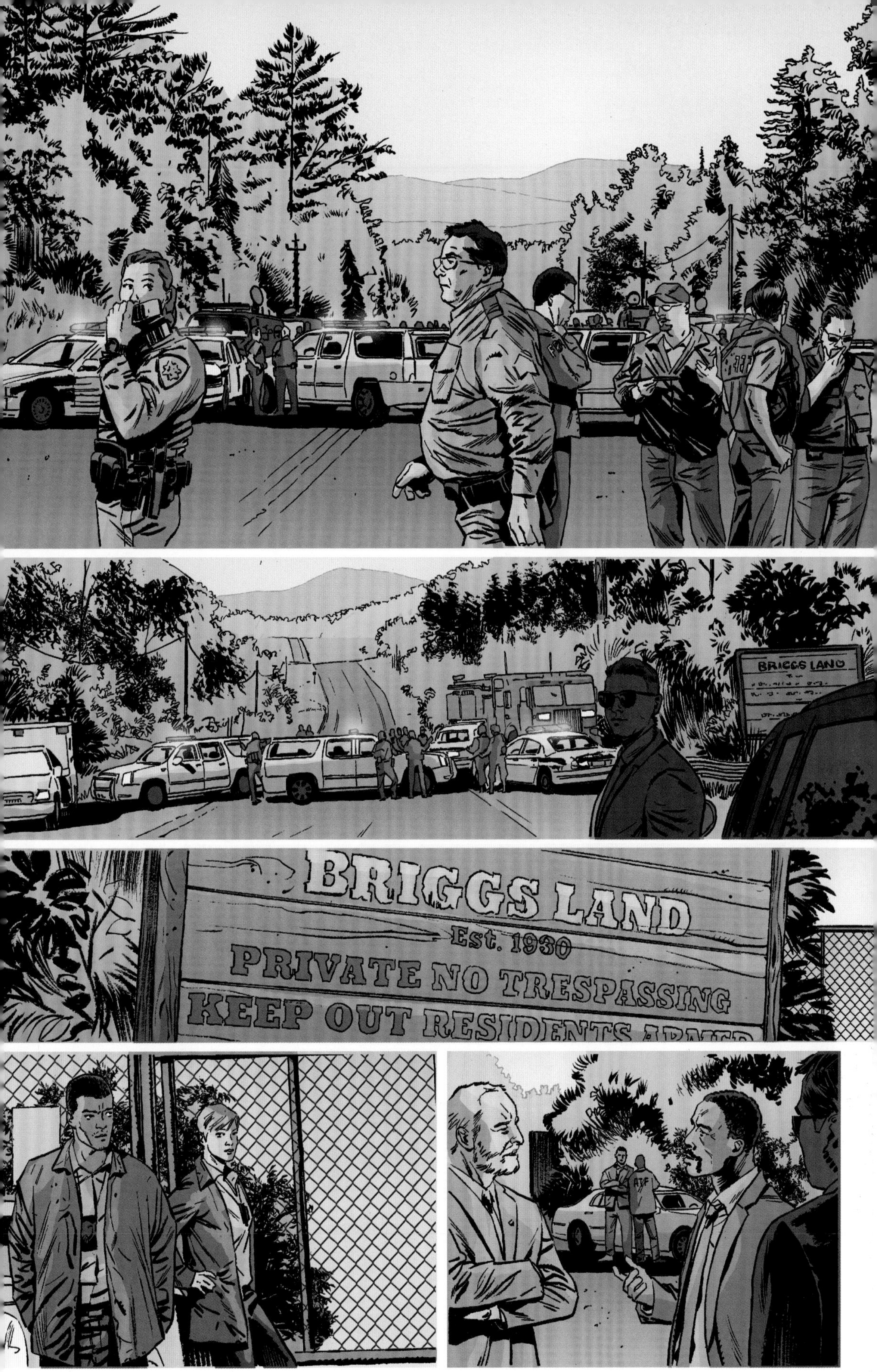
BRIGGS LAND
BRIGGS LAND
Est. 1930
PRIVATE NO TRESPASSING
KEEP OUT RESIDENTS
ATF

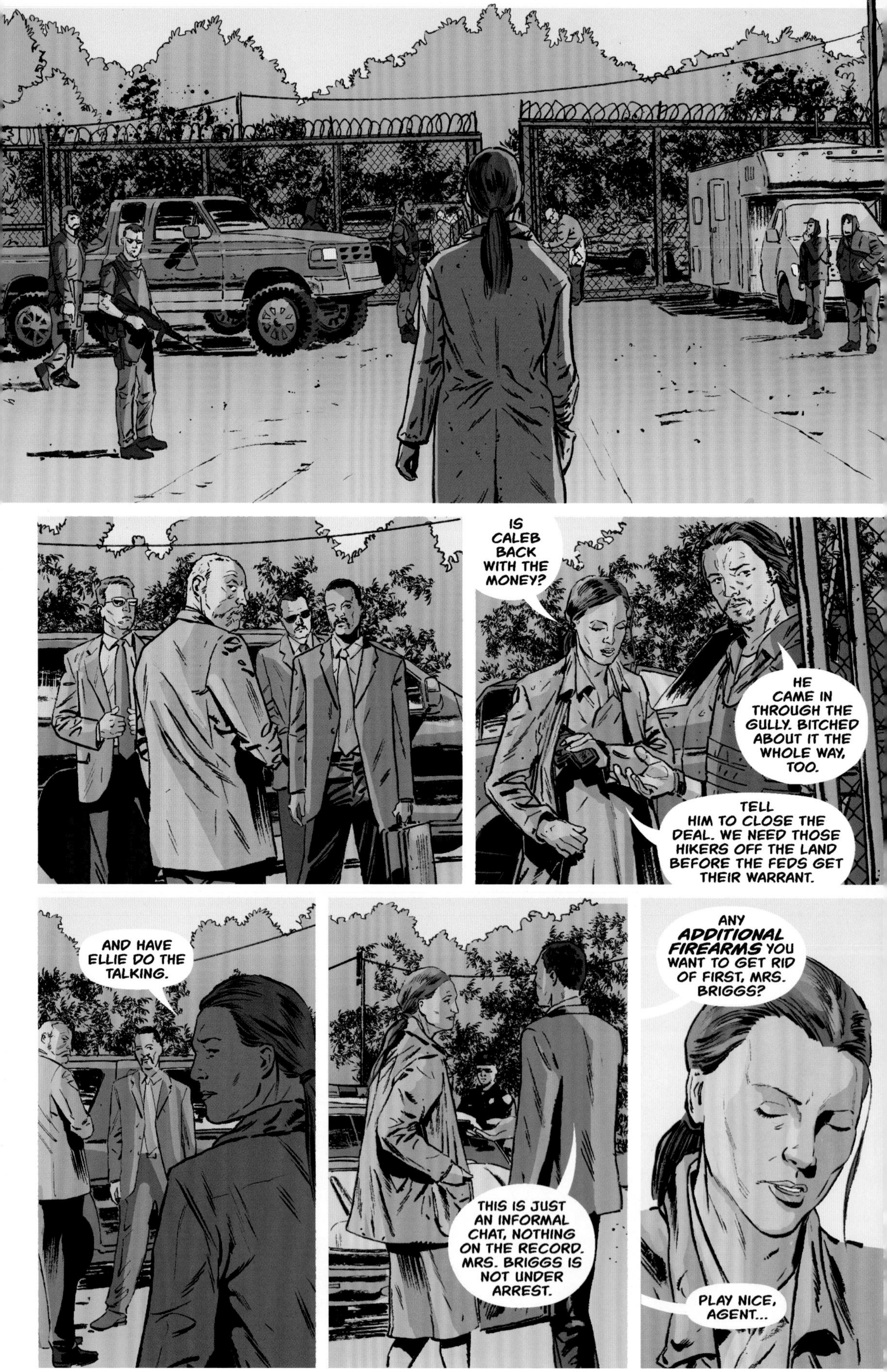
IS CALEB BACK WITH THE MONEY?
HE CAME IN THROUGH THE GULLY. BITCHED ABOUT IT THE WHOLE WAY, TOO.
TELL HIM TO CLOSE THE DEAL. WE NEED THOSE HIKERS OFF THE LAND BEFORE THE FEDS GET THEIR WARRANT.
AND HAVE ELLIE DO THE TALKING.
THIS IS JUST AN INFORMAL CHAT, NOTHING ON THE RECORD. MRS. BRIGGS IS NOT UNDER ARREST.
ANY ADDITIONAL FIREARMS YOU WANT TO GET RID OF FIRST, MRS. BRIGGS?
PLAY NICE, AGENT...

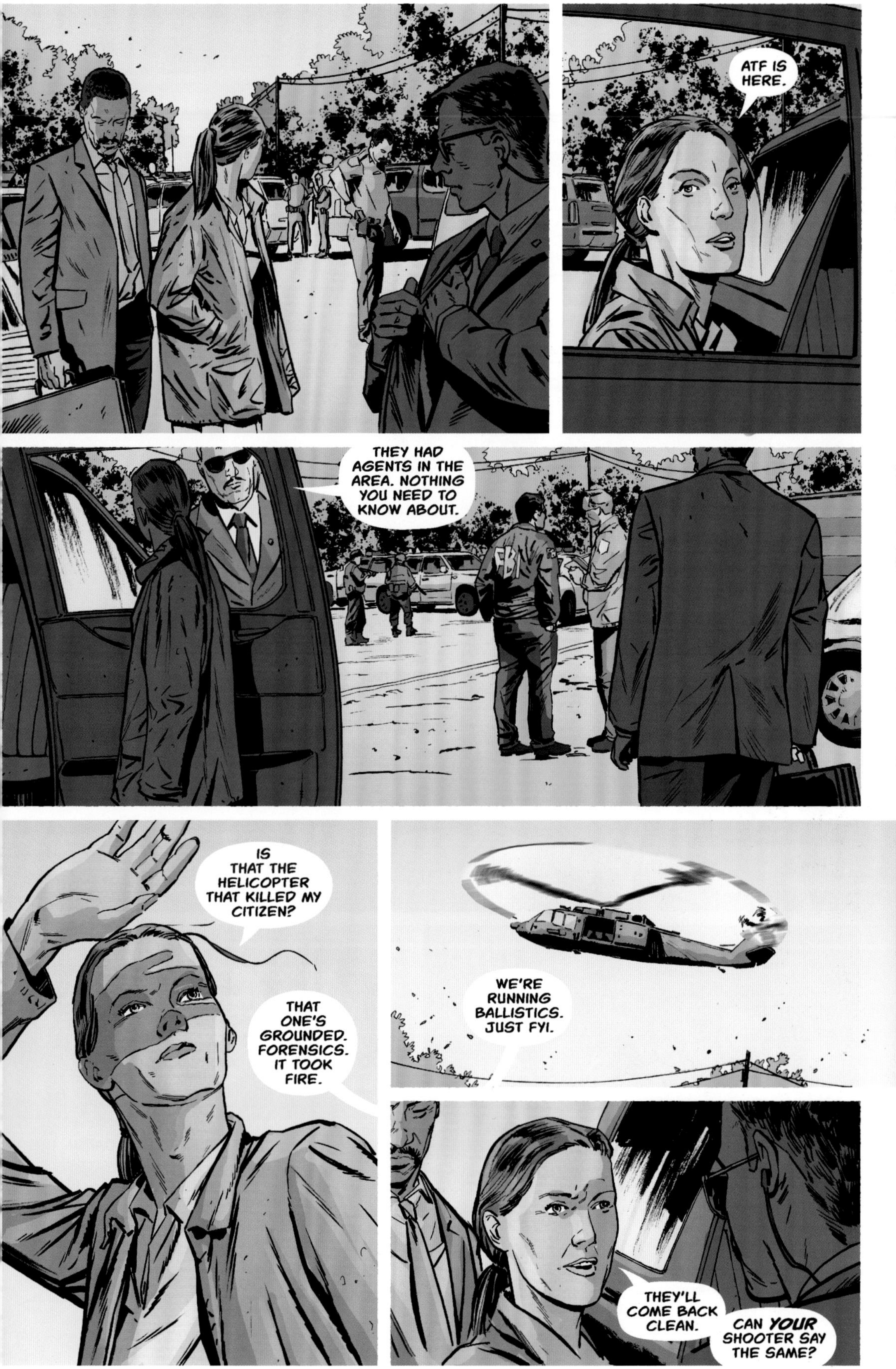

ATF IS HERE.
THEY HAD AGENTS IN THE AREA. NOTHING YOU NEED TO KNOW ABOUT.
FBI
IS THAT THE HELICOPTER THAT KILLED MY CITIZEN?
THAT ONE'S GROUNDED. FORENSICS. IT TOOK FIRE.
WE'RE RUNNING BALLISTICS. JUST FYI.
THEY'LL COME BACK CLEAN.
CAN YOUR SHOOTER SAY THE SAME?

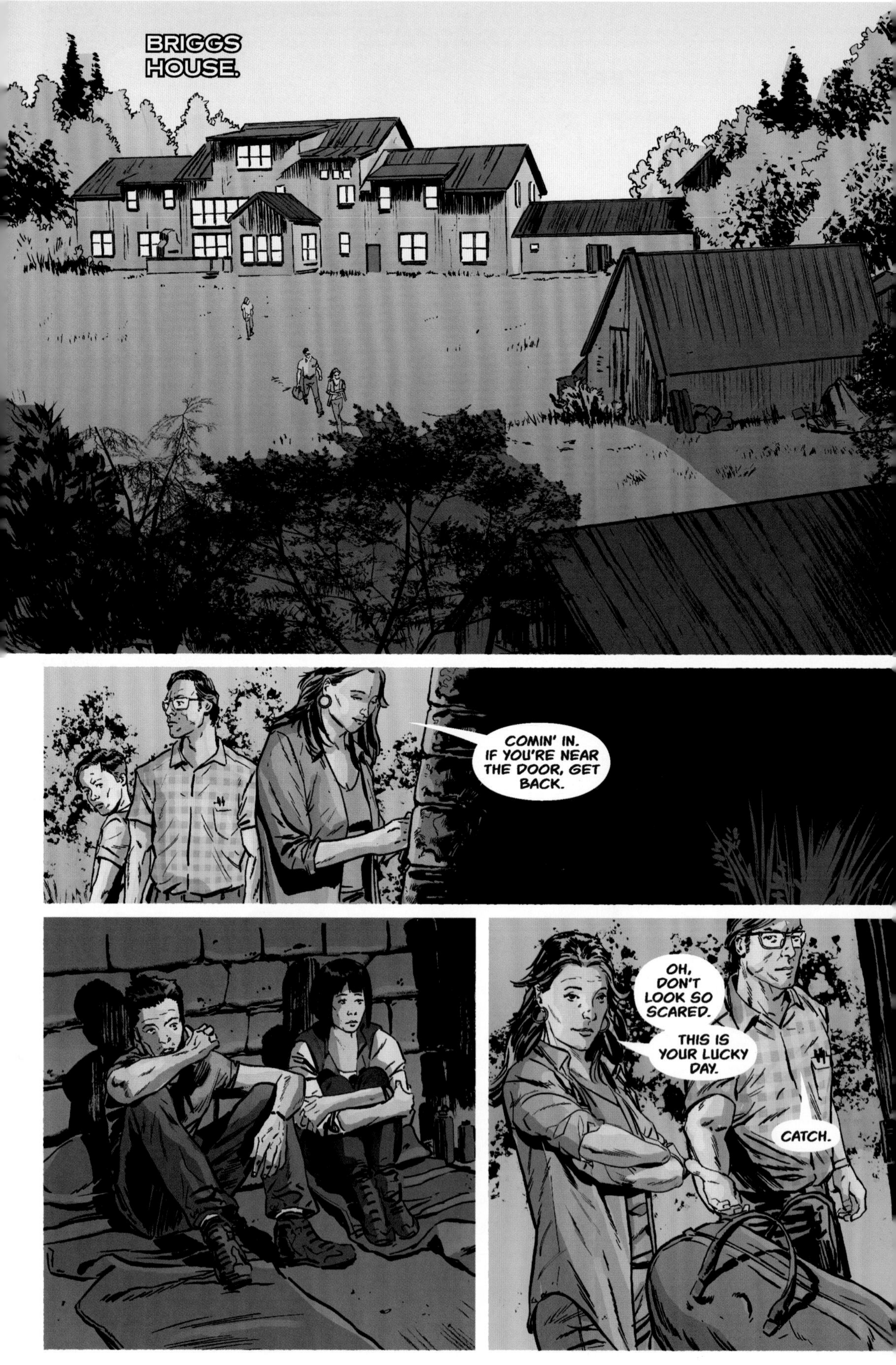
BRIGGS HOUSE.
COMIN' IN. IF YOU'RE NEAR THE DOOR, GET BACK.
OH, DON'T LOOK SO SCARED.
THIS IS YOUR LUCKY DAY.
CATCH.

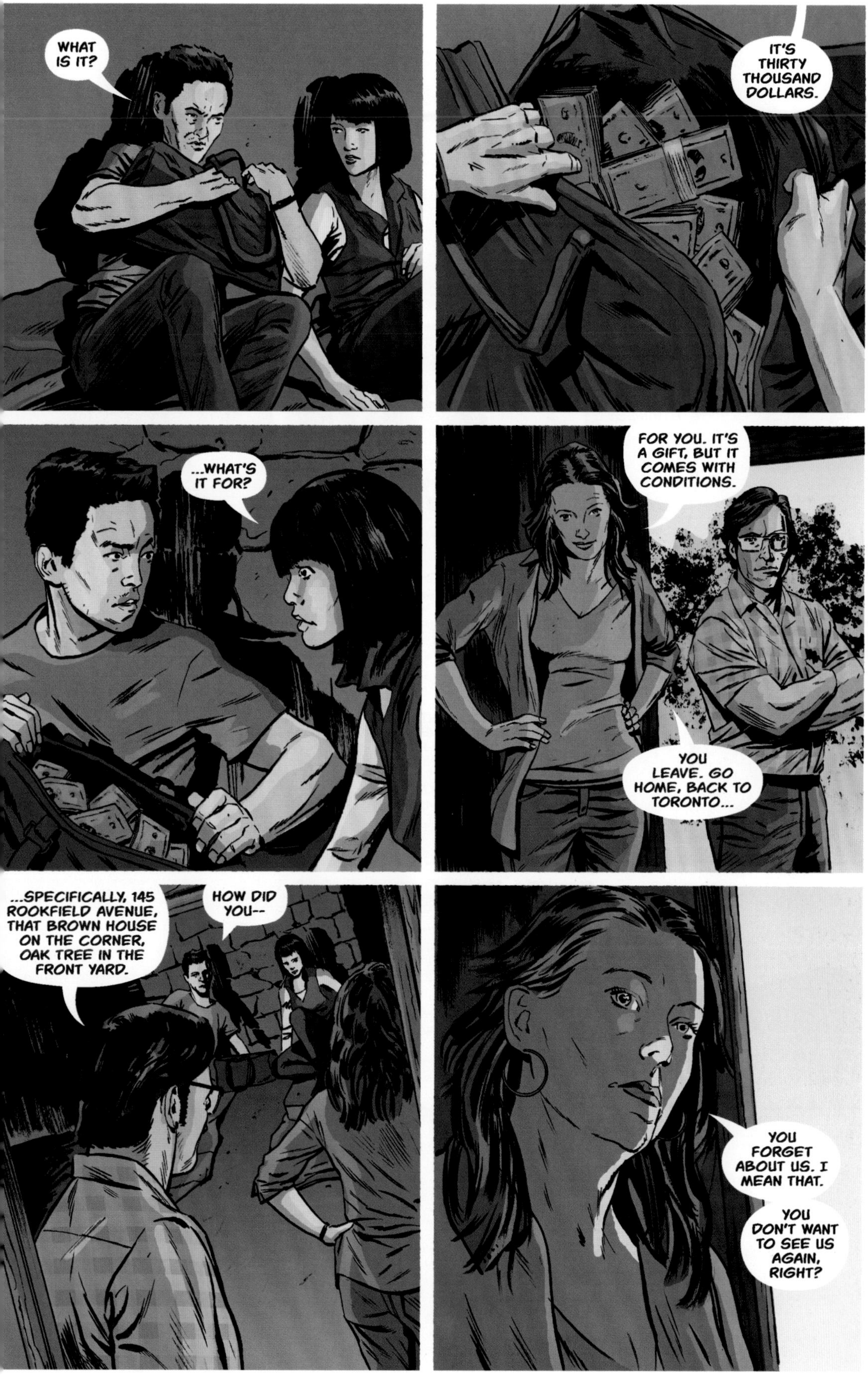
WHAT IS IT?
IT'S THIRTY THOUSAND DOLLARS.
...WHAT'S IT FOR?
FOR YOU. IT'S A GIFT, BUT IT COMES WITH CONDITIONS.
YOU LEAVE. GO HOME, BACK TO TORONTO...
...SPECIFICALLY, 145 ROOKFIELD AVENUE, THAT BROWN HOUSE ON THE CORNER, OAK TREE IN THE FRONT YARD.
HOW DID YOU--
YOU FORGET ABOUT US. I MEAN THAT.
YOU DON'T WANT TO SEE US AGAIN, RIGHT?

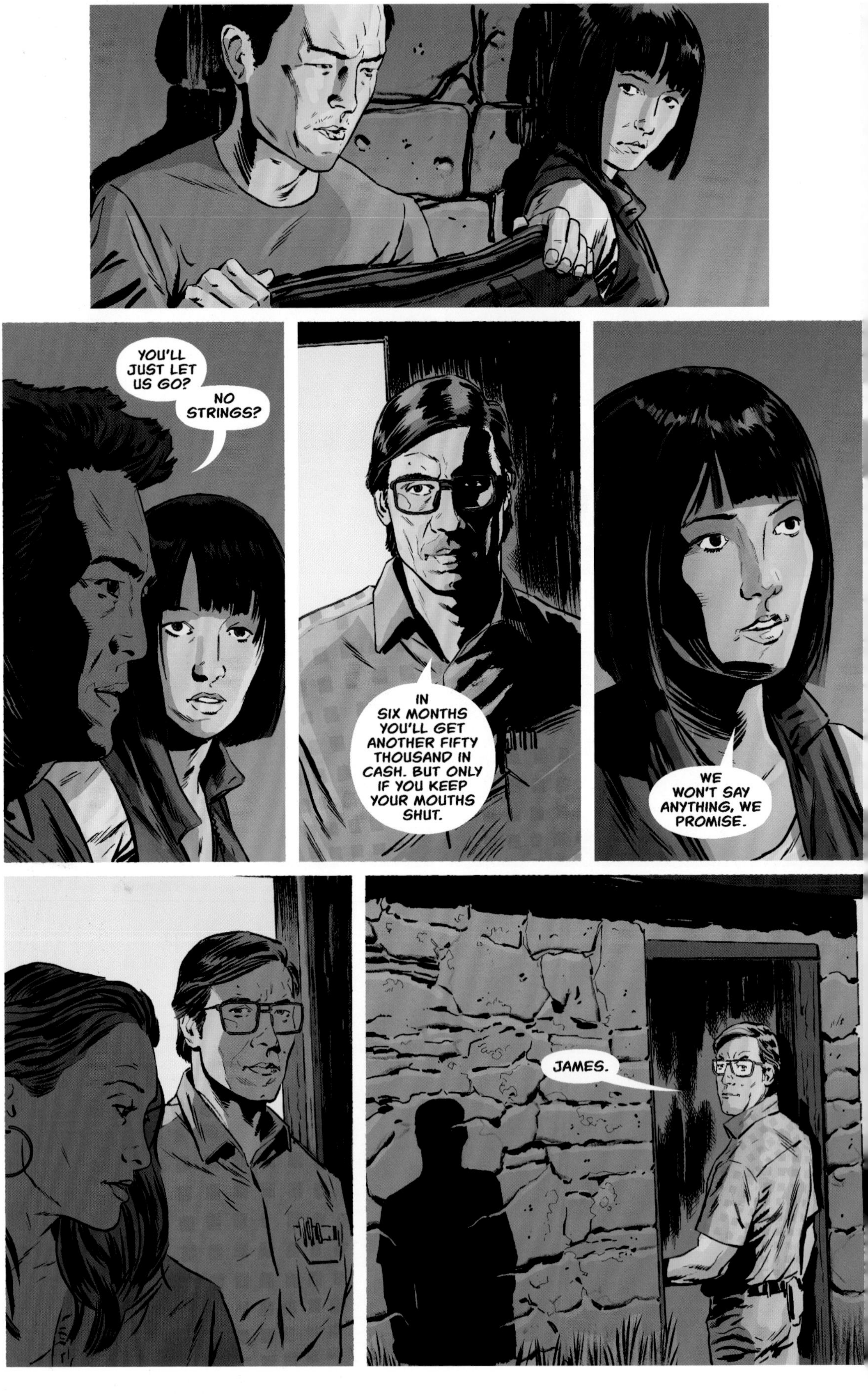
YOU'LL JUST LET US GO?
NO STRINGS?
IN SIX MONTHS YOU'LL GET ANOTHER FIFTY THOUSAND IN CASH. BUT ONLY IF YOU KEEP YOUR MOUTHS SHUT.
WE WON'T SAY ANYTHING, WE PROMISE.
JAMES.

TELL HER.

I TOOK YOUR PHONE.

I LOOKED AT IT. I HAVE A PRETTY GOOD MEMORY, SO I KNOW YOUR NUMBERS AND EMAILS. I ALSO KNOW YOUR CONTACTS, AND *THEIR* NUMBERS TOO.

AND I SAW YOUR PHOTOS.

WE WANT IT BACK.

WE DESTROYED IT. BUT HE'S TELLING THE TRUTH. I DON'T WANT YOU TO THINK YOU CAN HIDE FROM US BY JUST MOVING HOUSE.

WE DIDN'T ASK FOR THIS. WE DIDN'T MEAN TO COME ONTO YOUR LAND. IT WAS AN *ACCIDENT.*

AND *WE* FED YOU, WE DIDN'T HURT YOU, AND YOU'LL LEAVE HERE WITH A LOT OF MONEY.

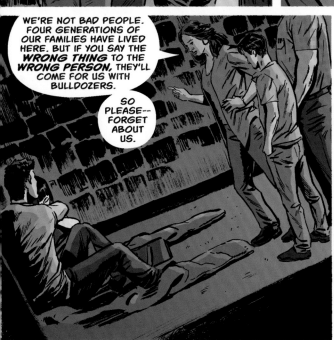

WE'RE NOT BAD PEOPLE. FOUR GENERATIONS OF OUR FAMILIES HAVE LIVED HERE. BUT IF YOU SAY THE *WRONG THING* TO THE *WRONG PERSON,* THEY'LL COME FOR US WITH BULLDOZERS.

SO PLEASE-- FORGET ABOUT US.

UNDERSTOOD.

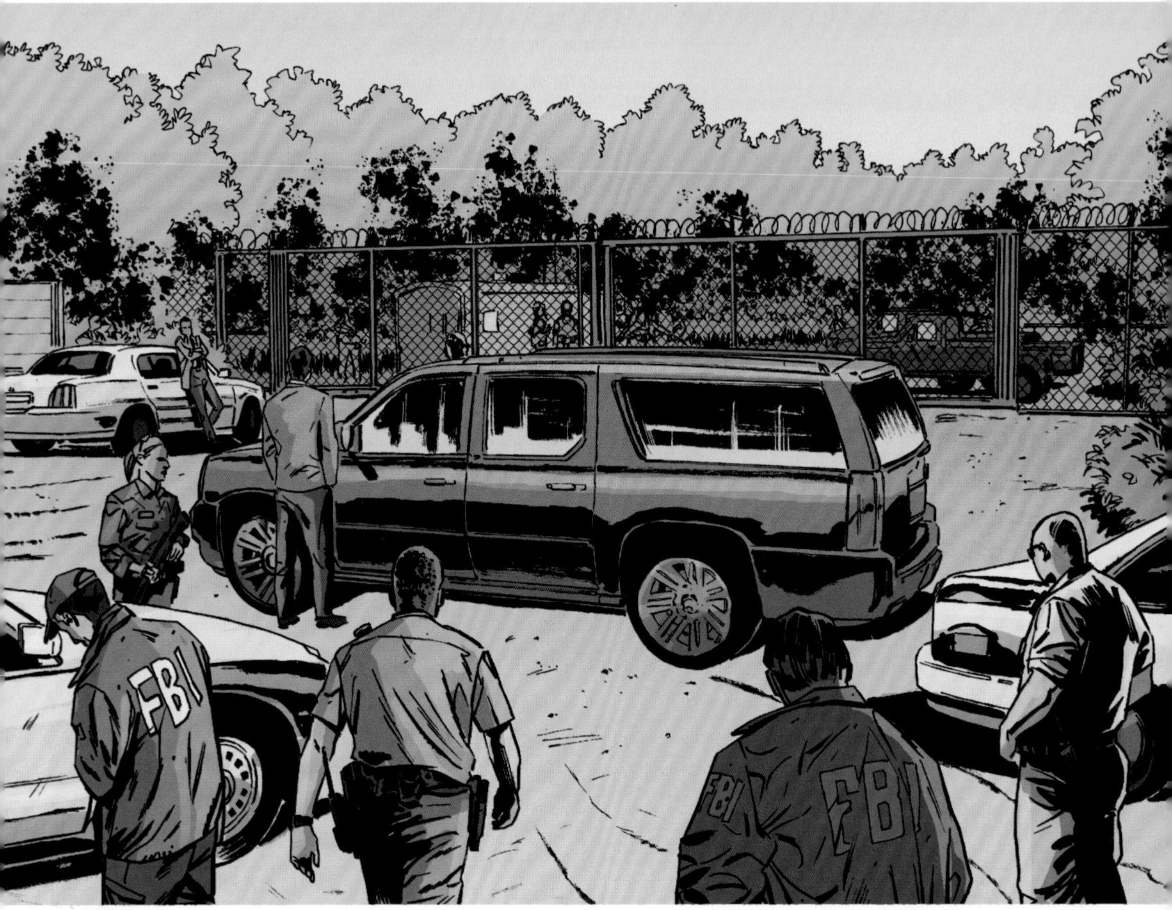
FBI
FBI

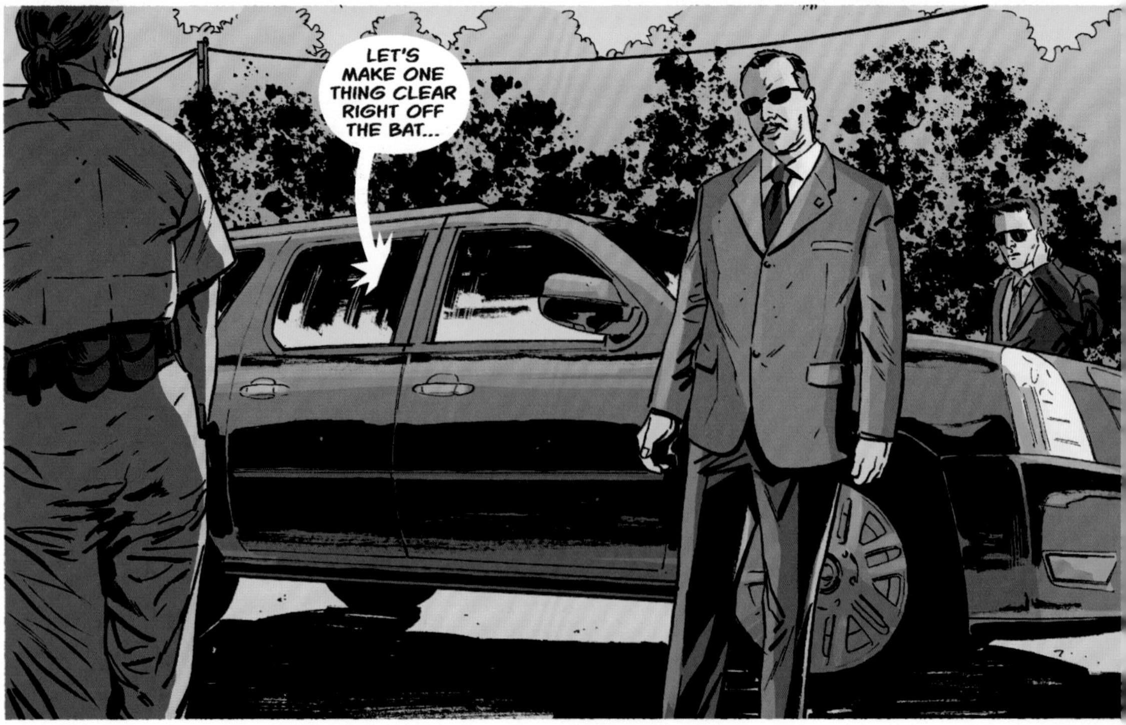
LET'S MAKE ONE THING CLEAR RIGHT OFF THE BAT...

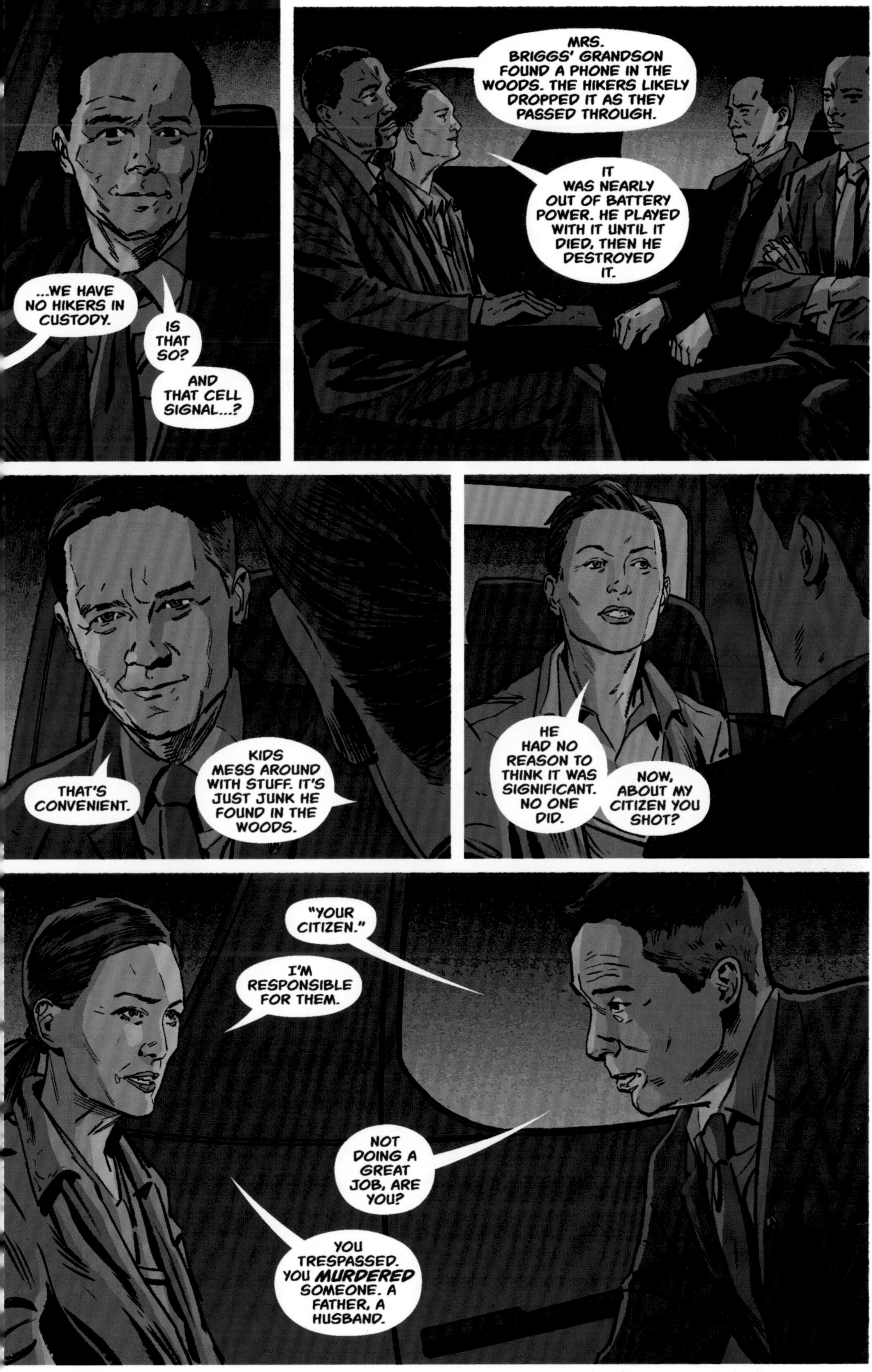
...WE HAVE NO HIKERS IN CUSTODY.
IS THAT SO?
AND THAT CELL SIGNAL...?
MRS. BRIGGS' GRANDSON FOUND A PHONE IN THE WOODS. THE HIKERS LIKELY DROPPED IT AS THEY PASSED THROUGH.
IT WAS NEARLY OUT OF BATTERY POWER. HE PLAYED WITH IT UNTIL IT DIED, THEN HE DESTROYED IT.
THAT'S CONVENIENT.
KIDS MESS AROUND WITH STUFF. IT'S JUST JUNK HE FOUND IN THE WOODS.
HE HAD NO REASON TO THINK IT WAS SIGNIFICANT. NO ONE DID.
NOW, ABOUT MY CITIZEN YOU SHOT?
"YOUR CITIZEN."
I'M RESPONSIBLE FOR THEM.
NOT DOING A GREAT JOB, ARE YOU?
YOU TRESPASSED. YOU MURDERED SOMEONE. A FATHER, A HUSBAND.

THIS LAND IS A TICKING **TIME BOMB**-- SOMETHING LIKE THIS WAS **BOUND** TO HAPPEN--

OKAY--

IT'S PRIVATE LAND-- NO DIFFERENT THAN YOUR BACKYARD--

OH, I THINK THERE'S **SOME** DIFFERENCE--

THAT'S ENOUGH--

--FUCKIN' **REDNECK DOMESTIC TERROR**--

COOL **IT!** FUCK'S SAKE.

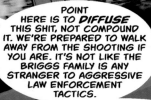

POINT HERE IS TO **DIFFUSE** THIS SHIT, NOT COMPOUND IT. WE'RE PREPARED TO WALK AWAY FROM THE SHOOTING IF YOU ARE. IT'S NOT LIKE THE BRIGGS FAMILY IS ANY STRANGER TO AGGRESSIVE LAW ENFORCEMENT TACTICS.

COST OF DOING BUSINESS, SO TO SPEAK.

YOU **KNOW** IF YOU GET THAT WARRANT AND SEND IN HUNDREDS OF AGENTS TO COMB MRS. BRIGGS PROPERTY, ALL THE INDIVIDUAL HOMES IN THAT VILLAGE, ALL THOSE FIREARMS...?

DO YOU REMEMBER RUBY RIDGE?

THAT WAS **ONE** HOUSE...

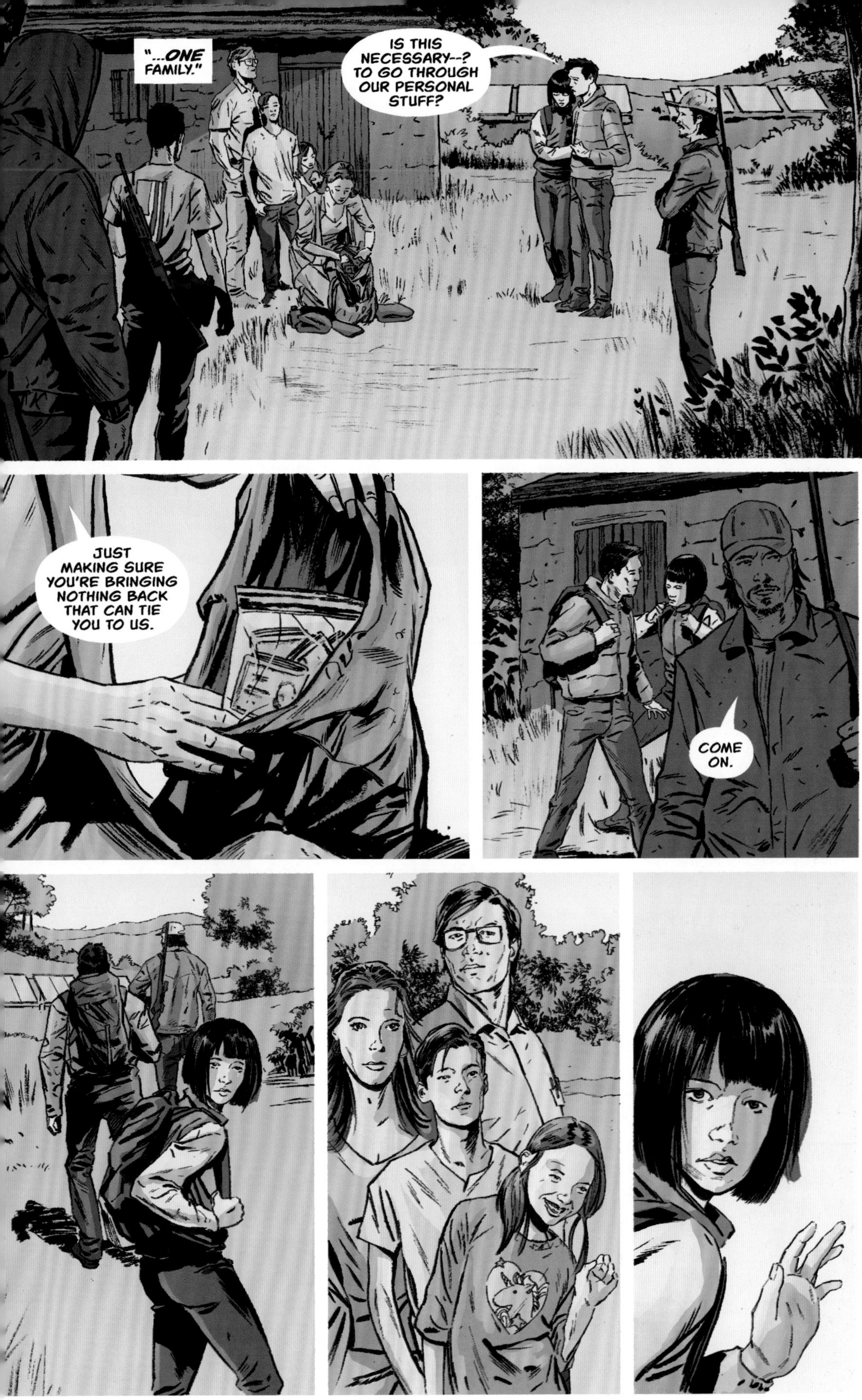
"...ONE FAMILY."
IS THIS NECESSARY--? TO GO THROUGH OUR PERSONAL STUFF?
JUST MAKING SURE YOU'RE BRINGING NOTHING BACK THAT CAN TIE YOU TO US.
COME ON.

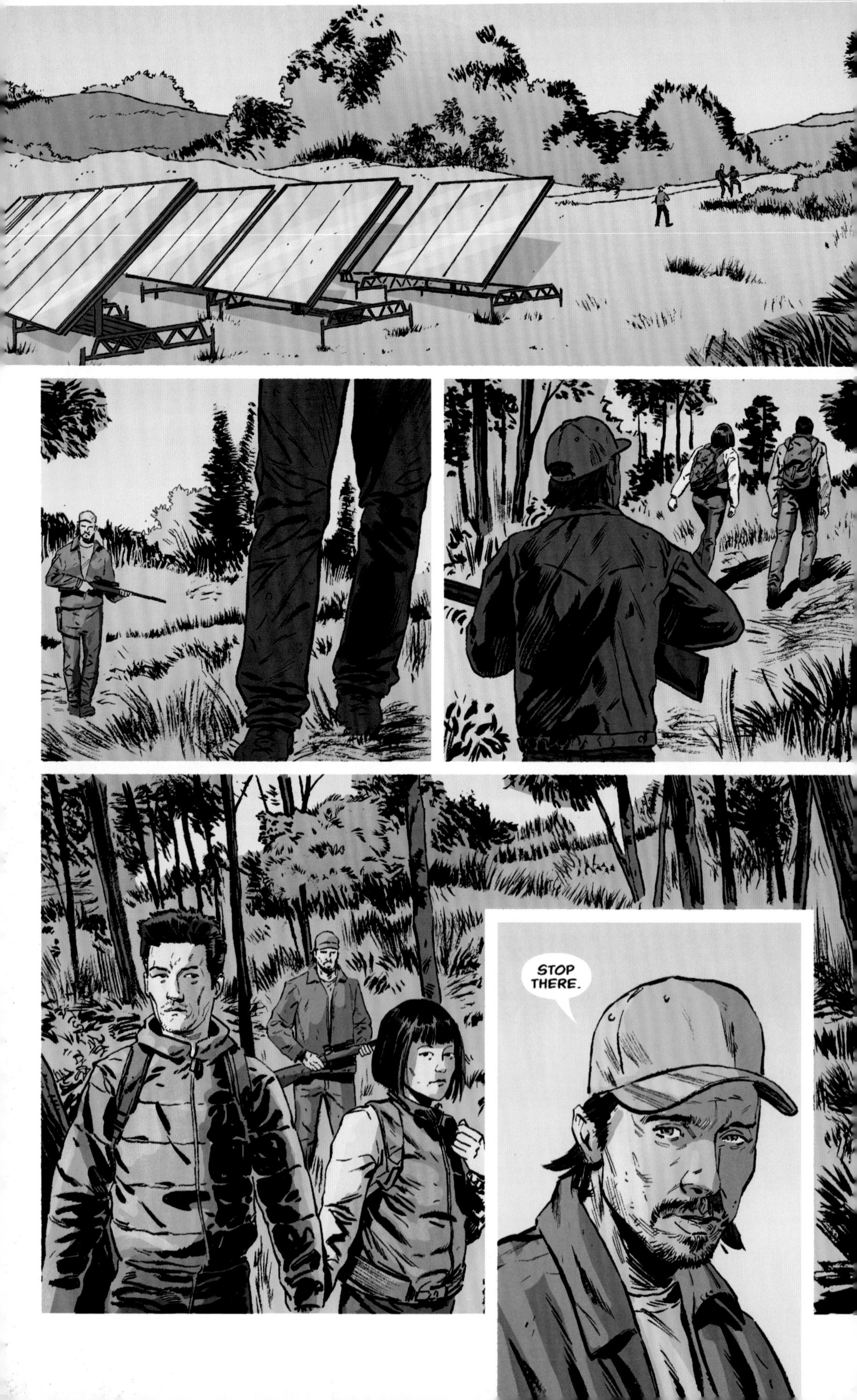
STOP THERE.

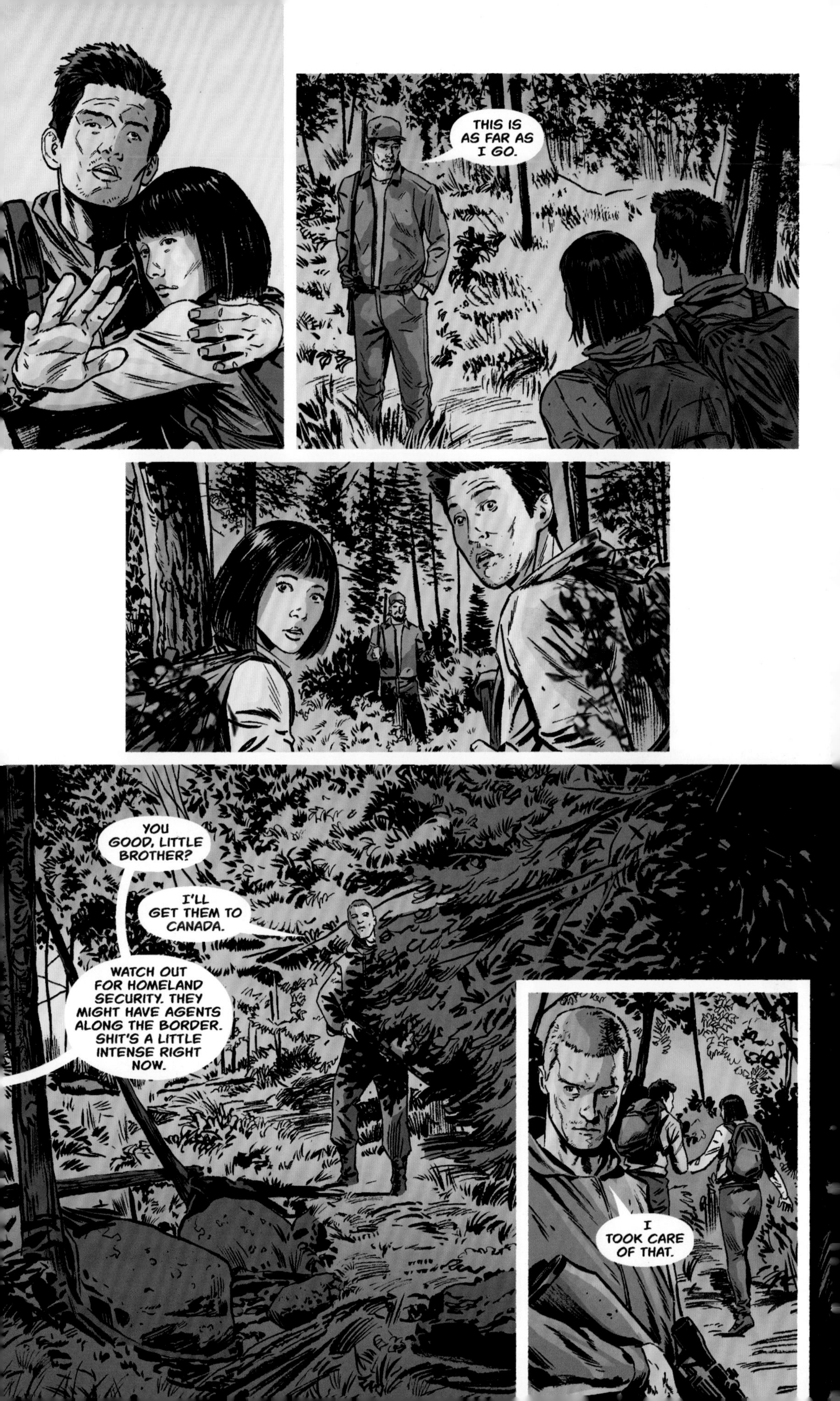
THIS IS AS FAR AS I GO.
YOU GOOD, LITTLE BROTHER?
I'LL GET THEM TO CANADA.
WATCH OUT FOR HOMELAND SECURITY. THEY MIGHT HAVE AGENTS ALONG THE BORDER. SHIT'S A LITTLE INTENSE RIGHT NOW.
I TOOK CARE OF THAT.

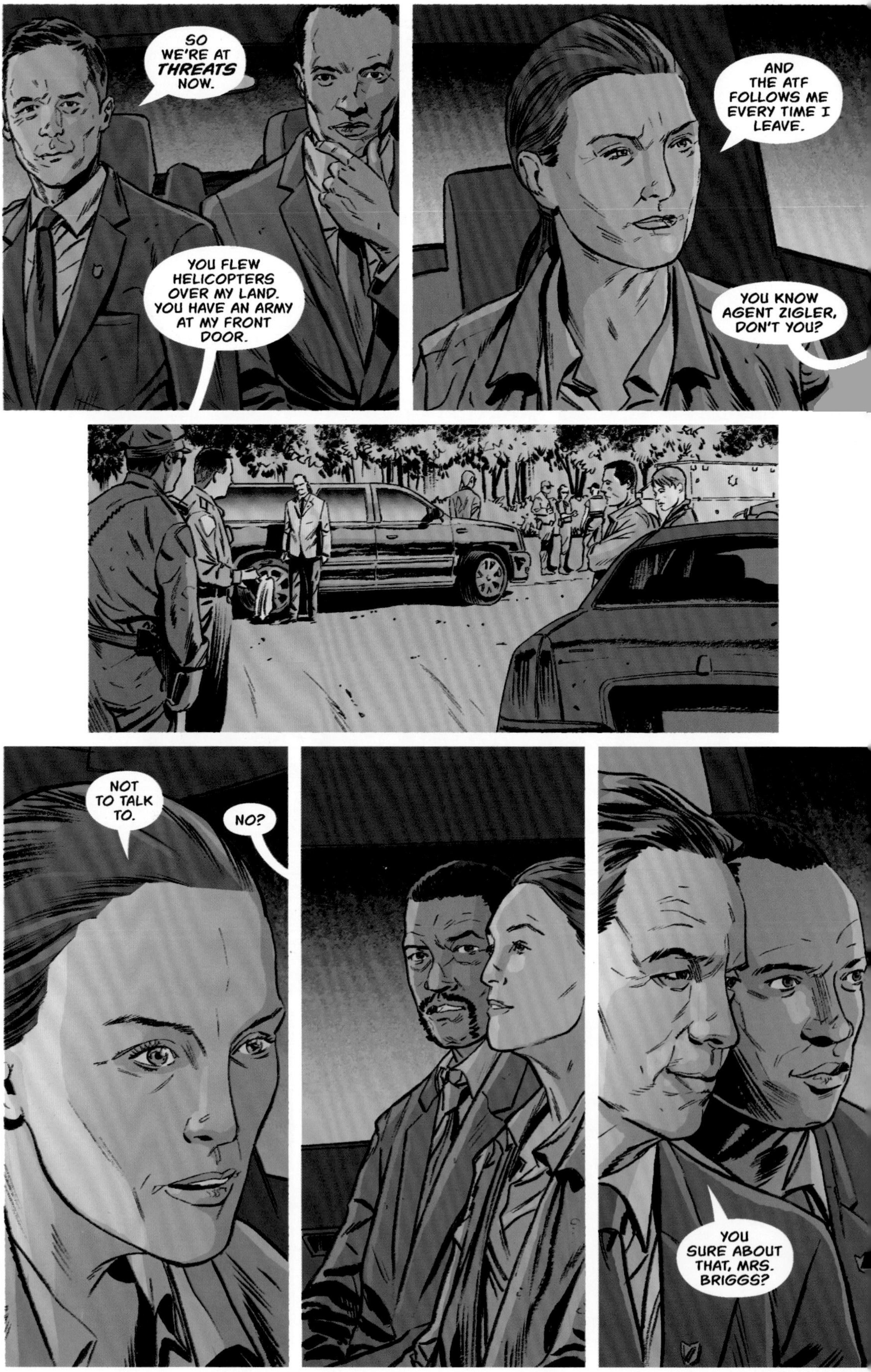

SO WE'RE AT *THREATS* NOW.
YOU FLEW HELICOPTERS OVER MY LAND. YOU HAVE AN ARMY AT MY FRONT DOOR.
AND THE ATF FOLLOWS ME EVERY TIME I LEAVE.
YOU KNOW AGENT ZIGLER, DON'T YOU?
NOT TO TALK TO.
NO?
YOU SURE ABOUT THAT, MRS. BRIGGS?

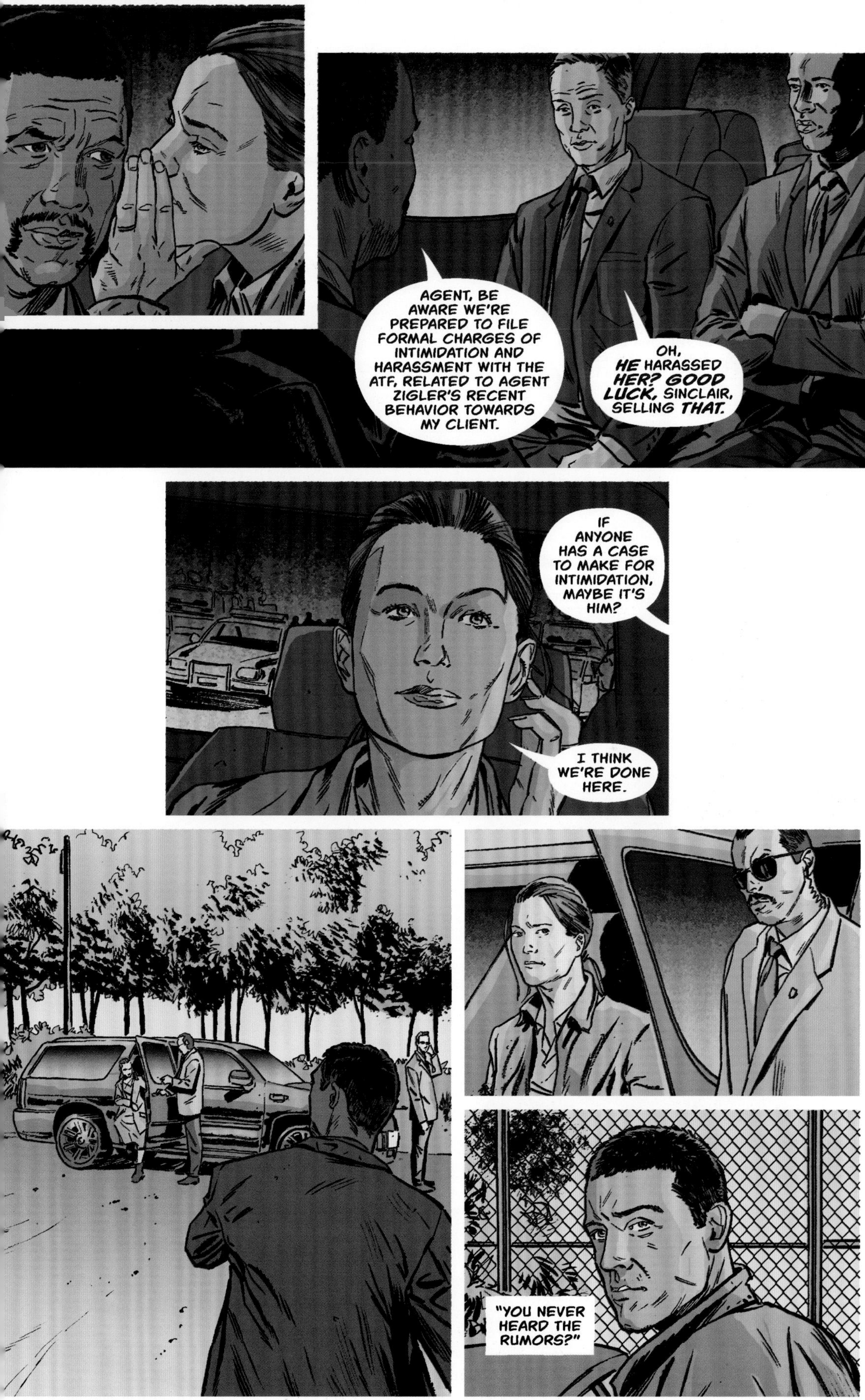
AGENT, BE AWARE WE'RE PREPARED TO FILE FORMAL CHARGES OF INTIMIDATION AND HARASSMENT WITH THE ATF, RELATED TO AGENT ZIGLER'S RECENT BEHAVIOR TOWARDS MY CLIENT.
OH, *HE* HARASSED *HER? GOOD LUCK,* SINCLAIR, SELLING *THAT.*
IF ANYONE HAS A CASE TO MAKE FOR INTIMIDATION, MAYBE IT'S HIM?
I THINK WE'RE DONE HERE.
"YOU NEVER HEARD THE RUMORS?"

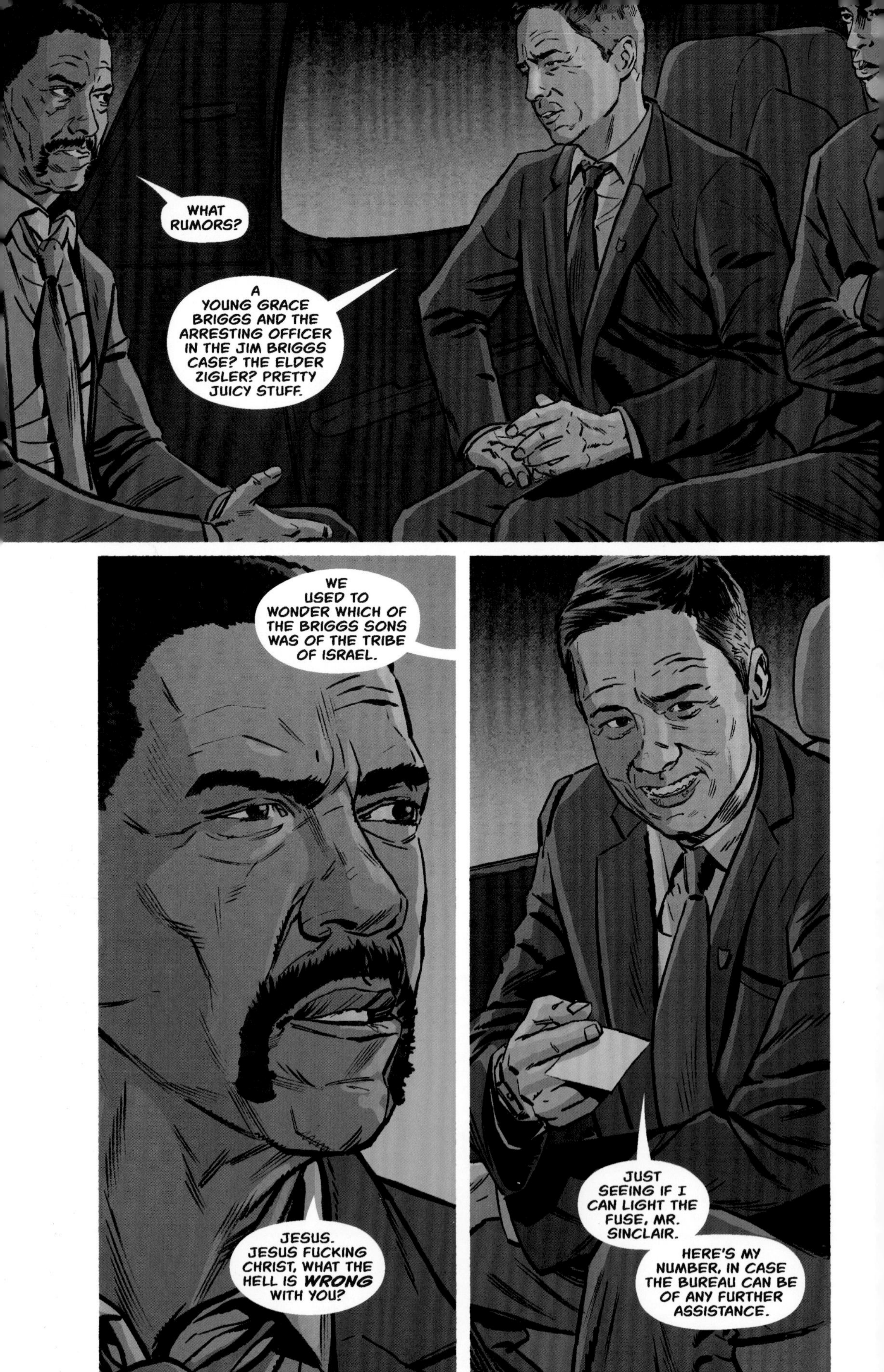
WHAT RUMORS?
A YOUNG GRACE BRIGGS AND THE ARRESTING OFFICER IN THE JIM BRIGGS CASE? THE ELDER ZIGLER? PRETTY JUICY STUFF.
WE USED TO WONDER WHICH OF THE BRIGGS SONS WAS OF THE TRIBE OF ISRAEL.
JESUS. JESUS FUCKING CHRIST, WHAT THE HELL IS *WRONG* WITH YOU?
JUST SEEING IF I CAN LIGHT THE FUSE, MR. SINCLAIR.
HERE'S MY NUMBER, IN CASE THE BUREAU CAN BE OF ANY FURTHER ASSISTANCE.

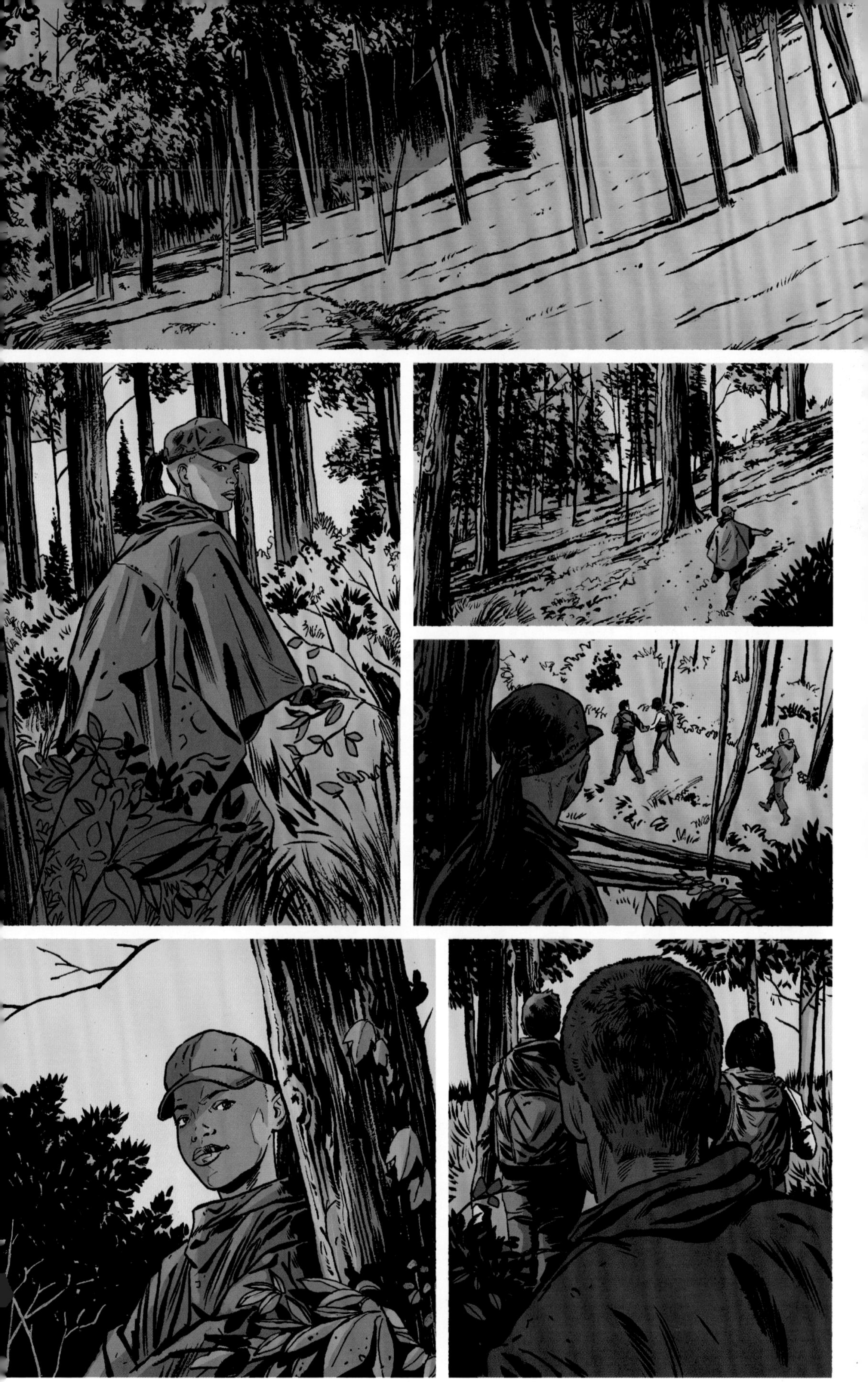

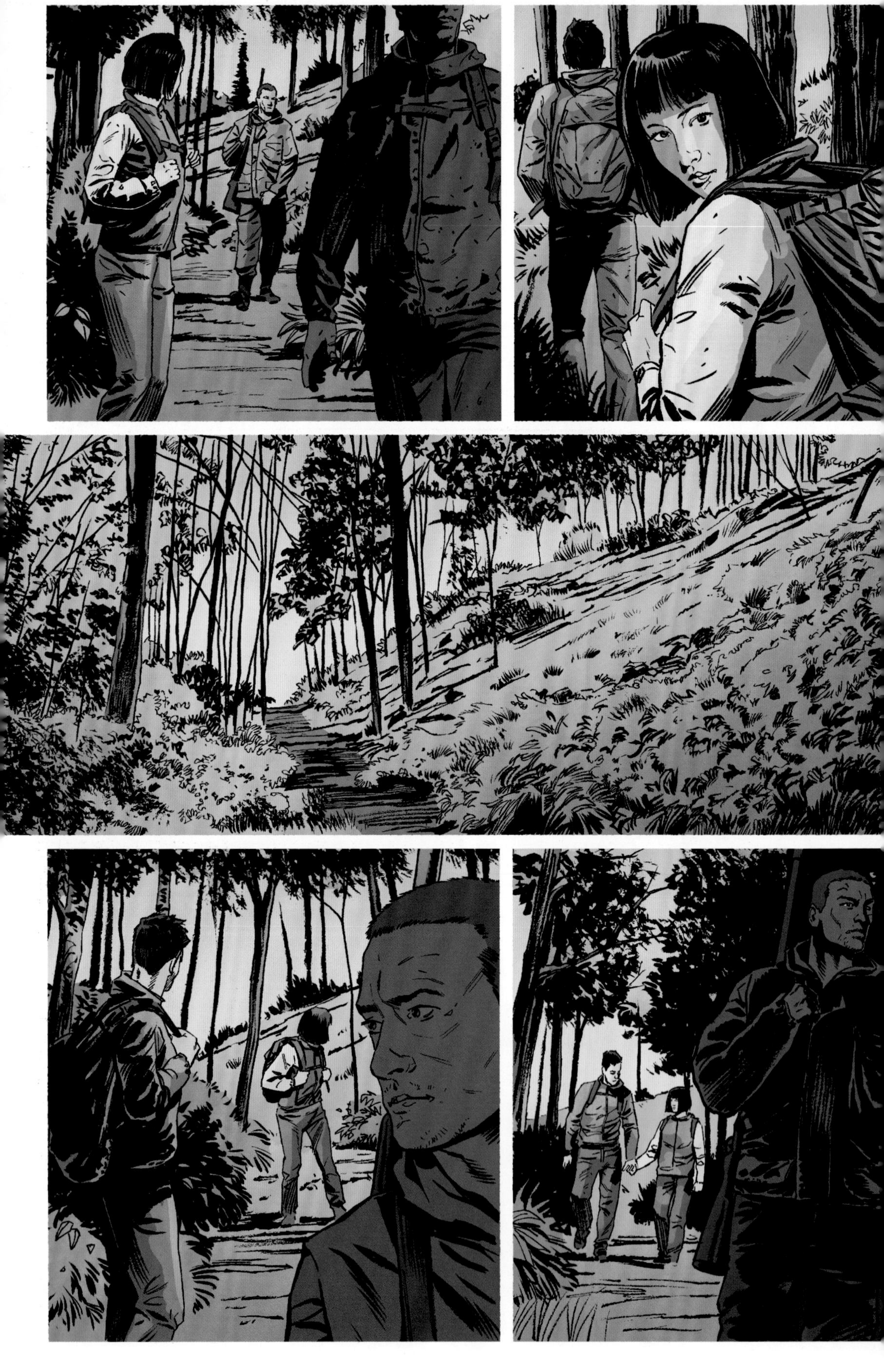

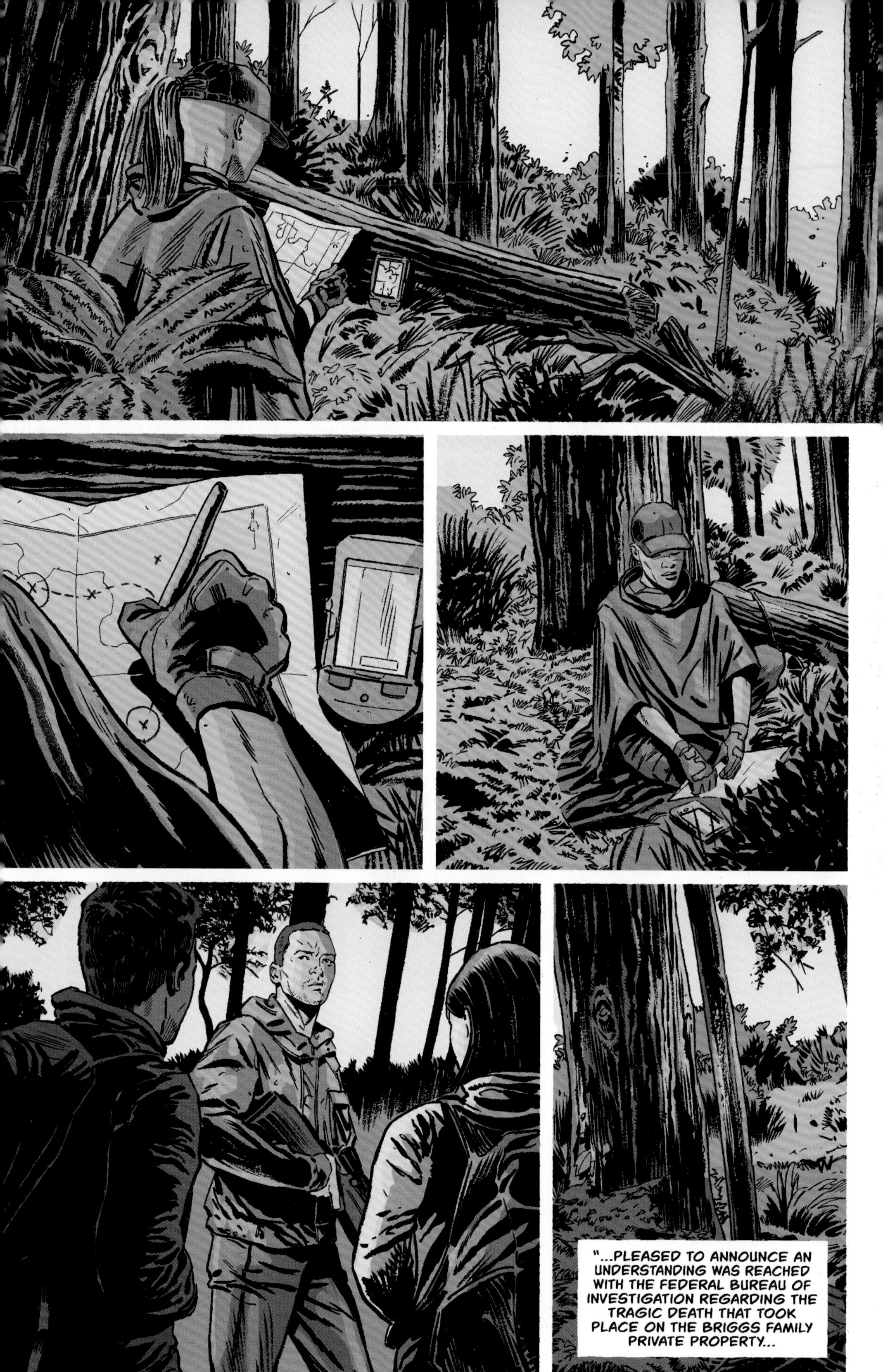
"...PLEASED TO ANNOUNCE AN UNDERSTANDING WAS REACHED WITH THE FEDERAL BUREAU OF INVESTIGATION REGARDING THE TRAGIC DEATH THAT TOOK PLACE ON THE BRIGGS FAMILY PRIVATE PROPERTY...

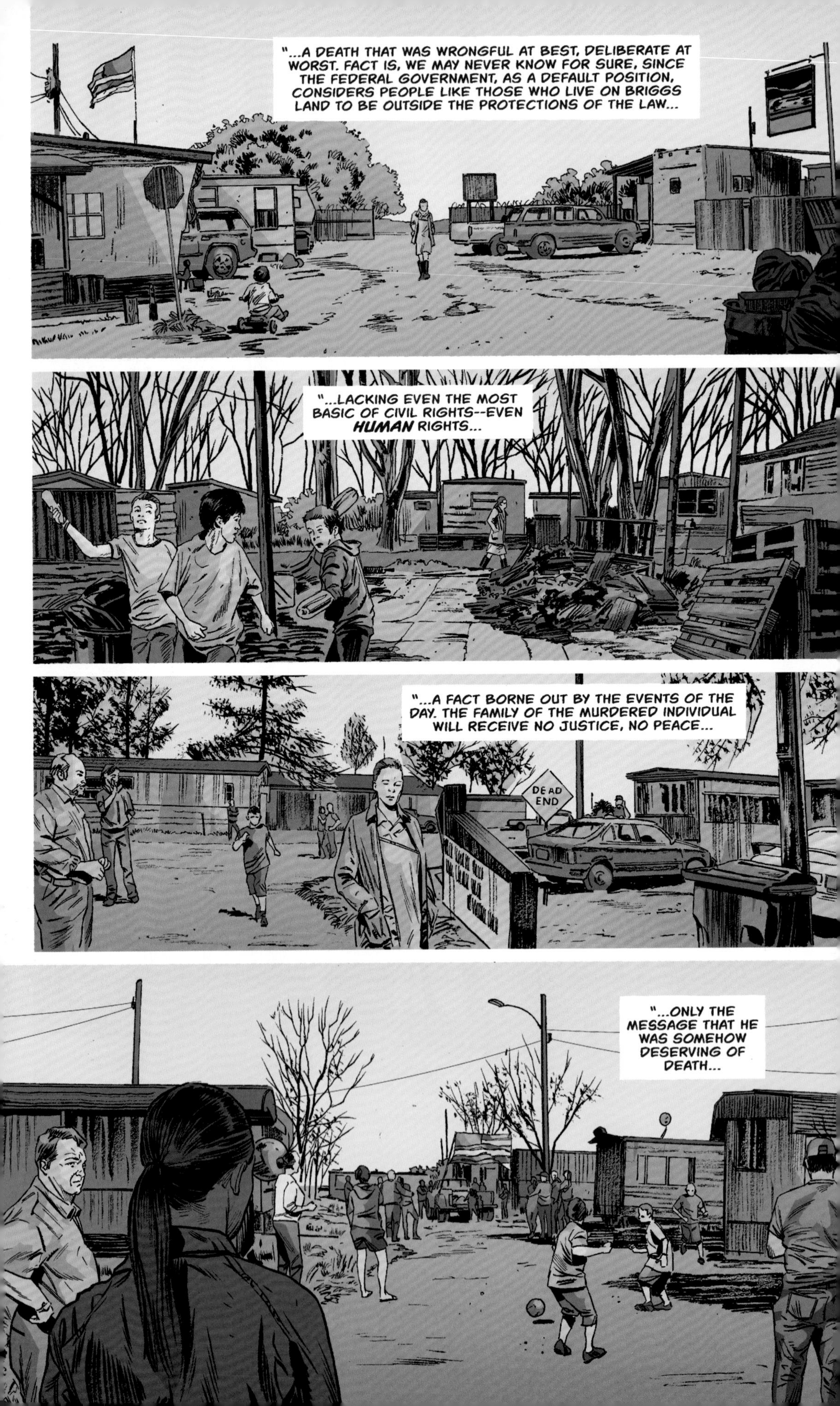
"...A DEATH THAT WAS WRONGFUL AT BEST, DELIBERATE AT WORST. FACT IS, WE MAY NEVER KNOW FOR SURE, SINCE THE FEDERAL GOVERNMENT, AS A DEFAULT POSITION, CONSIDERS PEOPLE LIKE THOSE WHO LIVE ON BRIGGS LAND TO BE OUTSIDE THE PROTECTIONS OF THE LAW...
"...LACKING EVEN THE MOST BASIC OF CIVIL RIGHTS--EVEN HUMAN RIGHTS...
"...A FACT BORNE OUT BY THE EVENTS OF THE DAY. THE FAMILY OF THE MURDERED INDIVIDUAL WILL RECEIVE NO JUSTICE, NO PEACE...
DEAD END
"...ONLY THE MESSAGE THAT HE WAS SOMEHOW DESERVING OF DEATH...

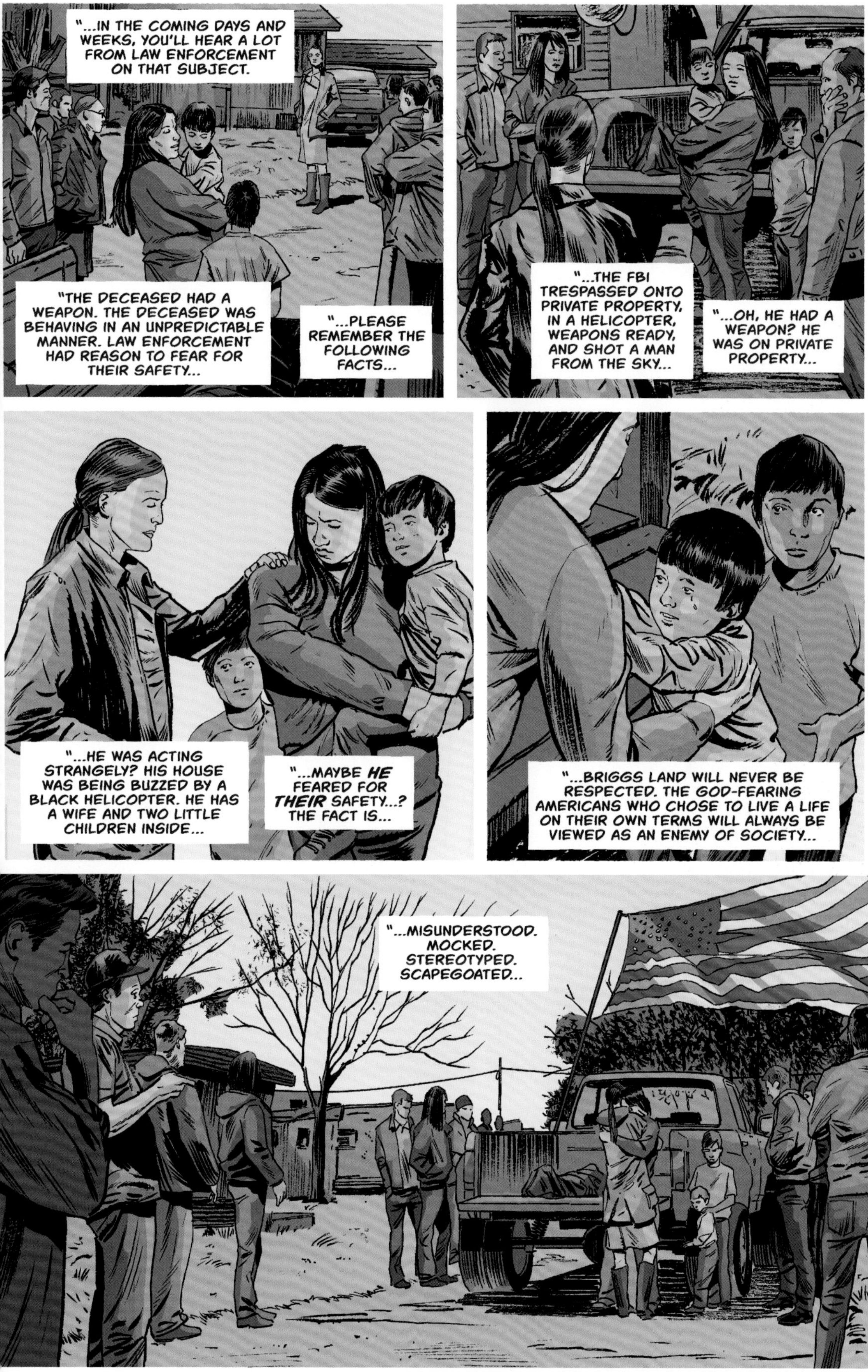
"...IN THE COMING DAYS AND WEEKS, YOU'LL HEAR A LOT FROM LAW ENFORCEMENT ON THAT SUBJECT.
"THE DECEASED HAD A WEAPON. THE DECEASED WAS BEHAVING IN AN UNPREDICTABLE MANNER. LAW ENFORCEMENT HAD REASON TO FEAR FOR THEIR SAFETY...
"...PLEASE REMEMBER THE FOLLOWING FACTS...
"...THE FBI TRESPASSED ONTO PRIVATE PROPERTY, IN A HELICOPTER, WEAPONS READY, AND SHOT A MAN FROM THE SKY...
"...OH, HE HAD A WEAPON? HE WAS ON PRIVATE PROPERTY...
"...HE WAS ACTING STRANGELY? HIS HOUSE WAS BEING BUZZED BY A BLACK HELICOPTER. HE HAS A WIFE AND TWO LITTLE CHILDREN INSIDE...
"...MAYBE ***HE*** FEARED FOR ***THEIR*** SAFETY...? THE FACT IS...
"...BRIGGS LAND WILL NEVER BE RESPECTED. THE GOD-FEARING AMERICANS WHO CHOSE TO LIVE A LIFE ON THEIR OWN TERMS WILL ALWAYS BE VIEWED AS AN ENEMY OF SOCIETY...
"...MISUNDERSTOOD. MOCKED. STEREOTYPED. SCAPEGOATED...

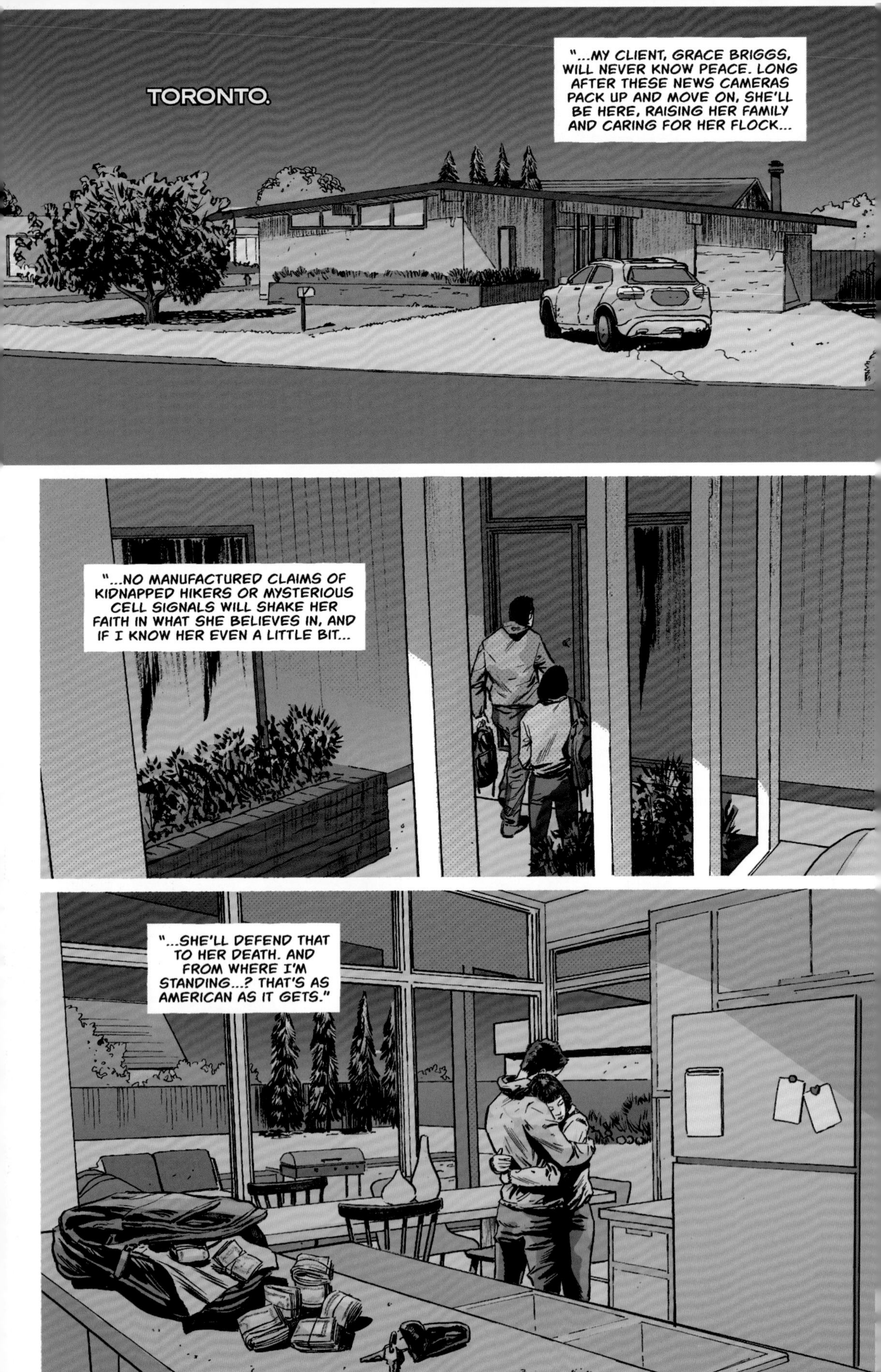
TORONTO.
"...MY CLIENT, GRACE BRIGGS, WILL NEVER KNOW PEACE. LONG AFTER THESE NEWS CAMERAS PACK UP AND MOVE ON, SHE'LL BE HERE, RAISING HER FAMILY AND CARING FOR HER FLOCK...
"...NO MANUFACTURED CLAIMS OF KIDNAPPED HIKERS OR MYSTERIOUS CELL SIGNALS WILL SHAKE HER FAITH IN WHAT SHE BELIEVES IN, AND IF I KNOW HER EVEN A LITTLE BIT...
"...SHE'LL DEFEND THAT TO HER DEATH. AND FROM WHERE I'M STANDING...? THAT'S AS AMERICAN AS IT GETS."

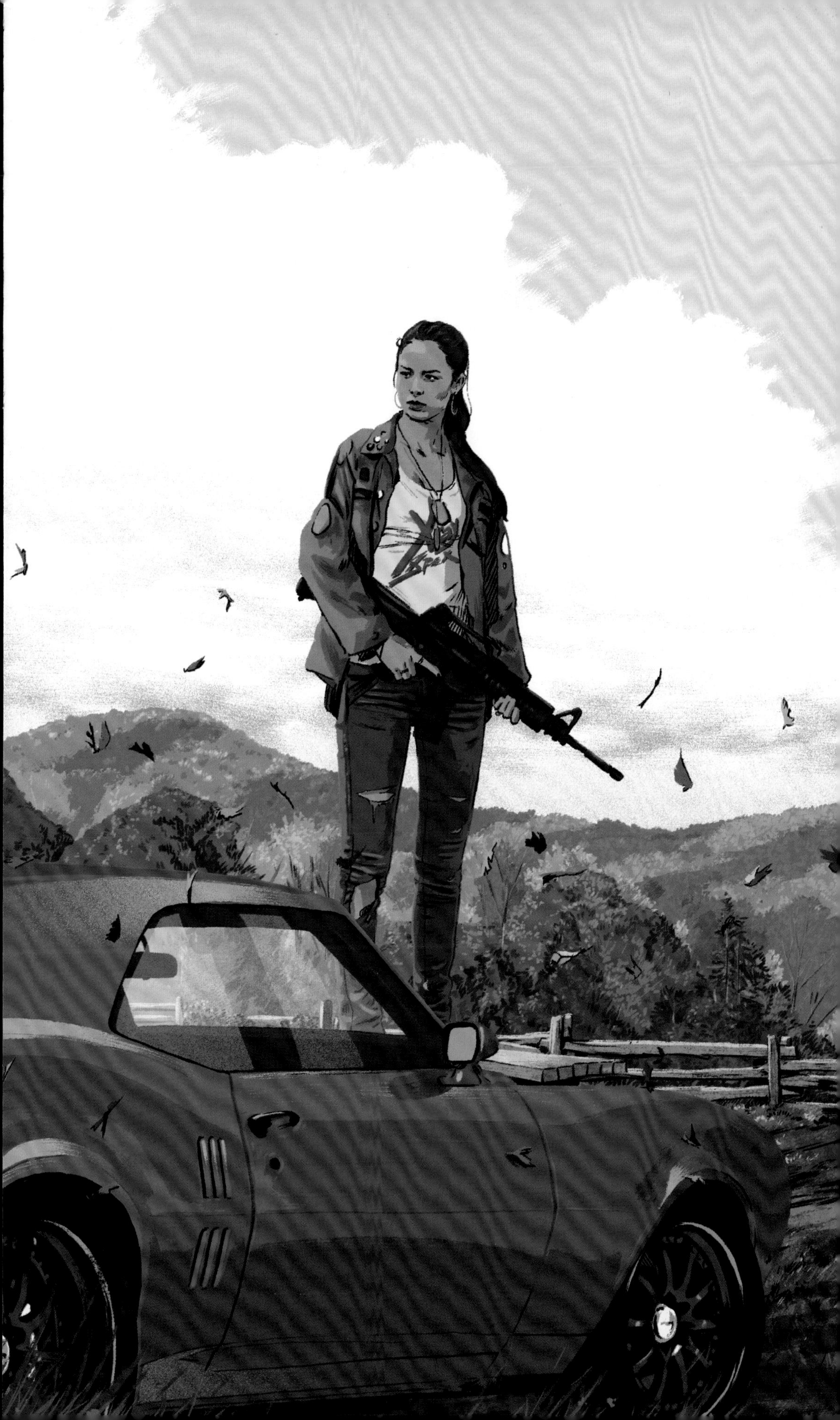

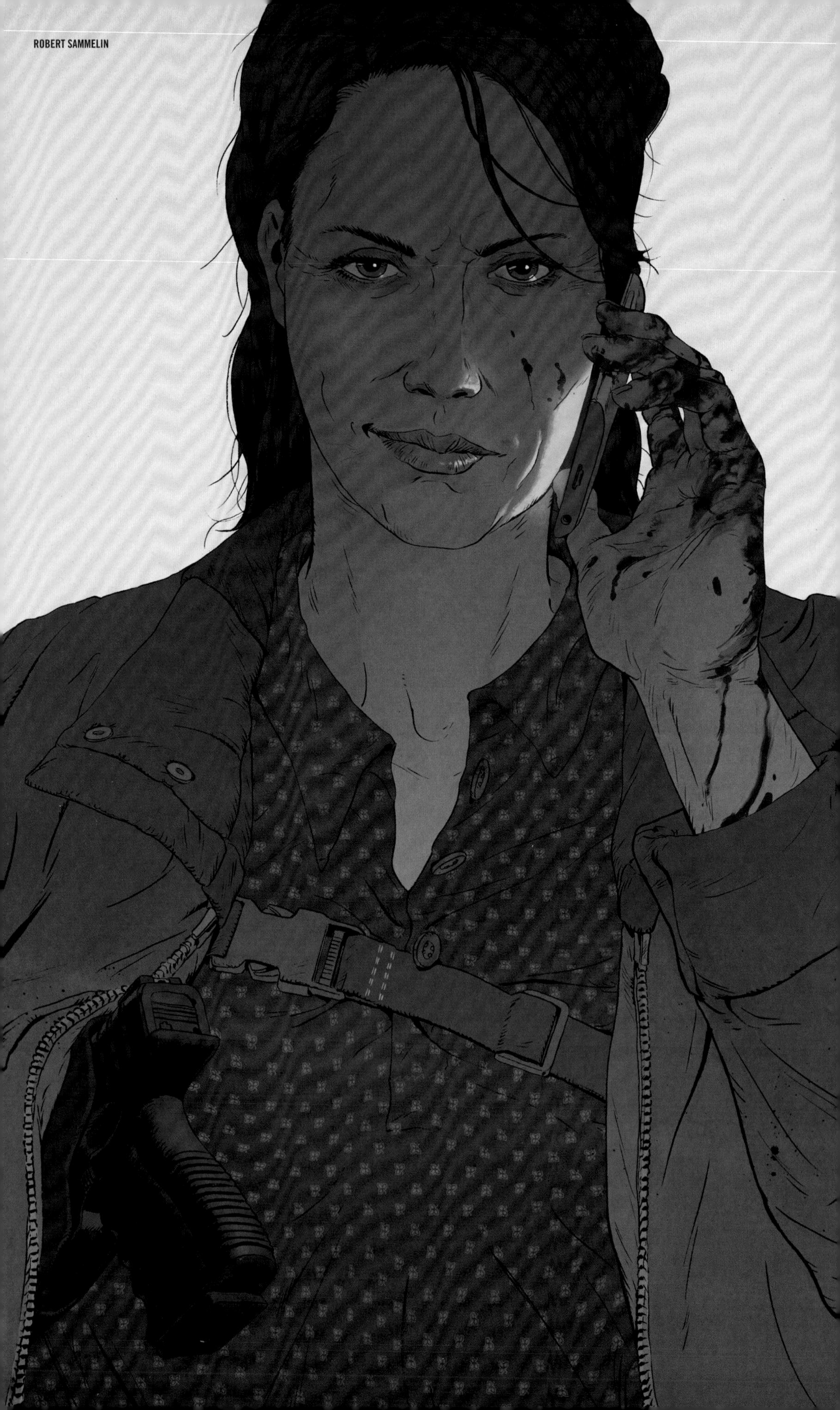

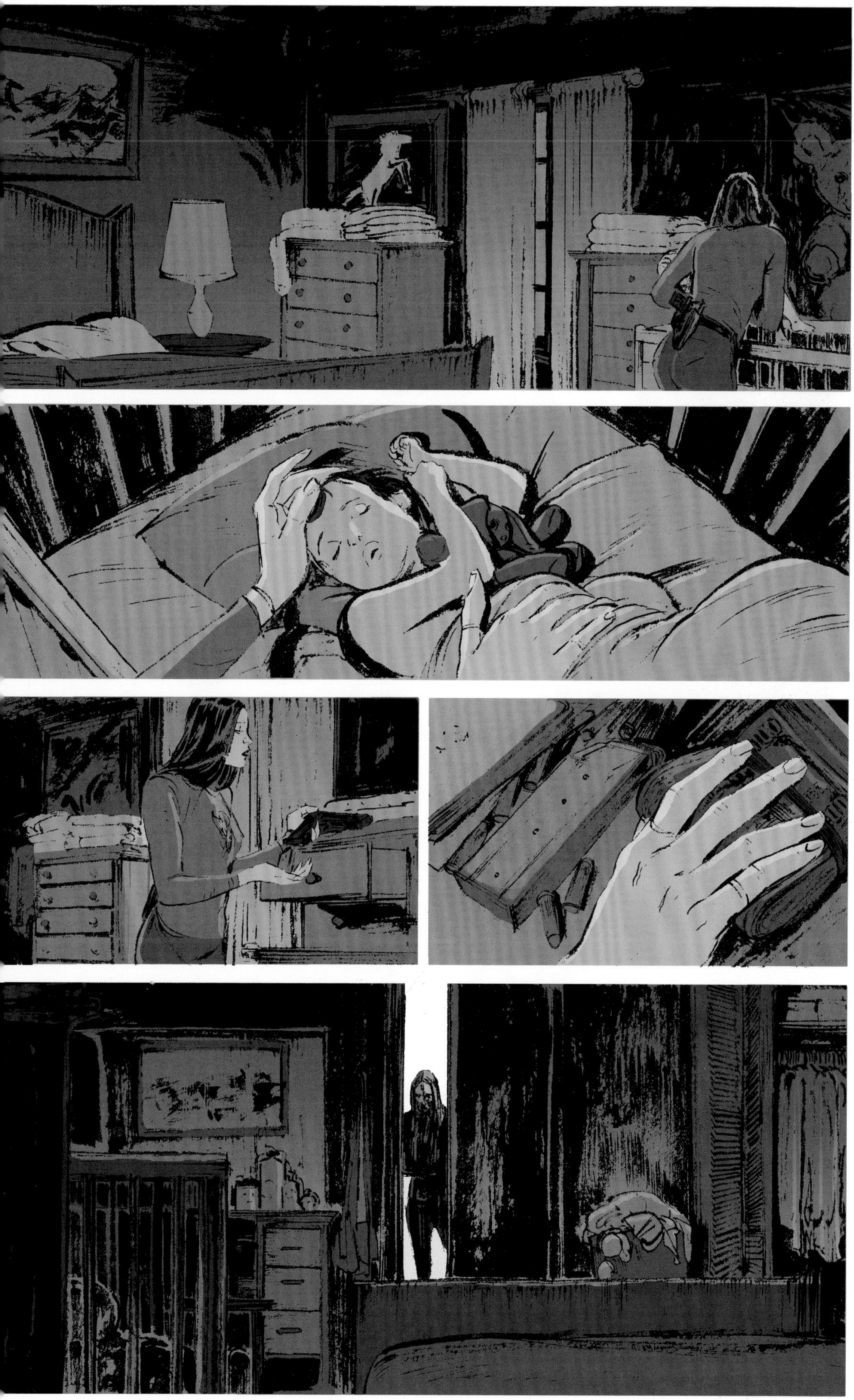

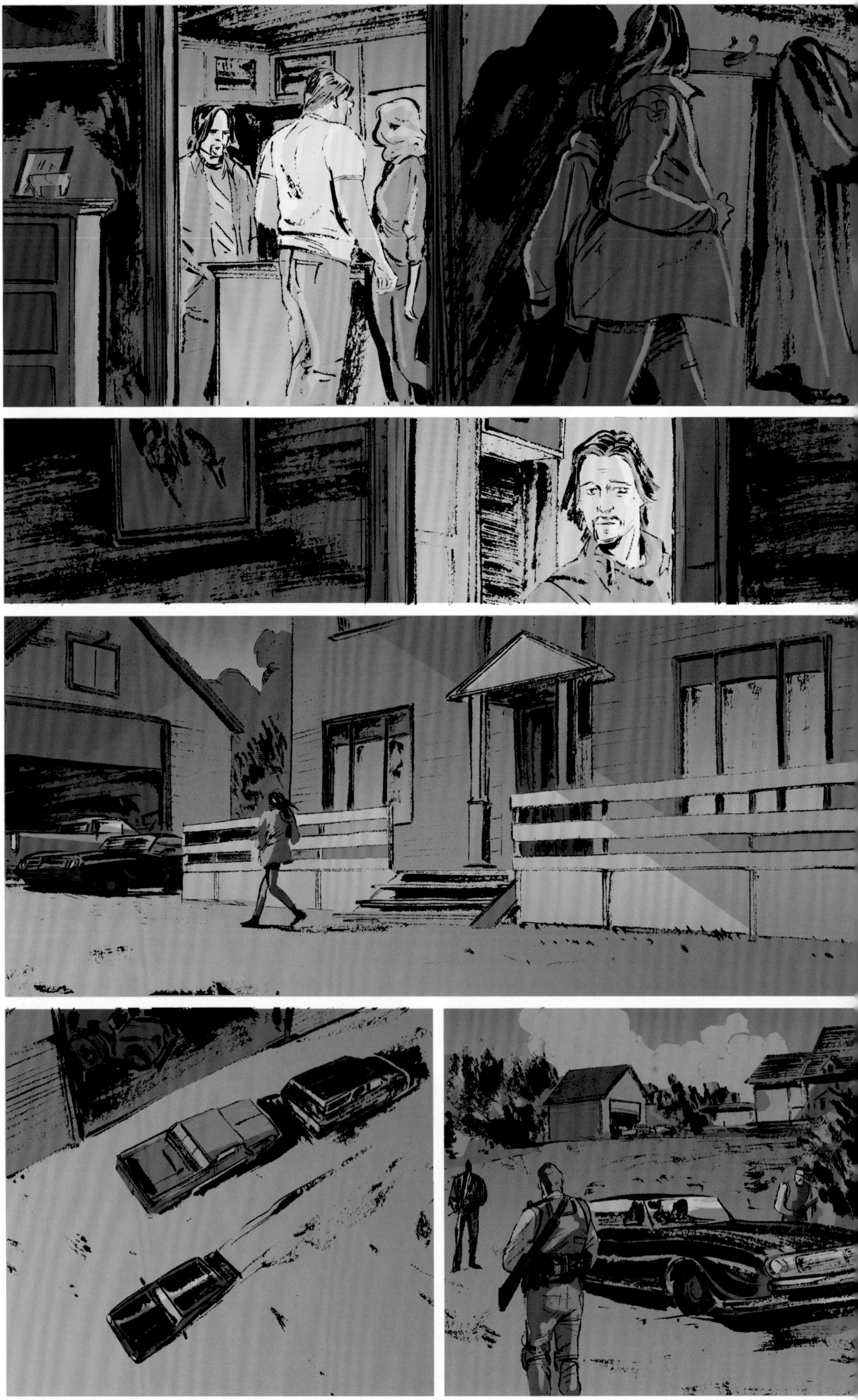

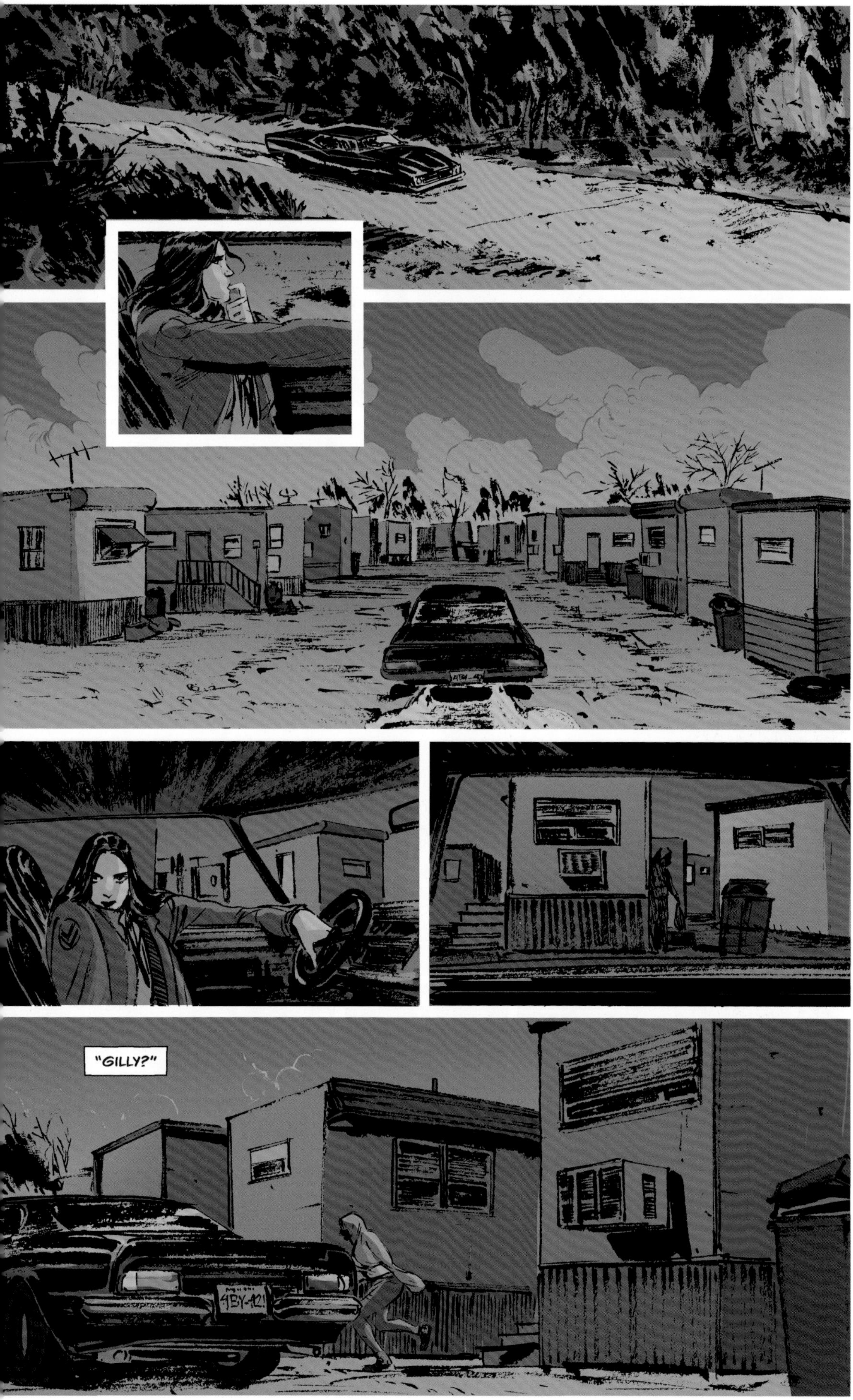
"GILLY?"

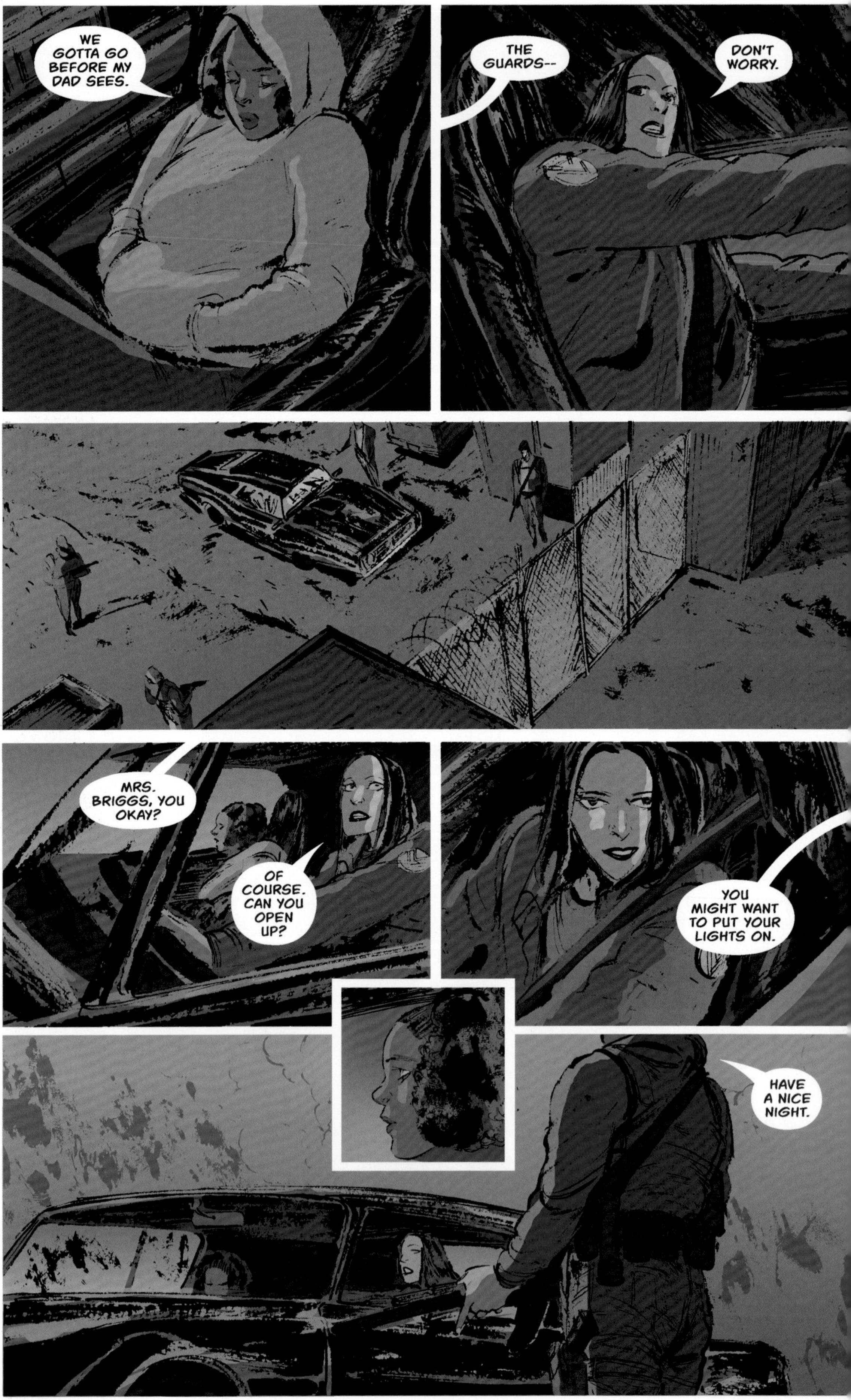
WE GOTTA GO BEFORE MY DAD SEES.
THE GUARDS--
DON'T WORRY.
MRS. BRIGGS, YOU OKAY?
OF COURSE. CAN YOU OPEN UP?
YOU MIGHT WANT TO PUT YOUR LIGHTS ON.
HAVE A NICE NIGHT.

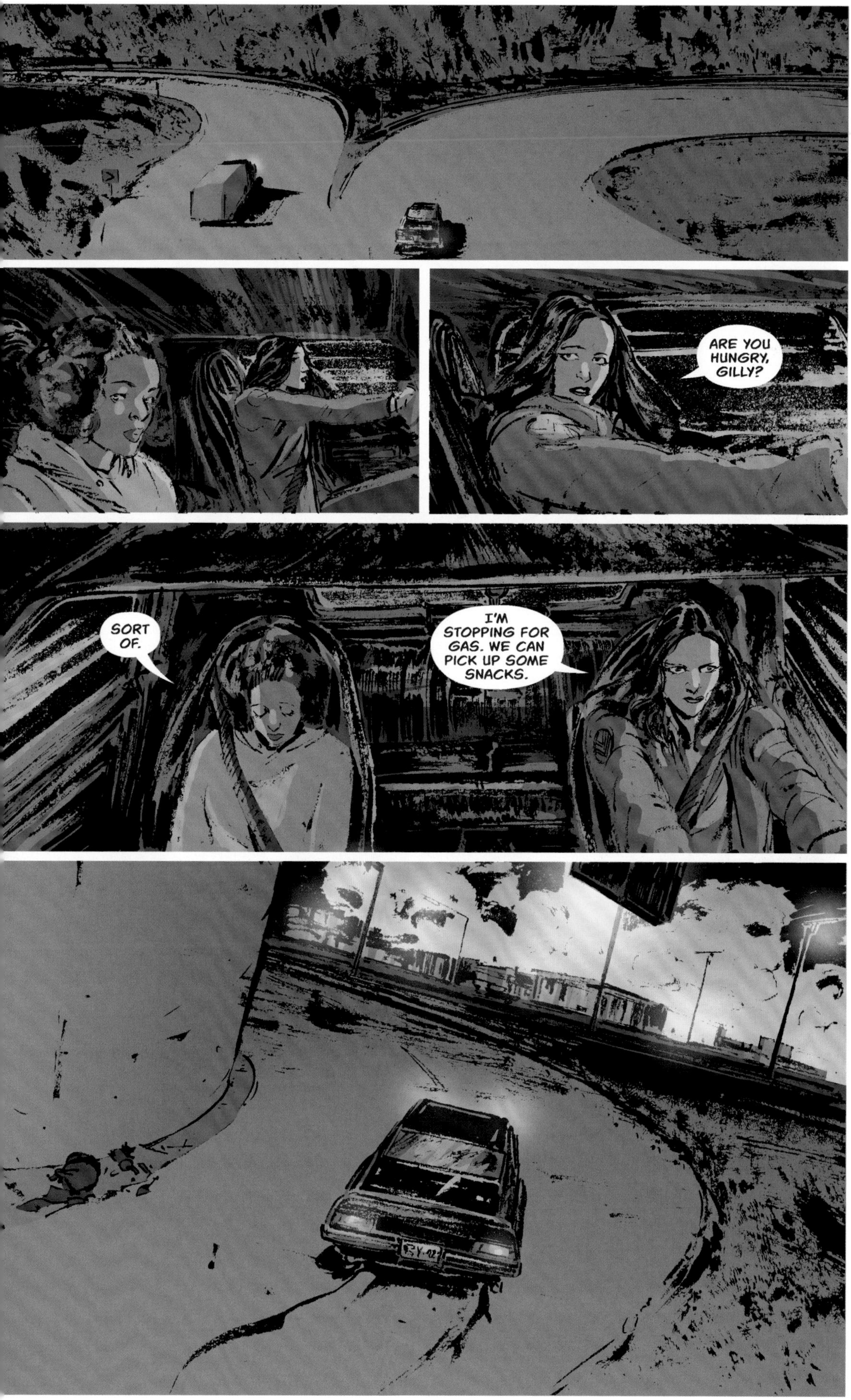
ARE YOU HUNGRY, GILLY?
SORT OF.
I'M STOPPING FOR GAS. WE CAN PICK UP SOME SNACKS.

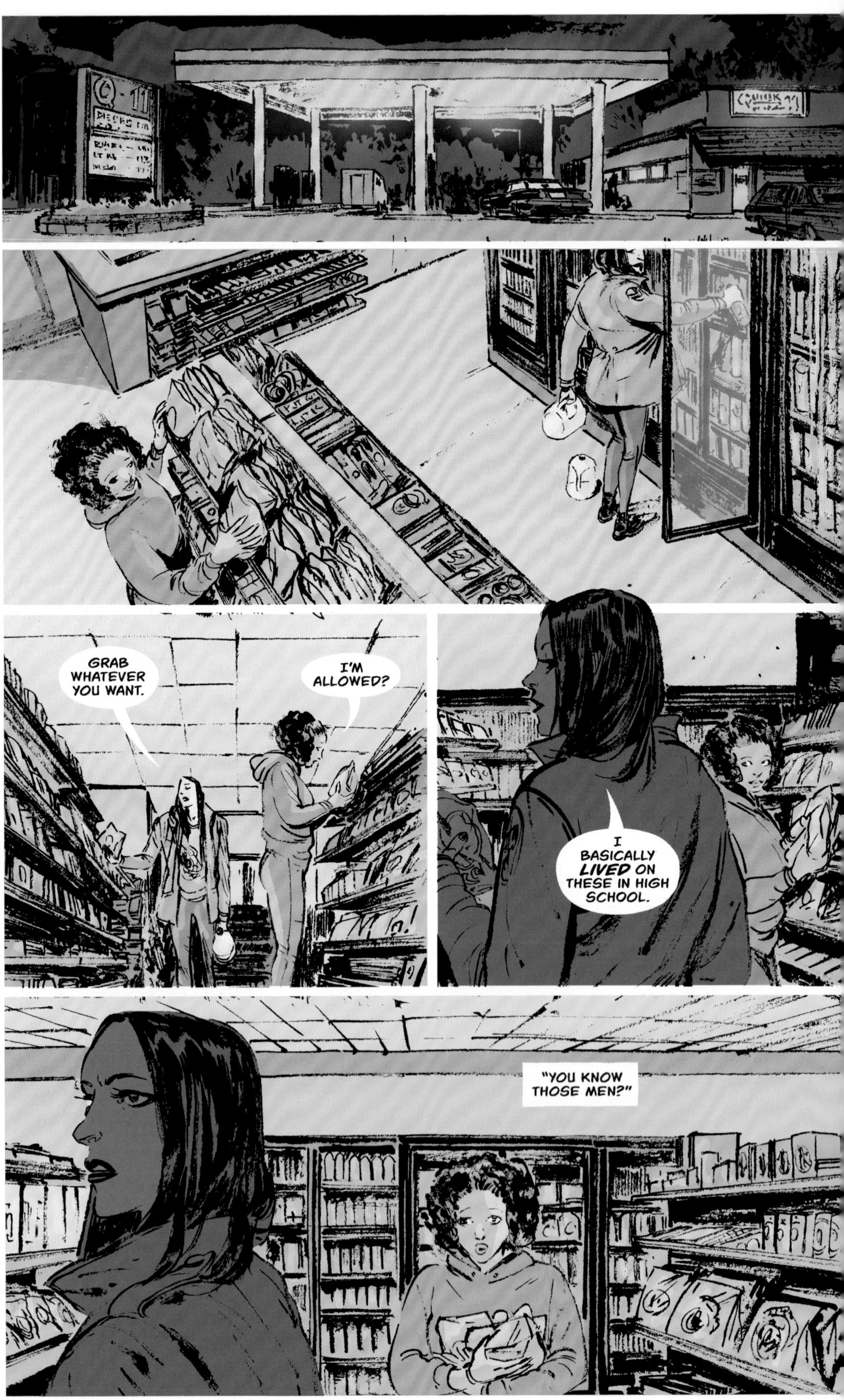
GRAB WHATEVER YOU WANT.
I'M ALLOWED?
I BASICALLY *LIVED* ON THESE IN HIGH SCHOOL.
"YOU KNOW THOSE MEN?"

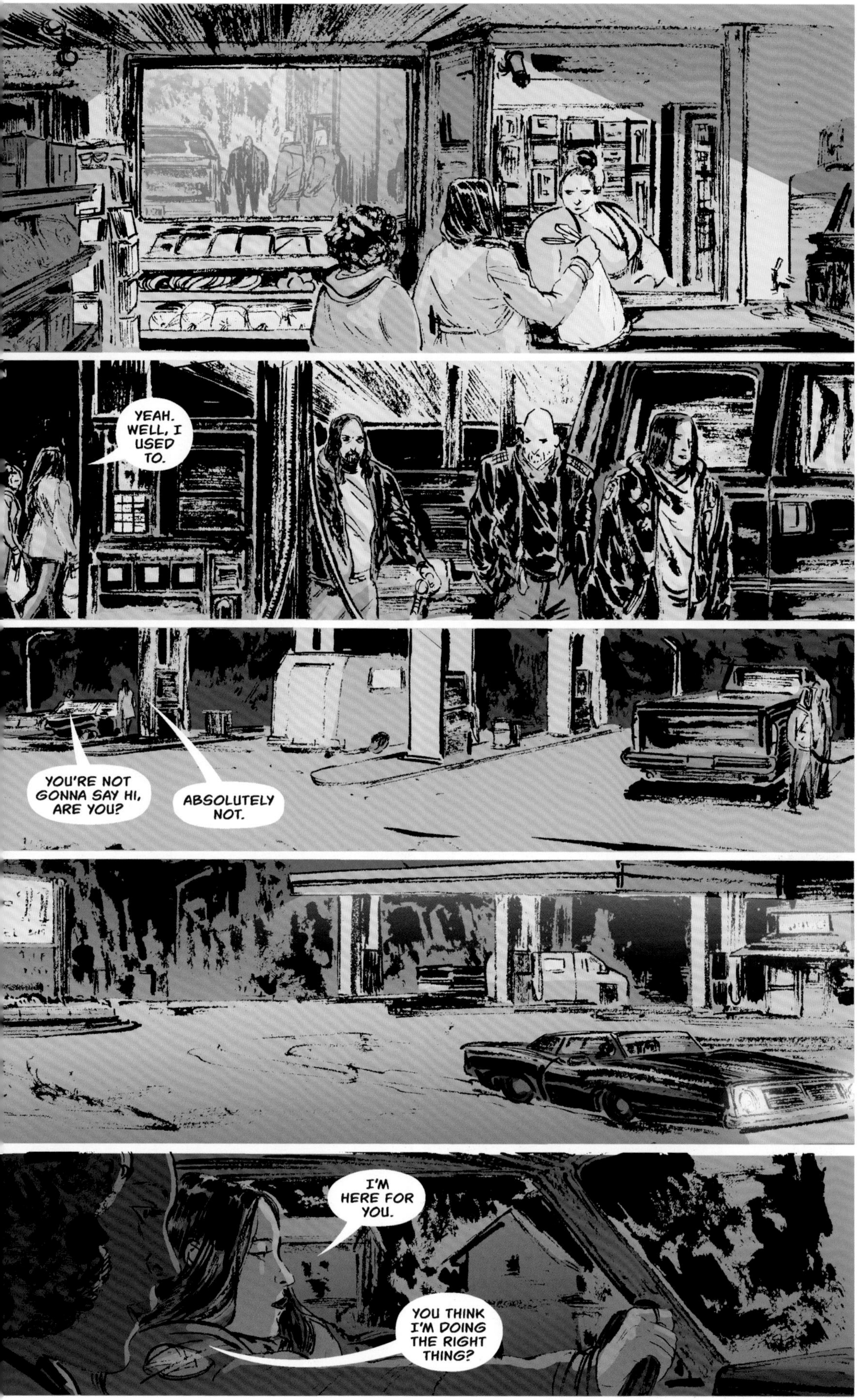
YEAH. WELL, I USED TO.
YOU'RE NOT GONNA SAY HI, ARE YOU?
ABSOLUTELY NOT.
I'M HERE FOR YOU.
YOU THINK I'M DOING THE RIGHT THING?

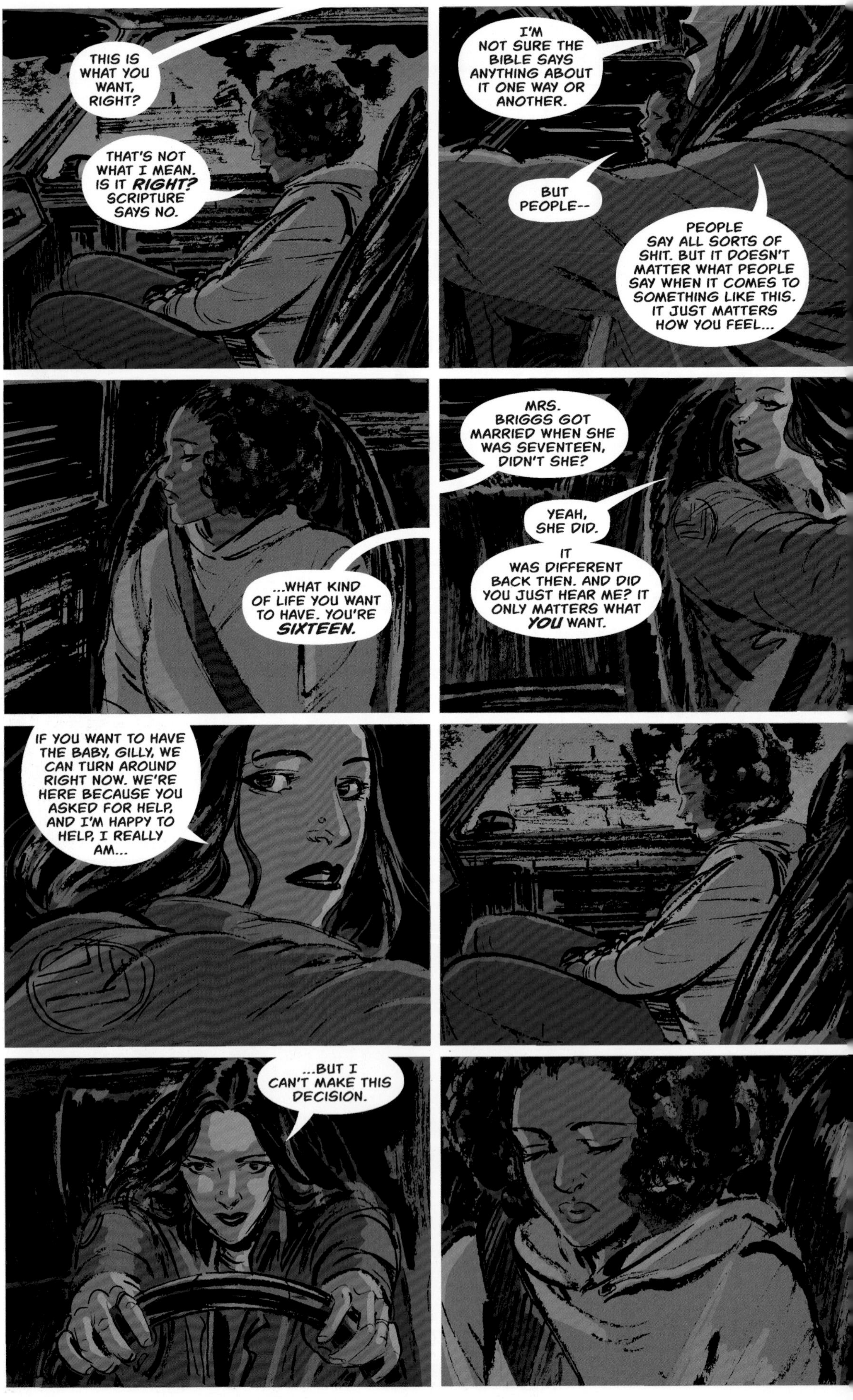
THIS IS WHAT YOU WANT, RIGHT?
THAT'S NOT WHAT I MEAN. IS IT RIGHT? SCRIPTURE SAYS NO.
I'M NOT SURE THE BIBLE SAYS ANYTHING ABOUT IT ONE WAY OR ANOTHER.
BUT PEOPLE--
PEOPLE SAY ALL SORTS OF SHIT. BUT IT DOESN'T MATTER WHAT PEOPLE SAY WHEN IT COMES TO SOMETHING LIKE THIS. IT JUST MATTERS HOW YOU FEEL...
...WHAT KIND OF LIFE YOU WANT TO HAVE. YOU'RE SIXTEEN.
MRS. BRIGGS GOT MARRIED WHEN SHE WAS SEVENTEEN, DIDN'T SHE?
YEAH, SHE DID.
IT WAS DIFFERENT BACK THEN. AND DID YOU JUST HEAR ME? IT ONLY MATTERS WHAT YOU WANT.
IF YOU WANT TO HAVE THE BABY, GILLY, WE CAN TURN AROUND RIGHT NOW. WE'RE HERE BECAUSE YOU ASKED FOR HELP, AND I'M HAPPY TO HELP, I REALLY AM...
...BUT I CAN'T MAKE THIS DECISION.

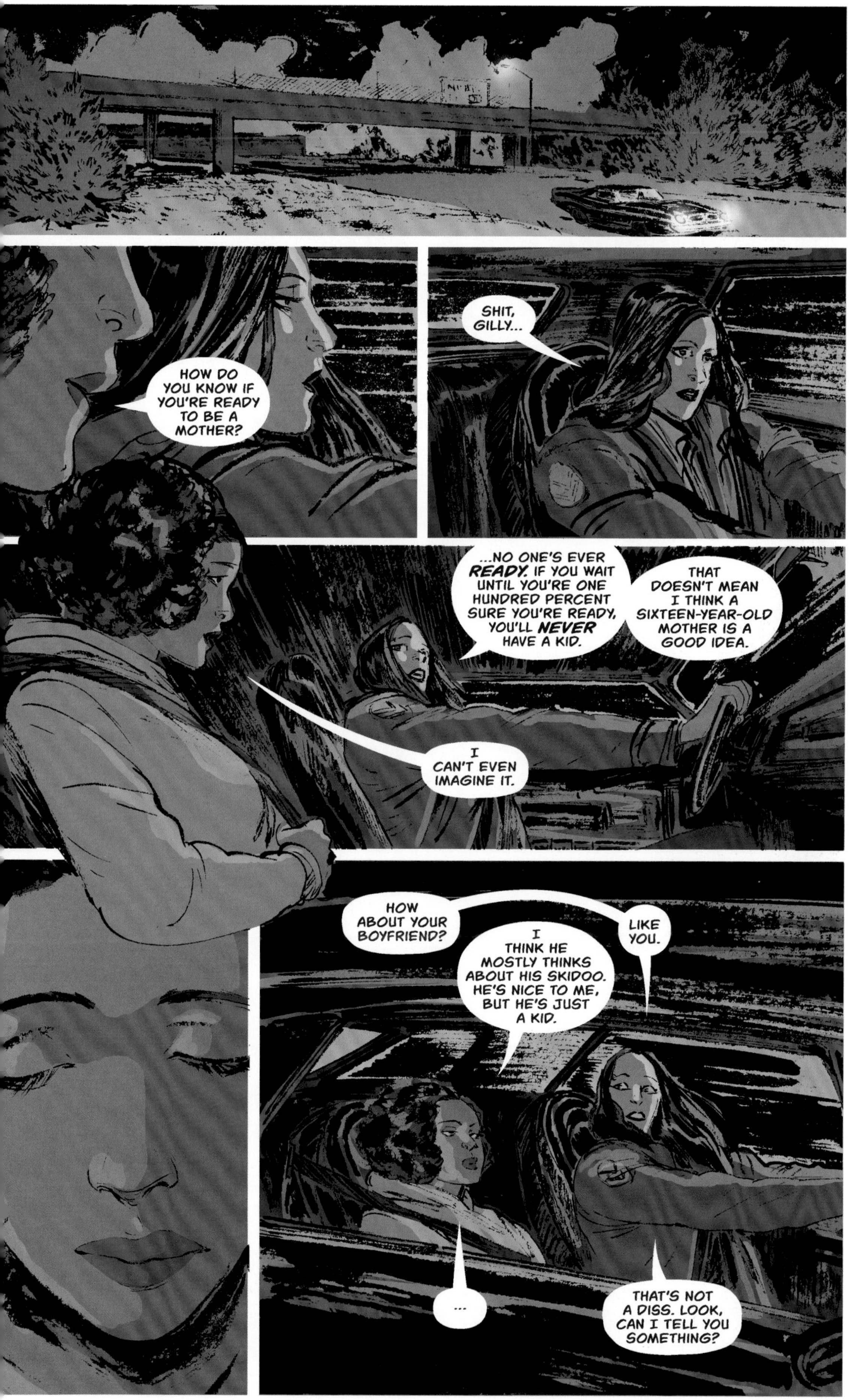
HOW DO YOU KNOW IF YOU'RE READY TO BE A MOTHER?
SHIT, GILLY...
...NO ONE'S EVER **READY.** IF YOU WAIT UNTIL YOU'RE ONE HUNDRED PERCENT SURE YOU'RE READY, YOU'LL **NEVER** HAVE A KID.
THAT DOESN'T MEAN I THINK A SIXTEEN-YEAR-OLD MOTHER IS A GOOD IDEA.
I CAN'T EVEN IMAGINE IT.
HOW ABOUT YOUR BOYFRIEND?
LIKE YOU.
I THINK HE MOSTLY THINKS ABOUT HIS SKIDOO. HE'S NICE TO ME, BUT HE'S JUST A KID.
...
THAT'S NOT A DISS. LOOK, CAN I TELL YOU SOMETHING?

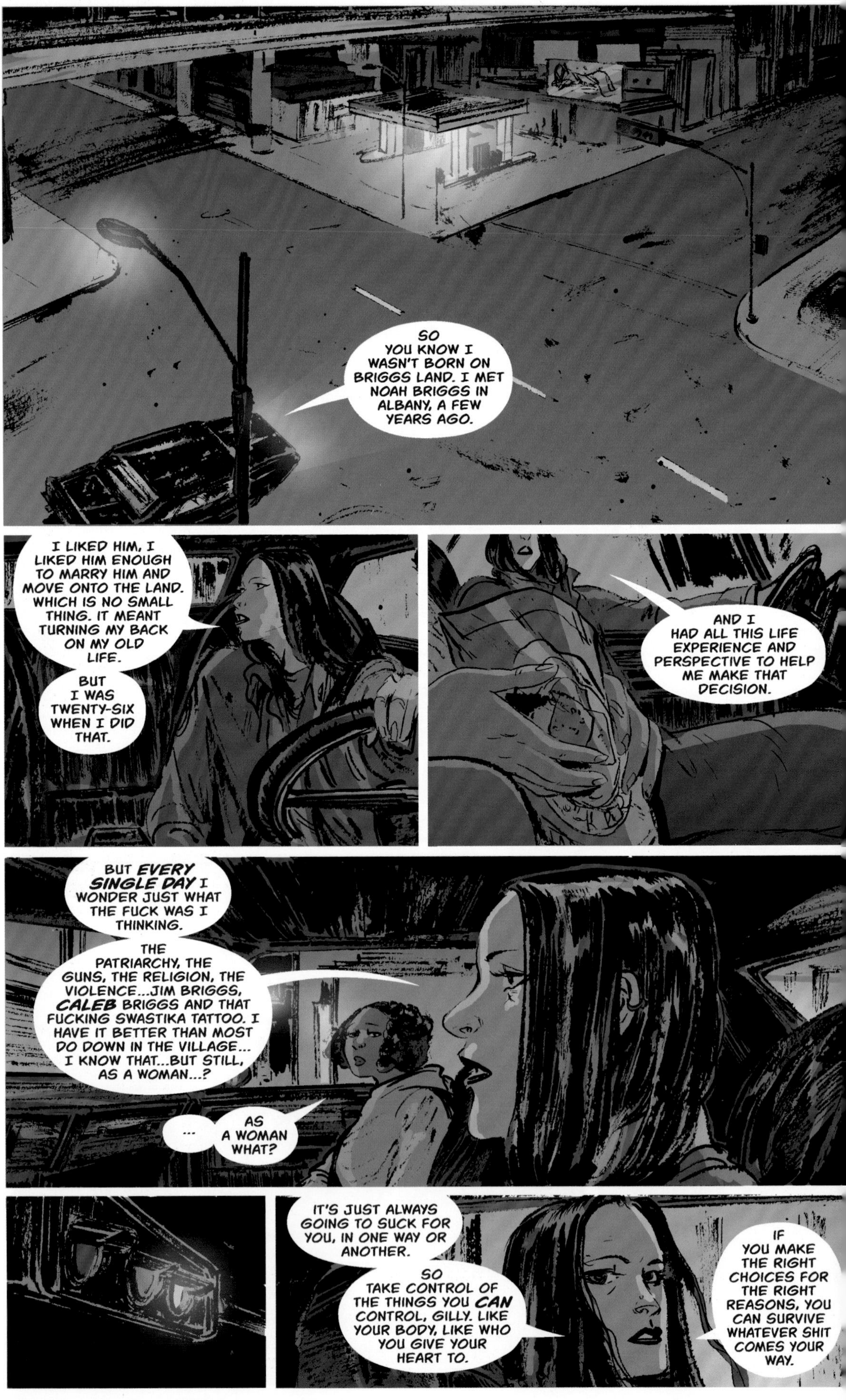
SO YOU KNOW I WASN'T BORN ON BRIGGS LAND. I MET NOAH BRIGGS IN ALBANY, A FEW YEARS AGO.
I LIKED HIM, I LIKED HIM ENOUGH TO MARRY HIM AND MOVE ONTO THE LAND. WHICH IS NO SMALL THING. IT MEANT TURNING MY BACK ON MY OLD LIFE.
BUT I WAS TWENTY-SIX WHEN I DID THAT.
AND I HAD ALL THIS LIFE EXPERIENCE AND PERSPECTIVE TO HELP ME MAKE THAT DECISION.
BUT EVERY SINGLE DAY I WONDER JUST WHAT THE FUCK WAS I THINKING.
THE PATRIARCHY, THE GUNS, THE RELIGION, THE VIOLENCE...JIM BRIGGS, CALEB BRIGGS AND THAT FUCKING SWASTIKA TATTOO. I HAVE IT BETTER THAN MOST DO DOWN IN THE VILLAGE... I KNOW THAT...BUT STILL, AS A WOMAN...?
...
AS A WOMAN WHAT?
IT'S JUST ALWAYS GOING TO SUCK FOR YOU, IN ONE WAY OR ANOTHER.
SO TAKE CONTROL OF THE THINGS YOU CAN CONTROL, GILLY. LIKE YOUR BODY, LIKE WHO YOU GIVE YOUR HEART TO.
IF YOU MAKE THE RIGHT CHOICES FOR THE RIGHT REASONS, YOU CAN SURVIVE WHATEVER SHIT COMES YOUR WAY.

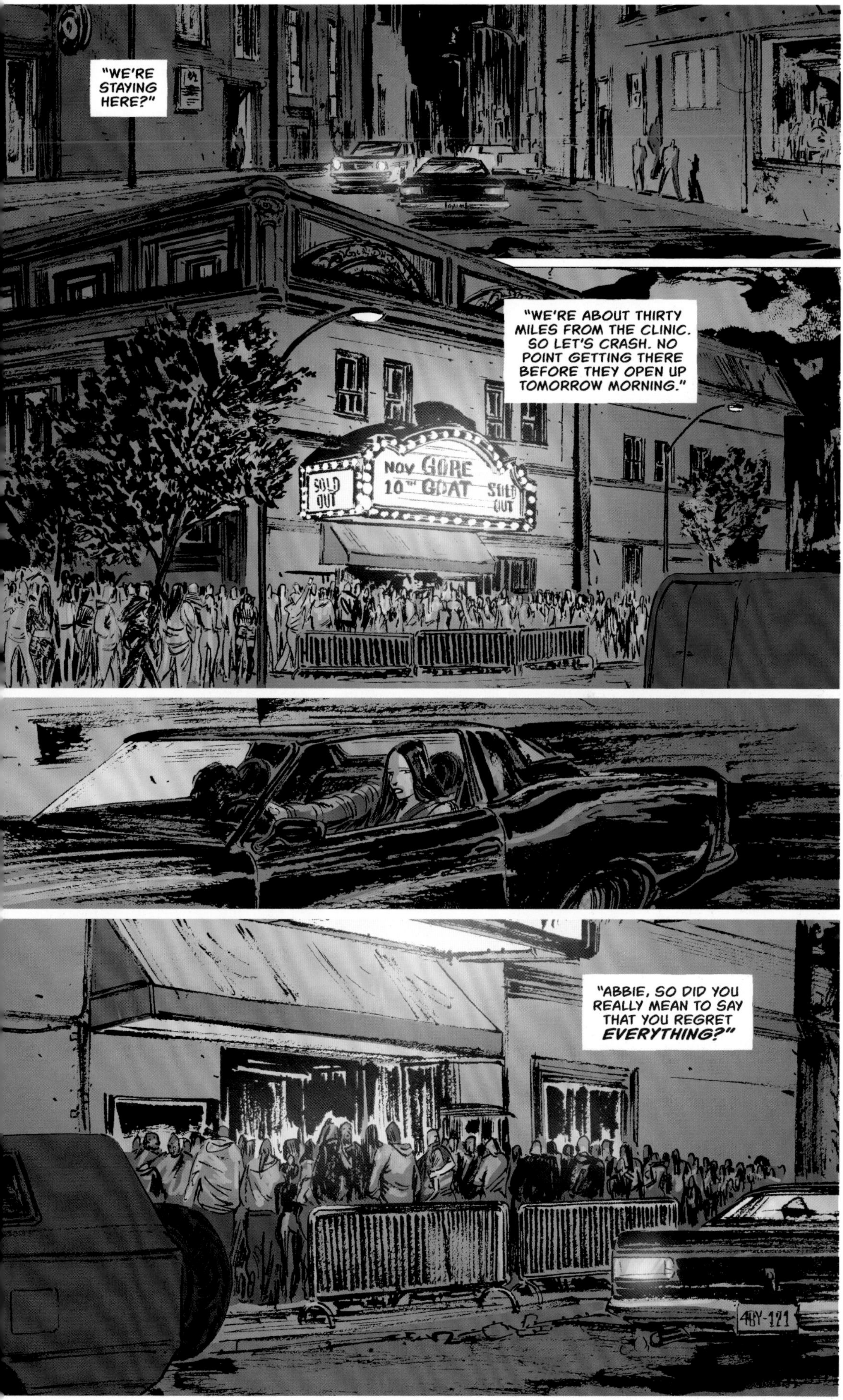
"WE'RE STAYING HERE?"
"WE'RE ABOUT THIRTY MILES FROM THE CLINIC. SO LET'S CRASH. NO POINT GETTING THERE BEFORE THEY OPEN UP TOMORROW MORNING."
SOLD OUT
NOV 10TH GORE GOAT
SOLD OUT
"ABBIE, SO DID YOU REALLY MEAN TO SAY THAT YOU REGRET *EVERYTHING?*"

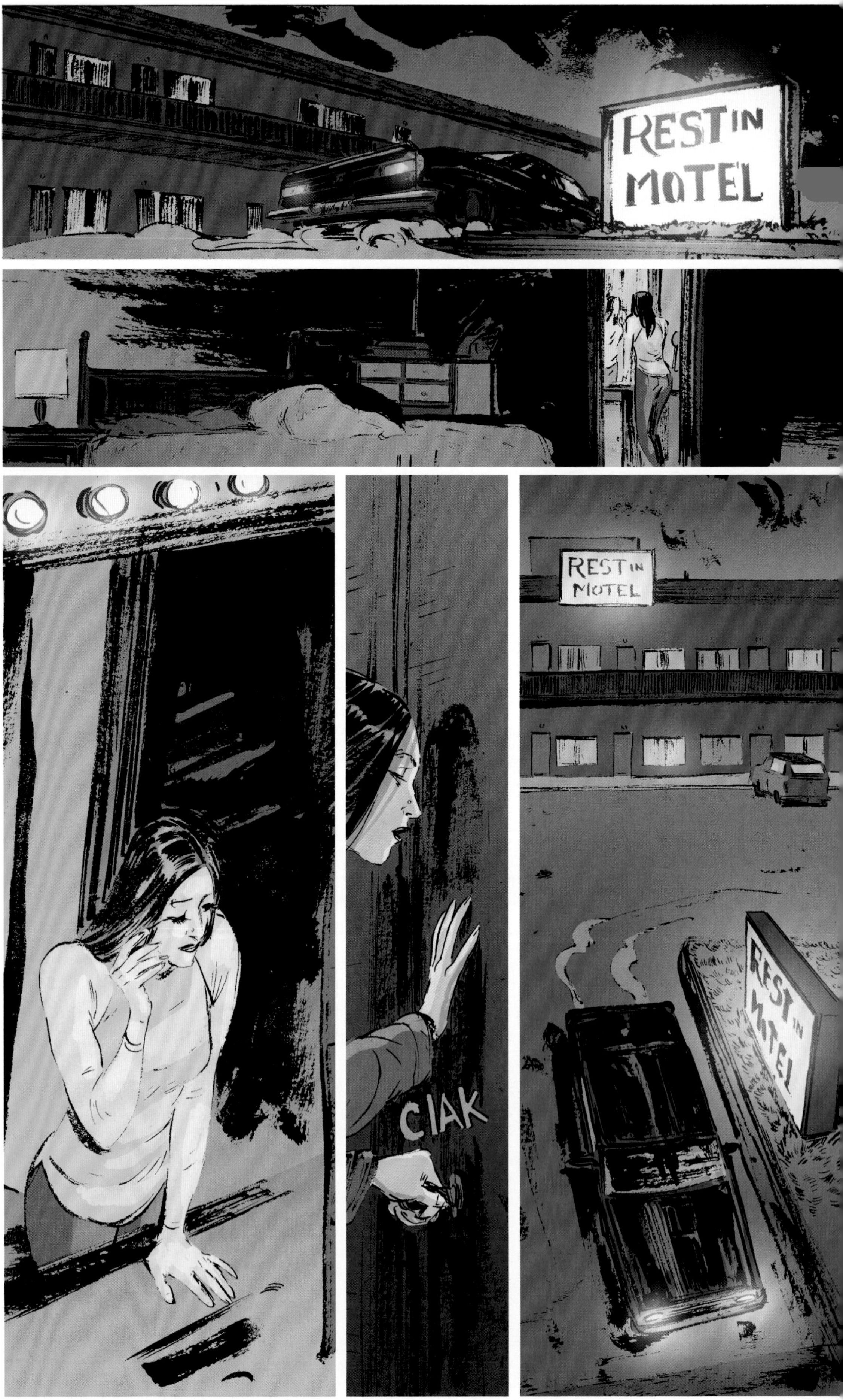
REST IN MOTEL
REST IN MOTEL
CIAK
REST IN MOTEL

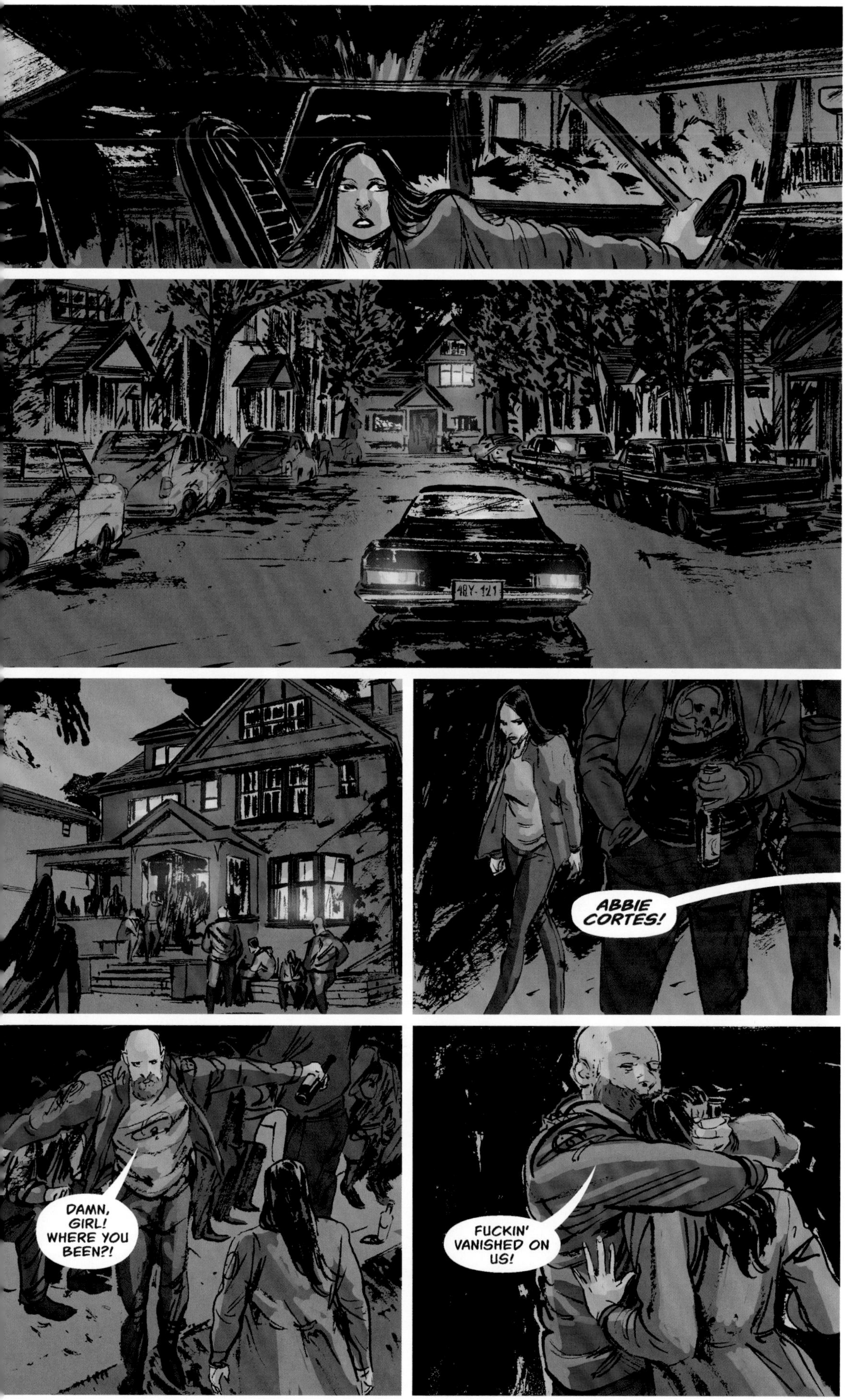
48Y-121
ABBIE CORTES!
DAMN, GIRL! WHERE YOU BEEN?!
FUCKIN' VANISHED ON US!

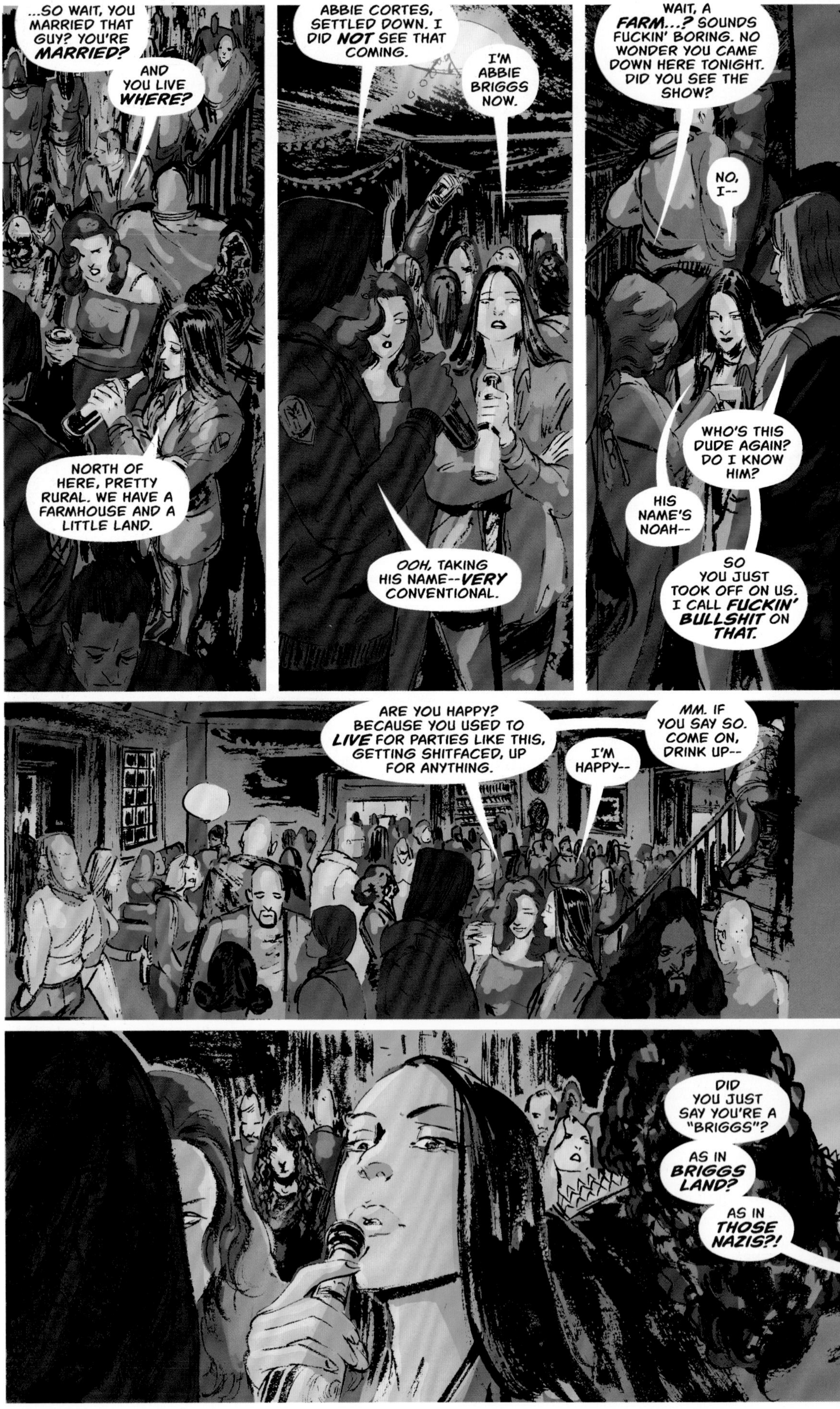
...SO WAIT, YOU MARRIED THAT GUY? YOU'RE MARRIED?
AND YOU LIVE WHERE?
NORTH OF HERE, PRETTY RURAL. WE HAVE A FARMHOUSE AND A LITTLE LAND.
ABBIE CORTES, SETTLED DOWN. I DID NOT SEE THAT COMING.
I'M ABBIE BRIGGS NOW.
OOH, TAKING HIS NAME--VERY CONVENTIONAL.
WAIT, A FARM...? SOUNDS FUCKIN' BORING. NO WONDER YOU CAME DOWN HERE TONIGHT. DID YOU SEE THE SHOW?
NO, I--
WHO'S THIS DUDE AGAIN? DO I KNOW HIM?
HIS NAME'S NOAH--
SO YOU JUST TOOK OFF ON US. I CALL FUCKIN' BULLSHIT ON THAT.
ARE YOU HAPPY? BECAUSE YOU USED TO LIVE FOR PARTIES LIKE THIS, GETTING SHITFACED, UP FOR ANYTHING.
I'M HAPPY--
MM. IF YOU SAY SO. COME ON, DRINK UP--
DID YOU JUST SAY YOU'RE A "BRIGGS"?
AS IN BRIGGS LAND?
AS IN THOSE NAZIS?!

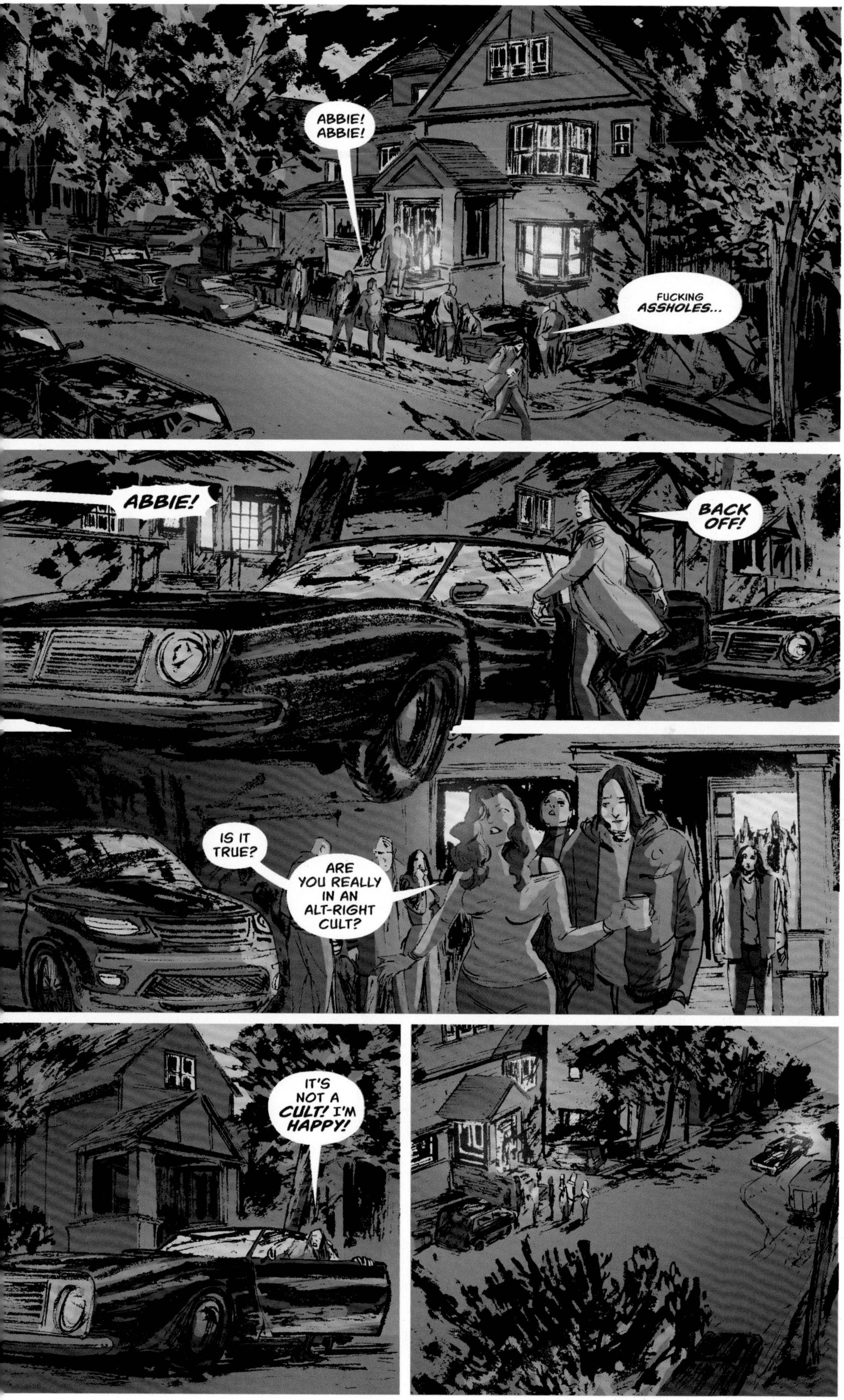
ABBIE! ABBIE!
FUCKING ASSHOLES...
ABBIE!
BACK OFF!
IS IT TRUE?
ARE YOU REALLY IN AN ALT-RIGHT CULT?
IT'S NOT A CULT! I'M HAPPY!

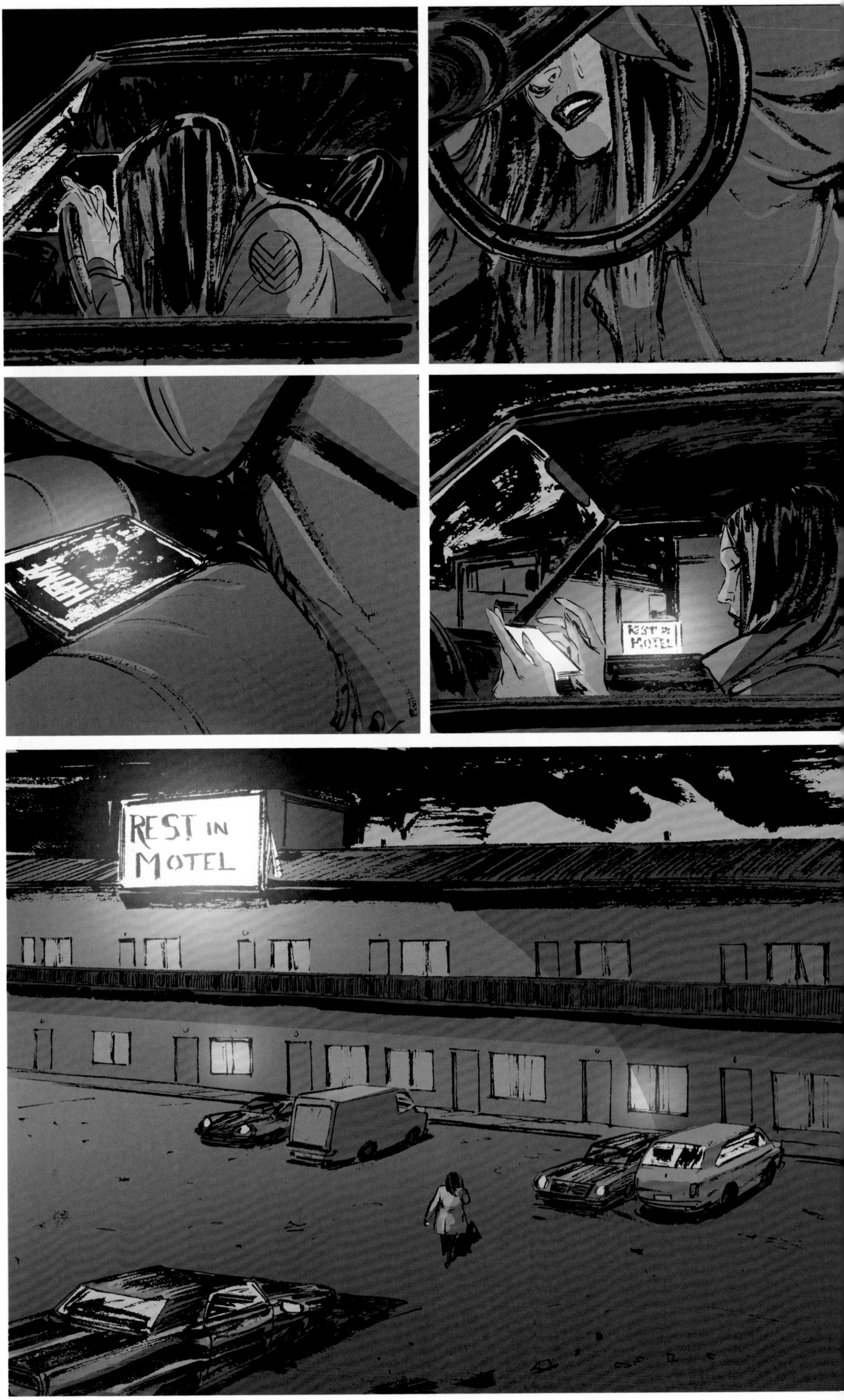
REST IN MOTEL
REST IN MOTEL

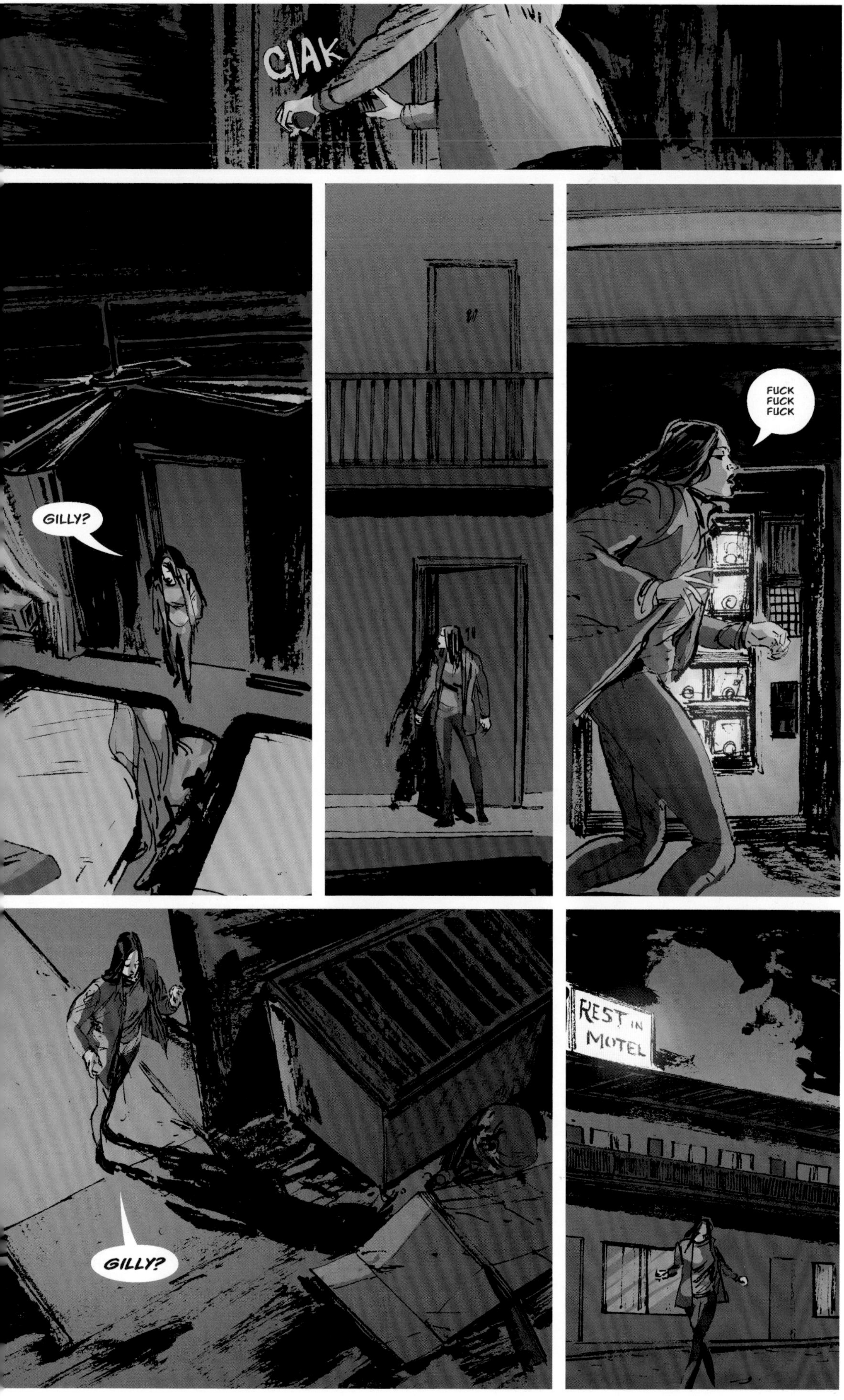
CIAK
GILLY?
FUCK
FUCK
FUCK
GILLY?
REST IN
MOTEL

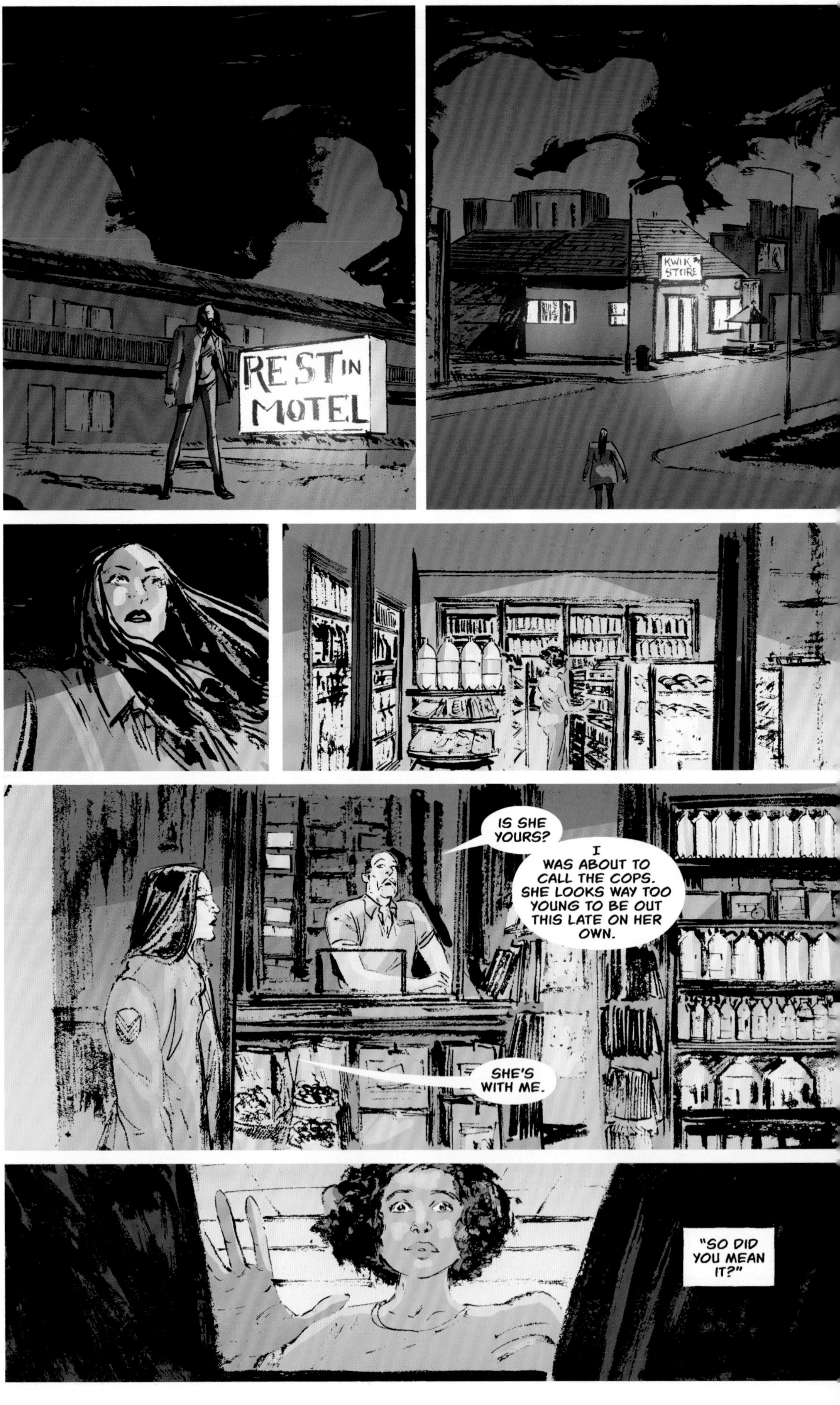
REST IN MOTEL
KWIK STORE
IS SHE YOURS?
I WAS ABOUT TO CALL THE COPS. SHE LOOKS WAY TOO YOUNG TO BE OUT THIS LATE ON HER OWN.
SHE'S WITH ME.
"SO DID YOU MEAN IT?"

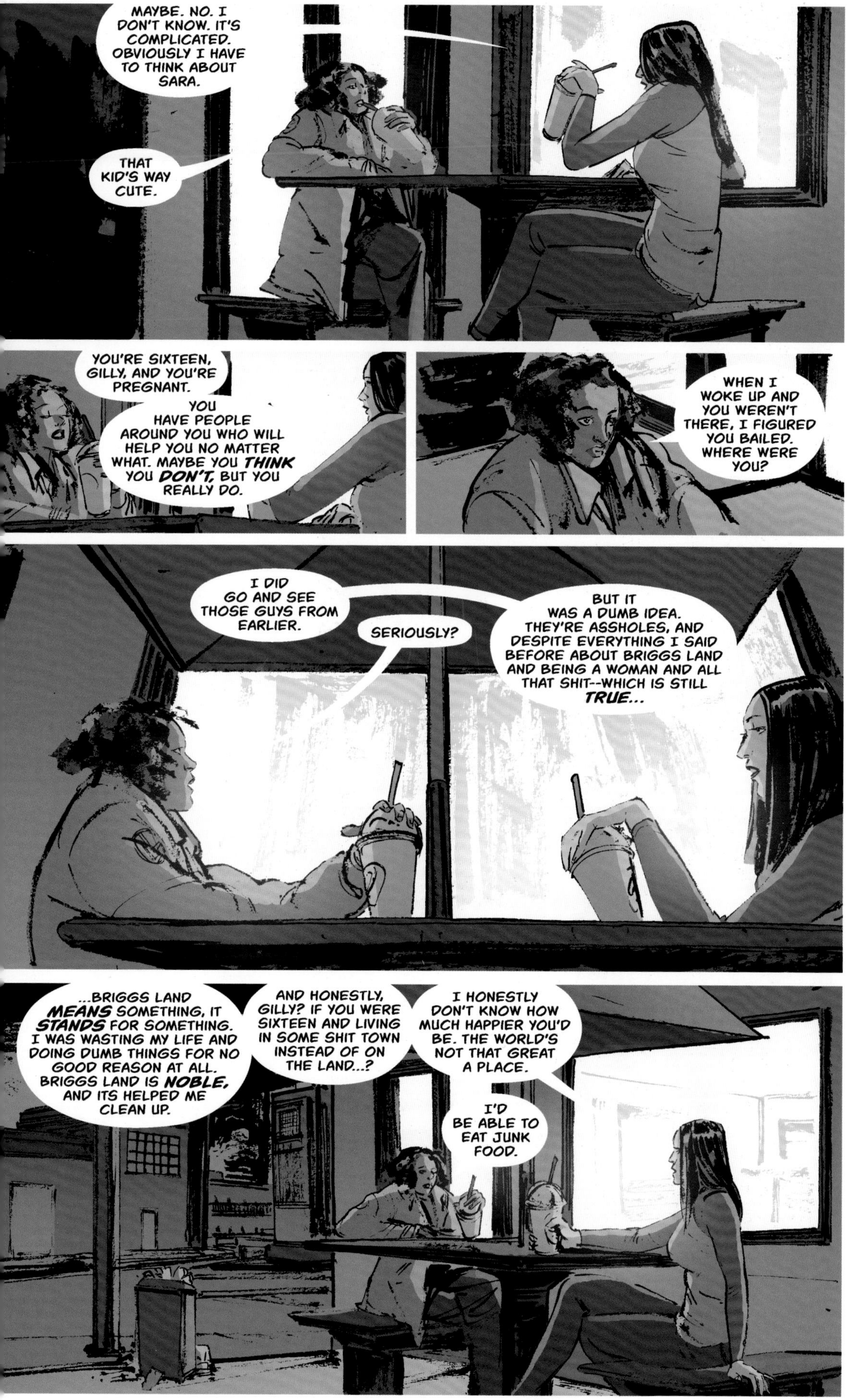
MAYBE. NO. I DON'T KNOW. IT'S COMPLICATED. OBVIOUSLY I HAVE TO THINK ABOUT SARA.
THAT KID'S WAY CUTE.
YOU'RE SIXTEEN, GILLY, AND YOU'RE PREGNANT.
YOU HAVE PEOPLE AROUND YOU WHO WILL HELP YOU NO MATTER WHAT. MAYBE YOU *THINK* YOU *DON'T,* BUT YOU REALLY DO.
WHEN I WOKE UP AND YOU WEREN'T THERE, I FIGURED YOU BAILED. WHERE WERE YOU?
I DID GO AND SEE THOSE GUYS FROM EARLIER.
SERIOUSLY?
BUT IT WAS A DUMB IDEA. THEY'RE ASSHOLES, AND DESPITE EVERYTHING I SAID BEFORE ABOUT BRIGGS LAND AND BEING A WOMAN AND ALL THAT SHIT--WHICH IS STILL *TRUE...*
...BRIGGS LAND *MEANS* SOMETHING, IT *STANDS* FOR SOMETHING. I WAS WASTING MY LIFE AND DOING DUMB THINGS FOR NO GOOD REASON AT ALL. BRIGGS LAND IS *NOBLE,* AND ITS HELPED ME CLEAN UP.
AND HONESTLY, GILLY? IF YOU WERE SIXTEEN AND LIVING IN SOME SHIT TOWN INSTEAD OF ON THE LAND...?
I HONESTLY DON'T KNOW HOW MUCH HAPPIER YOU'D BE. THE WORLD'S NOT THAT GREAT A PLACE.
I'D BE ABLE TO EAT JUNK FOOD.

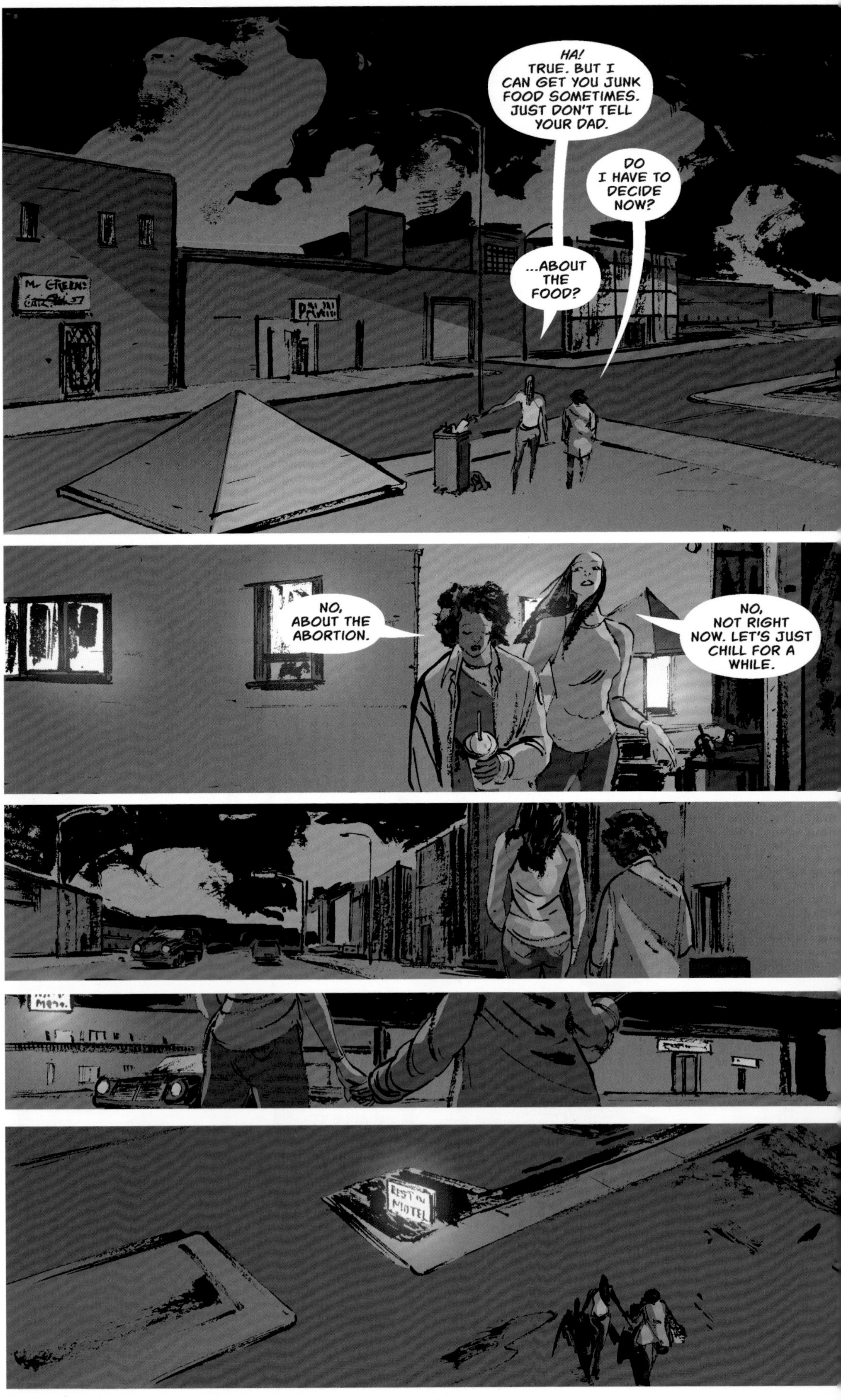
HA! TRUE. BUT I CAN GET YOU JUNK FOOD SOMETIMES. JUST DON'T TELL YOUR DAD.
...ABOUT THE FOOD?
DO I HAVE TO DECIDE NOW?
NO, ABOUT THE ABORTION.
NO, NOT RIGHT NOW. LET'S JUST CHILL FOR A WHILE.
REST IN MOTEL

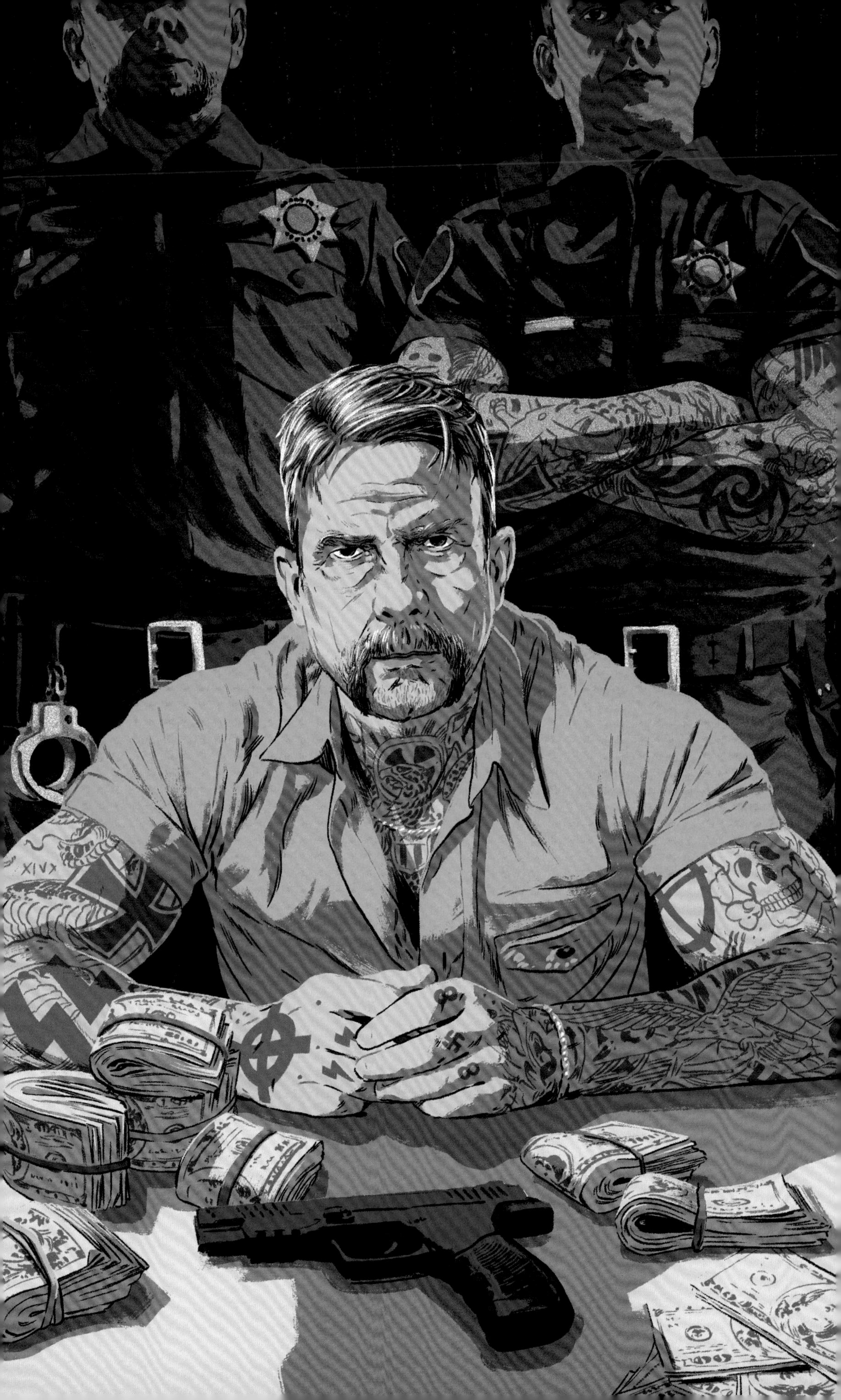

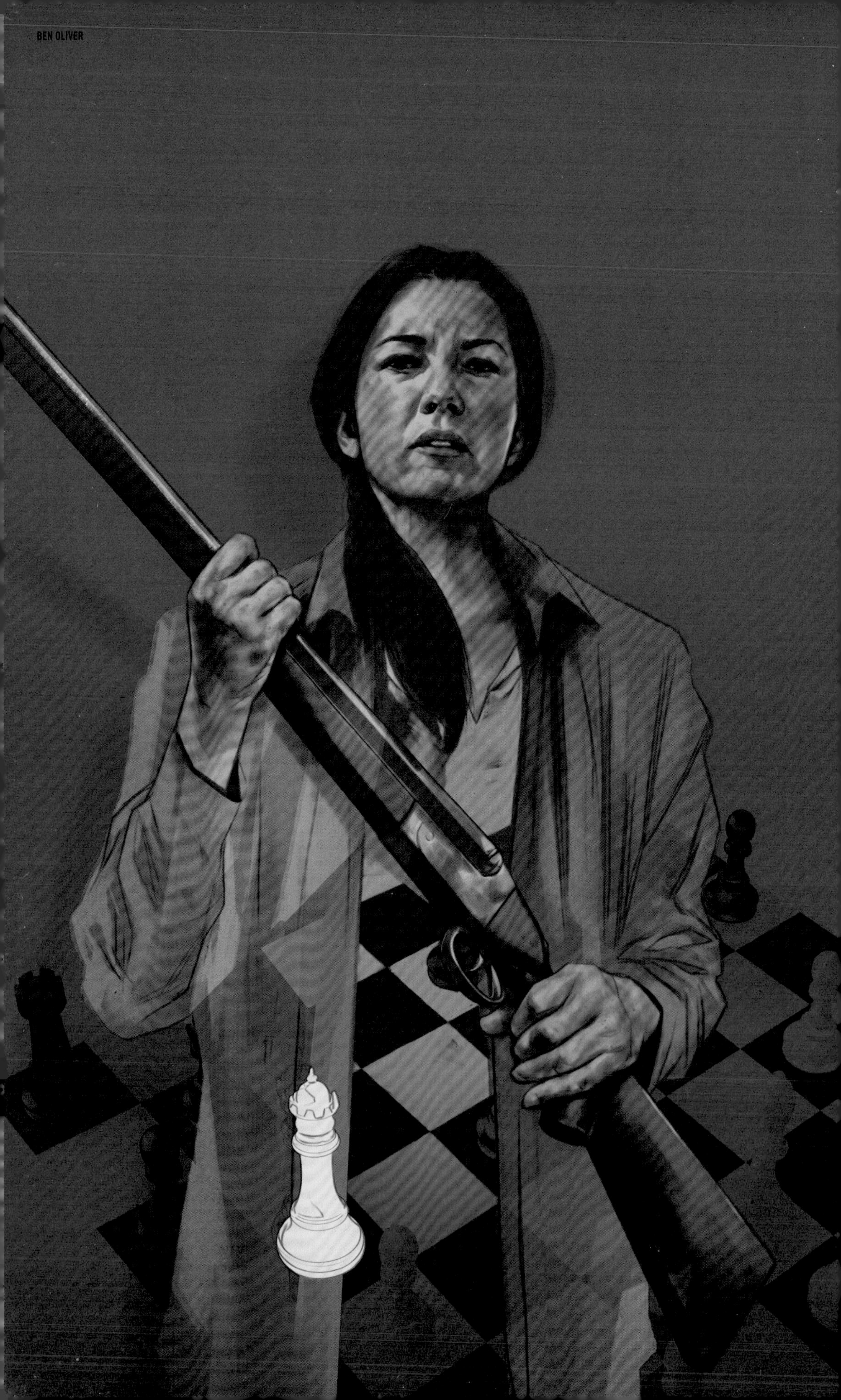
BEN OLIVER

UPSTATE
NEW YORK.

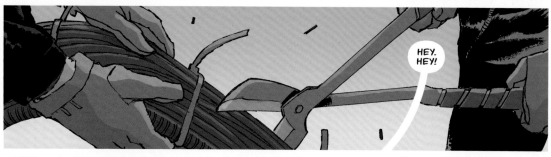

HEY.
HEY!

YOU
CAN'T BE
HERE.

THIS IS
PUBLIC LAND,
SO YEAH, WE
CAN.

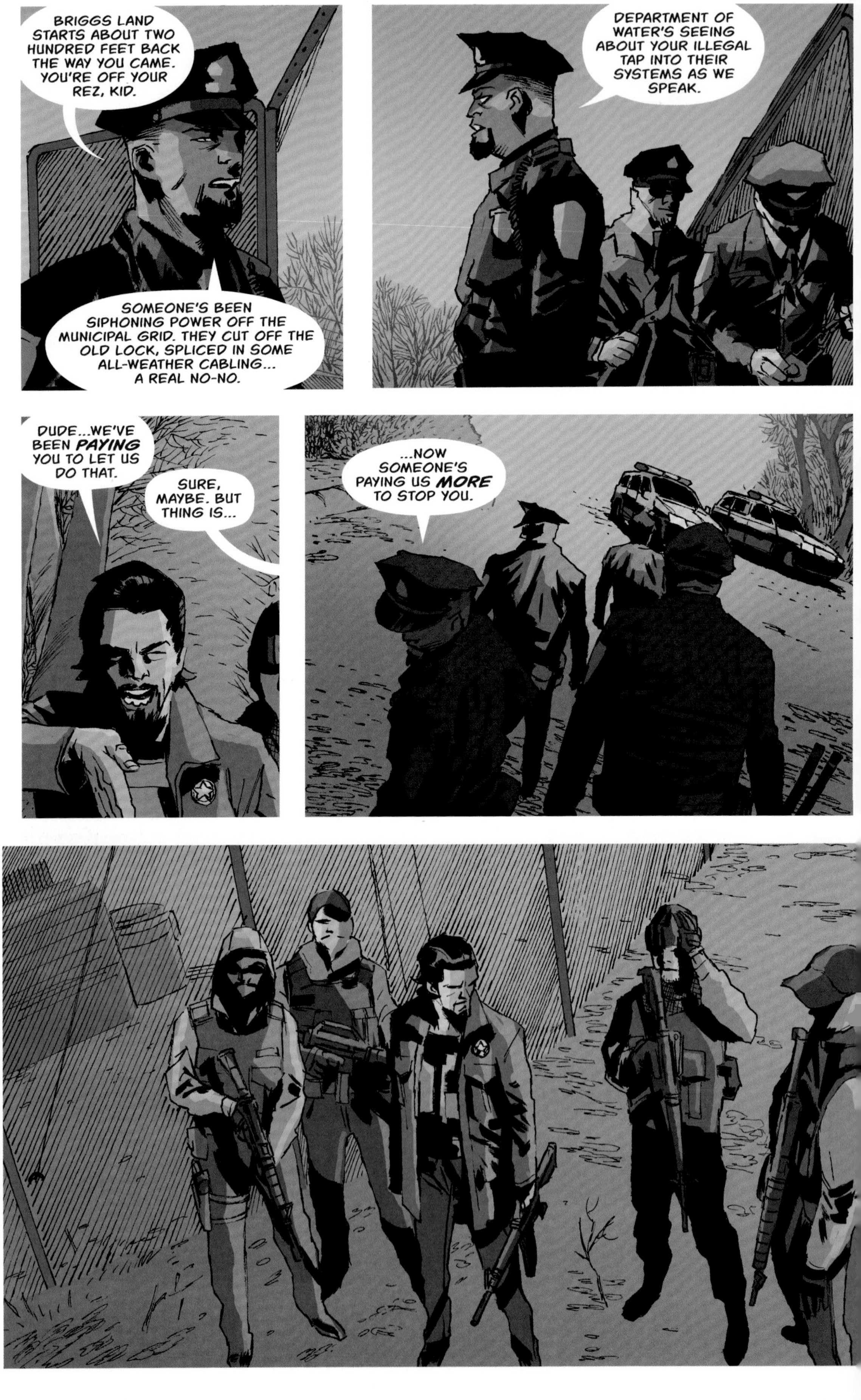
BRIGGS LAND STARTS ABOUT TWO HUNDRED FEET BACK THE WAY YOU CAME. YOU'RE OFF YOUR REZ, KID.
SOMEONE'S BEEN SIPHONING POWER OFF THE MUNICIPAL GRID. THEY CUT OFF THE OLD LOCK, SPLICED IN SOME ALL-WEATHER CABLING... A REAL NO-NO.
DEPARTMENT OF WATER'S SEEING ABOUT YOUR ILLEGAL TAP INTO THEIR SYSTEMS AS WE SPEAK.
DUDE...WE'VE BEEN **PAYING** YOU TO LET US DO THAT.
SURE, MAYBE. BUT THING IS...
...NOW SOMEONE'S PAYING US **MORE** TO STOP YOU.

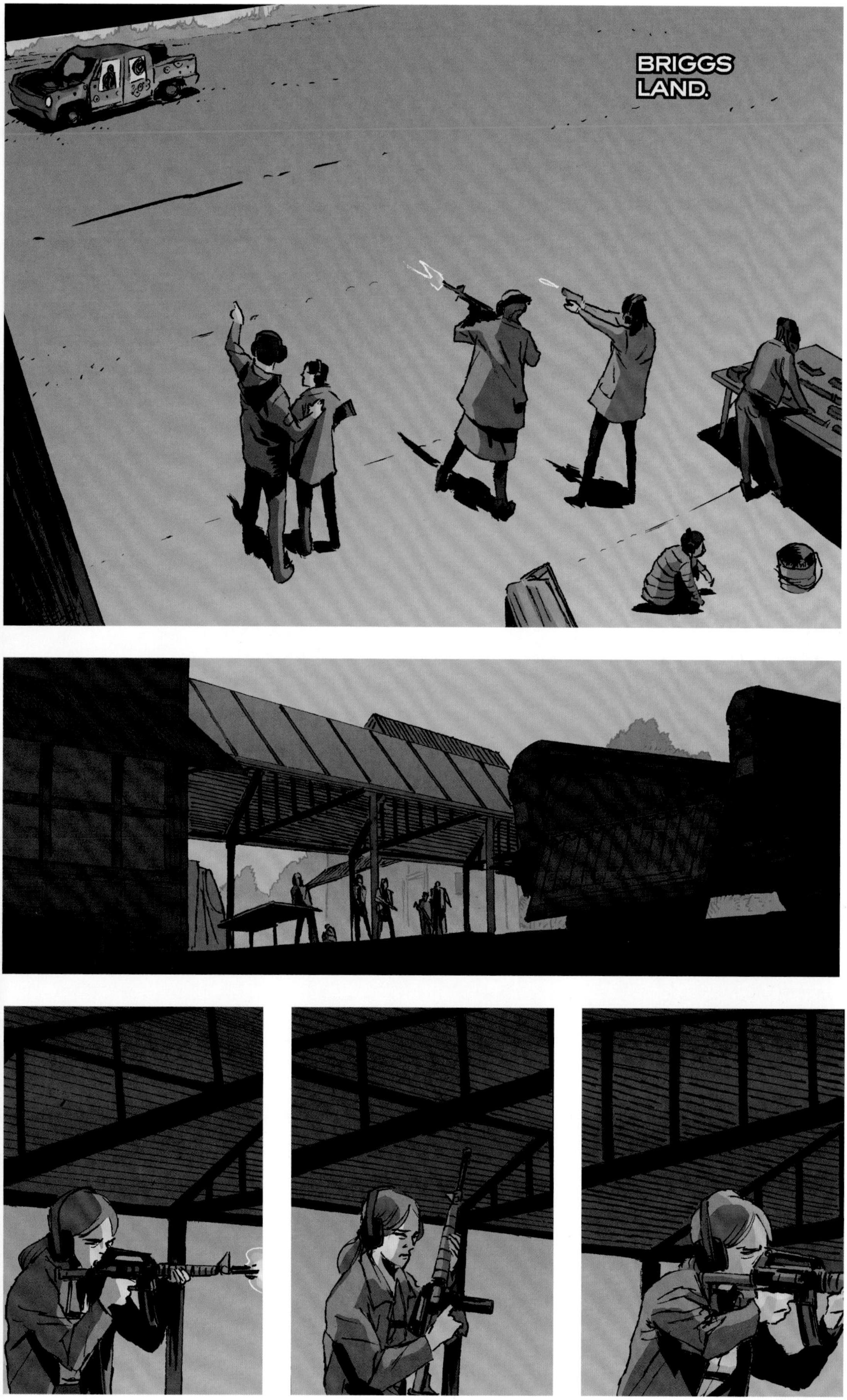
BRIGGS LAND.

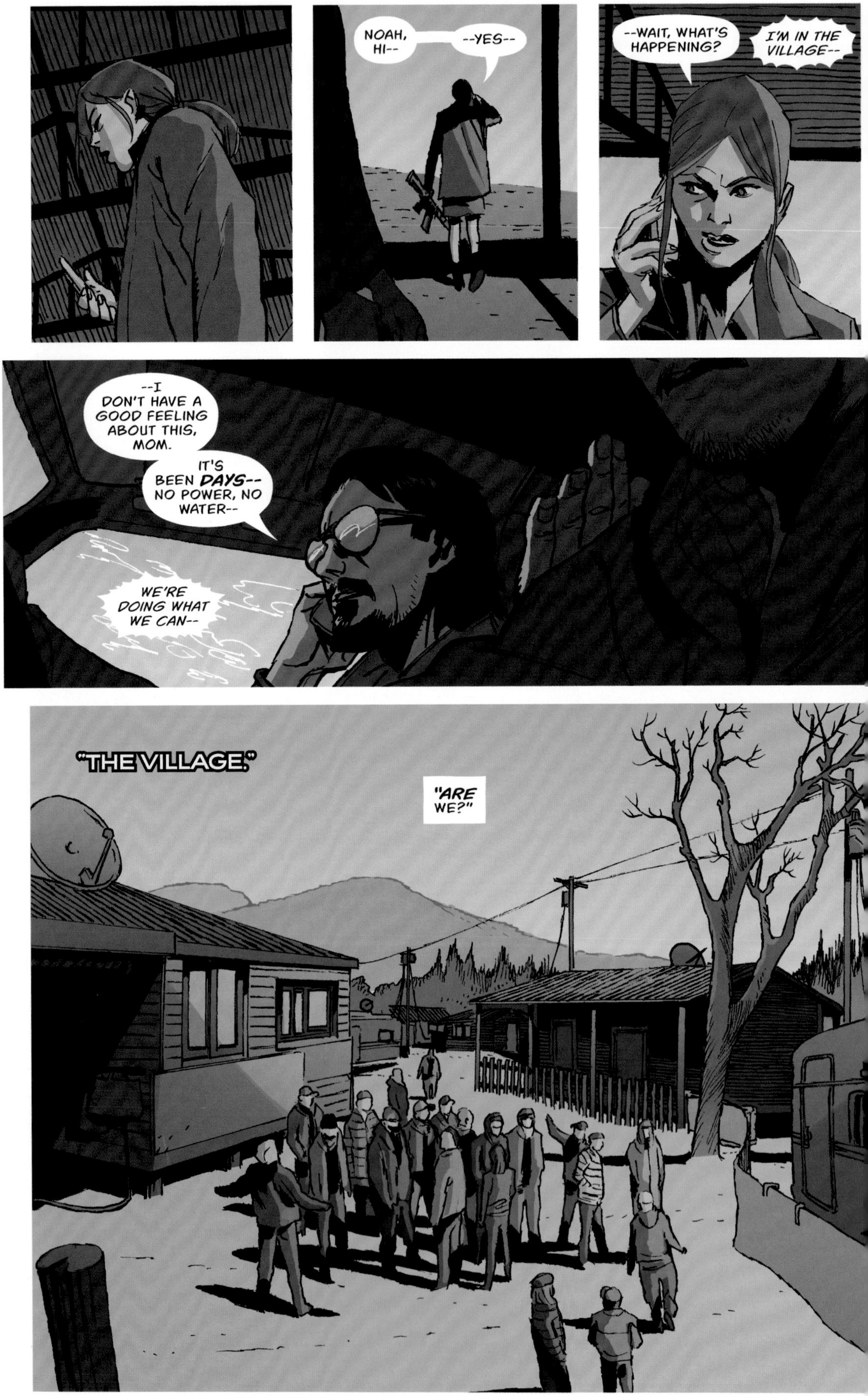

NOAH, HI--
--YES--
--WAIT, WHAT'S HAPPENING?
I'M IN THE VILLAGE--
--I DON'T HAVE A GOOD FEELING ABOUT THIS, MOM.
IT'S BEEN DAYS-- NO POWER, NO WATER--
WE'RE DOING WHAT WE CAN--
"THE VILLAGE."
"ARE WE?"

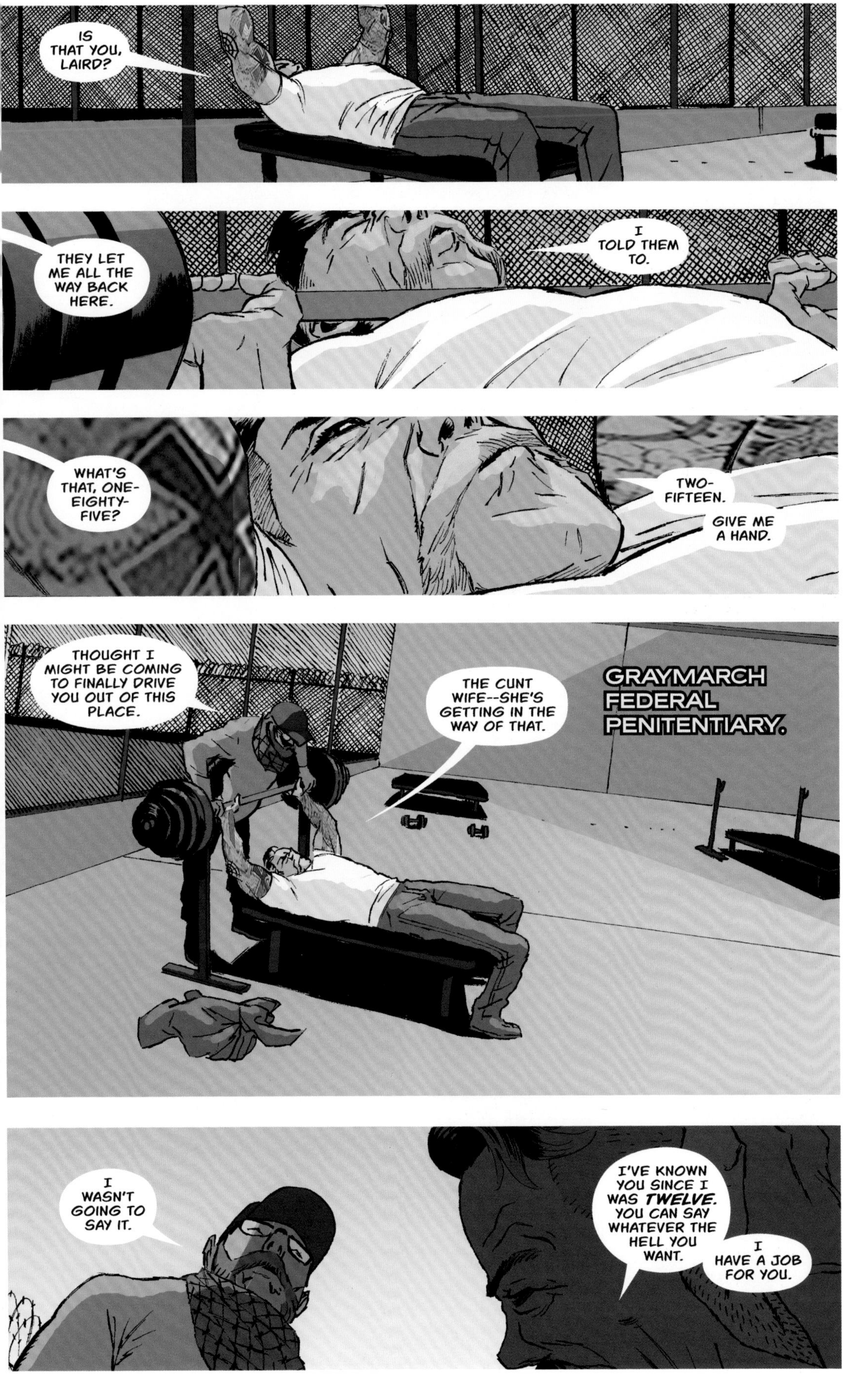
IS THAT YOU, LAIRD?
THEY LET ME ALL THE WAY BACK HERE.
I TOLD THEM TO.
WHAT'S THAT, ONE-EIGHTY-FIVE?
TWO-FIFTEEN.
GIVE ME A HAND.
THOUGHT I MIGHT BE COMING TO FINALLY DRIVE YOU OUT OF THIS PLACE.
THE CUNT WIFE--SHE'S GETTING IN THE WAY OF THAT.
GRAYMARCH FEDERAL PENITENTIARY.
I WASN'T GOING TO SAY IT.
I'VE KNOWN YOU SINCE I WAS *TWELVE.* YOU CAN SAY WHATEVER THE HELL YOU WANT.
I HAVE A JOB FOR YOU.

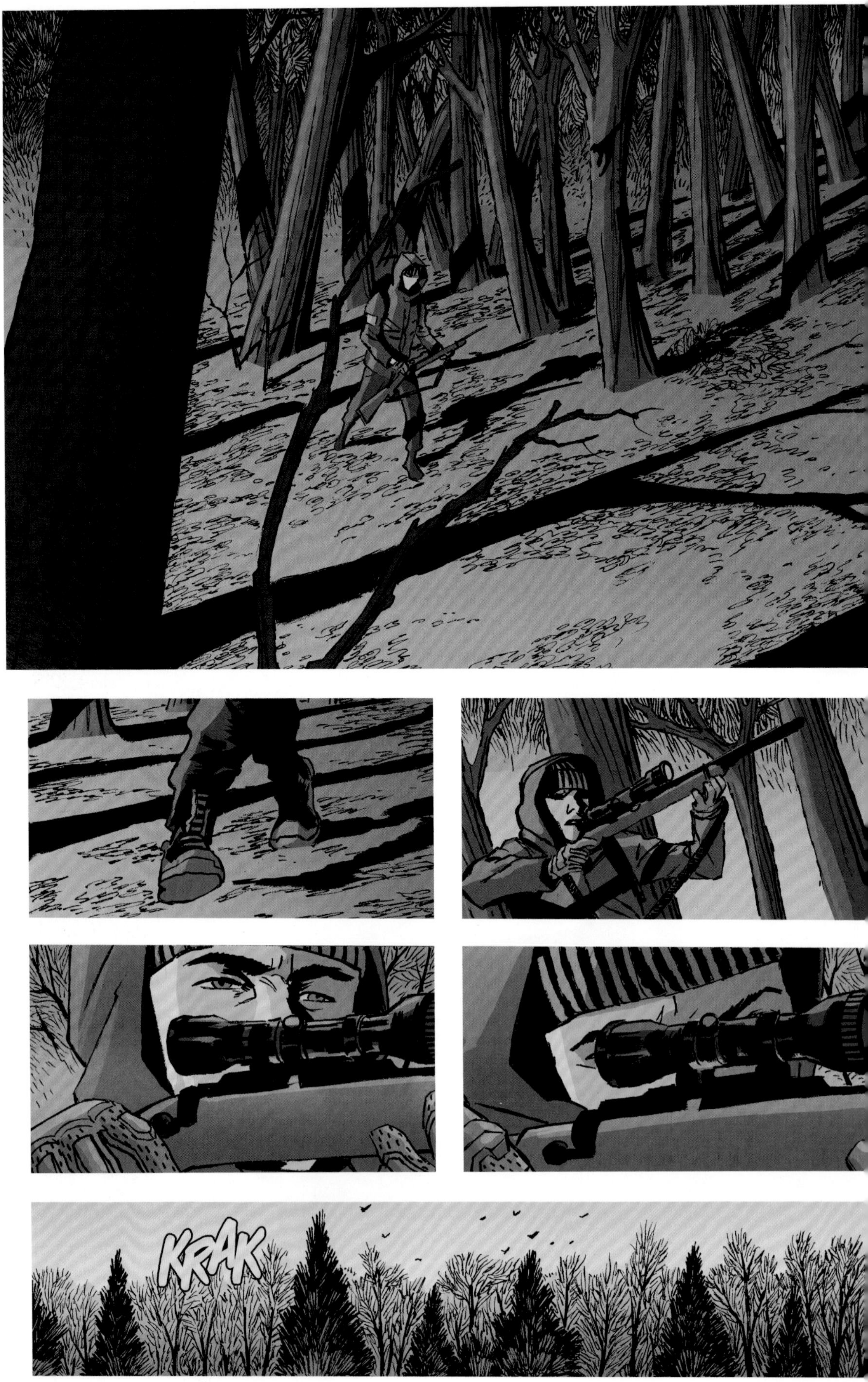
KRAK

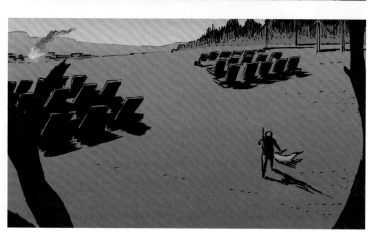

NOAH.

--NOT A GOOD TIME, ISAAC--

NOAH, I THINK THERE'S A FIRE DOWN IN THE VILLAGE.

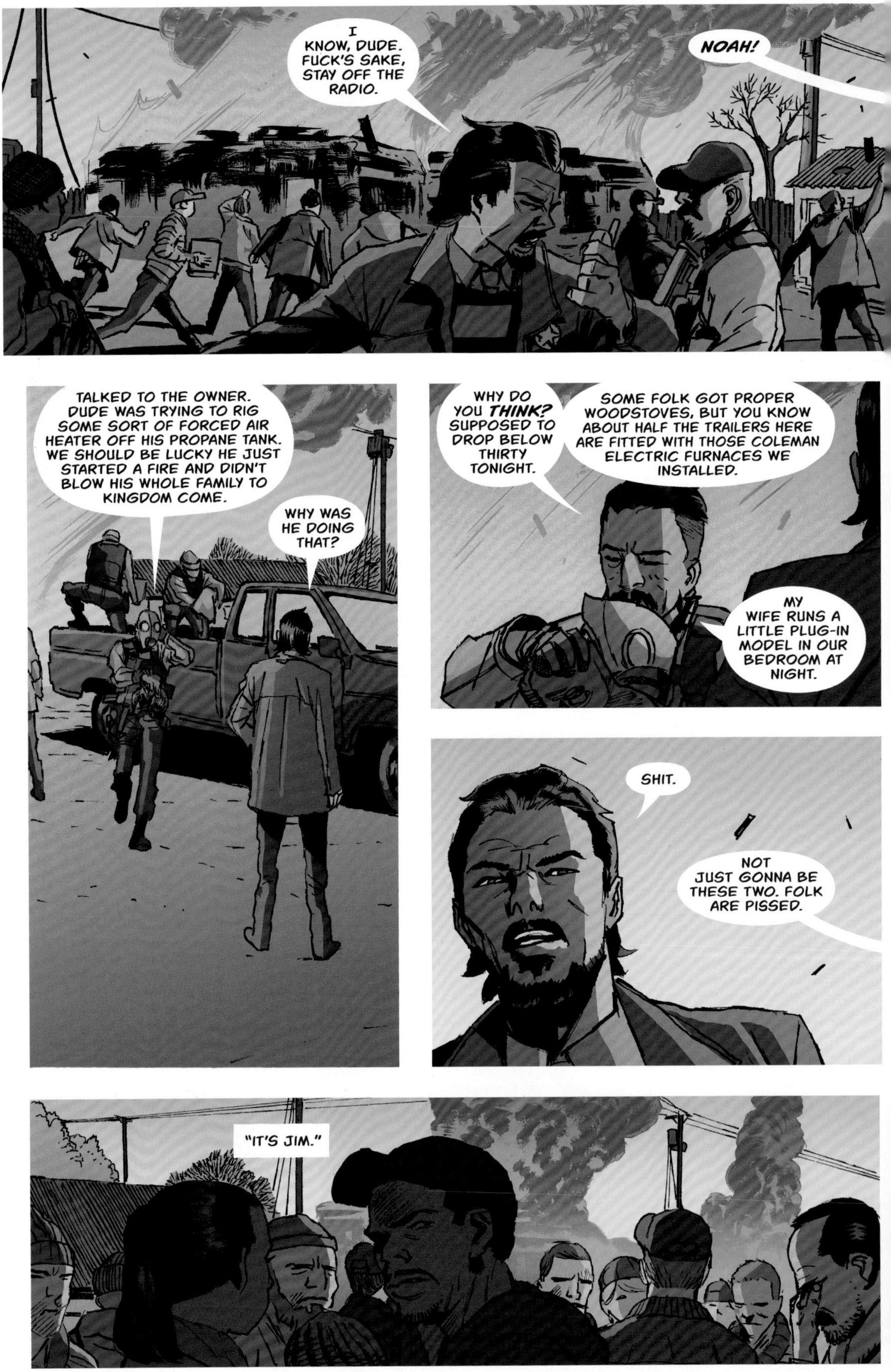
I KNOW, DUDE. FUCK'S SAKE, STAY OFF THE RADIO.
NOAH!
TALKED TO THE OWNER. DUDE WAS TRYING TO RIG SOME SORT OF FORCED AIR HEATER OFF HIS PROPANE TANK. WE SHOULD BE LUCKY HE JUST STARTED A FIRE AND DIDN'T BLOW HIS WHOLE FAMILY TO KINGDOM COME.
WHY WAS HE DOING THAT?
WHY DO YOU **THINK?** SUPPOSED TO DROP BELOW THIRTY TONIGHT.
SOME FOLK GOT PROPER WOODSTOVES, BUT YOU KNOW ABOUT HALF THE TRAILERS HERE ARE FITTED WITH THOSE COLEMAN ELECTRIC FURNACES WE INSTALLED.
MY WIFE RUNS A LITTLE PLUG-IN MODEL IN OUR BEDROOM AT NIGHT.
SHIT.
NOT JUST GONNA BE THESE TWO. FOLK ARE PISSED.
"IT'S JIM."

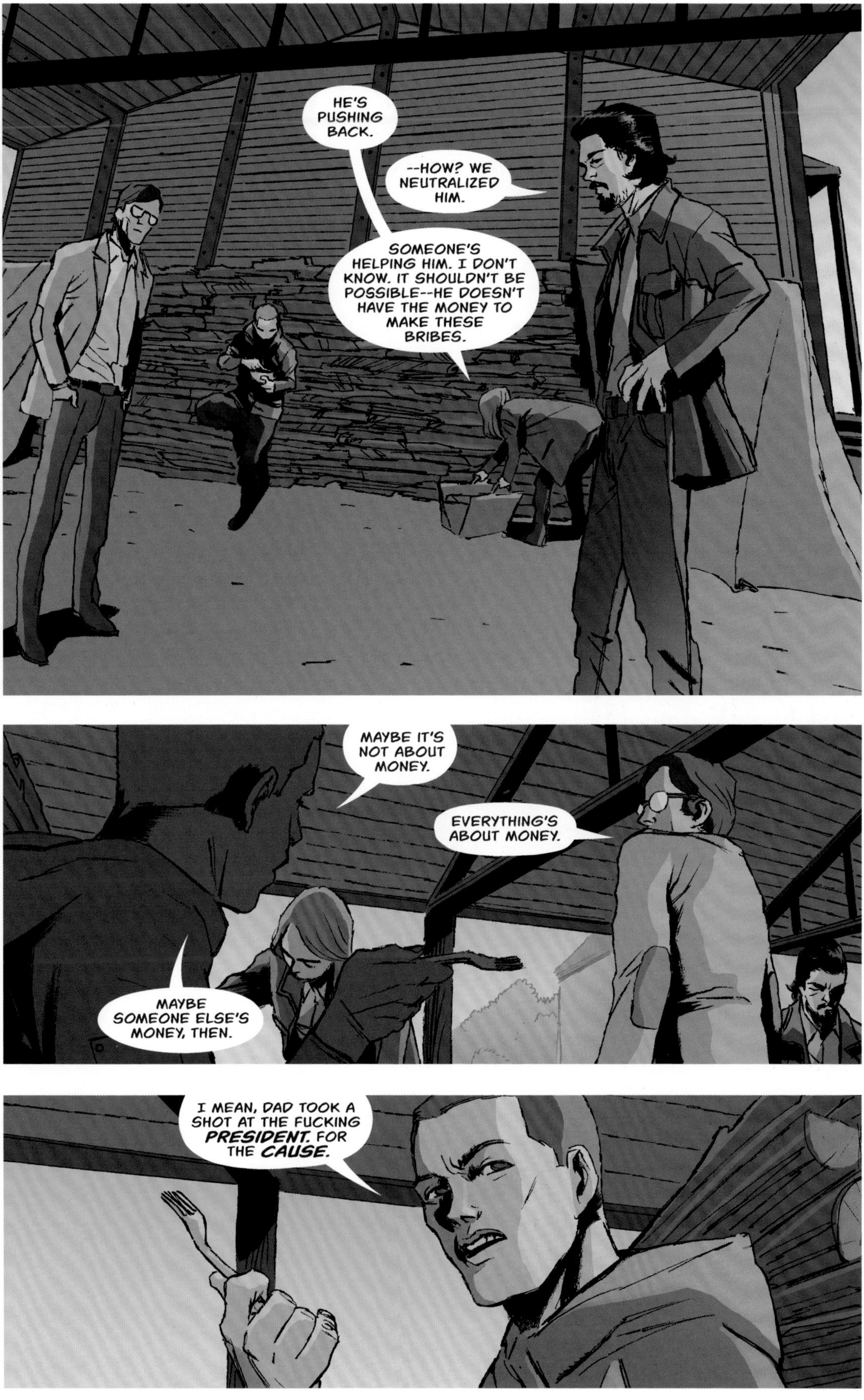
HE'S PUSHING BACK.
--HOW? WE NEUTRALIZED HIM.
SOMEONE'S HELPING HIM. I DON'T KNOW. IT SHOULDN'T BE POSSIBLE--HE DOESN'T HAVE THE MONEY TO MAKE THESE BRIBES.
MAYBE IT'S NOT ABOUT MONEY.
EVERYTHING'S ABOUT MONEY.
MAYBE SOMEONE ELSE'S MONEY, THEN.
I MEAN, DAD TOOK A SHOT AT THE FUCKING ***PRESIDENT.*** FOR THE ***CAUSE.***

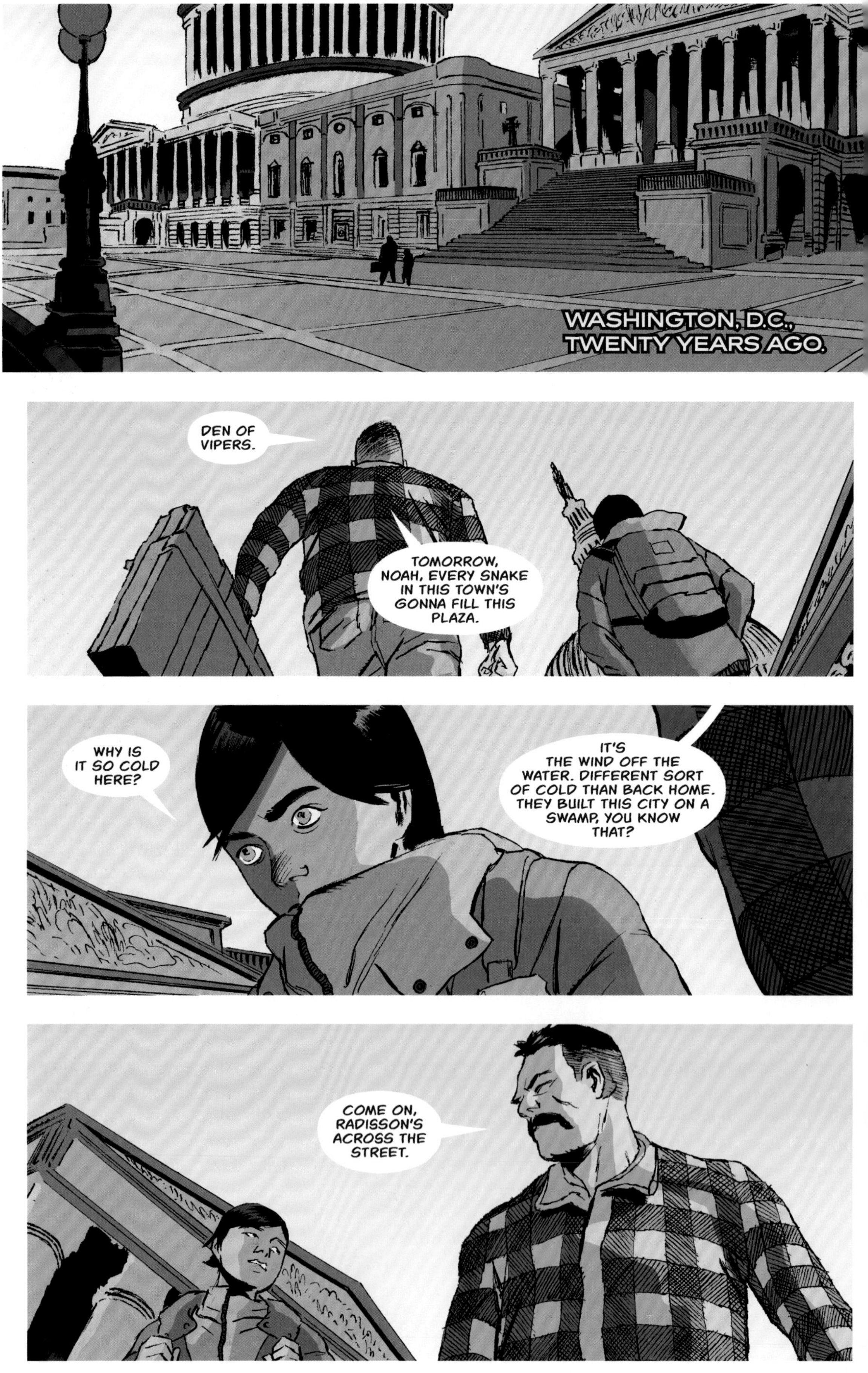
WASHINGTON, D.C., TWENTY YEARS AGO.
DEN OF VIPERS.
TOMORROW, NOAH, EVERY SNAKE IN THIS TOWN'S GONNA FILL THIS PLAZA.
WHY IS IT SO COLD HERE?
IT'S THE WIND OFF THE WATER. DIFFERENT SORT OF COLD THAN BACK HOME. THEY BUILT THIS CITY ON A SWAMP, YOU KNOW THAT?
COME ON, RADISSON'S ACROSS THE STREET.

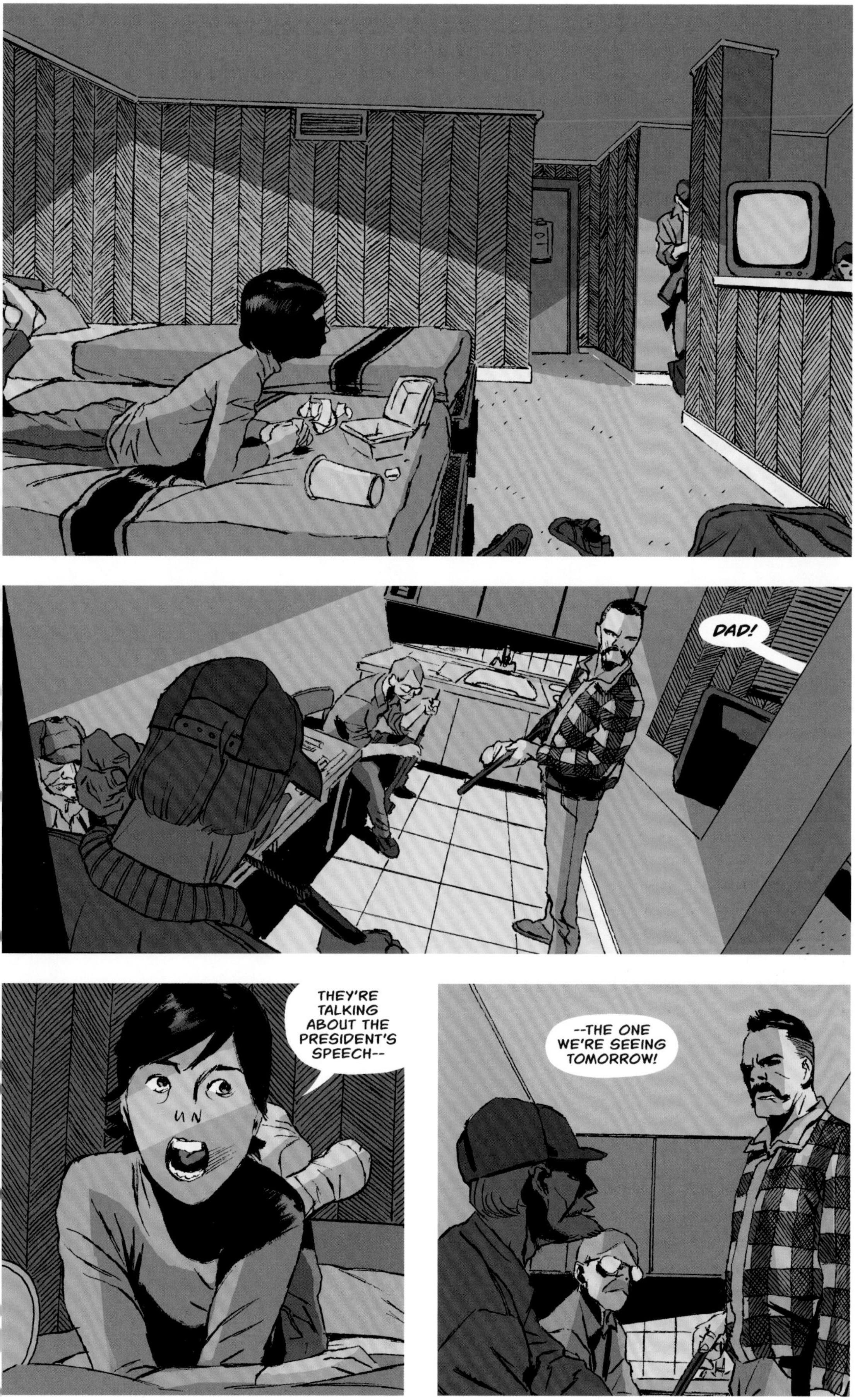
DAD!
THEY'RE TALKING ABOUT THE PRESIDENT'S SPEECH--
UN
--THE ONE WE'RE SEEING TOMORROW!

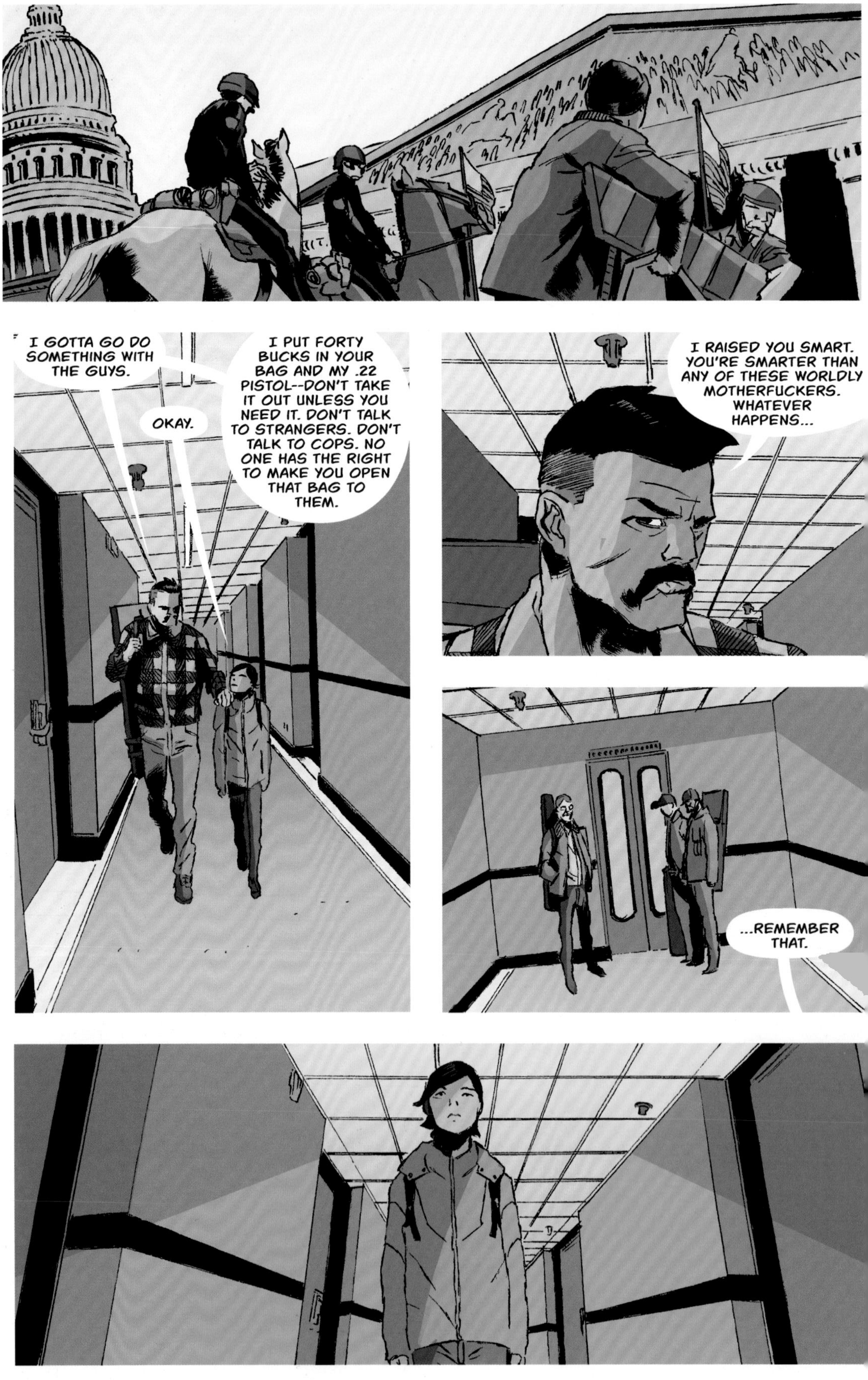
I GOTTA GO DO SOMETHING WITH THE GUYS.
OKAY.
I PUT FORTY BUCKS IN YOUR BAG AND MY .22 PISTOL--DON'T TAKE IT OUT UNLESS YOU NEED IT. DON'T TALK TO STRANGERS. DON'T TALK TO COPS. NO ONE HAS THE RIGHT TO MAKE YOU OPEN THAT BAG TO THEM.
I RAISED YOU SMART. YOU'RE SMARTER THAN ANY OF THESE WORLDLY MOTHERFUCKERS. WHATEVER HAPPENS...
...REMEMBER THAT.

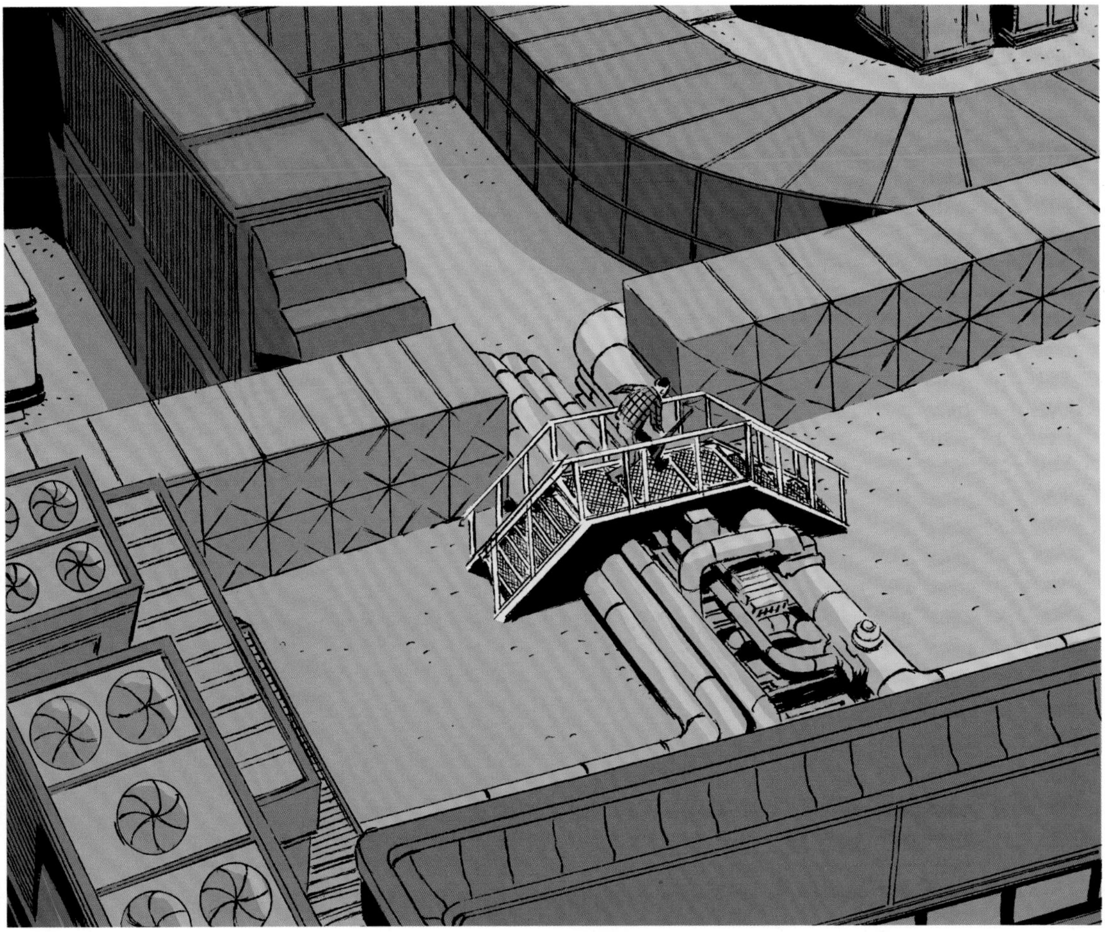

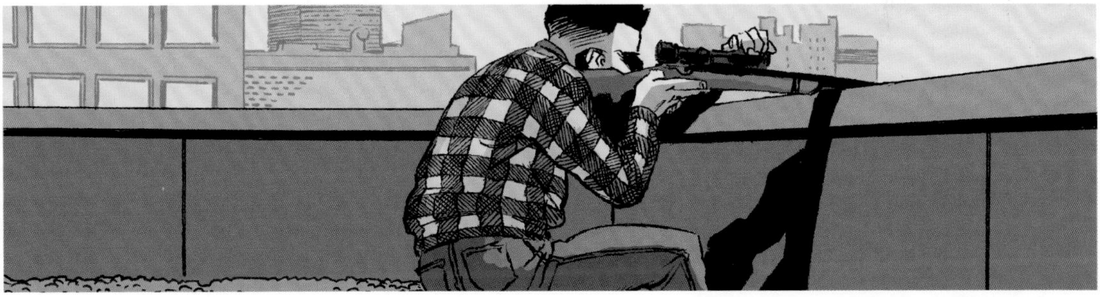

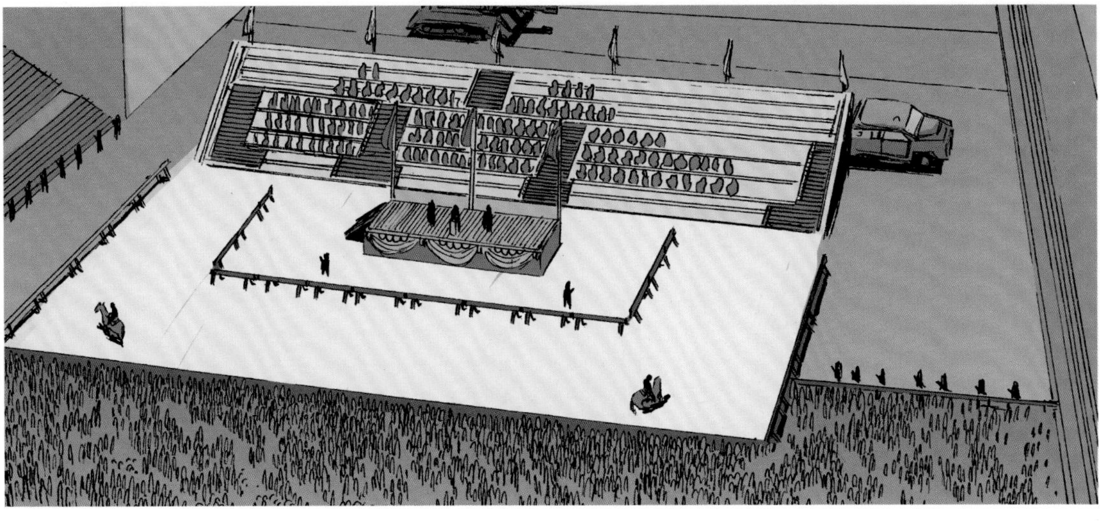

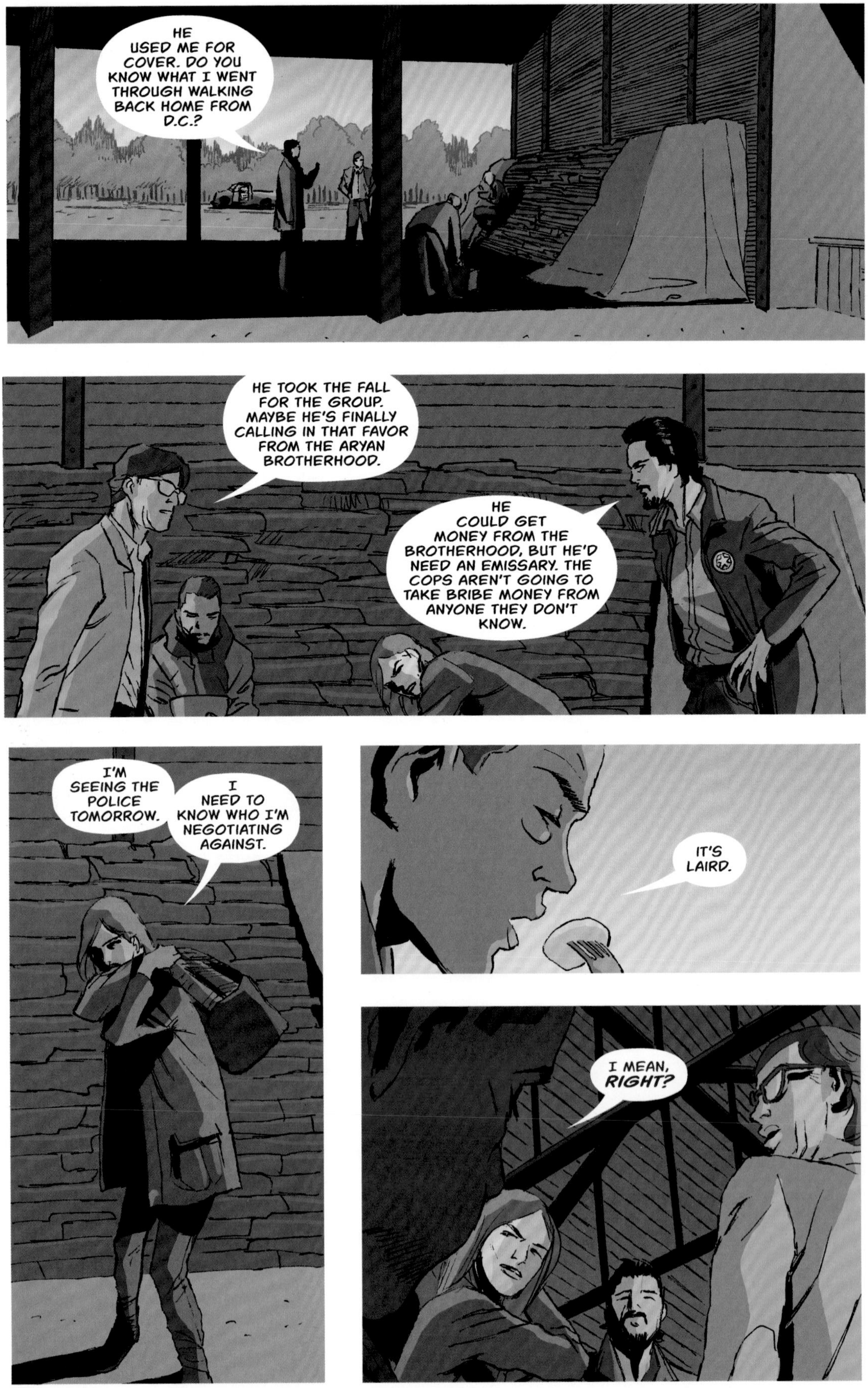
HE USED ME FOR COVER. DO YOU KNOW WHAT I WENT THROUGH WALKING BACK HOME FROM D.C.?
HE TOOK THE FALL FOR THE GROUP. MAYBE HE'S FINALLY CALLING IN THAT FAVOR FROM THE ARYAN BROTHERHOOD.
HE COULD GET MONEY FROM THE BROTHERHOOD, BUT HE'D NEED AN EMISSARY. THE COPS AREN'T GOING TO TAKE BRIBE MONEY FROM ANYONE THEY DON'T KNOW.
I'M SEEING THE POLICE TOMORROW.
I NEED TO KNOW WHO I'M NEGOTIATING AGAINST.
IT'S LAIRD.
I MEAN, *RIGHT?*

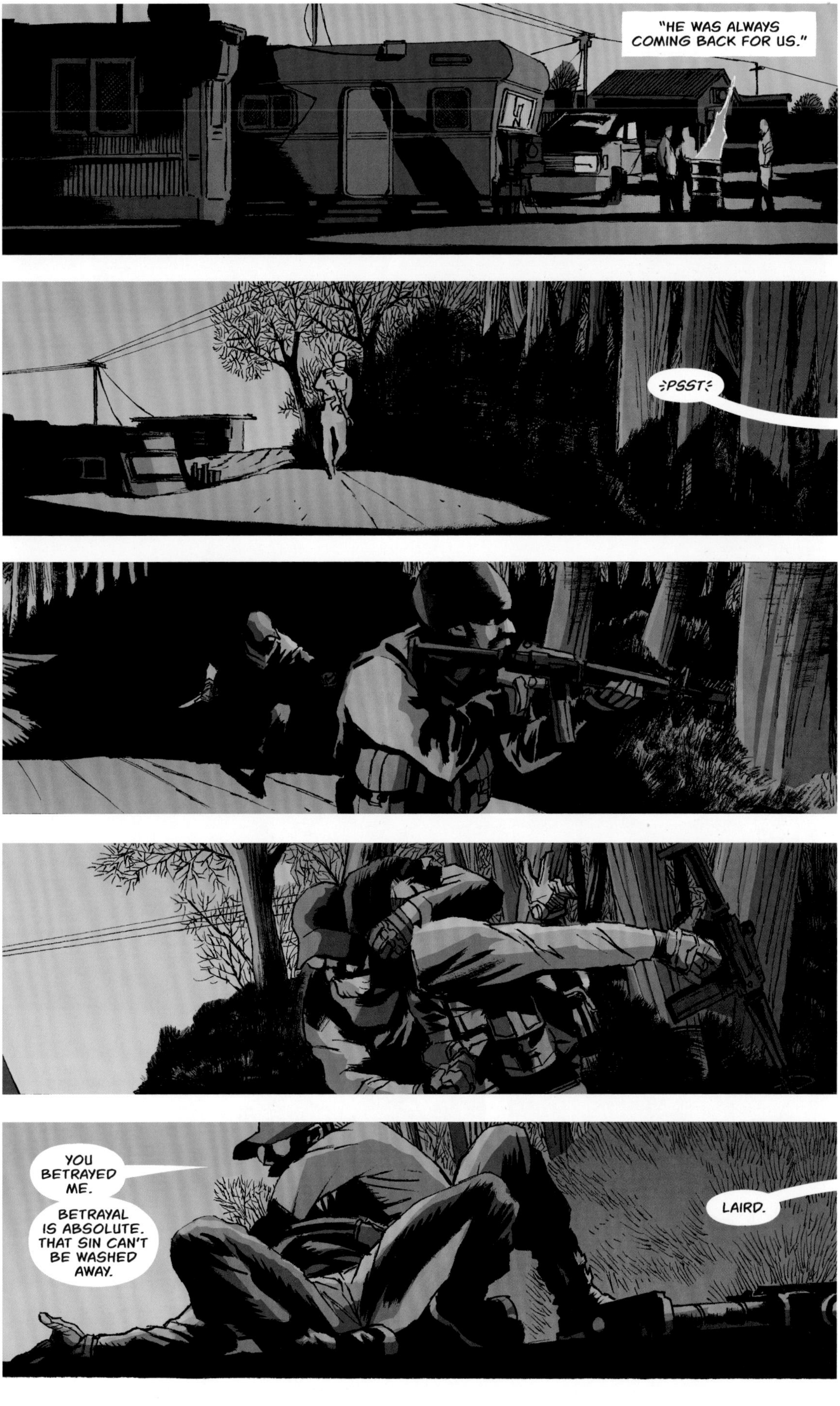
"HE WAS ALWAYS COMING BACK FOR US."
PSST
YOU BETRAYED ME.
BETRAYAL IS ABSOLUTE. THAT SIN CAN'T BE WASHED AWAY.
LAIRD.

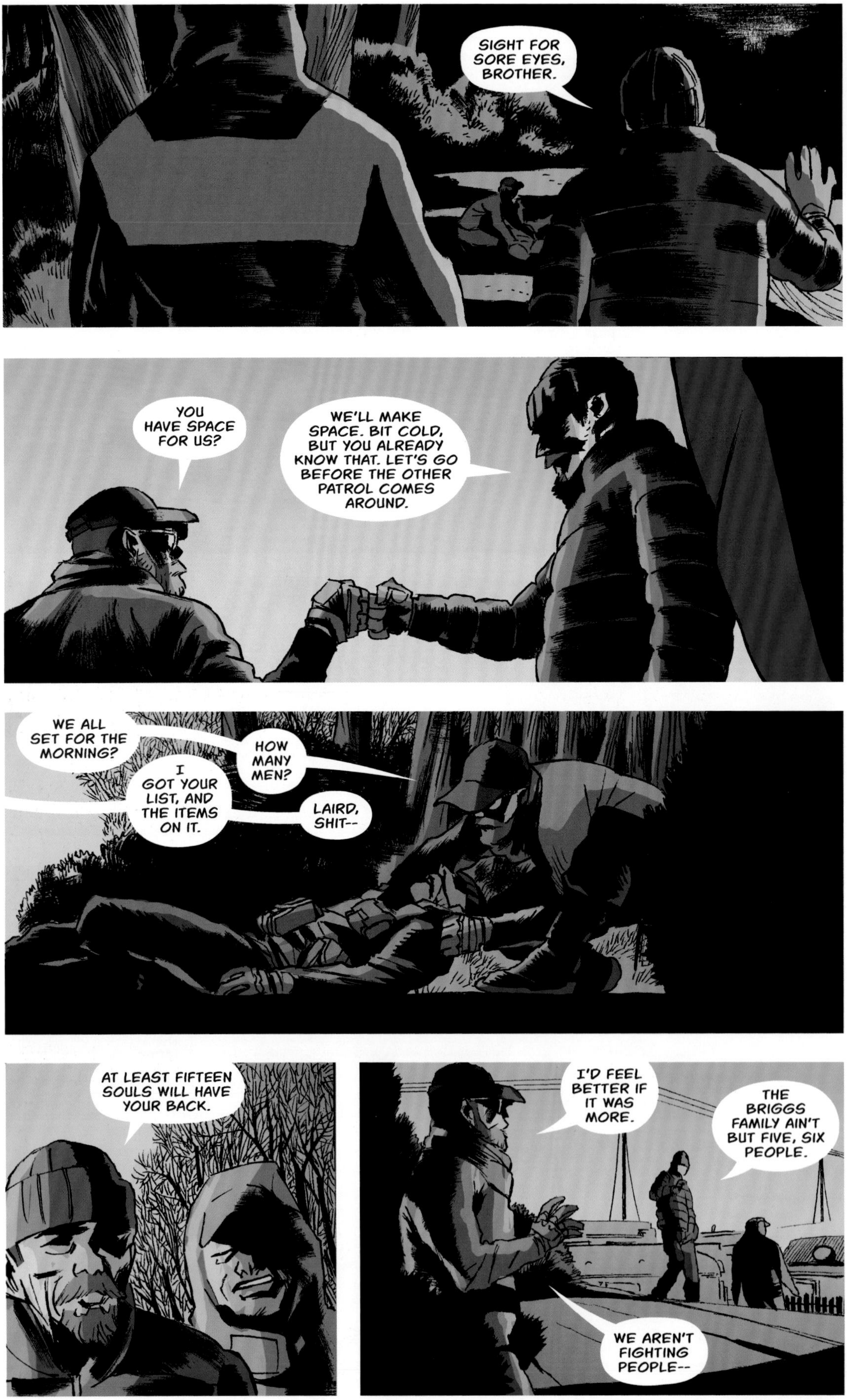
SIGHT FOR SORE EYES, BROTHER.
YOU HAVE SPACE FOR US?
WE'LL MAKE SPACE. BIT COLD, BUT YOU ALREADY KNOW THAT. LET'S GO BEFORE THE OTHER PATROL COMES AROUND.
WE ALL SET FOR THE MORNING?
I GOT YOUR LIST, AND THE ITEMS ON IT.
HOW MANY MEN?
LAIRD, SHIT--
AT LEAST FIFTEEN SOULS WILL HAVE YOUR BACK.
I'D FEEL BETTER IF IT WAS MORE.
THE BRIGGS FAMILY AIN'T BUT FIVE, SIX PEOPLE.
WE AREN'T FIGHTING PEOPLE--

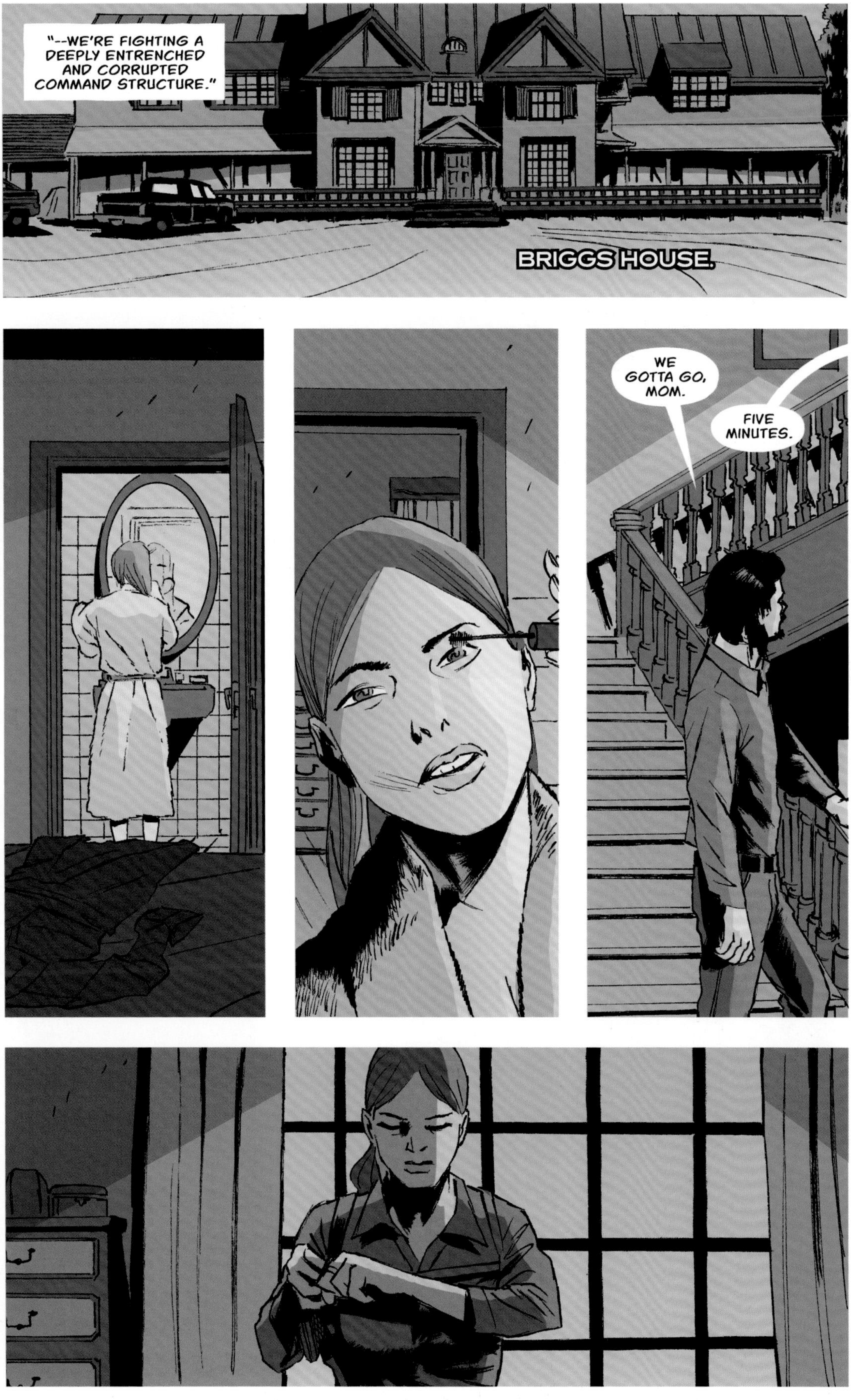
"--WE'RE FIGHTING A DEEPLY ENTRENCHED AND CORRUPTED COMMAND STRUCTURE."
BRIGGS HOUSE.
WE GOTTA GO, MOM.
FIVE MINUTES.

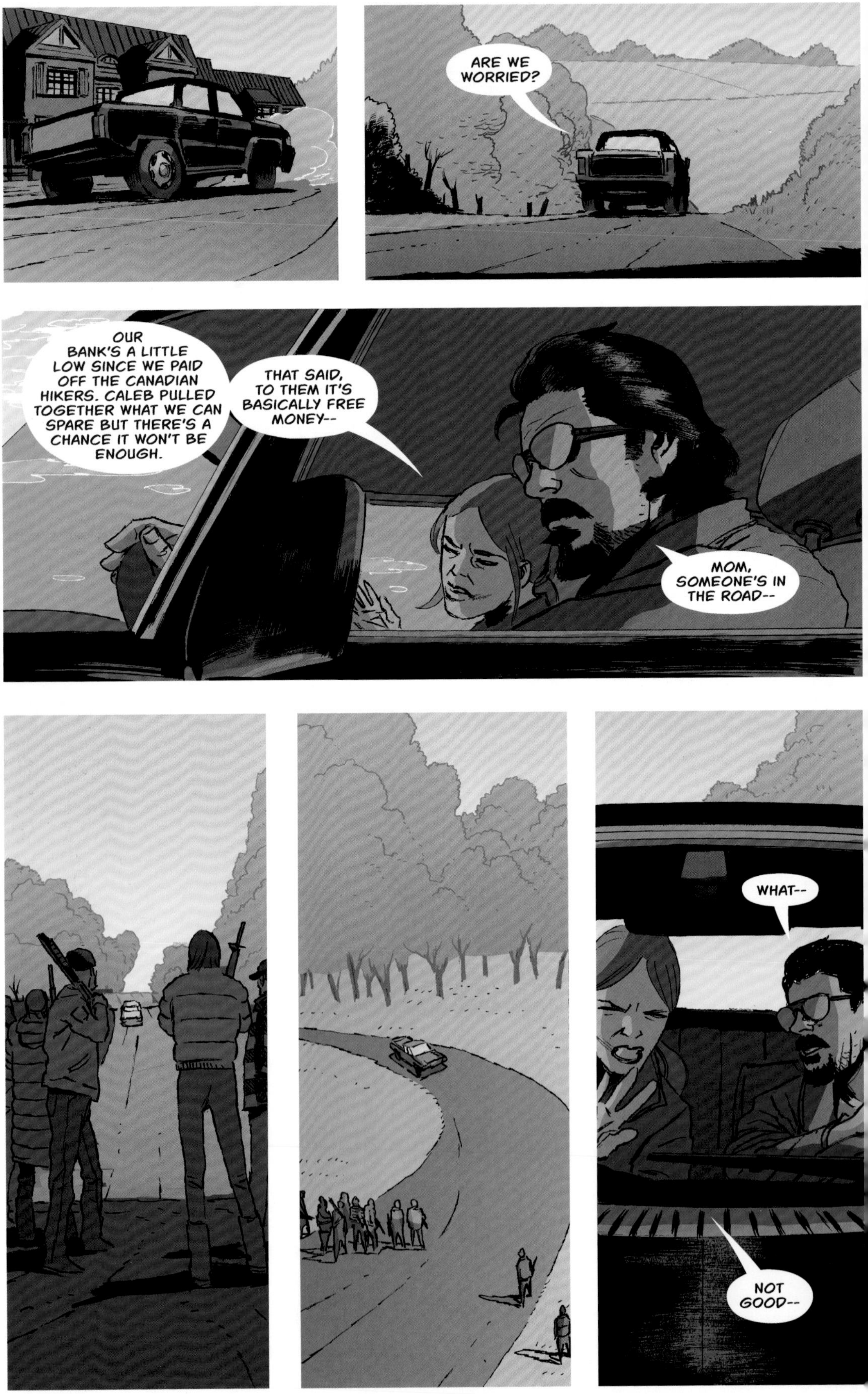
ARE WE WORRIED?
OUR BANK'S A LITTLE LOW SINCE WE PAID OFF THE CANADIAN HIKERS. CALEB PULLED TOGETHER WHAT WE CAN SPARE BUT THERE'S A CHANCE IT WON'T BE ENOUGH.
THAT SAID, TO THEM IT'S BASICALLY FREE MONEY--
MOM, SOMEONE'S IN THE ROAD--
WHAT--
NOT GOOD--

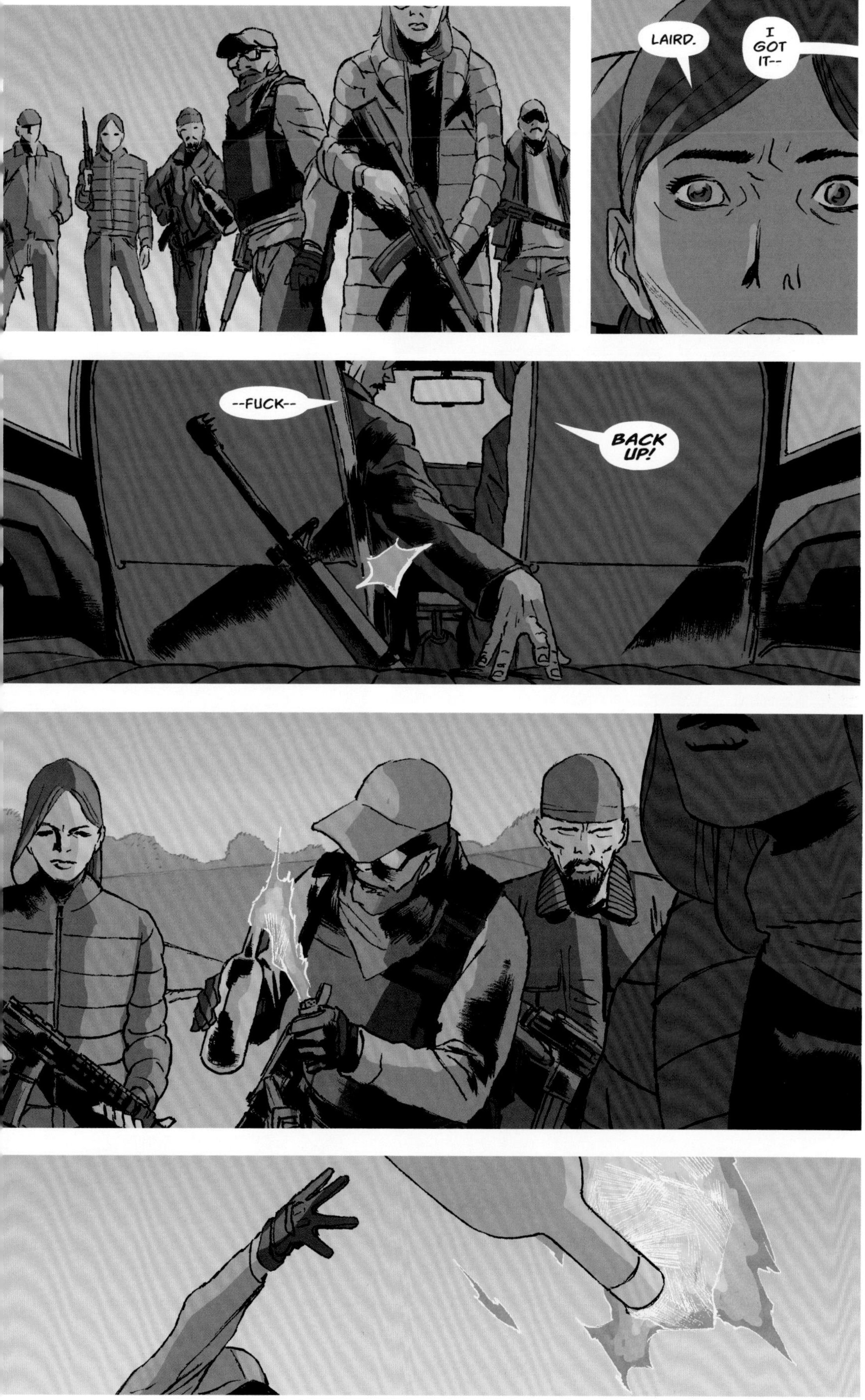
LAIRD.
I GOT IT--
--FUCK--
BACK UP!

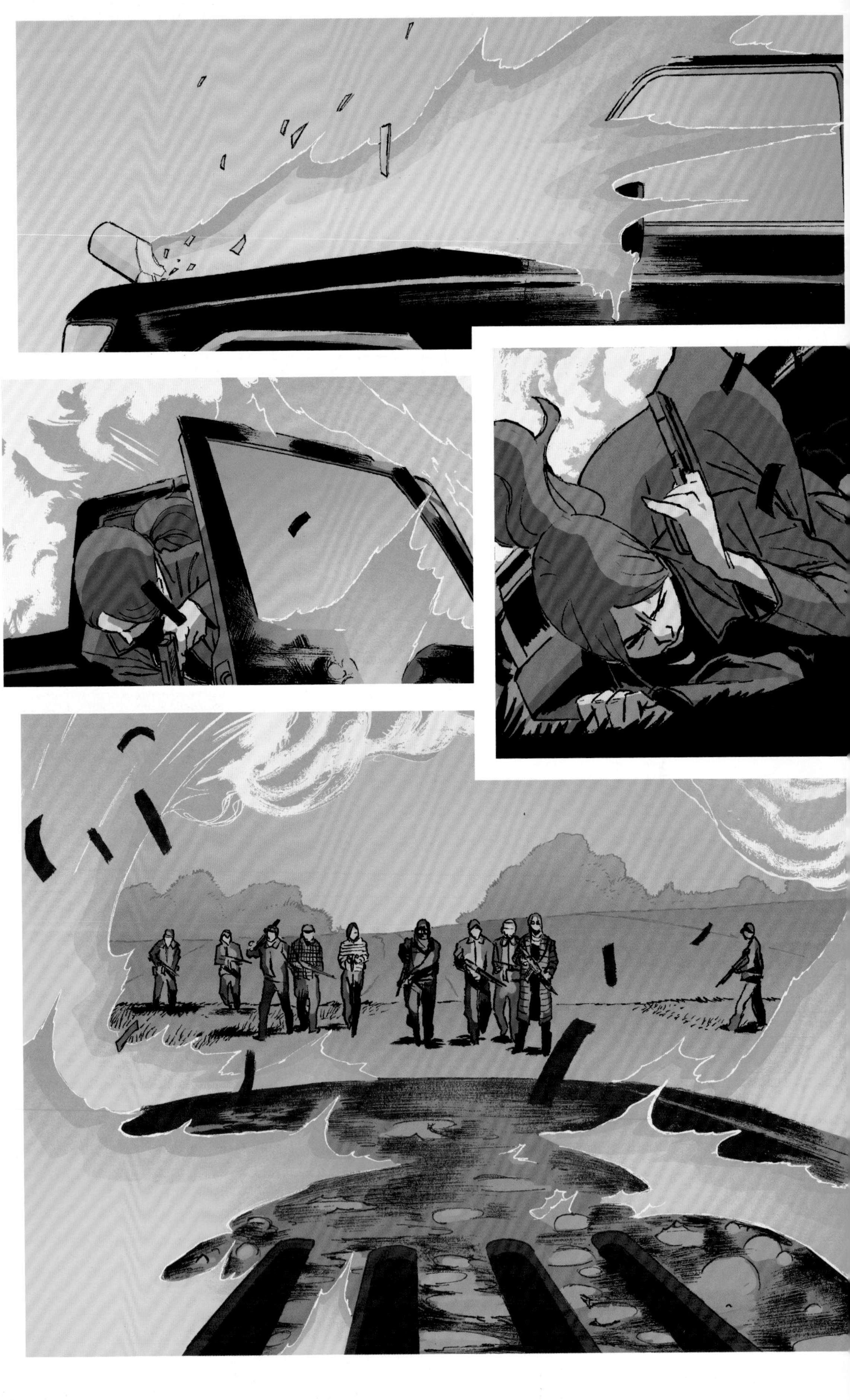

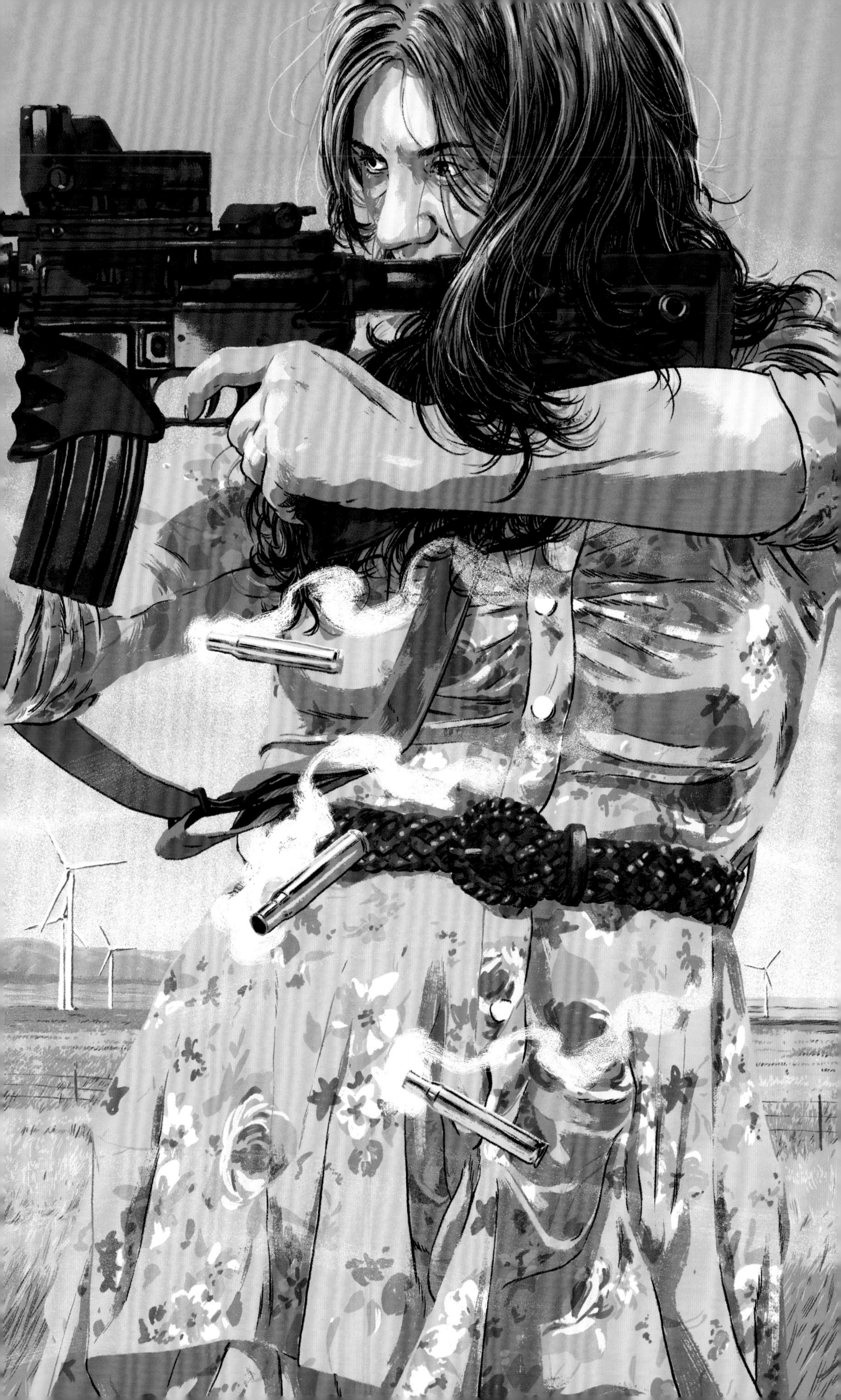

TRISTAN JONES

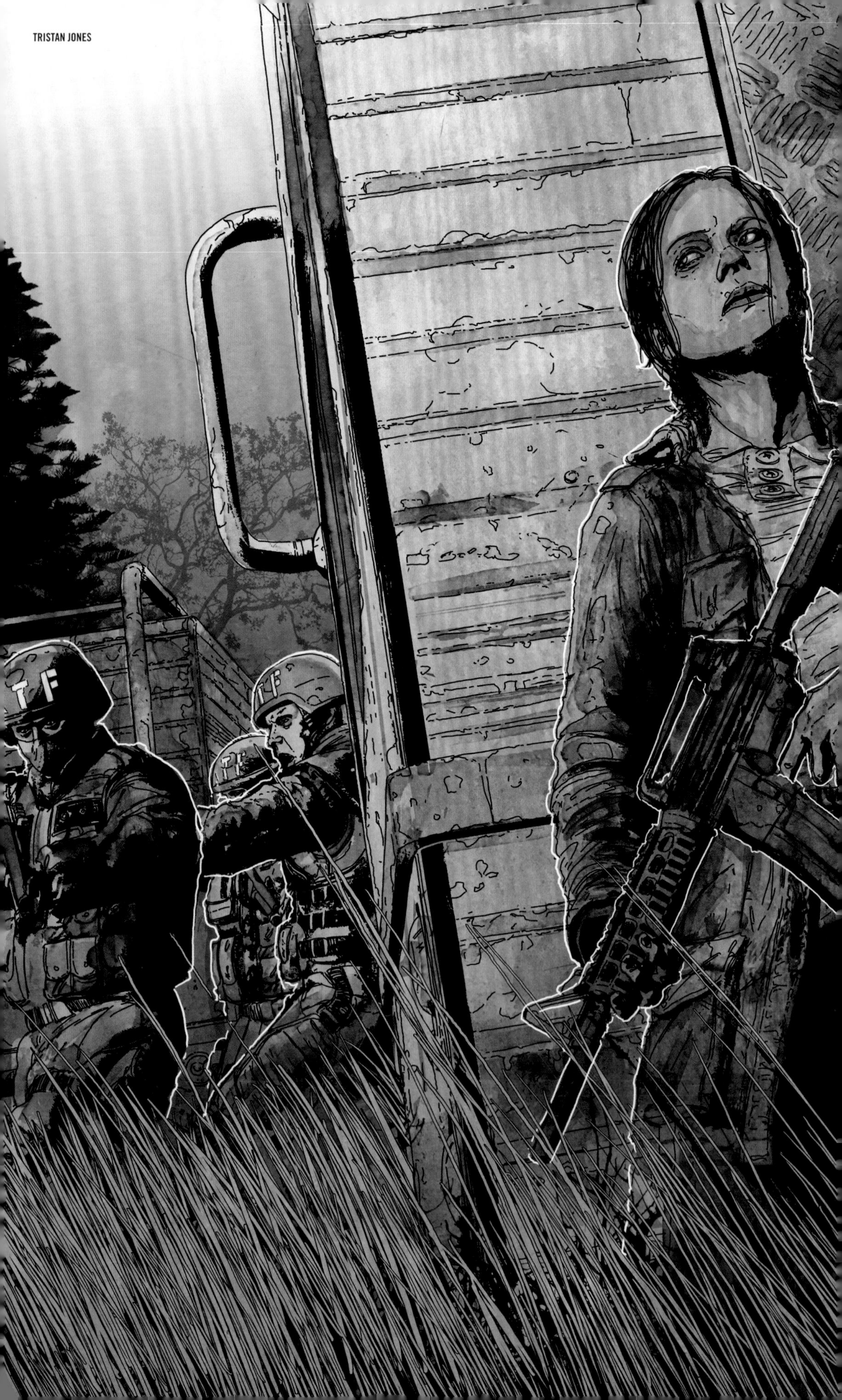

TF
TF
TF

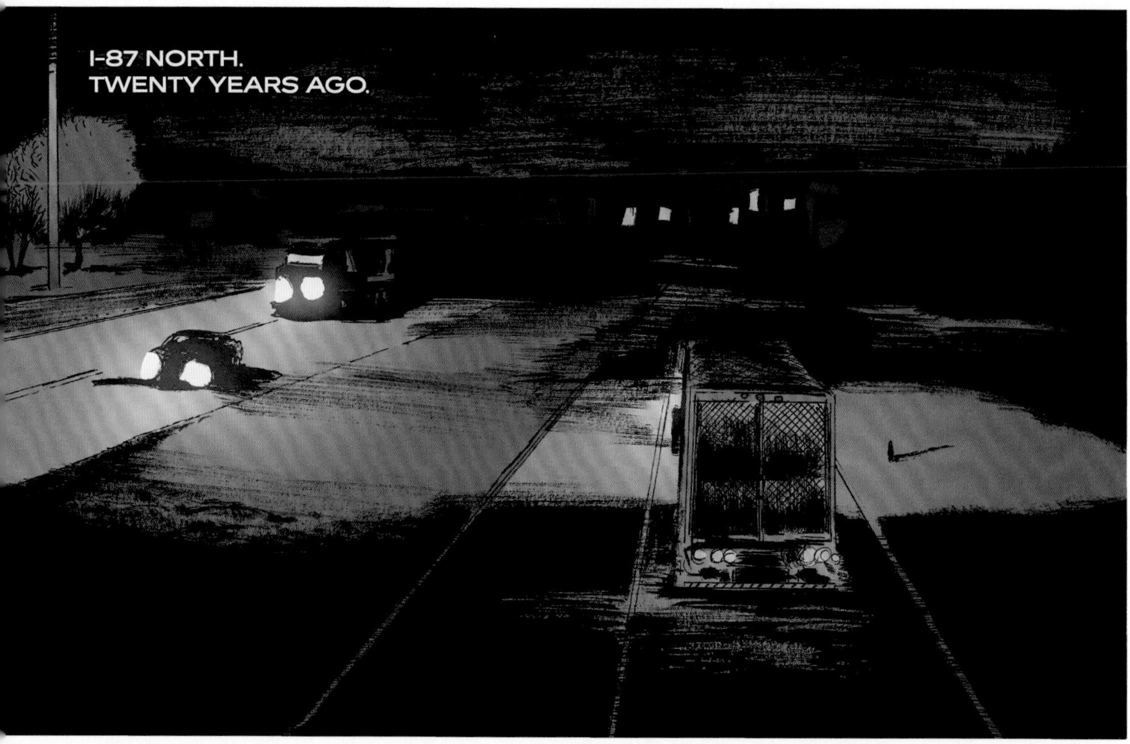
I-87 NORTH.
TWENTY YEARS AGO.

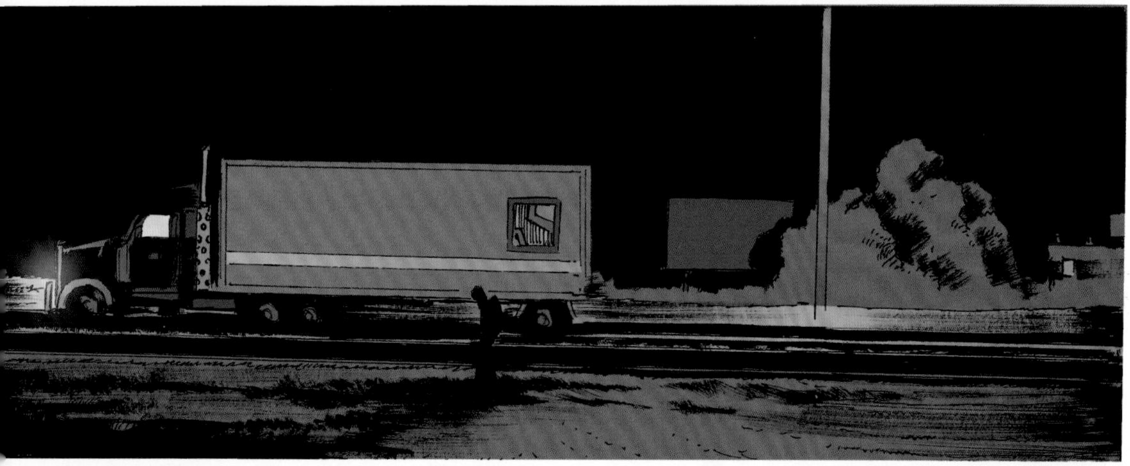

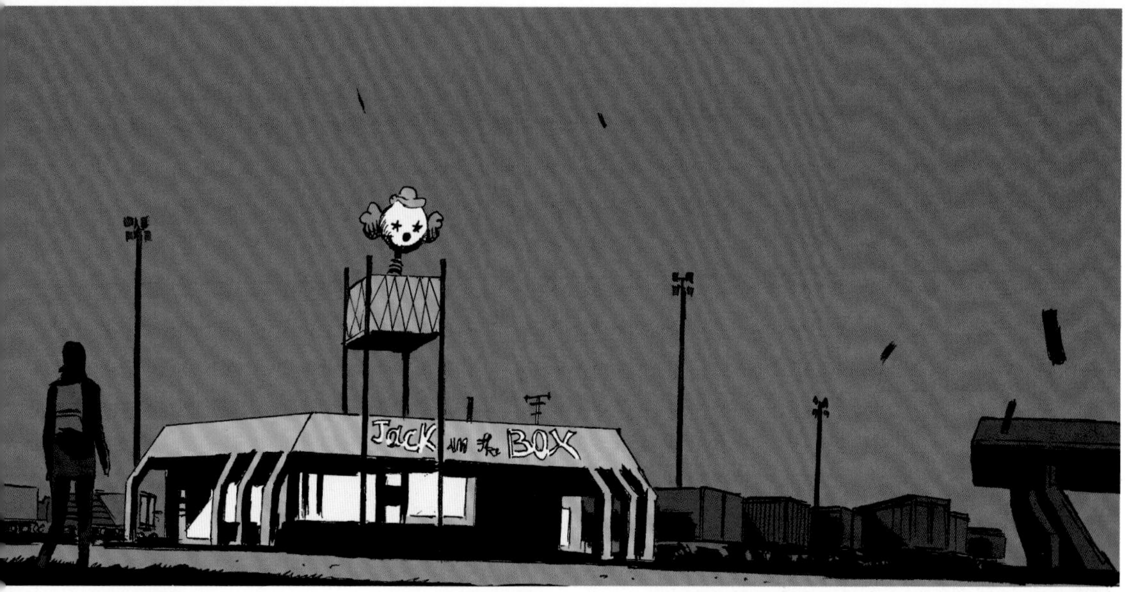
JACK in the BOX

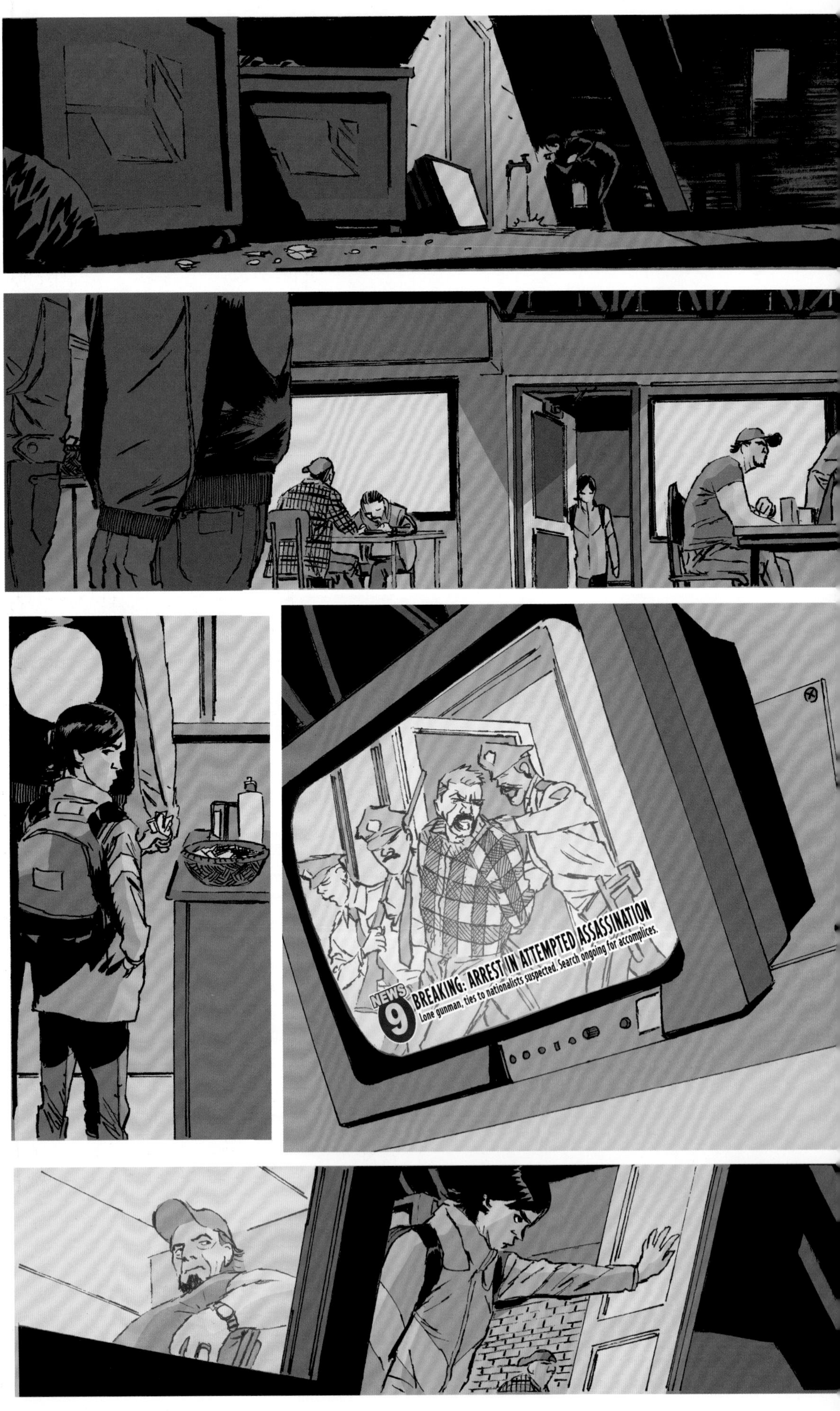
NEWS 9
BREAKING: ARREST IN ATTEMPTED ASSASSINATION
Lone gunman, ties to nationalists suspected. Search ongoing for accomplices.

HEY--

HEY, KID!

HEY, I DON'T WANNA HURT YOU--

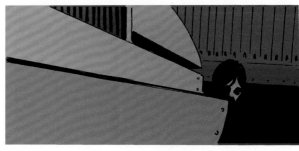

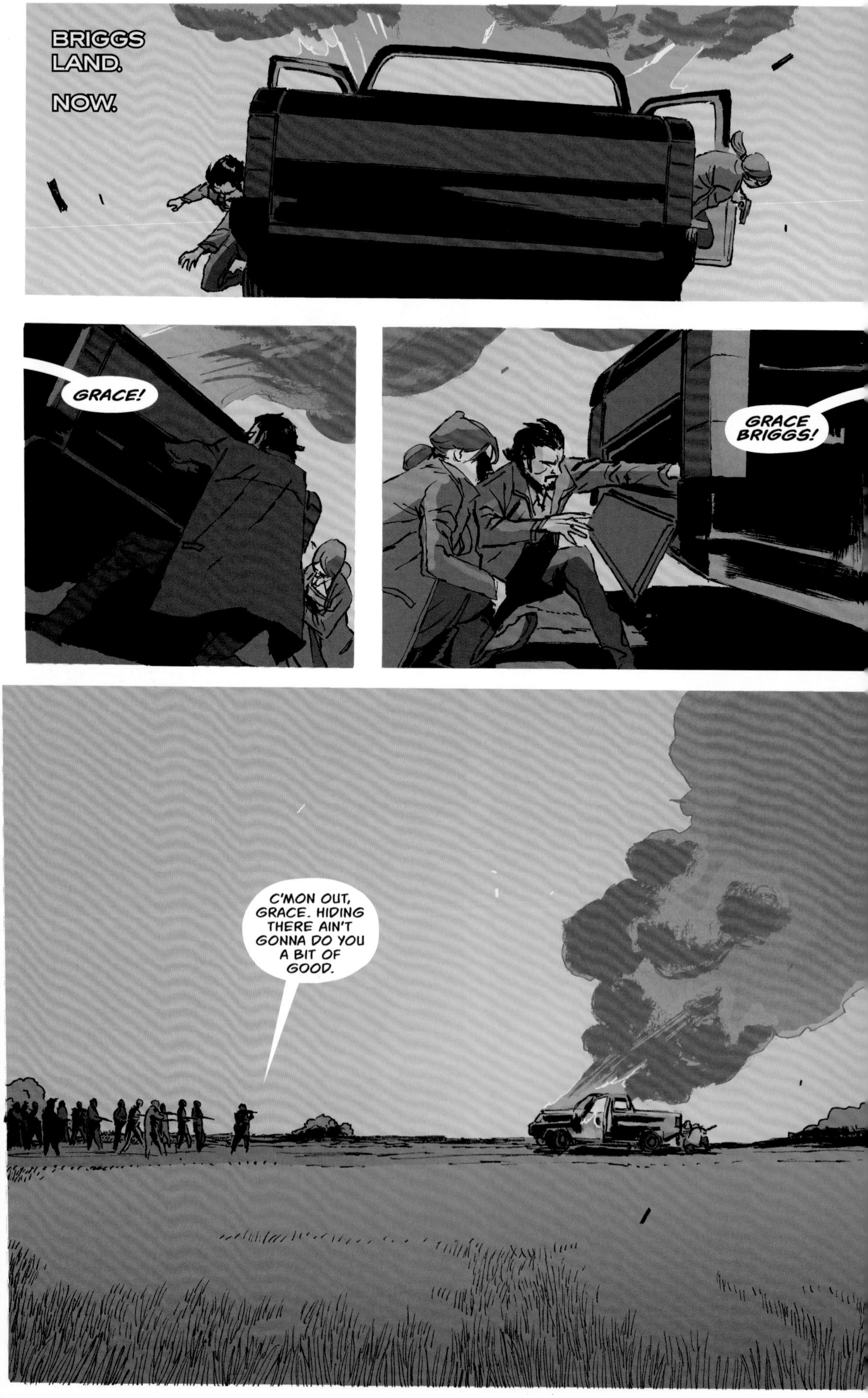
BRIGGS LAND.
NOW.
GRACE!
GRACE BRIGGS!
C'MON OUT, GRACE. HIDING THERE AIN'T GONNA DO YOU A BIT OF GOOD.

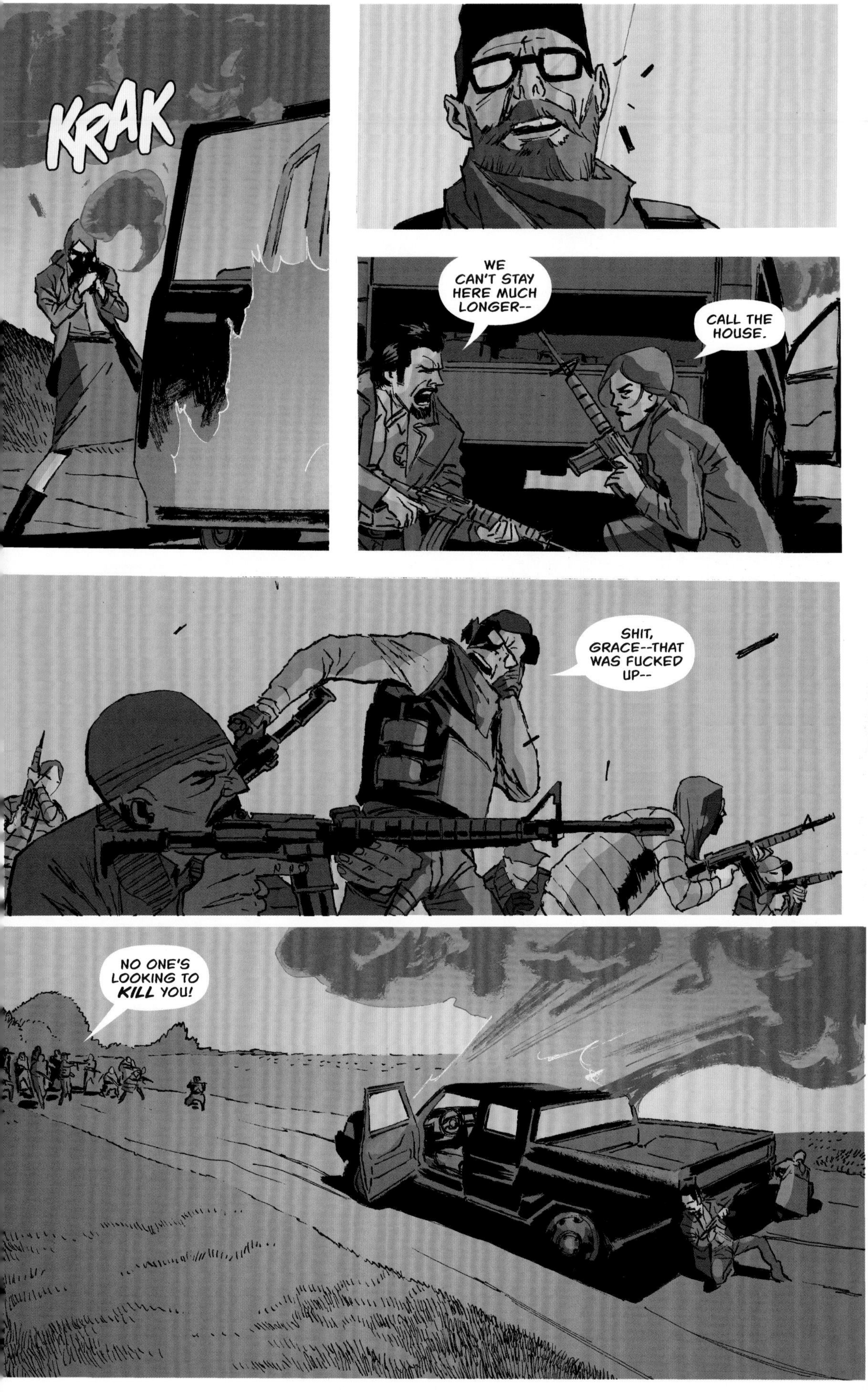
KRAK
WE CAN'T STAY HERE MUCH LONGER--
CALL THE HOUSE.
SHIT, GRACE--THAT WAS FUCKED UP--
NO ONE'S LOOKING TO *KILL* YOU!

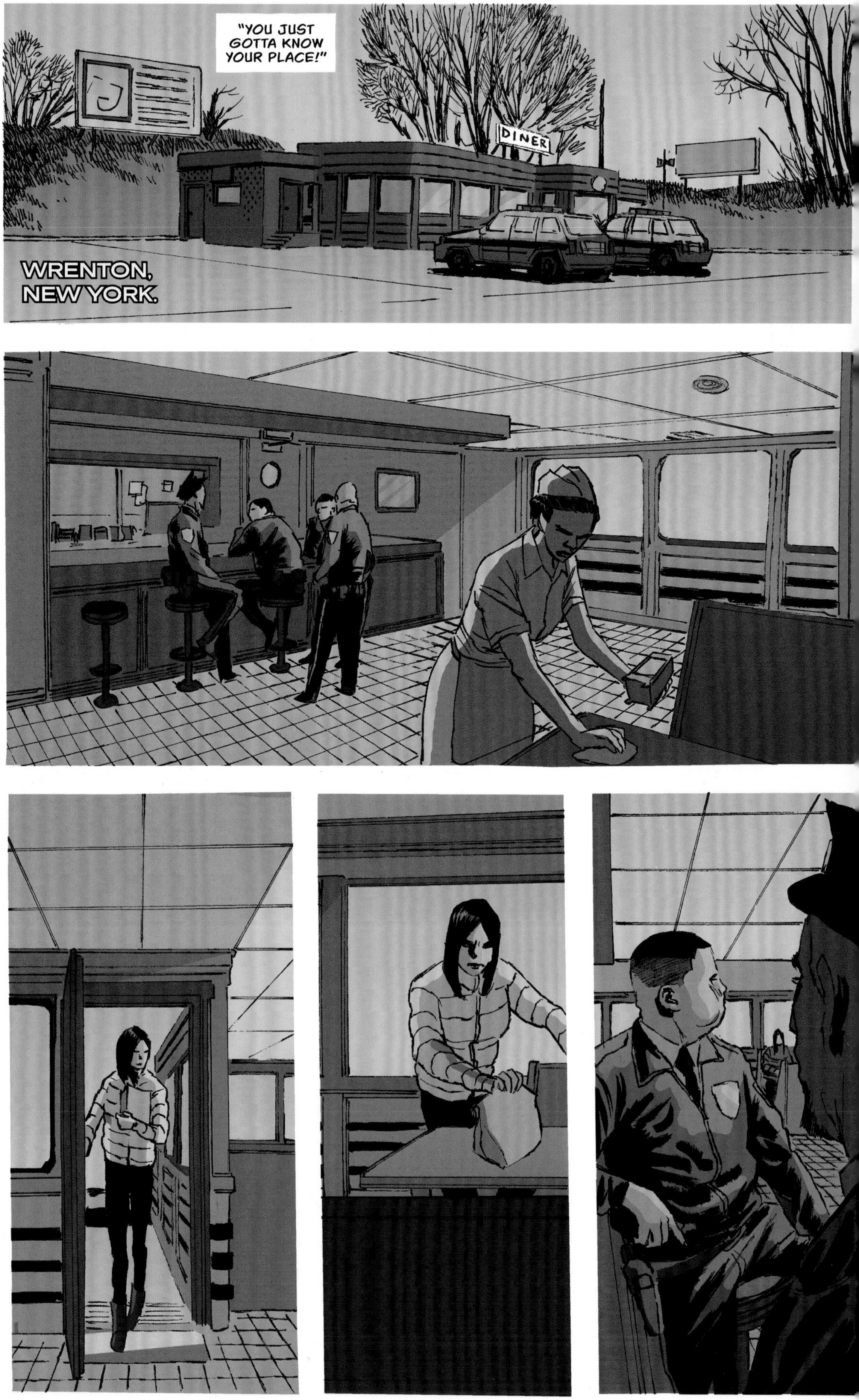
"YOU JUST GOTTA KNOW YOUR PLACE!"
DINER
WRENTON, NEW YORK.

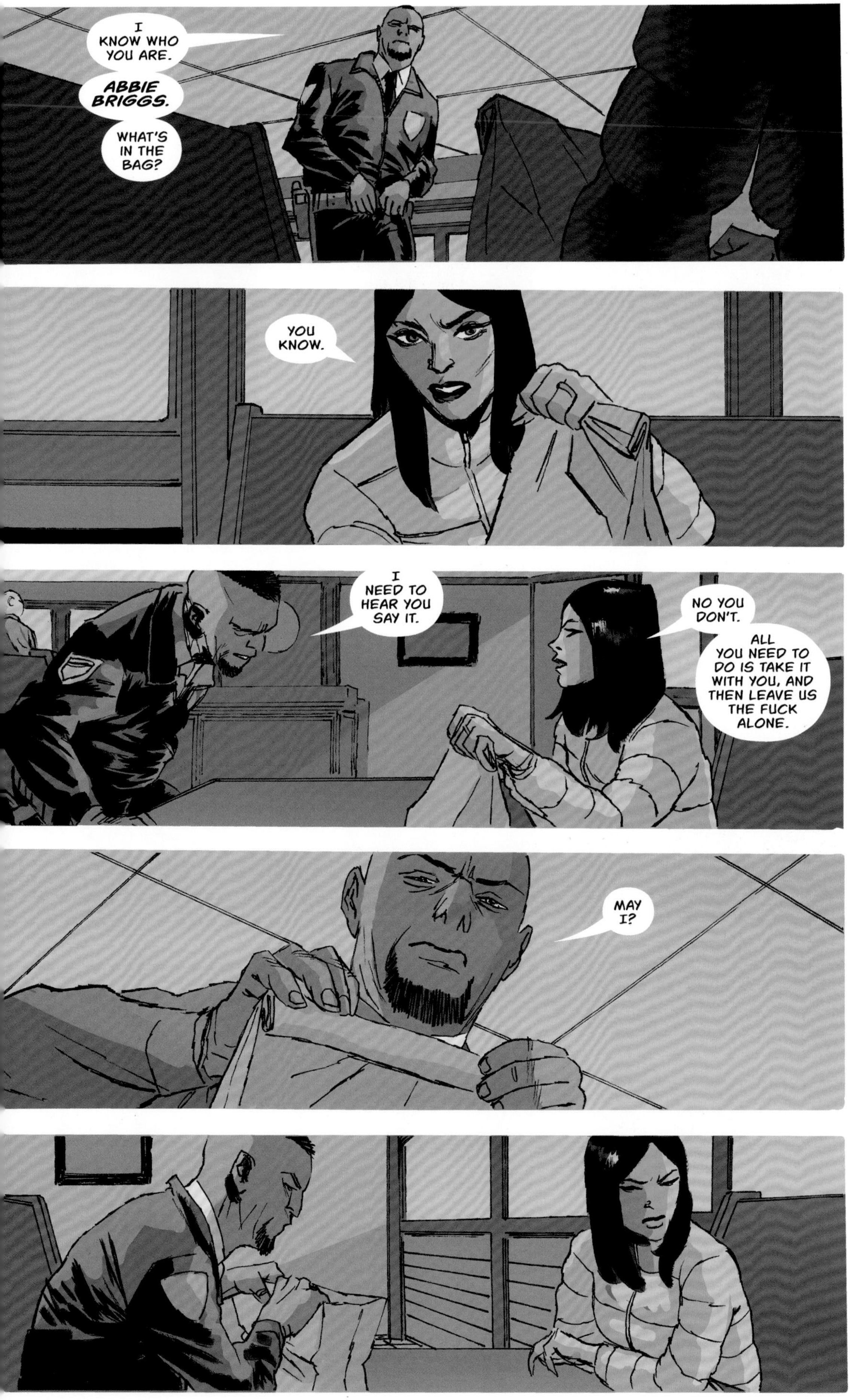
I KNOW WHO YOU ARE.
ABBIE BRIGGS.
WHAT'S IN THE BAG?
YOU KNOW.
I NEED TO HEAR YOU SAY IT.
NO YOU DON'T.
ALL YOU NEED TO DO IS TAKE IT WITH YOU, AND THEN LEAVE US THE FUCK ALONE.
MAY I?

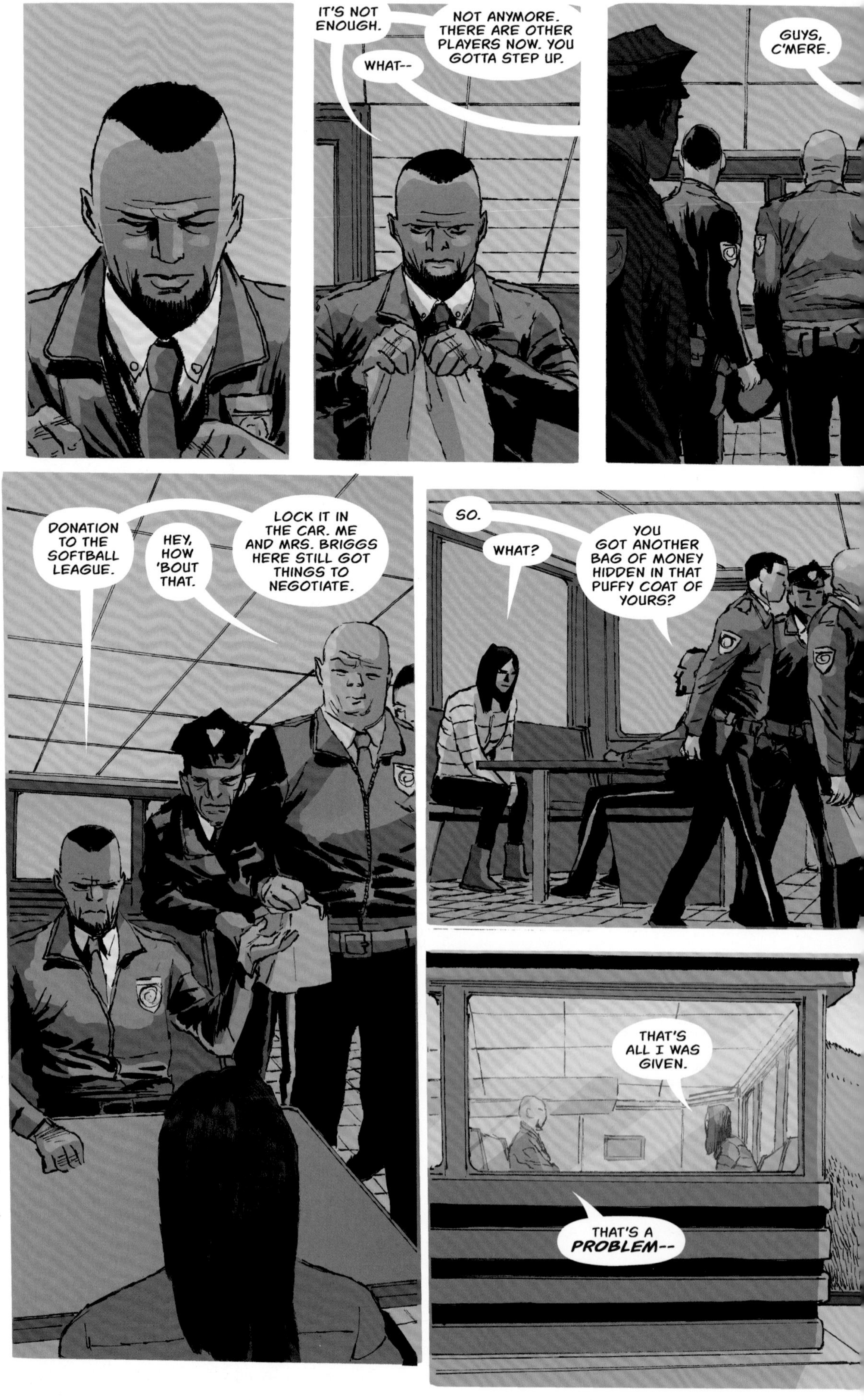
IT'S NOT ENOUGH.
WHAT--
NOT ANYMORE. THERE ARE OTHER PLAYERS NOW. YOU GOTTA STEP UP.
GUYS, C'MERE.
DONATION TO THE SOFTBALL LEAGUE.
HEY, HOW 'BOUT THAT.
LOCK IT IN THE CAR. ME AND MRS. BRIGGS HERE STILL GOT THINGS TO NEGOTIATE.
SO.
WHAT?
YOU GOT ANOTHER BAG OF MONEY HIDDEN IN THAT PUFFY COAT OF YOURS?
THAT'S ALL I WAS GIVEN.
THAT'S A *PROBLEM*--

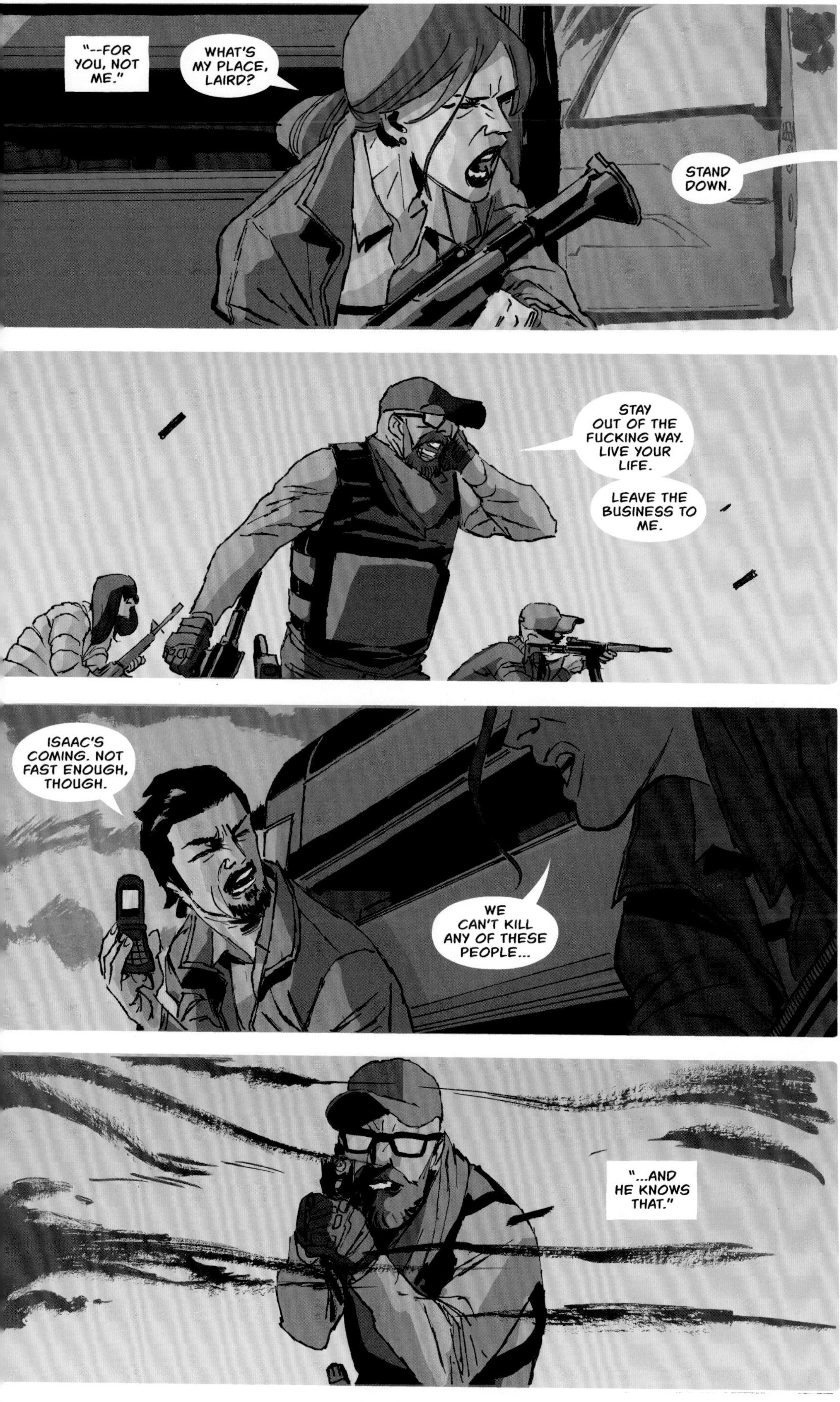
"--FOR YOU, NOT ME."
WHAT'S MY PLACE, LAIRD?
STAND DOWN.
STAY OUT OF THE FUCKING WAY. LIVE YOUR LIFE.
LEAVE THE BUSINESS TO ME.
ISAAC'S COMING. NOT FAST ENOUGH, THOUGH.
WE CAN'T KILL ANY OF THESE PEOPLE...
"...AND HE KNOWS THAT."

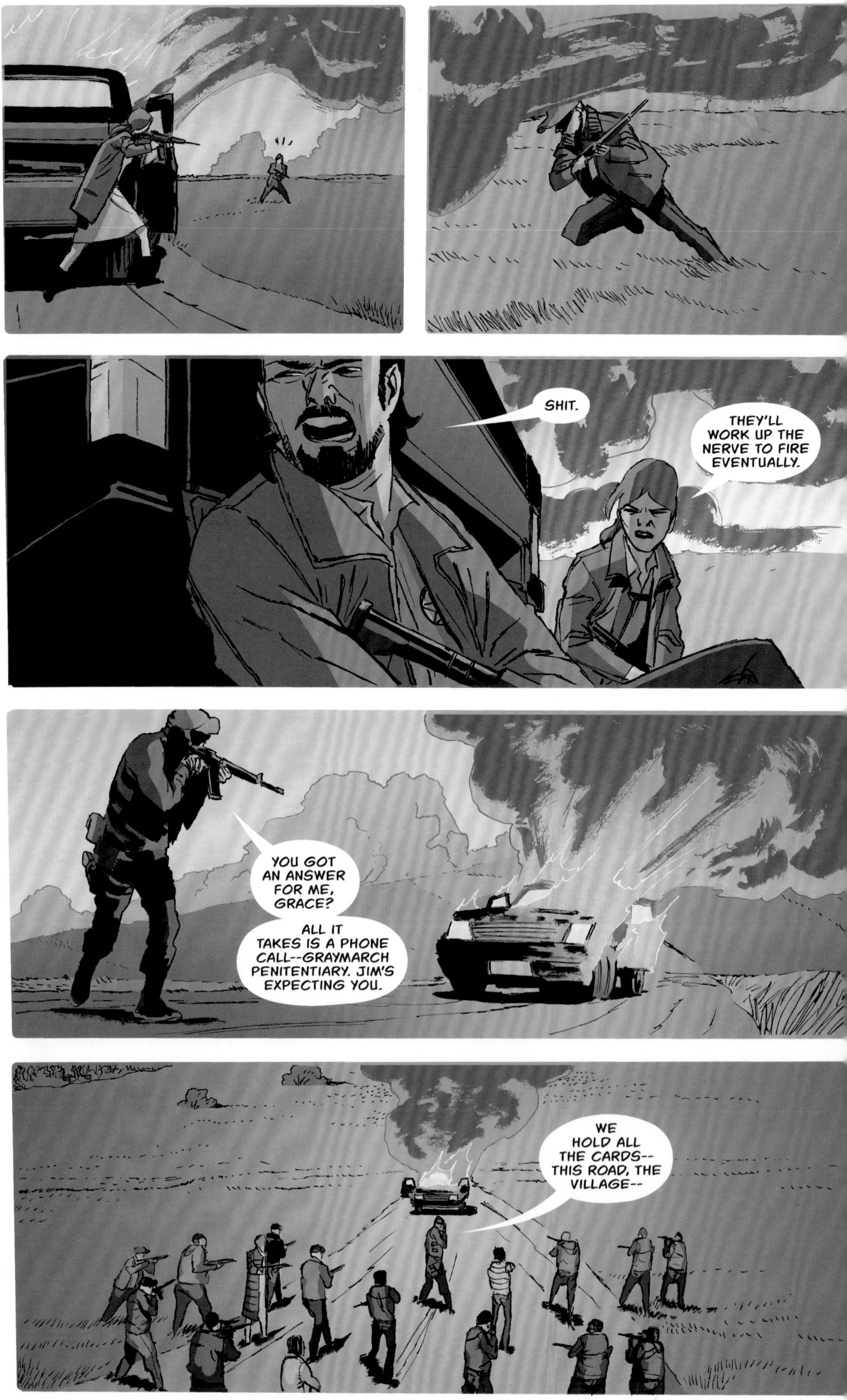
SHIT.
THEY'LL WORK UP THE NERVE TO FIRE EVENTUALLY.
YOU GOT AN ANSWER FOR ME, GRACE?
ALL IT TAKES IS A PHONE CALL--GRAYMARCH PENITENTIARY. JIM'S EXPECTING YOU.
WE HOLD ALL THE CARDS--THIS ROAD, THE VILLAGE--

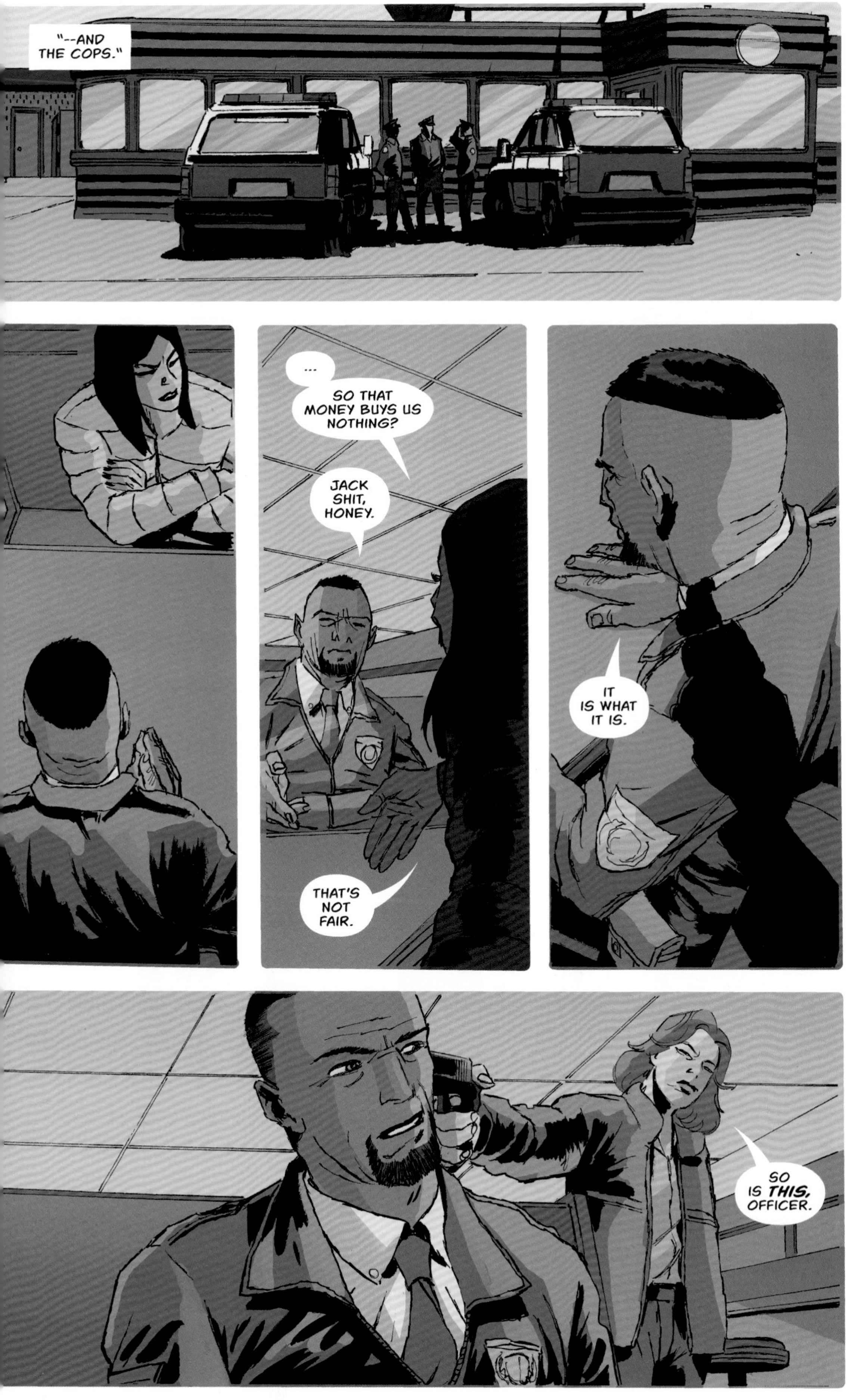
"--AND THE COPS."
...
SO THAT MONEY BUYS US NOTHING?
JACK SHIT, HONEY.
THAT'S NOT FAIR.
IT IS WHAT IT IS.
SO IS *THIS,* OFFICER.

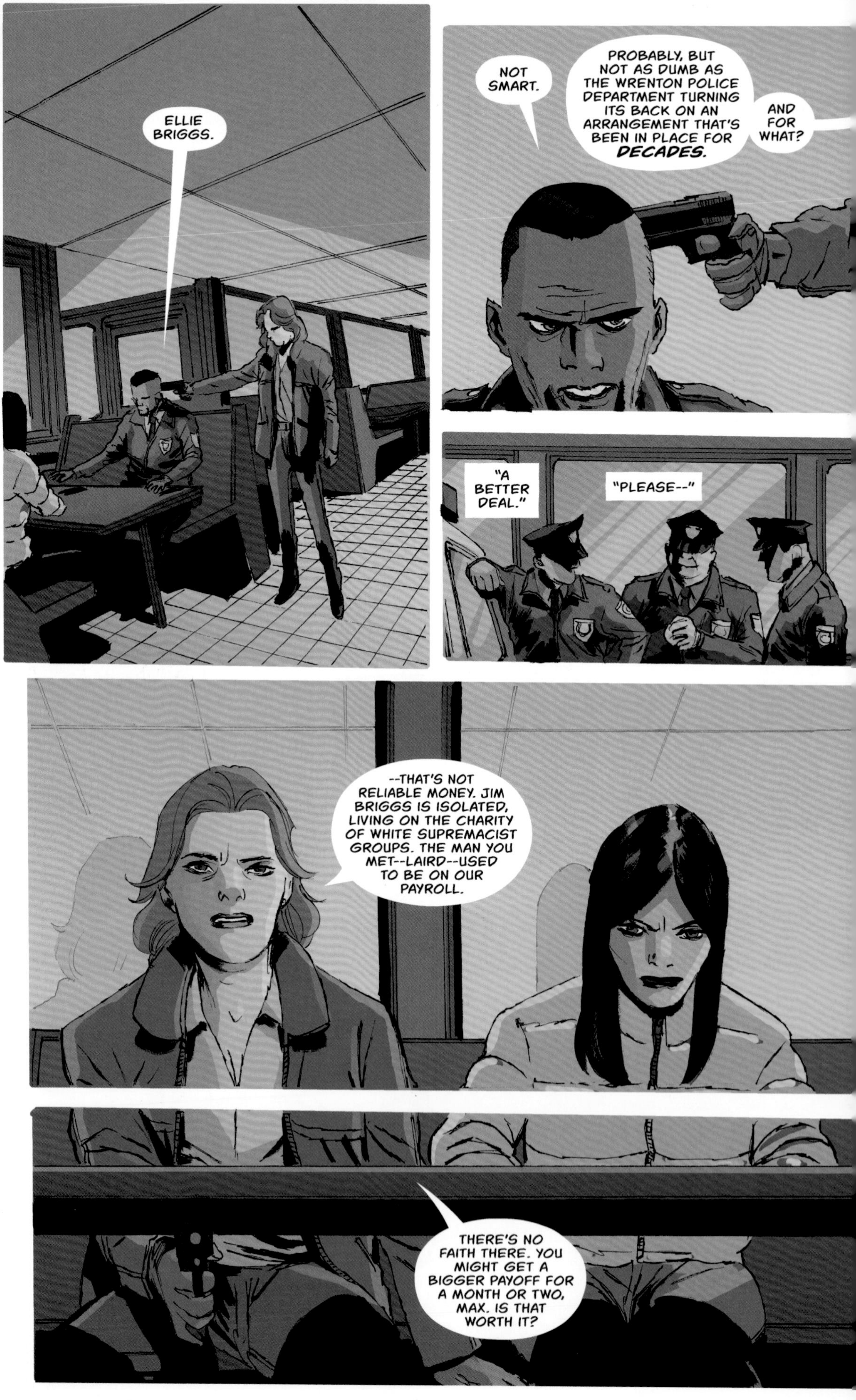
ELLIE BRIGGS.
NOT SMART.
PROBABLY, BUT NOT AS DUMB AS THE WRENTON POLICE DEPARTMENT TURNING ITS BACK ON AN ARRANGEMENT THAT'S BEEN IN PLACE FOR DECADES.
AND FOR WHAT?
"A BETTER DEAL."
"PLEASE--"
--THAT'S NOT RELIABLE MONEY. JIM BRIGGS IS ISOLATED, LIVING ON THE CHARITY OF WHITE SUPREMACIST GROUPS. THE MAN YOU MET--LAIRD--USED TO BE ON OUR PAYROLL.
THERE'S NO FAITH THERE. YOU MIGHT GET A BIGGER PAYOFF FOR A MONTH OR TWO, MAX. IS THAT WORTH IT?

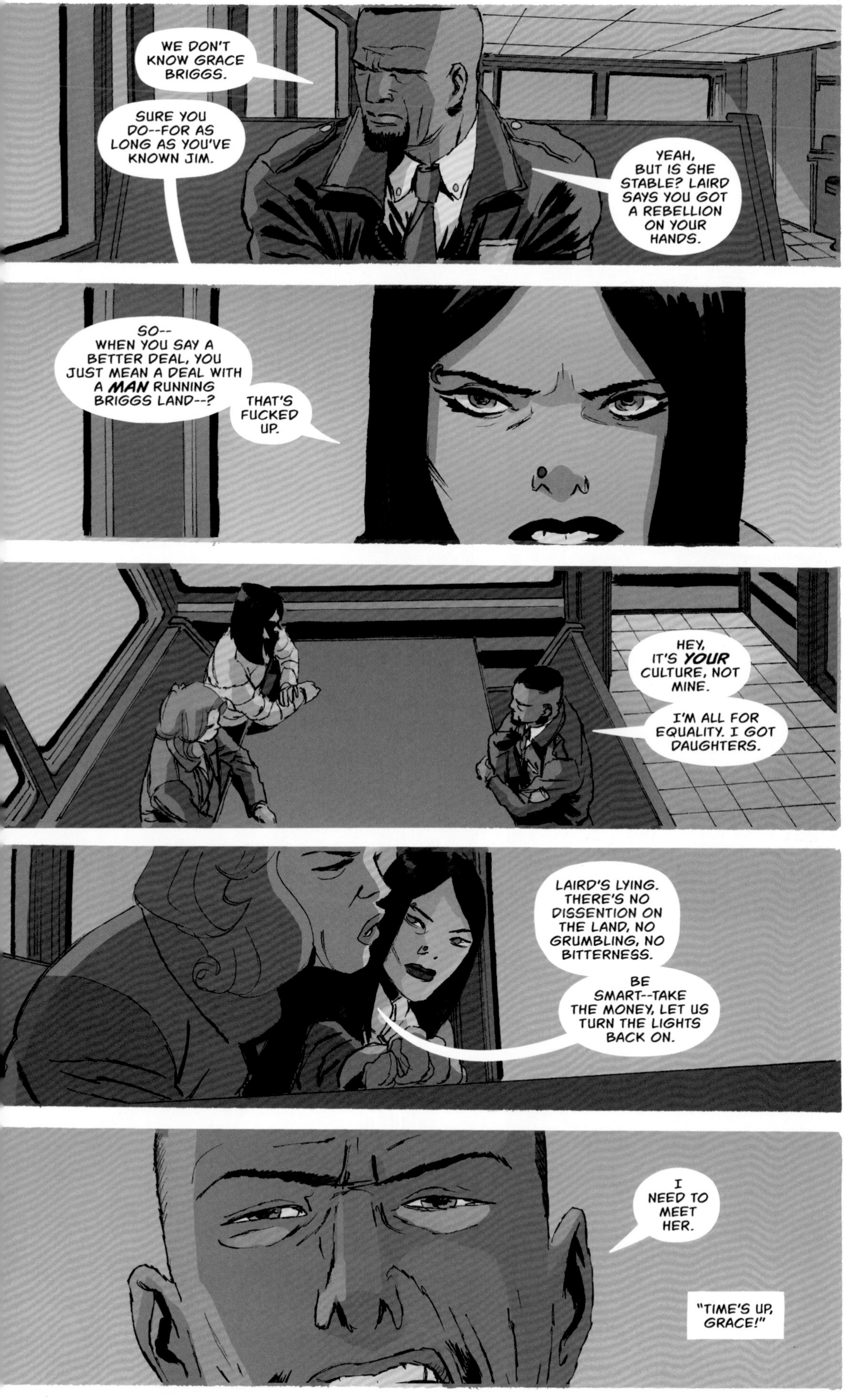
WE DON'T KNOW GRACE BRIGGS.
SURE YOU DO--FOR AS LONG AS YOU'VE KNOWN JIM.
YEAH, BUT IS SHE STABLE? LAIRD SAYS YOU GOT A REBELLION ON YOUR HANDS.
SO-- WHEN YOU SAY A BETTER DEAL, YOU JUST MEAN A DEAL WITH A MAN RUNNING BRIGGS LAND--?
THAT'S FUCKED UP.
HEY, IT'S YOUR CULTURE, NOT MINE.
I'M ALL FOR EQUALITY. I GOT DAUGHTERS.
LAIRD'S LYING. THERE'S NO DISSENTION ON THE LAND, NO GRUMBLING, NO BITTERNESS.
BE SMART--TAKE THE MONEY, LET US TURN THE LIGHTS BACK ON.
I NEED TO MEET HER.
"TIME'S UP, GRACE!"

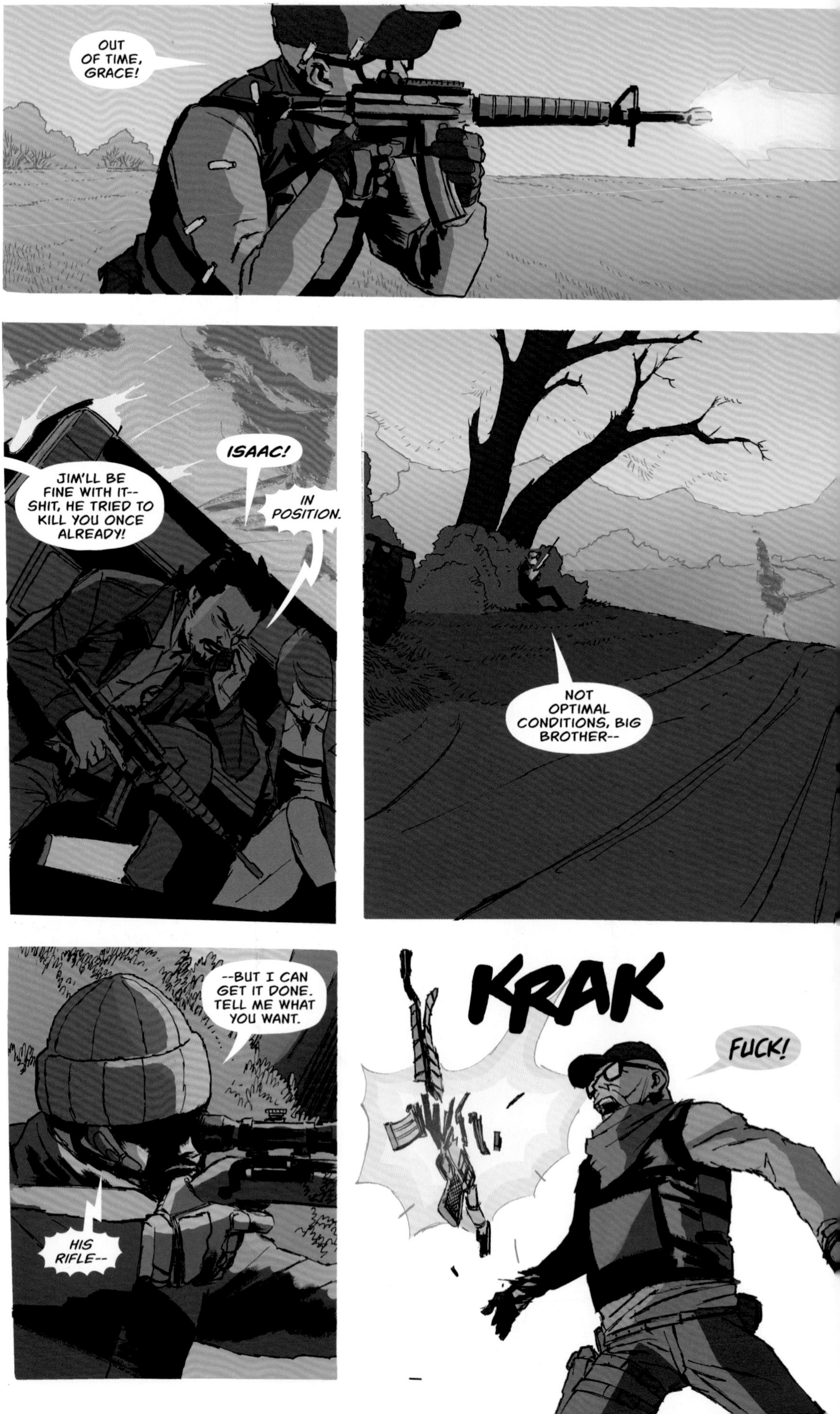
OUT OF TIME, GRACE!
JIM'LL BE FINE WITH IT-- SHIT, HE TRIED TO KILL YOU ONCE ALREADY!
ISAAC!
IN POSITION.
NOT OPTIMAL CONDITIONS, BIG BROTHER--
--BUT I CAN GET IT DONE. TELL ME WHAT YOU WANT.
HIS RIFLE--
KRAK
FUCK!

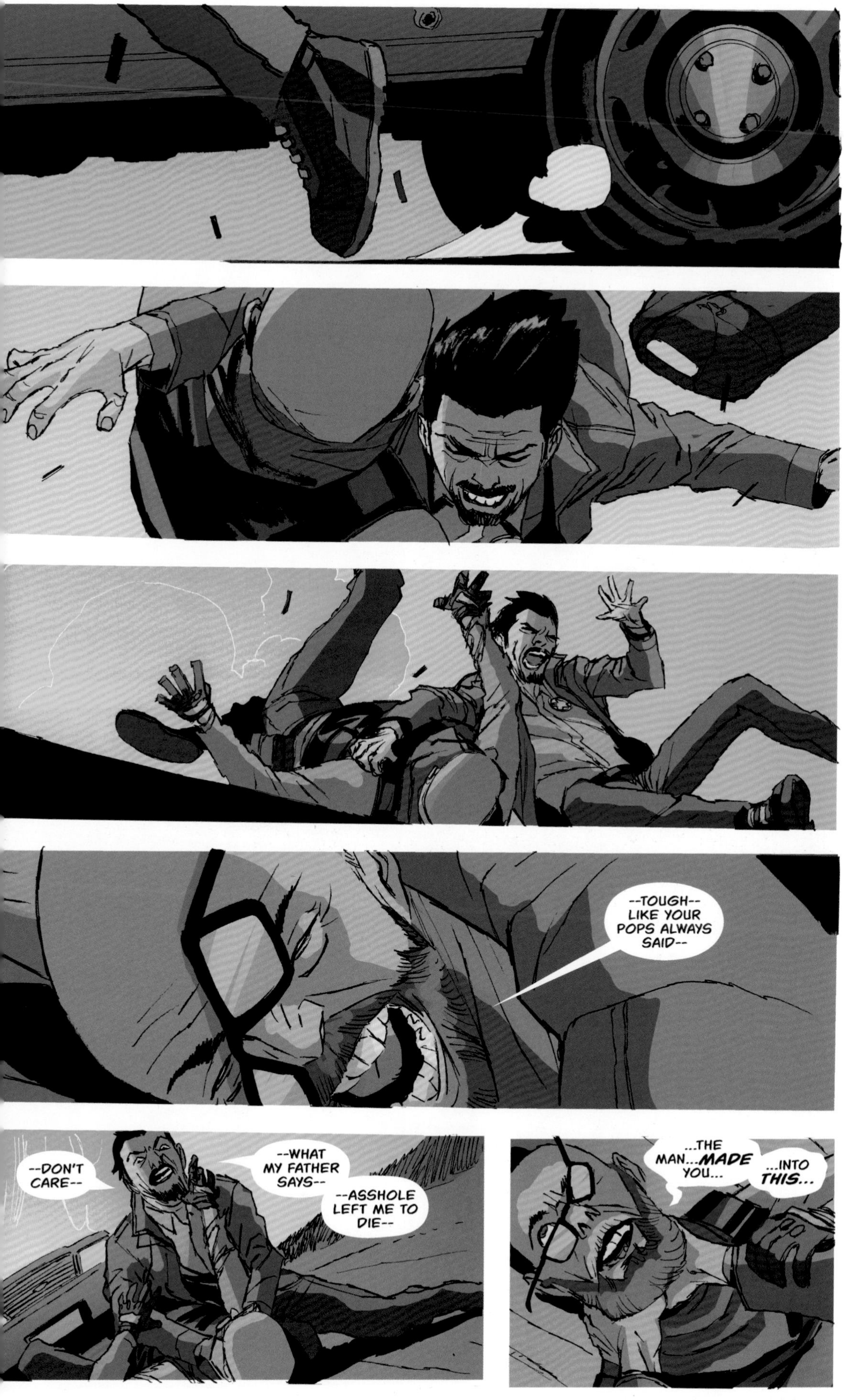
--TOUGH-- LIKE YOUR POPS ALWAYS SAID--
--DON'T CARE--
--WHAT MY FATHER SAYS--
--ASSHOLE LEFT ME TO DIE--
...THE MAN...MADE YOU...
...INTO THIS...

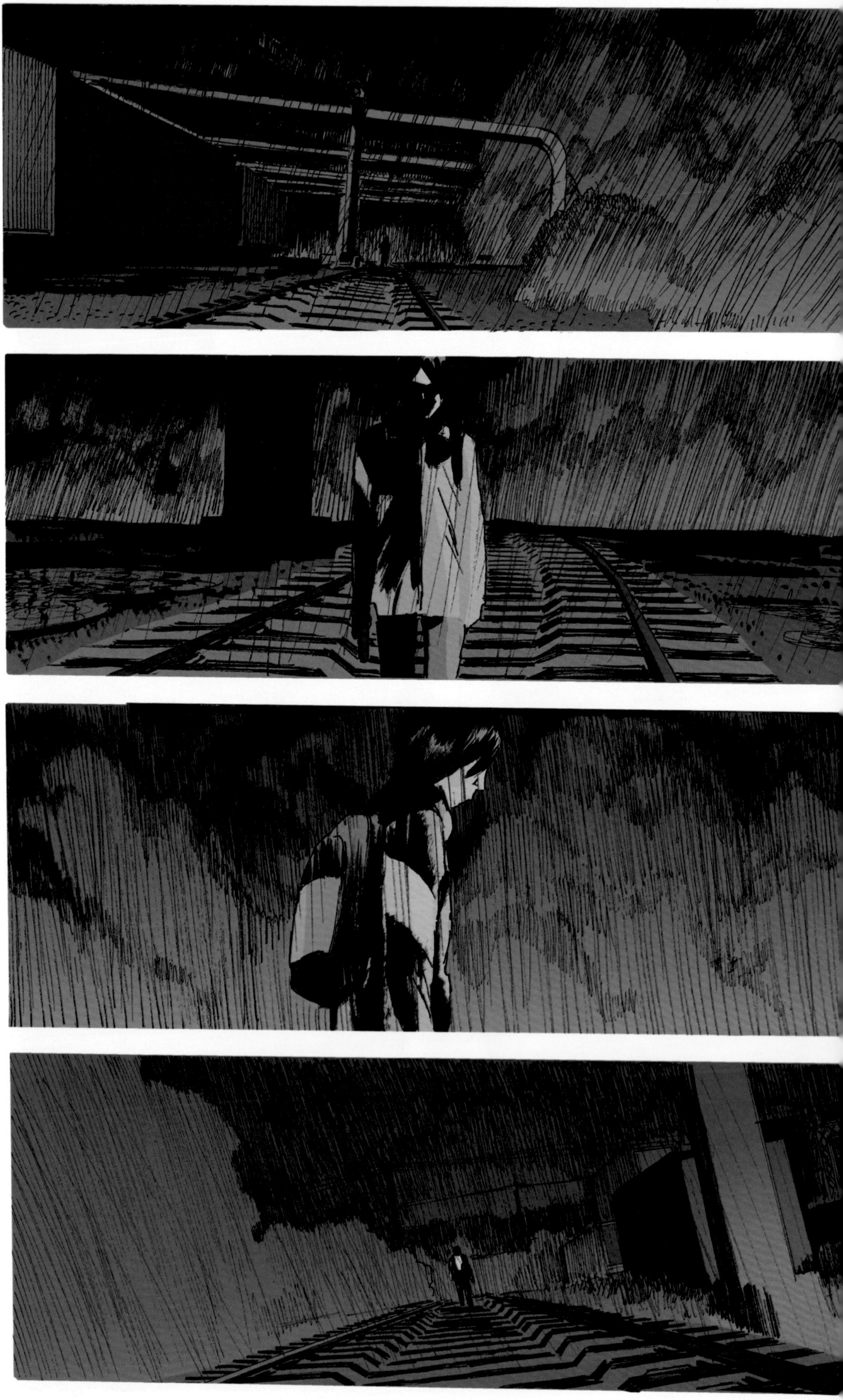

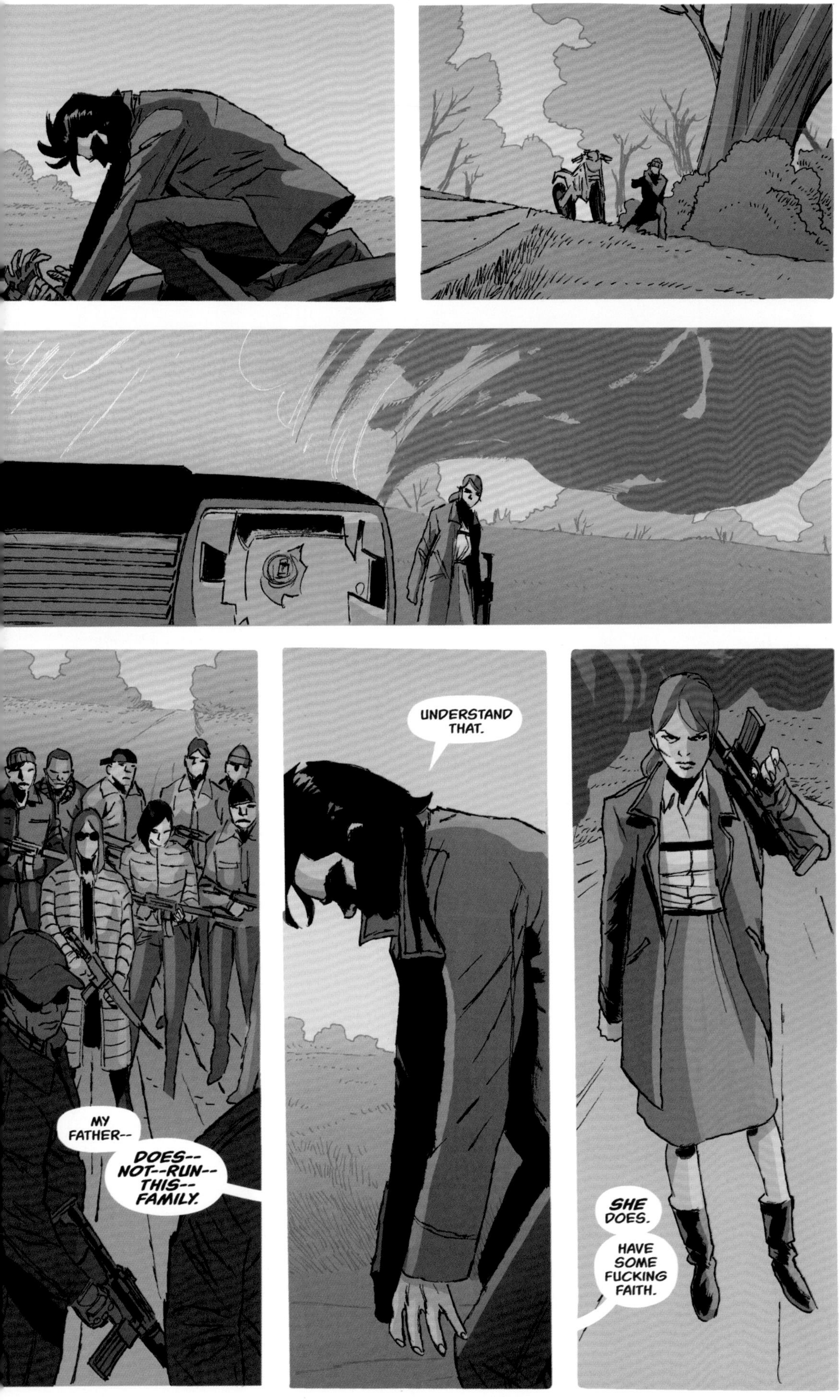
MY FATHER--
DOES-- NOT--RUN-- THIS-- FAMILY.
UNDERSTAND THAT.
SHE DOES.
HAVE SOME FUCKING FAITH.

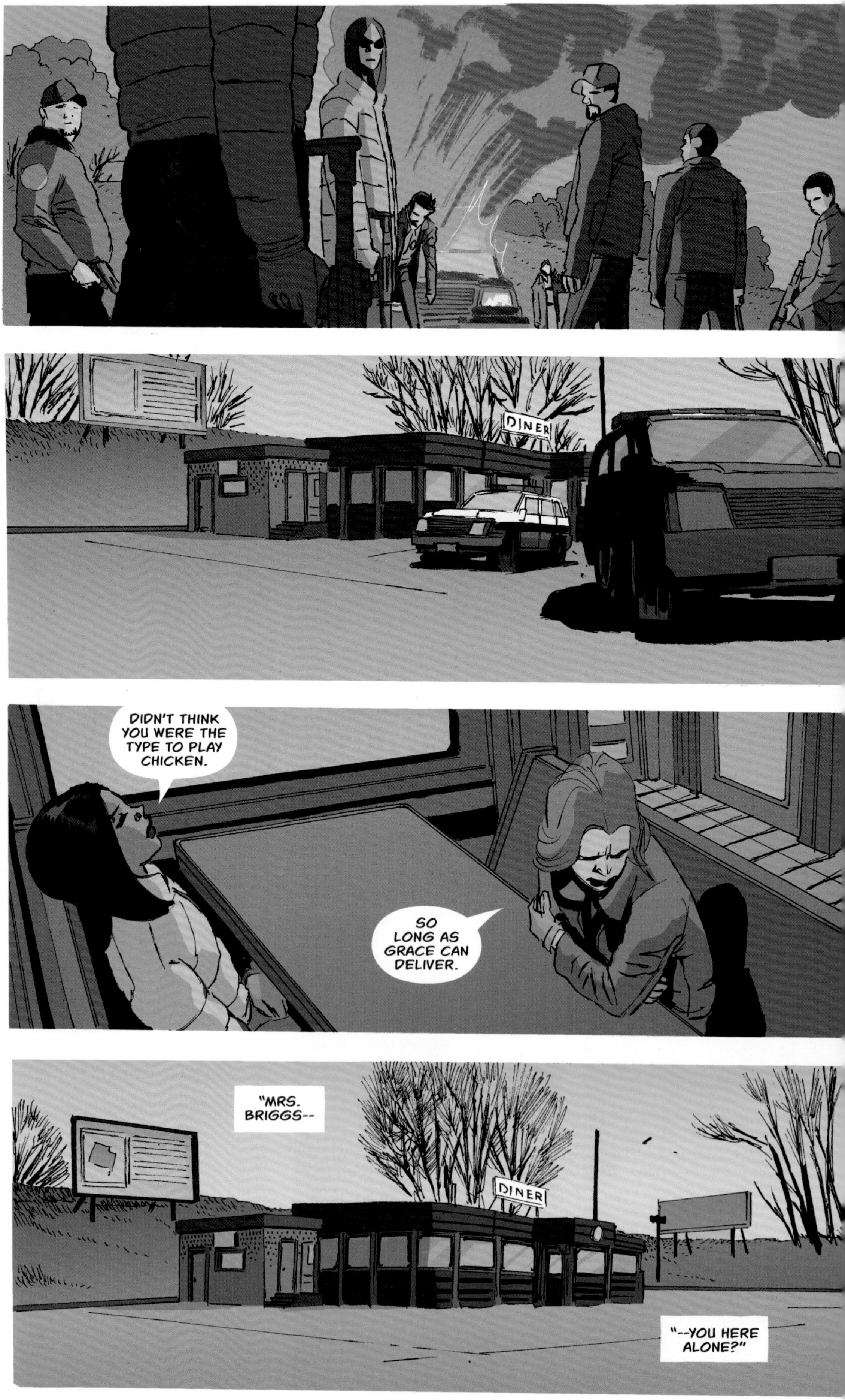
DINER
DIDN'T THINK YOU WERE THE TYPE TO PLAY CHICKEN.
SO LONG AS GRACE CAN DELIVER.
"MRS. BRIGGS--
DINER
"--YOU HERE ALONE?"

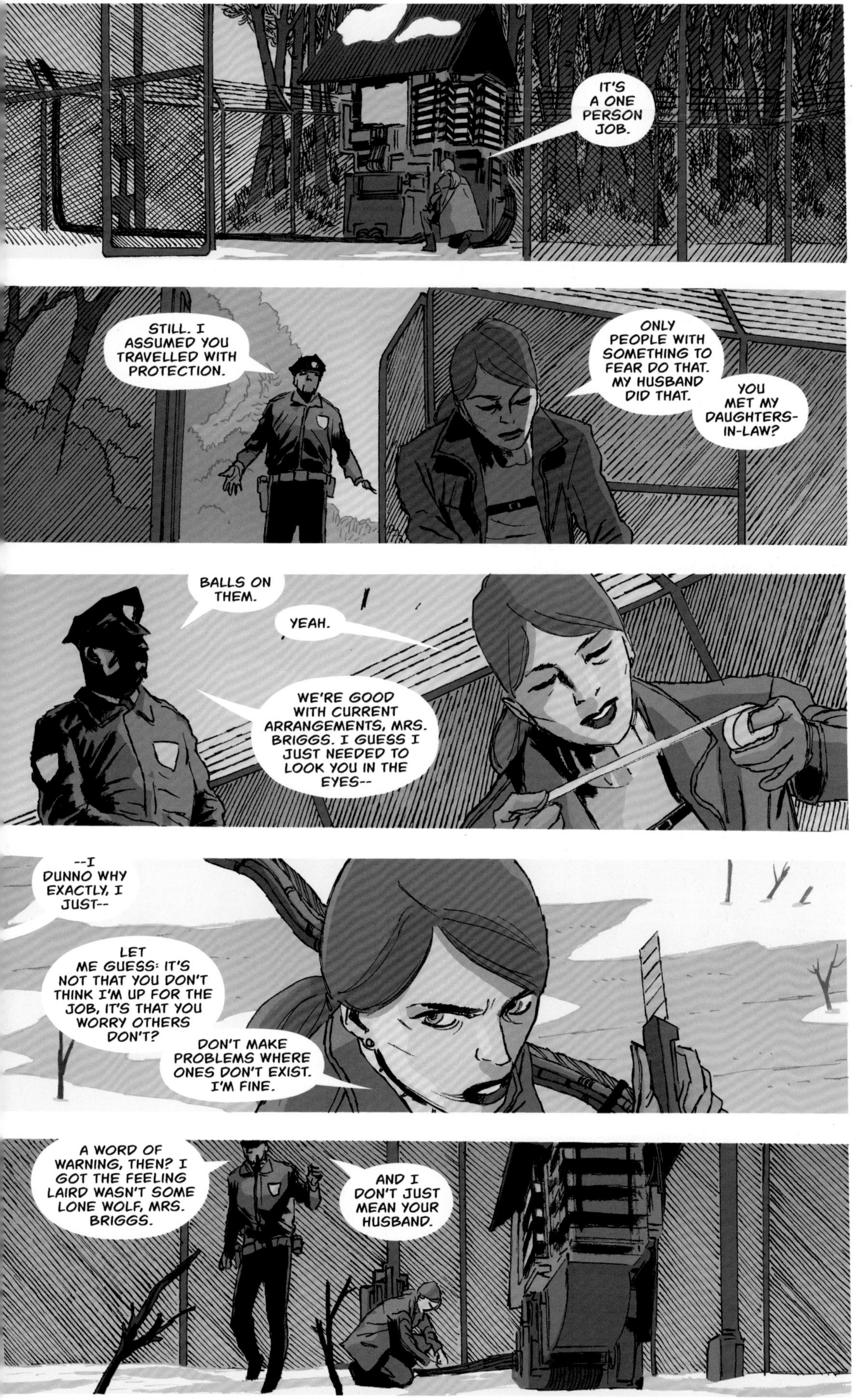
IT'S A ONE PERSON JOB.
STILL. I ASSUMED YOU TRAVELLED WITH PROTECTION.
ONLY PEOPLE WITH SOMETHING TO FEAR DO THAT. MY HUSBAND DID THAT.
YOU MET MY DAUGHTERS-IN-LAW?
BALLS ON THEM.
YEAH.
WE'RE GOOD WITH CURRENT ARRANGEMENTS, MRS. BRIGGS. I GUESS I JUST NEEDED TO LOOK YOU IN THE EYES--
--I DUNNO WHY EXACTLY, I JUST--
LET ME GUESS: IT'S NOT THAT YOU DON'T THINK I'M UP FOR THE JOB, IT'S THAT YOU WORRY OTHERS DON'T?
DON'T MAKE PROBLEMS WHERE ONES DON'T EXIST. I'M FINE.
A WORD OF WARNING, THEN? I GOT THE FEELING LAIRD WASN'T SOME LONE WOLF, MRS. BRIGGS.
AND I DON'T JUST MEAN YOUR HUSBAND.

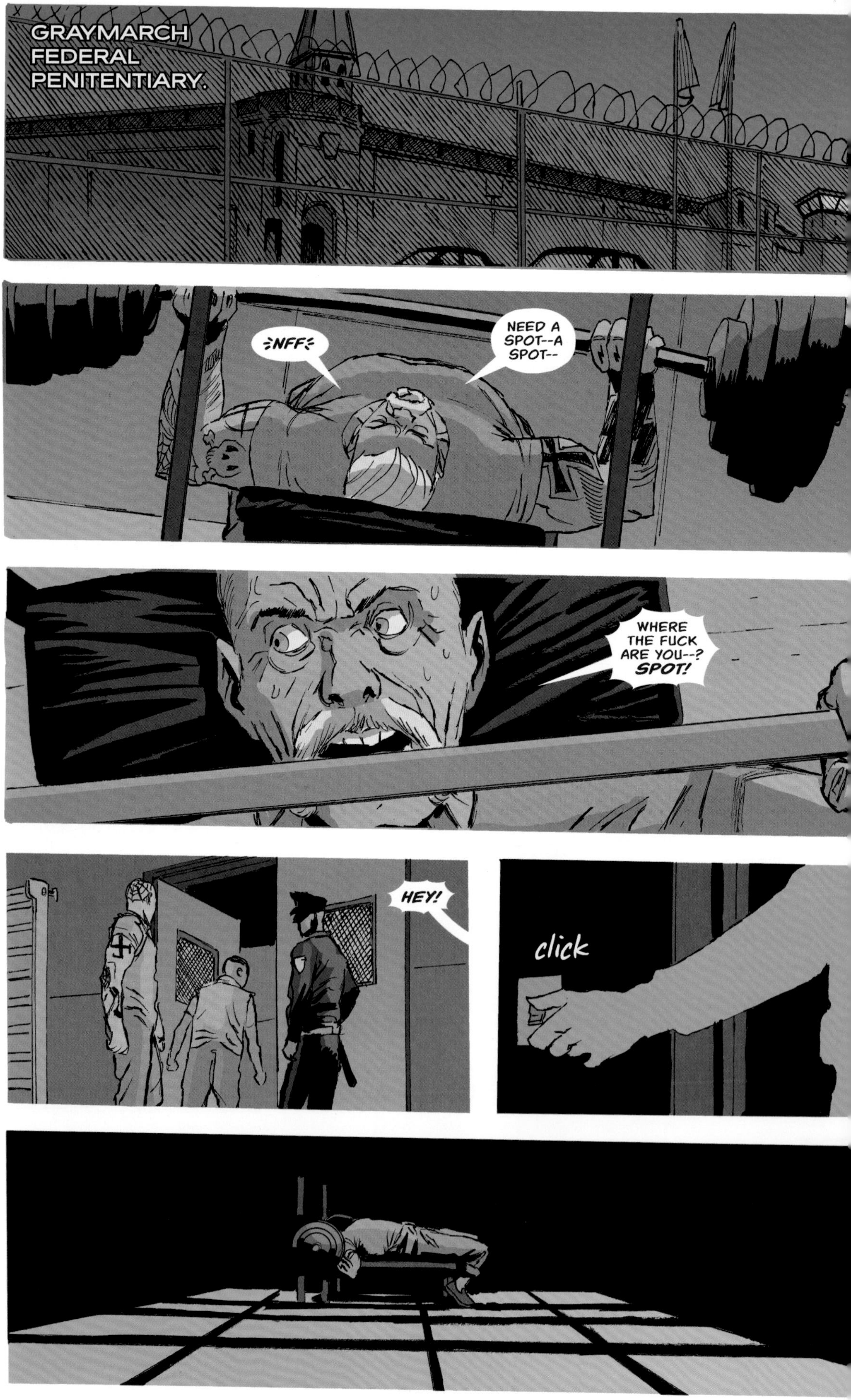
GRAYMARCH FEDERAL PENITENTIARY.
NFF
NEED A SPOT--A SPOT--
WHERE THE FUCK ARE YOU--? SPOT!
HEY!
click

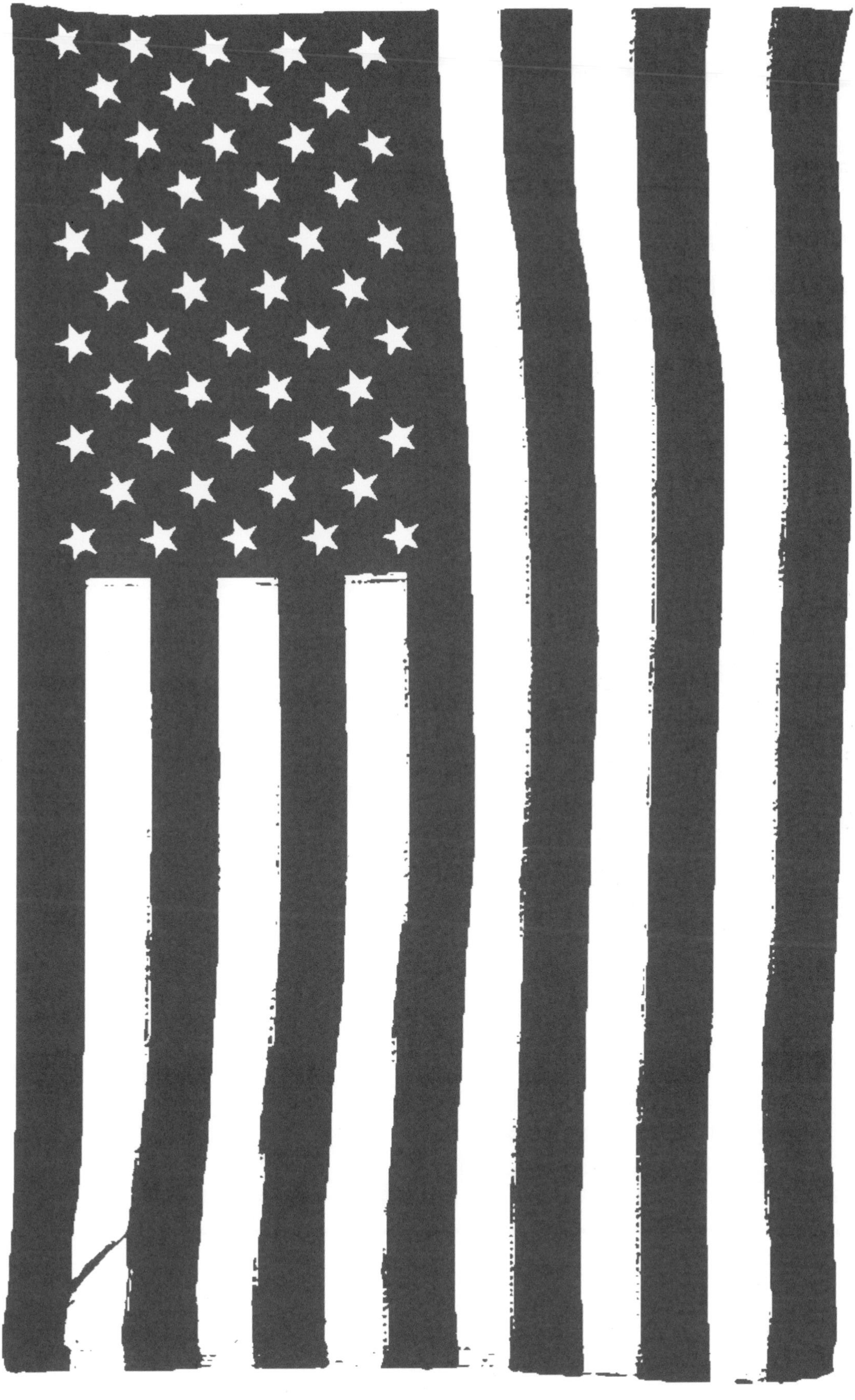

THE VILLAGE

THIS STORY OCCURS BETWEEN *BRIGGS LAND: STATE OF GRACE*
CHAPTER TWO AND CHAPTER THREE.

SCRIPT / BRIAN WOOD

ART / WERTHER DELL'EDERA

COLORS / LEE LOUGHRIDGE

LETTERING / NATE PIEKOS OF BLAMBOT®

BRIGGS LAND CREATED BY BRIAN WOOD

BRIGGS LAND

AN AMERICAN FAMILY UNDER SIEGE

THE VILLAGE

Briggs Land created by Brian Wood

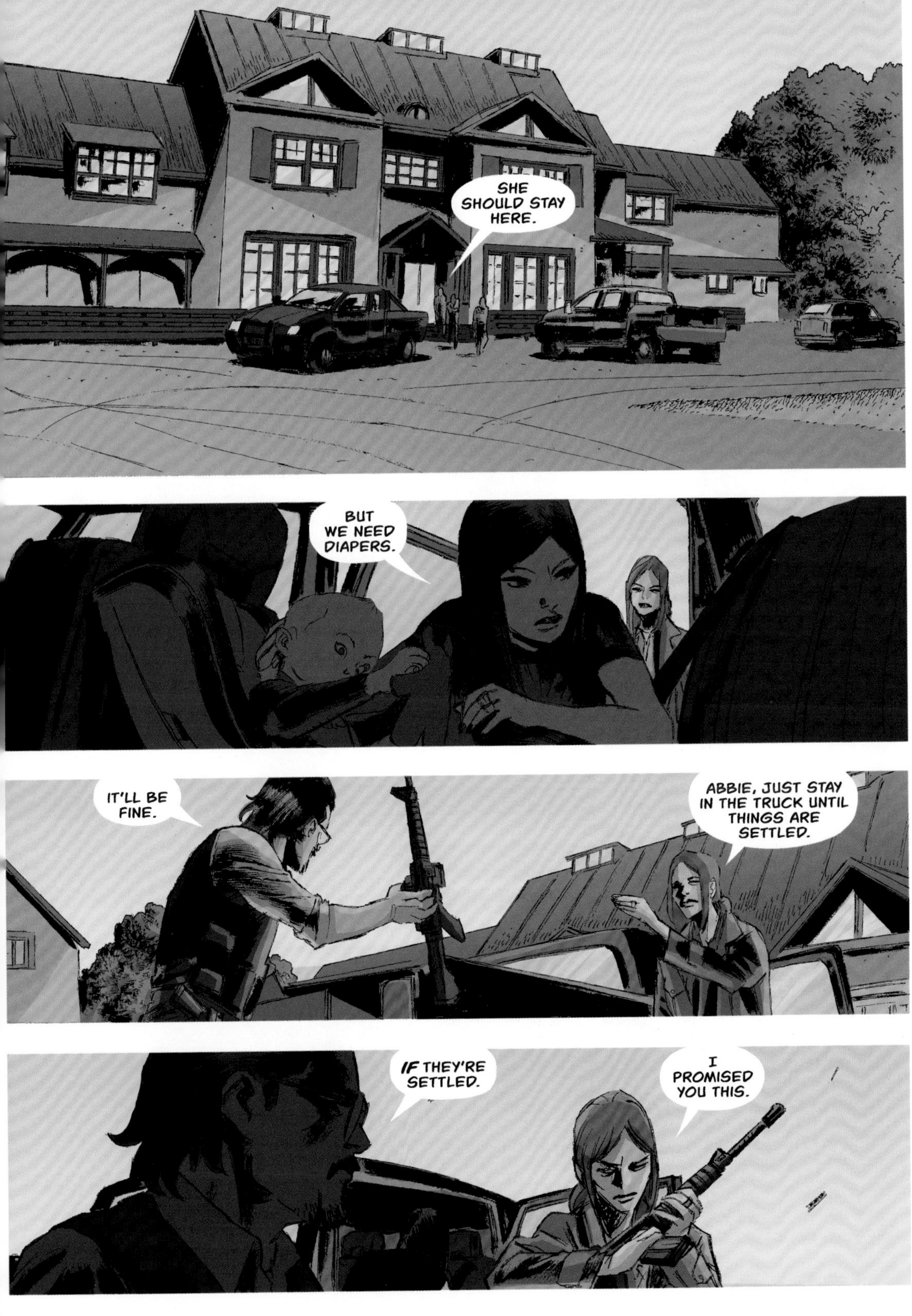

SHE SHOULD STAY HERE.
BUT WE NEED DIAPERS.
IT'LL BE FINE.
ABBIE, JUST STAY IN THE TRUCK UNTIL THINGS ARE SETTLED.
IF THEY'RE SETTLED.
I PROMISED YOU THIS.

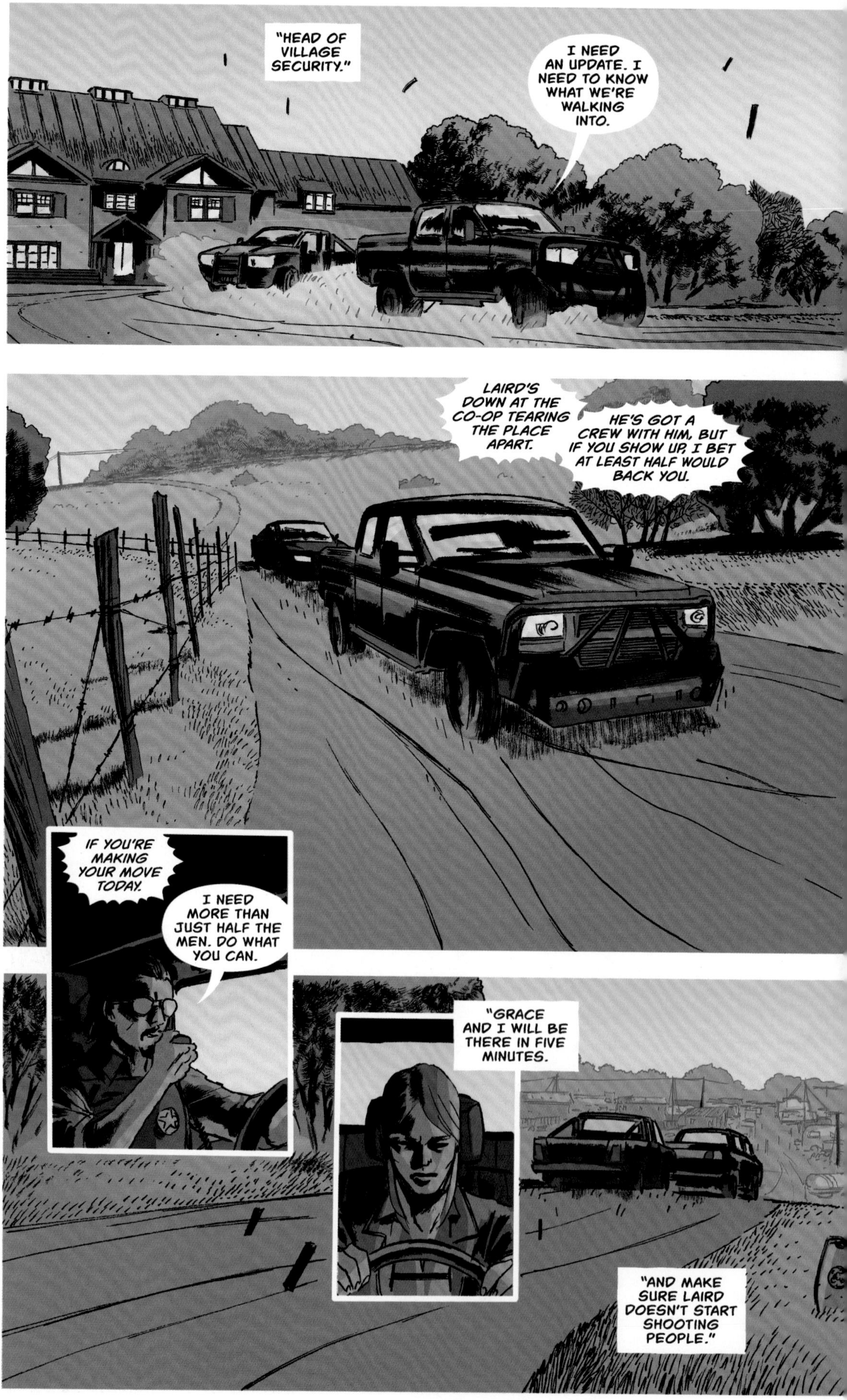
"HEAD OF VILLAGE SECURITY."
I NEED AN UPDATE. I NEED TO KNOW WHAT WE'RE WALKING INTO.
LAIRD'S DOWN AT THE CO-OP TEARING THE PLACE APART.
HE'S GOT A CREW WITH HIM, BUT IF YOU SHOW UP, I BET AT LEAST HALF WOULD BACK YOU.
IF YOU'RE MAKING YOUR MOVE TODAY.
I NEED MORE THAN JUST HALF THE MEN. DO WHAT YOU CAN.
"GRACE AND I WILL BE THERE IN FIVE MINUTES.
"AND MAKE SURE LAIRD DOESN'T START SHOOTING PEOPLE."

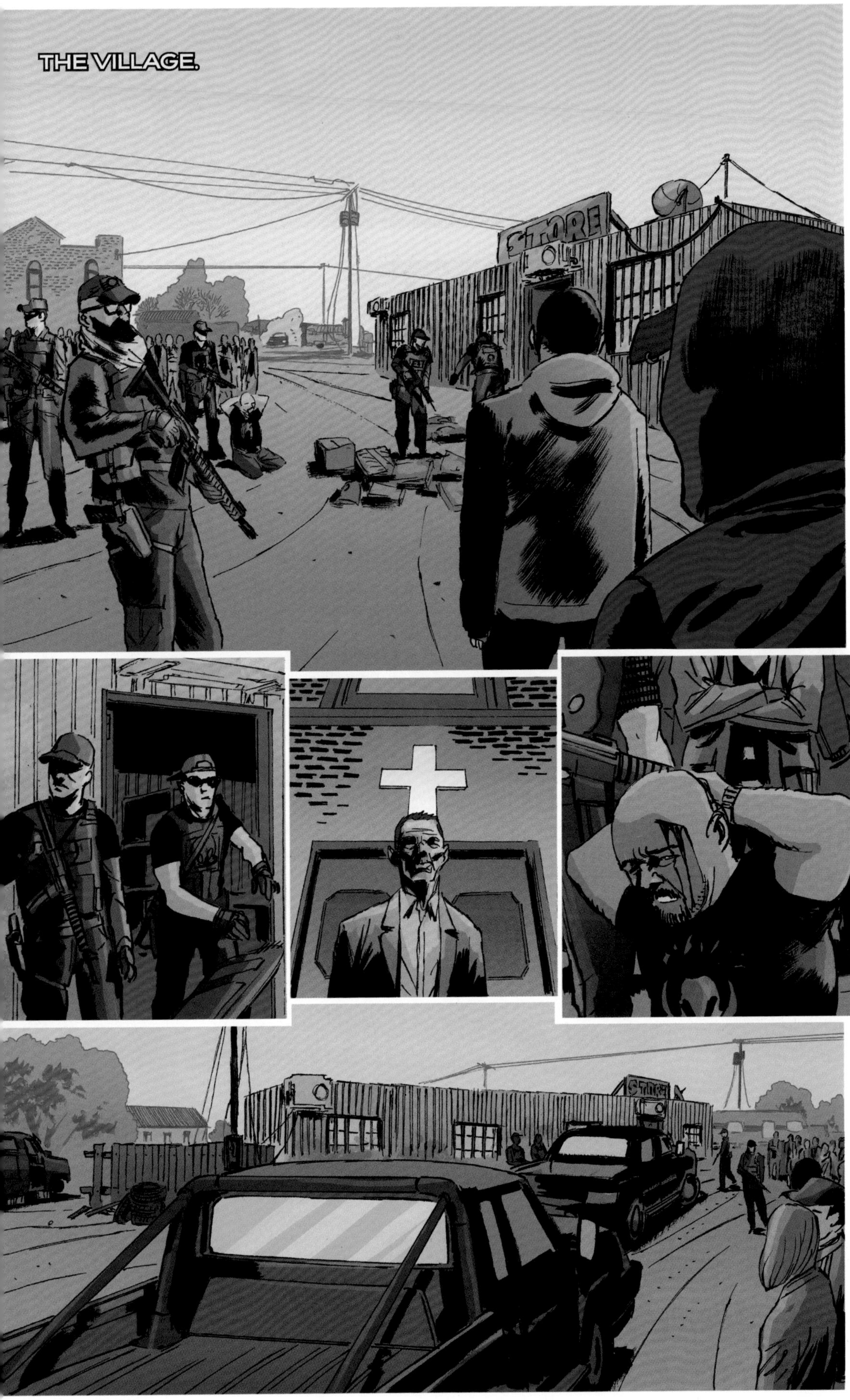
THE VILLAGE.
STORE
STORE

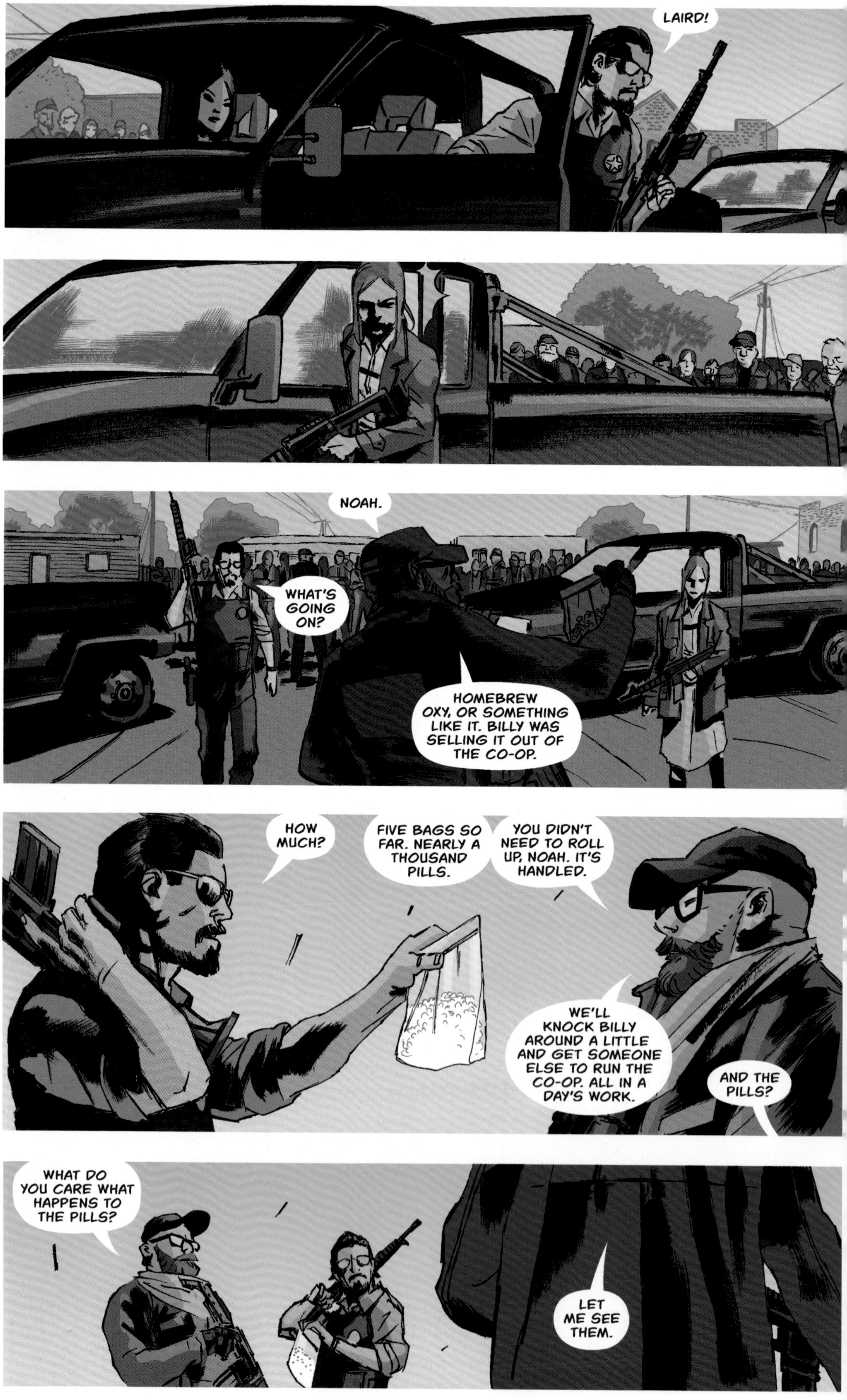
LAIRD!
NOAH.
WHAT'S GOING ON?
HOMEBREW OXY, OR SOMETHING LIKE IT. BILLY WAS SELLING IT OUT OF THE CO-OP.
HOW MUCH?
FIVE BAGS SO FAR. NEARLY A THOUSAND PILLS.
YOU DIDN'T NEED TO ROLL UP, NOAH. IT'S HANDLED.
WE'LL KNOCK BILLY AROUND A LITTLE AND GET SOMEONE ELSE TO RUN THE CO-OP. ALL IN A DAY'S WORK.
AND THE PILLS?
WHAT DO YOU CARE WHAT HAPPENS TO THE PILLS?
LET ME SEE THEM.

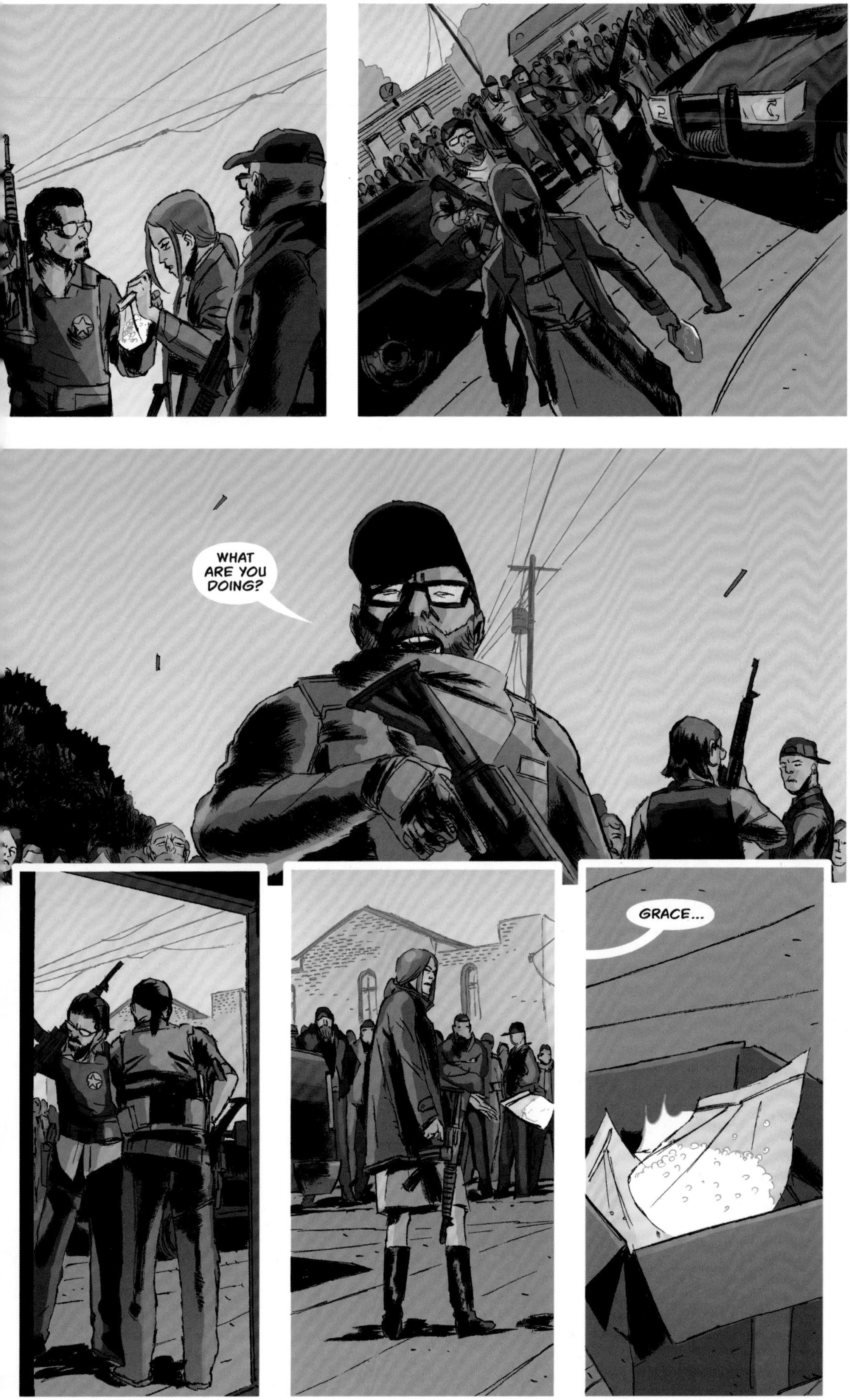

WHAT ARE YOU DOING?
GRACE...

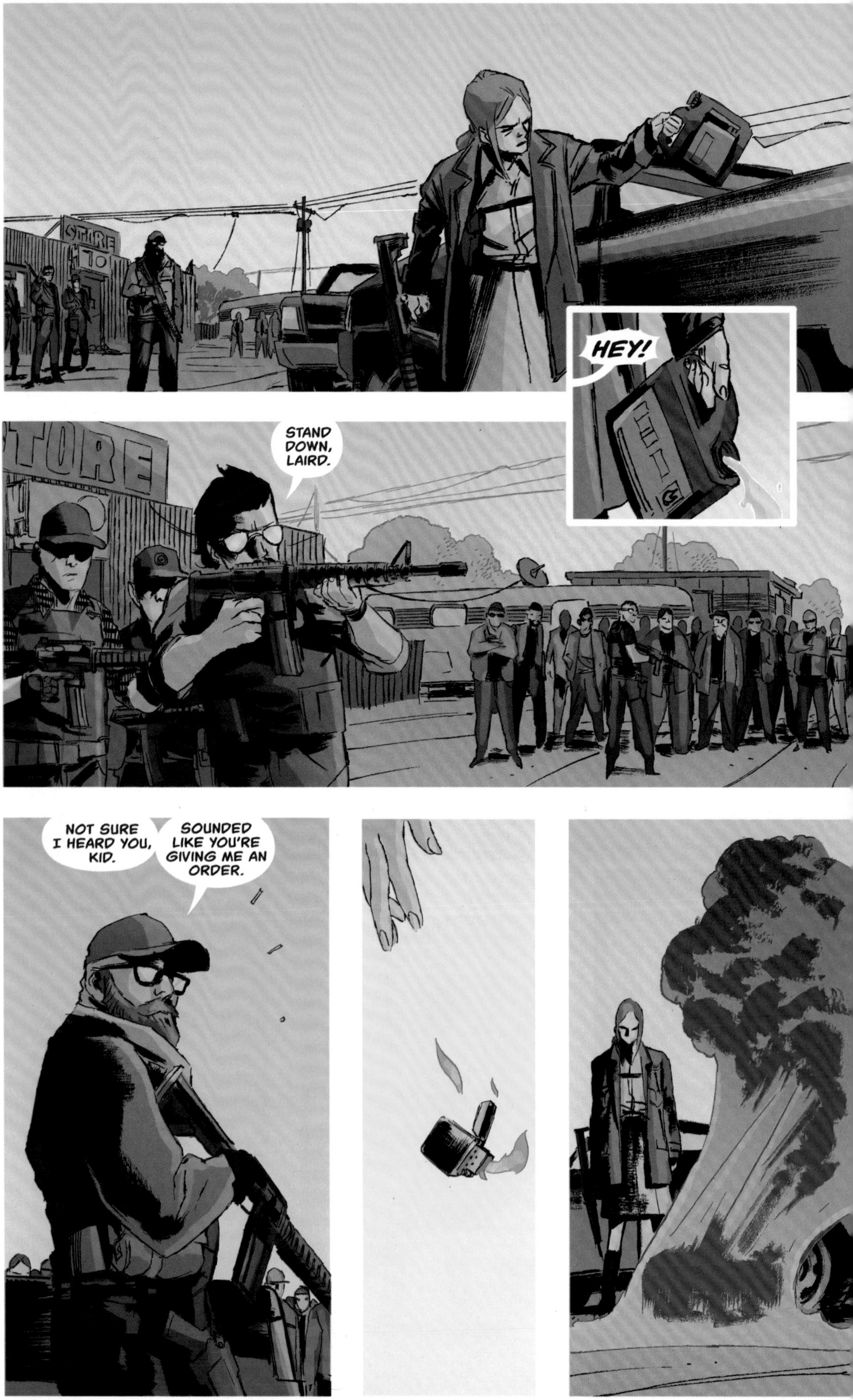
STORE
HEY!
STAND DOWN, LAIRD.
STORE
NOT SURE I HEARD YOU, KID.
SOUNDED LIKE YOU'RE GIVING ME AN ORDER.

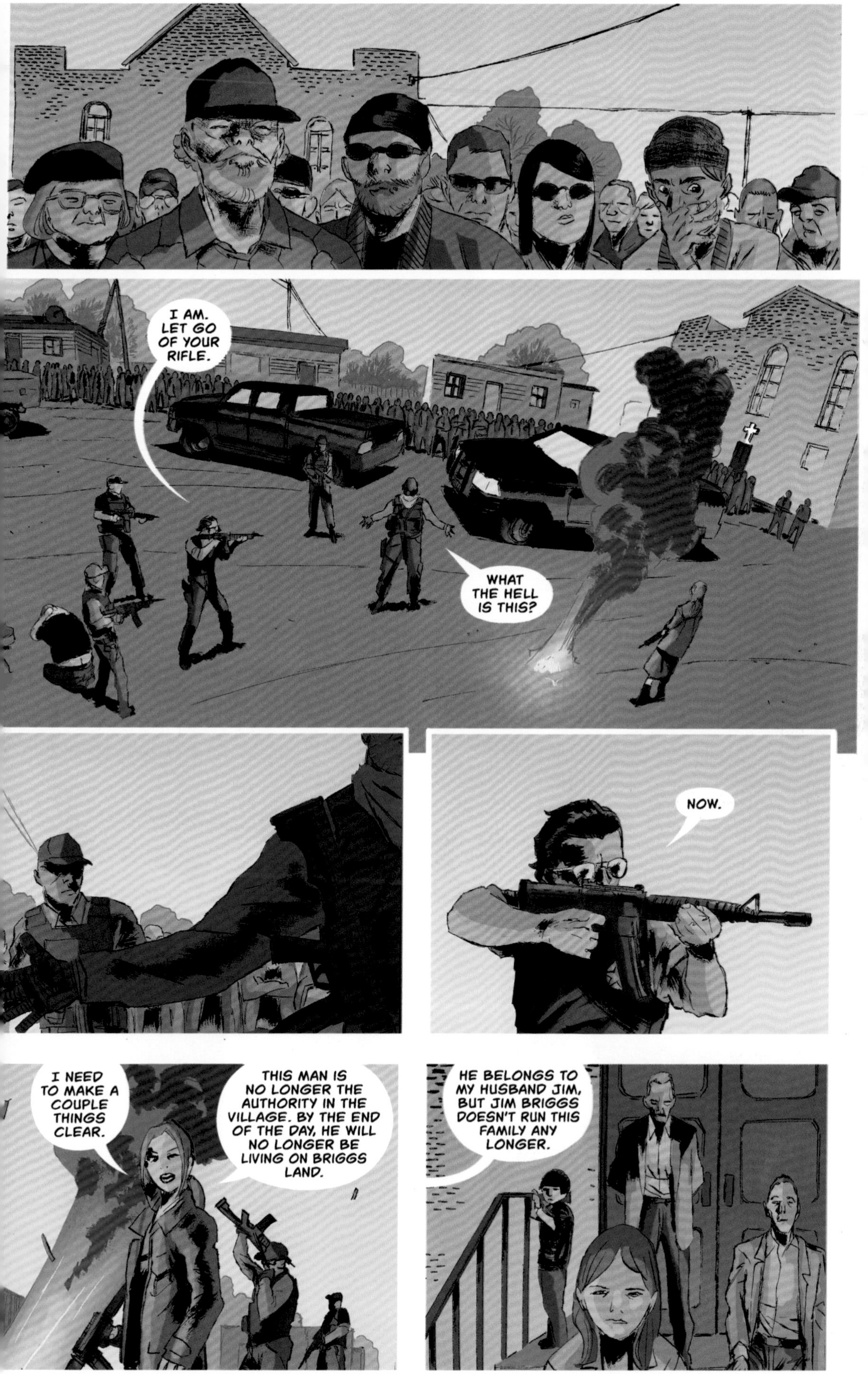

I AM. LET GO OF YOUR RIFLE.
WHAT THE HELL IS THIS?
NOW.
I NEED TO MAKE A COUPLE THINGS CLEAR.
THIS MAN IS NO LONGER THE AUTHORITY IN THE VILLAGE. BY THE END OF THE DAY, HE WILL NO LONGER BE LIVING ON BRIGGS LAND.
HE BELONGS TO MY HUSBAND JIM, BUT JIM BRIGGS DOESN'T RUN THIS FAMILY ANY LONGER.

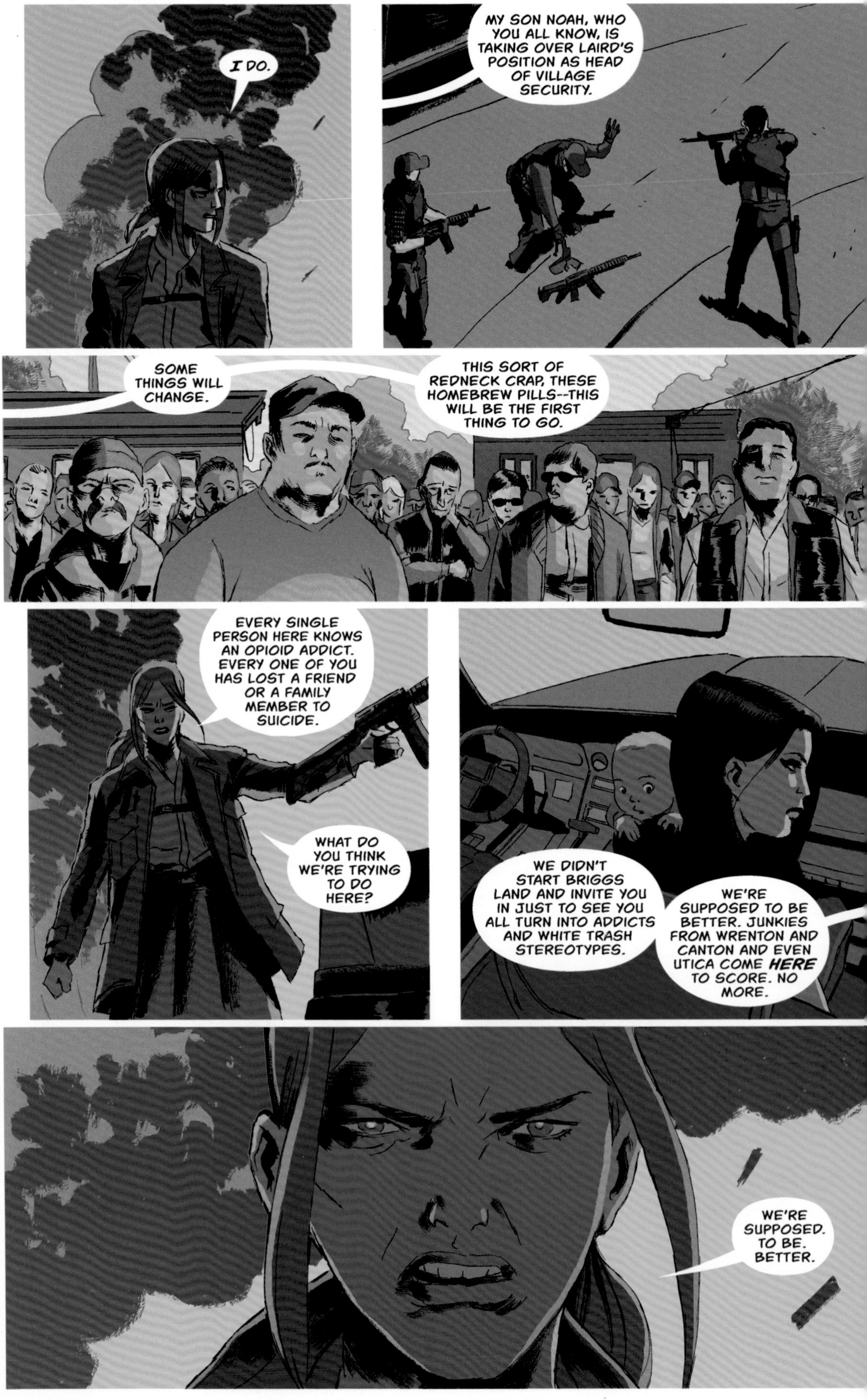
I DO.
MY SON NOAH, WHO YOU ALL KNOW, IS TAKING OVER LAIRD'S POSITION AS HEAD OF VILLAGE SECURITY.
SOME THINGS WILL CHANGE.
THIS SORT OF REDNECK CRAP, THESE HOMEBREW PILLS--THIS WILL BE THE FIRST THING TO GO.
EVERY SINGLE PERSON HERE KNOWS AN OPIOID ADDICT. EVERY ONE OF YOU HAS LOST A FRIEND OR A FAMILY MEMBER TO SUICIDE.
WHAT DO YOU THINK WE'RE TRYING TO DO HERE?
WE DIDN'T START BRIGGS LAND AND INVITE YOU IN JUST TO SEE YOU ALL TURN INTO ADDICTS AND WHITE TRASH STEREOTYPES.
WE'RE SUPPOSED TO BE BETTER. JUNKIES FROM WRENTON AND CANTON AND EVEN UTICA COME *HERE* TO SCORE. NO MORE.
WE'RE SUPPOSED. TO BE. BETTER.

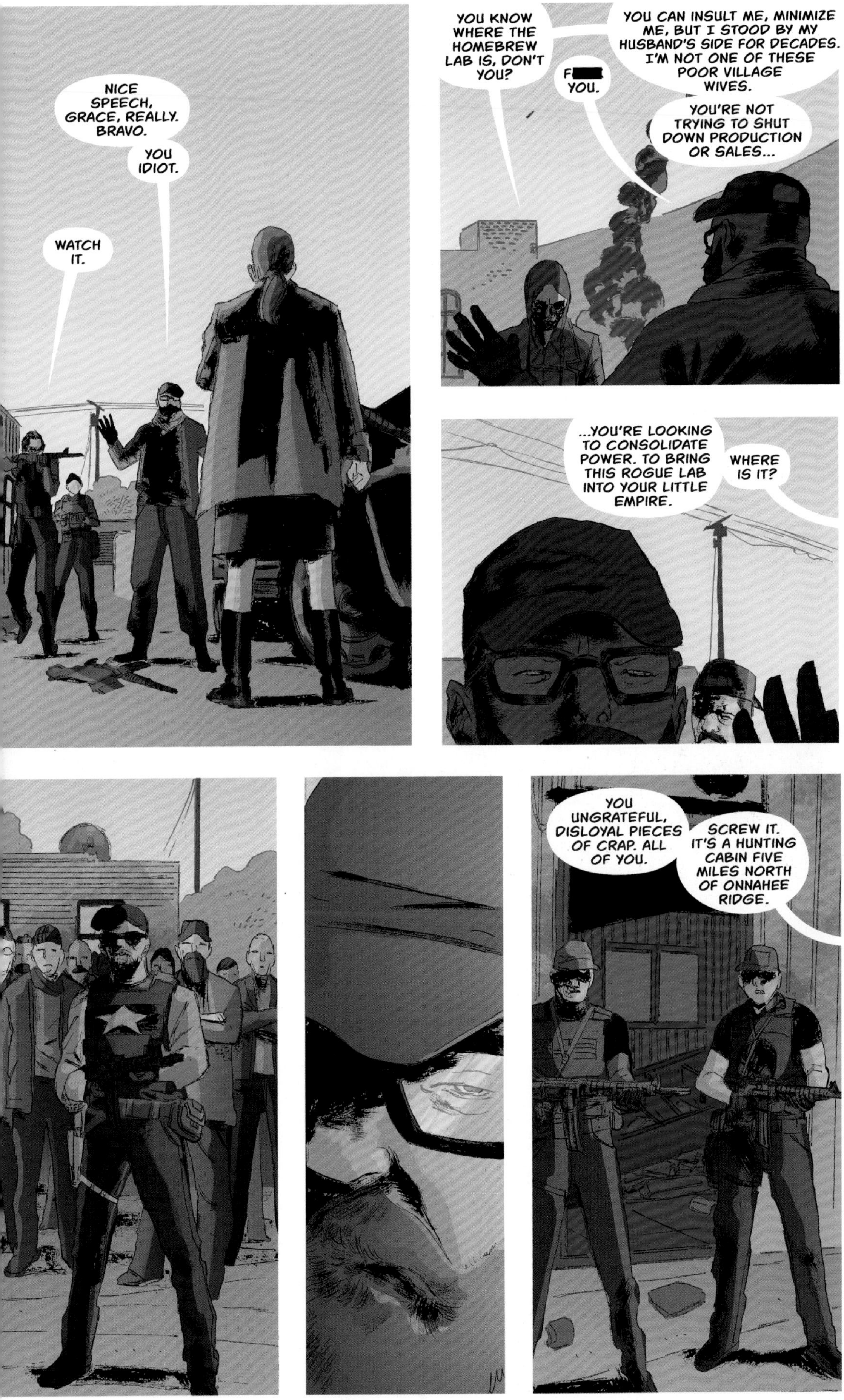
NICE SPEECH, GRACE, REALLY. BRAVO.
YOU IDIOT.
WATCH IT.
YOU KNOW WHERE THE HOMEBREW LAB IS, DON'T YOU?
F[redacted] YOU.
YOU CAN INSULT ME, MINIMIZE ME, BUT I STOOD BY MY HUSBAND'S SIDE FOR DECADES. I'M NOT ONE OF THESE POOR VILLAGE WIVES.
YOU'RE NOT TRYING TO SHUT DOWN PRODUCTION OR SALES...
...YOU'RE LOOKING TO CONSOLIDATE POWER. TO BRING THIS ROGUE LAB INTO YOUR LITTLE EMPIRE.
WHERE IS IT?
YOU UNGRATEFUL, DISLOYAL PIECES OF CRAP. ALL OF YOU.
SCREW IT. IT'S A HUNTING CABIN FIVE MILES NORTH OF ONNAHEE RIDGE.

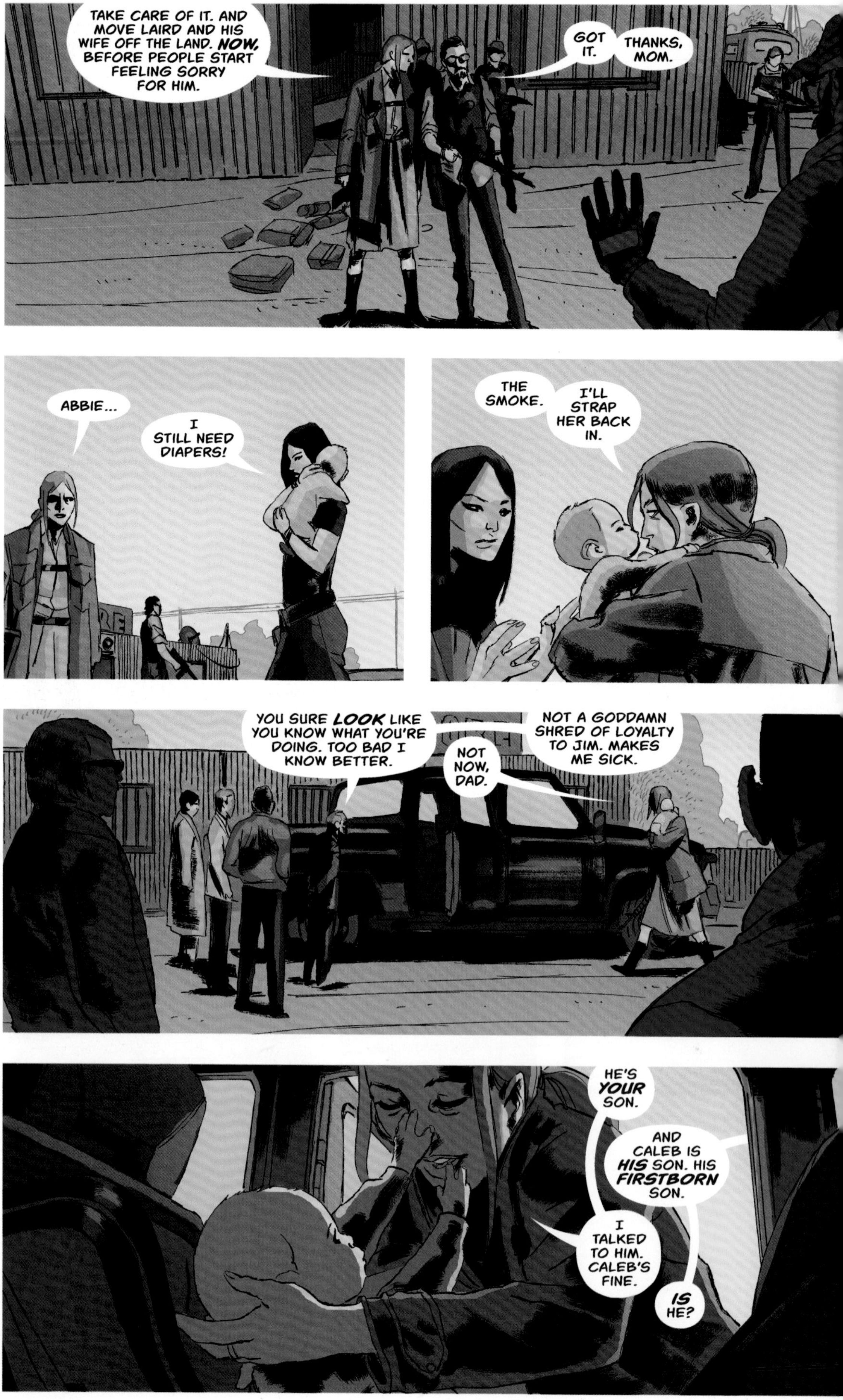
TAKE CARE OF IT. AND MOVE LAIRD AND HIS WIFE OFF THE LAND. NOW, BEFORE PEOPLE START FEELING SORRY FOR HIM.
GOT IT.
THANKS, MOM.
ABBIE...
I STILL NEED DIAPERS!
THE SMOKE.
I'LL STRAP HER BACK IN.
YOU SURE LOOK LIKE YOU KNOW WHAT YOU'RE DOING. TOO BAD I KNOW BETTER.
NOT A GODDAMN SHRED OF LOYALTY TO JIM. MAKES ME SICK.
NOT NOW, DAD.
HE'S YOUR SON.
AND CALEB IS HIS SON. HIS FIRSTBORN SON.
I TALKED TO HIM. CALEB'S FINE.
IS HE?

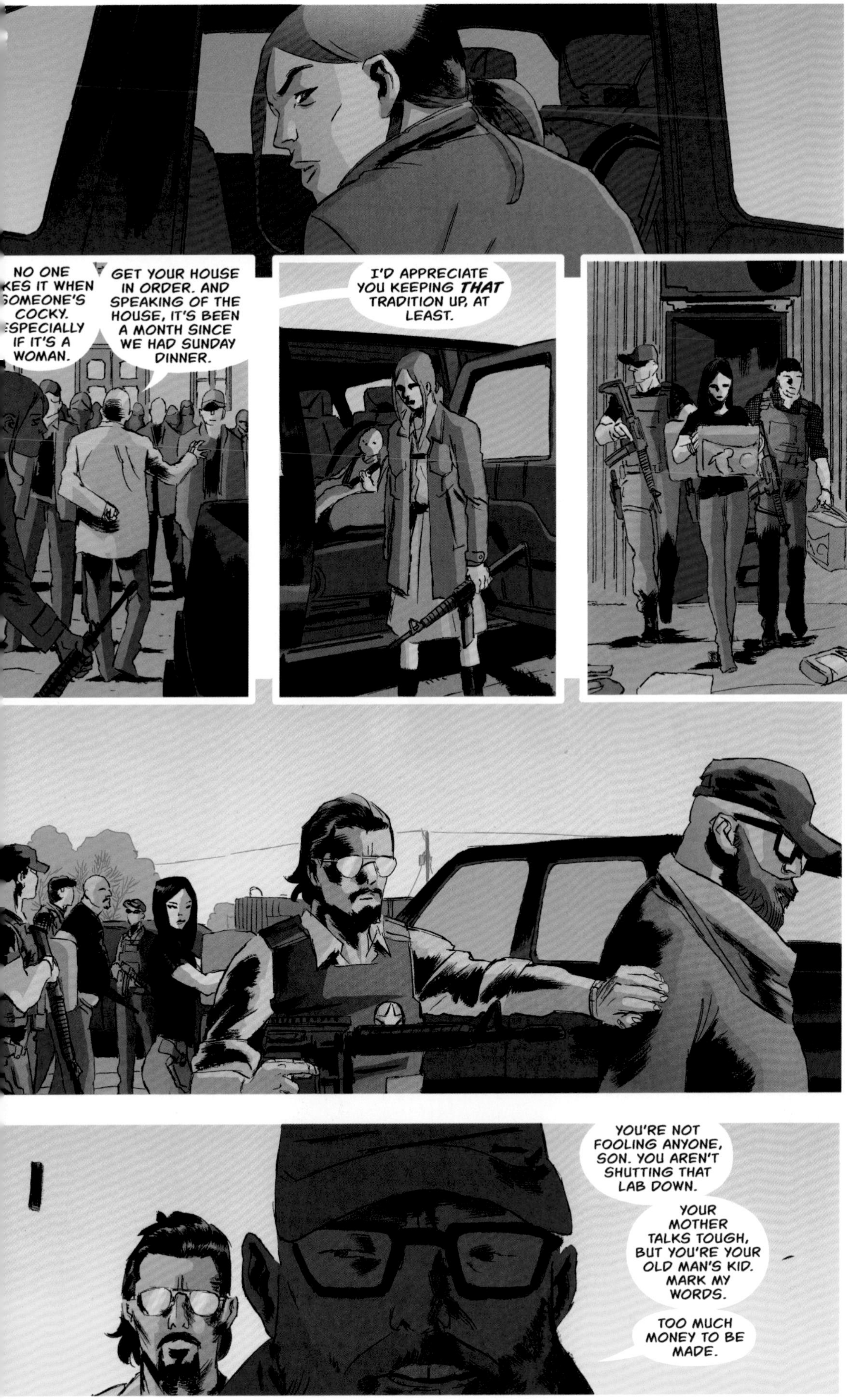
NO ONE
KES IT WHEN
SOMEONE'S
COCKY.
ESPECIALLY
IF IT'S A
WOMAN.
GET YOUR HOUSE IN ORDER. AND SPEAKING OF THE HOUSE, IT'S BEEN A MONTH SINCE WE HAD SUNDAY DINNER.
I'D APPRECIATE YOU KEEPING *THAT* TRADITION UP, AT LEAST.
YOU'RE NOT FOOLING ANYONE, SON. YOU AREN'T SHUTTING THAT LAB DOWN.
YOUR MOTHER TALKS TOUGH, BUT YOU'RE YOUR OLD MAN'S KID. MARK MY WORDS.
TOO MUCH MONEY TO BE MADE.

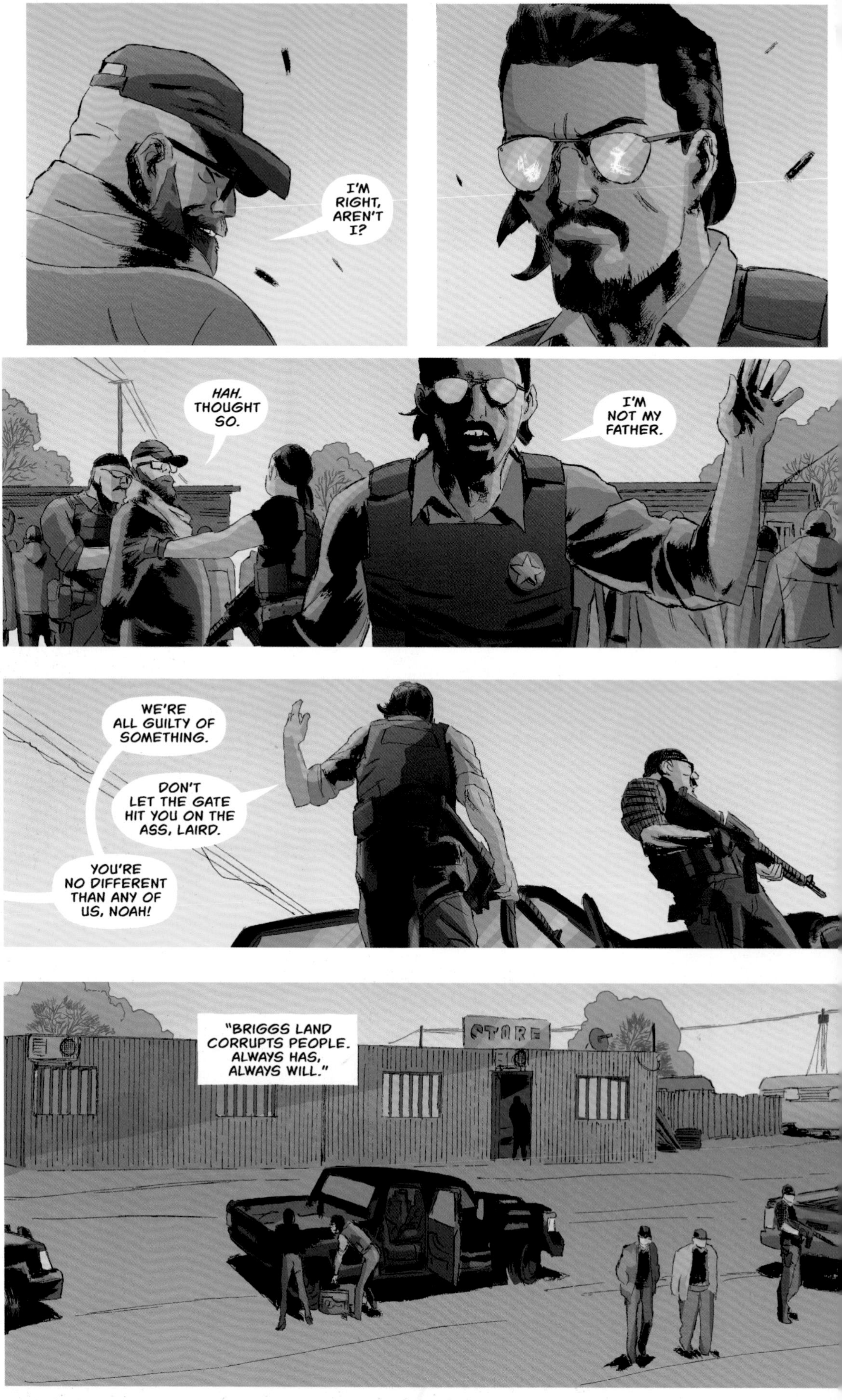
I'M RIGHT, AREN'T I?
HAH. THOUGHT SO.
I'M NOT MY FATHER.
WE'RE ALL GUILTY OF SOMETHING.
DON'T LET THE GATE HIT YOU ON THE ASS, LAIRD.
YOU'RE NO DIFFERENT THAN ANY OF US, NOAH!
"BRIGGS LAND CORRUPTS PEOPLE. ALWAYS HAS, ALWAYS WILL."
STORE

More great

NOIR AND ESPIONAGE

from Dark Horse Books

BLACKSAD

BLACKSAD

JUAN DÍAZ CANALES AND JUANJO GUARNIDO

The *Blacksad* books first took Europe by storm in 2000 and sold over 200,000 copies in France alone. Now Dark Horse presents the beautifully painted stories of private investigator John Blacksad, up to his feline ears in mystery, digging into the backstories behind murders, child abductions, and nuclear secrets.

ISBN 978-1-59582-393-9
$29.99

MIND MGMT
matt kindt
VOLUME ONE: THE MANAGER

MIND MGMT VOLUME 1

MATT KINDT

A young journalist stumbles onto a big story—the top-secret Mind Management program. Her ensuing journey involves weaponized psychics, hypnotic advertising, talking dolphins, and seemingly immortal pursuers. But in a world where people can rewrite reality itself, can she trust anything she sees?

ISBN 978-1-59582-797-5
$19.99

THE BLACK BEETLE
IN "NO WAY OUT"
A Mystery Tale by FRANCESCO FRANCAVILLA

THE BLACK BEETLE VOLUME 1: NO WAY OUT

FRANCESCO FRANCAVILLA

Follow Francesco Francavilla's critically acclaimed pulp hero the Black Beetle—Colt City's sleuthing sentinel—as he searches island prisons, dank sewers, and swanky nightclubs for the mysterious man known as Labyrinto.

ISBN 978-1-61655-202-2
$19.99

GREEN RIVER KILLER
A TRUE DETECTIVE STORY
JEFF JENSEN | JONATHAN CASE

GREEN RIVER KILLER: A TRUE DETECTIVE STORY

JEFF JENSEN AND JONATHAN CASE

The story of one of America's most notorious killers is revealed in this true-crime comic unlike any other! Written by case detective Tom Jensen's own son, acclaimed entertainment writer Jeff Jensen, this is the ultimate insider's account of America's most prolific serial killer.

ISBN 978-1-59582-560-5
$24.99

AVAILABLE AT YOUR LOCAL COMICS SHOP OR BOOKSTORE • TO FIND A COMICS SHOP IN YOUR AREA, CALL 1-888-266-4226
For more information or to order direct: • On the web: DarkHorse.com • E-mail: mailorder@darkhorse.com • Phone: 1-800-862-0052 Mon.–Fri. 9 AM to 5 PM Pacific Time.

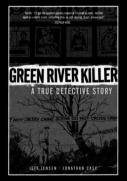